Research Methods and Design in Sport Management

Damon P. S. Andrew, PhD

College of Health and Human Services
Troy University

Paul M. Pedersen, PhD

School of Health, Physical Education, and Recreation
Indiana University

Chad D. McEvoy, EdD

School of Kinesiology and Recreation
Illinois State University

Human Kinetics

Library of Congress Cataloging-in-Publication Data

Andrew, Damon P.S., 1976-
  Research methods and design in sport management / by Damon P.S. Andrew, Paul M.
Pedersen, and Chad D. McEvoy.
    p. cm.
  Includes bibliographical references and index.
  ISBN-13: 978-0-7360-7385-1 (hard cover)
  ISBN-10: 0-7360-7385-X (hard cover)
  1. Sports--Mangement--Research. 2. Sports administration--Research. I.
Pedersen, Paul Mark. II. McEvoy, Chad D., 1971- III. Title.
  GV13.A55 2011
  796.06'9dc22

                          2010039551

ISBN: 978-0-7360-7385-1

The Web addresses cited in this text were current as of September 2010, unless otherwise noted.

Acquisitions Editor: Myles Schrag; **Developmental Editor:** Judy Park; **Assistant Editor:** Brendan
Shea; **Copyeditor:** Tom Tiller; **Indexer:** Bobbi Swanson; **Permission Manager:** Dalene Reeder; **Graphic
Designer:** Fred Starbird; **Graphic Artist:** Dawn Sills; **Cover Designer:** Keith Blomberg; **Photographer
(cover):** Troy University Photography Dept.; **Art Manager:** Kelly Hendren; **Associate Art Manager:** Alan
L. Wilborn; **Illustrations:** © Human Kinetics; **Printer:** Total Printing Systems

Printed in the United States of America   10 9

The paper in this book is certified under a sustainable forestry program.

Human Kinetics
P.O. Box 5076
Champaign, IL 61825-5076
Website: www.HumanKinetics.com

In the United States, email info@hkusa.com or call 800-747-4457.
In Canada, email info@hkcanada.com.
In the United Kingdom/Europe, email hk@hkeurope.com.

For information about Human Kinetics' coverage in other areas of the world,
please visit our website: **www.HumanKinetics.com**

E4407

Contents

Part IV Statistical Methods in Sport Management 199

Preface

On November 13, 2009, an industry panel consisting of John Bolton (general manager of the BOK Center and Tulsa Convention Center), Pat Gallagher (former president of the San Francisco Giants Enterprises), and Steve Zito (senior vice president of operations and management for the Memphis Grizzlies and FedEx Forum) addressed the audience at the 2009 Sport Entertainment and Venues Tomorrow Conference in Columbia, South Carolina. The topic for their panel was "Have You Been Served? Customer-Centric Services as a Marketing Tool." As each of these industry experts explained how the marketing function had gradually shifted from segmented marketing to customer-centric marketing during the 21st century, it became very clear to the audience that research was the engine behind this paradigm shift. Each member of the panel explained in detail how his organization used methods such as customer surveys, interviews, and focus groups to learn more about existing customers and prospective customers. Decisions made within their organizations were not based on hunches or even experienced guesses—those decisions were data driven. Not surprisingly, as we enter the second decade of the 21st century, successful sport organizations are those that collect, analyze, interpret, and apply data. At the conclusion of their presentation, these panel members emphasized that the successful sport manager in the future must possess and consistently apply research skills. Accordingly, the process of sport management education must continually be adapted to meet the needs of the industry, and it is our hope that this text helps spawn the next generation of data-driven sport managers.

This text meets the needs of upper-level undergraduate and graduate sport management students and serves as a reference for sport management scholars and practitioners in the field. The first two sections of the text are organized in a manner that allows you to understand the research process from beginning to end before delving into the specific methods of qualitative, quantitative, and mixed-methods research that are presented in the last two parts of the book. As such, it is an ideal tutorial for those embarking on a research project, thesis, or dissertation. Using our collective experience in teaching research methods classes, we incorporated multiple applied examples of past research by some of the leading sport management scholars in the world. Accordingly, special attention is devoted to the process of reading and understanding research in the field so that you are prepared to comprehend and apply research long after reading our text. Finally, in accordance with its applied focus, the book features step-by-step procedures for analyzing data, including SPSS statistical software procedures for quantitative analyses. At the end of each chapter you'll find a featured called Research Methods and Design in Action. The journal articles in these features discuss terms that relate specifically to the concepts described within the chapter; the circled terms in the text excerpt section are those discussed within the chapter and highlighted with the *Journal of Sport Management* icon. These articles and the discussion questions that follow them are aimed at teaching you how to effectively consume and evaluate research. You can find the full articles on the Human Kinetics Web site at www.humankinetics.com/products/all-products/Research-Methods-and-Design-in-Sport-Management.

Part I of the text begins with an introduction to research in sport management (both qualitative and quantitative in nature) along with a discussion of the ethical issues associated with research projects. Chapter 1 defines the concept of research and outlines five general themes in which research can be classified: application, objectives, type of information sought, presence of data, and the data source analyzed. In addition, two philosophical approaches to research are defined as well as four paradigms, or mind-sets, of research inquiry. The evolution and status of sport management research are delineated. Chapter 2 addresses ethical issues in research by detailing the history of human subjects' protection and the development of the Nuremberg Code. The chapter also reviews commonly accepted ethical principles and guidelines for research, including beneficence and nonmaleficence, fidelity and responsibility, integrity, justice, and respect

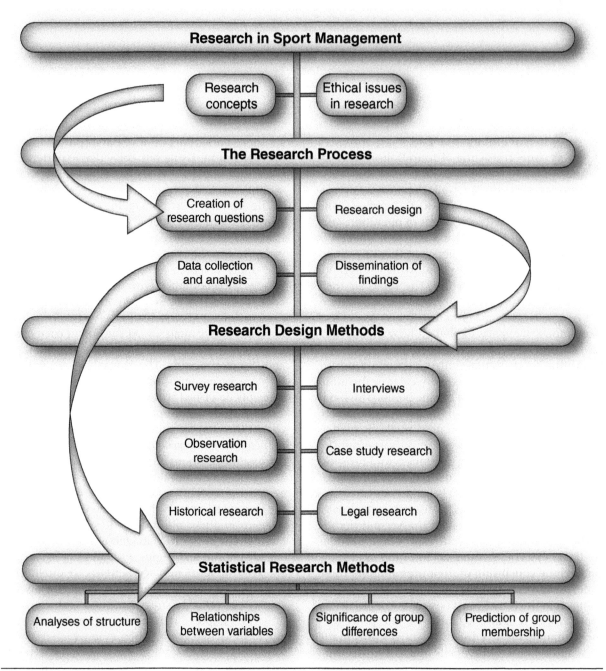

Flowchart of book organization.

for people's rights and dignity. Topics such as the institutional review board, informed consent, and scientific dishonesty are explained.

Part II introduces the research process, a step-by-step process of addressing one or more research questions. The processes of selecting a topic, reviewing the literature, developing a conceptual framework, focusing research questions, and outlining hypotheses are covered in chapter 3. Chapter 4 describes the various types of research designs and how one would go about selecting a research

design tailored to the research question. Specific issues including the selection of an appropriate sample size, sampling strategies, and establishing reliability and validity are also discussed. Chapter 5 focuses on data collection and analysis, including such topics as nonresponse bias, data preparation, scales of measurement, the concept of statistical significance, Type I and Type II errors, statistical power, effect size, and an overview of descriptive and inferential statistics. Finally, chapter 6 delineates the various research dissemination options, including academic presentations, scholarly journals, and research reports.

Part III introduces common research designs used by sport management students, scholars, researchers, and practitioners. A chapter is devoted to each of the following six common designs: surveys, interviews and focus groups, observation approaches, case studies, historical analysis, and legal analysis. Cumulatively, these designs allow for the assessment of data through quantitative, qualitative, or mixed-methods approaches. We extend special appreciation to Stephen Dittmore (chapter 8, Interviews) and Anita Moorman and John Grady (chapter 12, Legal Research) for their content expertise and authorship of respective chapters in this section. Indeed, chapter 12 is particularly noteworthy because it serves as the first-ever description of sport law research methods, another void filled by this text.

Finally, given that the field of sport management relies heavily on statistical methods, part IV of this text is dedicated to the presentation of these techniques according to their general purpose. Accordingly, part IV includes chapters that address analyses of structure, relationships between variables, significance of group differences, and prediction of group membership. In grouping the analyses by purpose, our goal is to create a user-friendly text through the acknowledgment that sport managers tend to use research to investigate an existing situation or provide solutions to an existing problem. Throughout part IV, we provide procedural steps for conducting each analysis by means of SPSS, a

statistical software package that is used widely by sports management researchers and at prominent universities and colleges. Chapter 13 discusses Cronbach's alpha, exploratory factor analysis, principal component analysis, and confirmatory factor analysis. Chapter 14 addresses bivariate correlation, simple linear regression, multiple regression, and path analysis. Chapter 15 covers the t-test, one-way analysis of variance (ANOVA), one-way analysis of covariance (ANCOVA), factorial ANOVA, factorial ANCOVA, one-way multivariate analysis of variance (MANOVA), one-way multivariate analysis of covariance (MANCOVA), factorial MANOVA, and factorial MANCOVA. Finally, chapter 16 addresses discriminant analysis, logistic regression, and cluster analysis.

A wise professor once said, "There are no completed manuscripts—there are only published and unpublished manuscripts." This quote acknowledges that every draft of a manuscript or book, even the final draft, is still a draft. The meaning of this quote is not often lost on professors, many of whom have either developed perfectionist qualities during their doctoral studies or possessed them before their higher education experiences began! Indeed, this textbook is the result of over four years of our cumulative efforts. Though we are hopeful the first edition will have a significant impact on the field, we are already dreaming up ways to make the book better in future editions. As such, we invite you to join us in this process by contacting us directly should you have any ideas for improvement of the text, whether in structure or in content.

Acknowledgments

This textbook to dedicated to Dr. John Kovaleski, who first encouraged me to pursue an academic career, and Dr. Robert (Bob) Heitman, who sparked a passion for research methods and design in me that burns even brighter today. I am most appreciative to my colleagues (Paul, Chad, Steve, Anita, and John) who added their considerable talent to this first edition, as well as the good folks at Human Kinetics who believed in and supported this project. I would also like to acknowledge the faculty, staff, and students at Jefferson Davis Community College, University of South Alabama, University of Florida, Florida State University, University of Louisville, University of Tennessee, and Troy University, who have collectively pushed me over the years to improve on a daily basis. I owe a deep debt of gratitude to my parents, William and Debra Andrew, my sisters, Ivy and Pamela, and my grandmother, Janie Owen, who unselfishly sacrificed to ensure my college education. I would also like to thank my wife, Tera, for her unconditional love and guidance, and my daughter, Clare. I also render gratitude to my in-laws and extended family for their understanding and support throughout the writing of this textbook. Finally, I offer humble praise to my Creator for His many blessings.

—Damon P. S. Andrew, Ph.D.

I sincerely appreciate Dr. Damon Andrew's invitation and leadership, Dr. Chad McEvoy's collaboration, and Myles Schrag's guidance regarding this textbook. I'm also very thankful for the support I received during this endeavor from my Indiana University colleagues (Drs. Larry Fielding, Gary Sailes, Choonghoon Lim, Galen Clavio, Patrick Walsh, and Antonio Williams), chair (Dr. David Koceja), and dean (Dr. Mohammad Torabi). Lastly, I could not have participated in this extensive project without the approval and encouragement of my family (Jen, Hallie, Zack, Brock, and Carlie). I'm grateful to you all.

—Paul M. Pedersen, Ph.D.

I would like to thank all those at Human Kinetics involved in publishing this book. In particular, I want to highlight the efforts of Myles Schrag and Judy Park. Thank you to my students and faculty peers at Illinois State University. My colleagues and friends in our Sport Management Program, Nels Popp and Brent Beggs, make the endeavor of building a great program a truly enjoyable experience. To our students, helping you learn about our industry and chase after your dreams of working in sport is extremely rewarding. Thanks also to my wonderful family – to my wife Kerry for being so supportive and for being such a terrific partner and mother, and to our boys Andy and Luke (and soon one more), who bring a smile to my face each and every day. I look forward to sharing my love of sport with you in the years to come. Finally, thank you to Damon and Paul for including me in this project. It was great to work with you both.

—Chad D. McEvoy, Ed.D.

Introduction to Research in Sport Management

To some extent, we are all affected by research; indeed, it is challenging to make it through even a few hours without using a tangible object that was developed through countless hours of research, whether it be a communication device, a form of transportation, or even a mattress that promises more comfortable rest. In today's world, organizations that are able to efficiently acquire, process, and apply information stand out as leaders of our global society. Contemporary managers are less willing to make important decisions based on hunches or guesses, and data-driven decision making is now the gold standard for accomplished leaders. As a result, if the sport industry—currently entrenched as a top 10 global industry in scope, magnitude, and financial impact—is to retain this lofty position or even rise higher, its future must be guided by sport managers who base their management decisions on sound research findings.

As its title suggests, part I of this textbook focuses on the basics of understanding and conducting research in sport management. Just as an athlete must possess basic knowledge about a sport and its rules in order to be successful, this part of the book provides two chapters addressing the nature of research (chapter 1) and its ethical boundaries (chapter 2). Chapter 1 defines the concept of research and outlines five general aspects by which research can be classified: application, objectives, type of information sought, presence of data, and data source. The chapter also defines two philosophical approaches to research and four paradigms (mind-sets) of research inquiry; in addition, it delineates the evolution and status of sport management research. Chapter 2 addresses ethical issues in research by detailing the history of human subject protection and the development of the Nuremberg Code. It also reviews commonly accepted ethical principles and guidelines for research, including beneficence, nonmaleficence, fidelity, responsibility, integrity, justice, and respect for people's rights and dignity. Finally, the chapter explores several other topics, including institutional review boards, informed consent, and scientific dishonesty.

Research Concepts in Sport Management

Learning Objectives

After studying this chapter, you should be able to do the following:

- Understand the need for sport managers to be consumers of research
- List prominent subdisciplines and contexts of sport management research
- Provide a general description of the purposes of research
- Distinguish between theories, principles, and facts
- Classify research according to application, objective, type of information sought, presence of data, and data source
- Discuss the philosophical approaches to research
- Understand the four research paradigms that influence a researcher's approach to study design
- Comment on the evolution and status of sport management research

It is difficult to find an area in society that is unaffected by current and ongoing research efforts. Television ads promote and distinguish between products and services of all types based on research conducted by trained professionals. For example, which medication is most effective at treating a particular kind of infection? Which automobile performs best in crash tests? What is the president's approval rating? The examples are endless and they affect us every day.

Not surprisingly, the field of sport management also relies upon research in order to advance its knowledge base. Sport managers are often called upon to address important issues for their organizations, and many of these questions require research before they can be answered (see the related highlight box for a list of key topics in sport management). For example, a sport manager might be asked to address questions such as the following: What is the average income of our fans? How does our team's fan base fit with a particular sponsor's target market? What kinds of services do our customers want? Such questions affect the financial stability of sport organizations, and the sport managers called upon to answer them must become acquainted with basic research methods. All of us, then, are affected by research—both generally as consumers and specifically in our particular fields of study. With that in mind, this text gives you a systematic overview of basic research methods and statistics in order to help you develop your ability to understand, conduct, and consume research.

Sport management students need to develop research competencies in order to become true professionals who can keep up with the latest industry trends long after their formal educational training is complete. In order to become effective decision makers, sport managers must avail themselves of the best and most recent knowledge available; that is, they must become consumers of research. This approach is vastly superior to the alternative of relying on tradition, trial and error, or bias in order to reach a conclusion. Sport managers must be able not only to interpret and apply the results of a study but also to judge the quality of the research used to produce those results. In a world filled with false and misleading advertising, true professionals can tell the difference between legitimate and nonlegitimate claims of effectiveness for a product or service. A good understanding of the research process might also enhance your life in less obvious ways. It might, for example, positively affect the way in which you develop a personal financial plan, select an important internship, organize for an extended trip, or even purchase common household products.

Research Topics in Sport Management

Research topics are typically derived from the various sport management subdisciplines, then applied to one of the various contexts, or focus areas, of sport.

Subdisciplines

- Communication and media relations in sport
  - Technology and the media
  - Integrating public relations with strategic management
  - Creating public relations campaigns
  - Managing relationships between sport organizations and the media
  - Crisis communication
  - Developing organizational media
  - Direct contact tactics
  - Internal communication
  - Organizational behavior and theory in sport
  - Organizational structure
  - Interorganizational relationships
  - Strategic alliances
  - Human resources and labor management relationships
  - Analyzing and managing change
  - Diversity in sport organizations
- Sport economics
  - Economic impact of star players
  - Supply and demand in sport
  - Impact of sport on local economies
  - Labor markets and sport
  - Regulation of sport
  - Antitrust issues in sport

(continued)

- Sport finance
  - Debt and equity financing
  - Capital budgeting
  - Grant applications
  - Taxation and legal issues
  - Fundraising
  - Financial planning
  - Revenue streams
  - Exit strategy
- Sport marketing
  - Sport participant behavior
  - Sport spectator behavior
  - Pricing concepts and strategies
  - Promotions
  - Distribution concepts
  - Market segmentation and targeting
  - Managing sport brands
- Sport sponsorship and sales
  - Sport consumer incentivization
  - Training of ticket sales staff
  - Customer service and retention
  - Sport sponsorship sales and activation
  - Sport licensing
  - Ecommerce
  - Sport brand communication
- Sport facility and event management
  - Event planning
  - Risk management
  - Venue ownership and management
  - Venue operations (e.g., concessionaires, parking attendants)
  - Security, safety, and medical services
  - Maintenance issues
  - Retail sales
  - Postevent evaluation

- Sport law
  - Negligence and liability
  - Discrimination
  - Doping
  - Employment and labor law
  - Athlete agreements
  - Copyright and trademark
  - Commercial agreements
- Sport governance
  - International sport organizations
  - League operations
  - Government involvement in sport and policy issues
  - Corporate social responsibility
  - Health and humanitarian goals in communities
- Sport ethics
  - Ethics and morals
  - Sources and moderators of ethical decision making
  - Ethical principles for sport and recreation
  - Human interaction
  - Agent accountability
  - Rendering of moral judgment

Contexts

- Amateur sport
  - Youth sport
  - High school sport
  - Collegiate sport
  - International and Olympic sport
- Professional sport
- Disability sport
- Lifestyle sport
  - Health and fitness
  - Recreational sport
- Sport education
- Athletic equipment and apparel

Research Defined

Research is important to society, and much attention has been devoted to defining it. Definitions of research vary in their complexity, but each is correct in its own way. Several scholars have attempted to define research as it relates to sport organizations. For example, Li, Pitts, and Quarterman (2008, p. 4) have defined sport management research as "a scientific, purposeful, systematic and rigorous method of collecting, analyzing, and interpreting data objectively or subjectively about some characteristic in order to gain new knowledge or add to the existing knowledge base of the field of sport organization management studies." This definition implies that true research expands the knowledge base of one's field. Gratton and Jones (2010, p. 4) define **research** simply as "a systematic process of discovery and advancement of human knowledge."

The more concise definition offered by Gratton and Jones contains several key descriptors of research. First, research is a systematic process, which implies that it involves multiple premeditated steps completed in a certain order. Research is typically generated by a specific research question, hypothesis, or problem and is complimented by a specific plan or procedure, otherwise known as the research process. Second, research involves discovery, which implies that it generates new information. Research aims to increase understanding by interpreting facts and reaching conclusions based on those facts and on a reasoned argument. Finally, research results in the "advancement of human knowledge." This phrase suggests that research should not merely discover new facts but should generate information that, when applied, advances our understanding. In this way, research can be considered reiterative, in that it is based on previous knowledge, which it aims to advance, but it may also develop further research questions. Part II of this textbook focuses on application of the research process.

We must also make clear the reasons for undertaking research, and Hussey and Hussey (1997) have summarized the various purposes of research. First, research can be used to investigate an existing situation—for example, soccer violence and hooliganism in Europe (Frosdick & Marsh, 2005). A second purpose of research is to provide solutions to a specific problem. For instance, if a sporting goods retailer is struggling with employee turnover, the manager might undertake research into methods for enhancing employee commitment, such as providing more intrinsically satisfying tasks and organizational support (Todd & Andrew, 2006).

Third, research can be conducted to explore and analyze general issues. For example, sport has for many years been identified as an activity that can help participants develop positive behavior patterns. Indeed, the term *sportsmanship* implies positive behavior rooted in sporting activity. However, if sport helps participants develop positive behavior, why do some professional athletes, who participate in thousands of hours of sport activity, engage in negative behavior? Scholars have recognized that sportsmanship behavior can be encouraged by using benefits-based programs (Wells et al., 2008), which implies that the organization of activities is a crucial component in determining behavioral outcomes.

Fourth, research can be used to construct or create a new procedure or system. For example, the tragic events of September 11, 2001, have influenced the ways in which sport facility managers approach security issues. Indeed, research entities such as the National Center for Spectator Sports Safety & Security at the University of Southern Mississippi now exist to build security awareness, improve sport security policies and procedures, and enhance emergency response, evacuation, and recovery operations in the case of a terrorist incident, natural disaster, or other crowd management issue (see www.ncs4.com). A fifth purpose of research is to explain a new phenomenon. For instance, fantasy sport leagues benefited from the rise of the Internet in the mid-1990s. A decade later, the Fantasy Sports Trade Association (2008) estimated that nearly 30 million people of age 12 and above in the United States and Canada were playing fantasy sports. Recent fantasy sport research has examined the phenomenon in terms of participant motivation (Dwyer, Kim, & Gray, 2008; Lee, Seo, & Green, 2008) and legal aspects (Evans, 2008; Grady, 2007). Another purpose of research is to generate new knowledge. As new sports and trends emerge, researchers collect data to allow sport managers to make informed decisions. For example, the emerging sport of mixed martial arts (MMA) now competes favorably with college football games, NASCAR, and the U.S. Open tennis tournament in terms of television ratings (Pishna, 2007). Not surprisingly, research has emerged that highlights the uniqueness of MMA consumer motivations as compared with those of team sport fans (Kim, Greenwell, Andrew, Lee, & Mahony, 2008), as well as cross-national differences in MMA consumer motivations (Kim, Andrew, & Greenwell, 2009).

Research is not limited to only one of the purposes just discussed; rather, two or more of these purposes can be combined in a single project. Research also provides a vehicle for distinguishing between theories, principles, and facts. A **theory** is an explanation of a phenomenon that can be used to make testable predictions supported by prior research. Theories are generally based on similar outcomes of a number of studies that lead a researcher to notice an overall pattern of results. Further research may either support or not support a theory or portions of a theory; if it does not, then a modified theory will be needed. In contrast, principles and facts undergo much higher levels of research scrutiny. A **principle** is a collection of thoroughly tested theories that can be used to guide behavior (e.g., dietary guidelines, weight training principles). A **fact** is a notion so firmly supported by evidence that there is no longer a compelling reason to continue testing it. In essence, a fact that is supported by overwhelming evidence has such an extremely high probability of being true that researchers treat it as if it simply is true. The quantity and quality of research conducted about a particular phenomenon, therefore, determines whether the resulting conclusions are considered to represent theory, principle, or fact. Decision makers who base their conclusions on facts are taking a lesser risk than are those who use principles or theories as a basis for their decisions.

Types of Research

Research can be classified from five perspectives: (1) the *application* of the research study, (2) the *objectives* of the research, (3) the *type of information sought*, (4) the *presence of data*, and (5) the *data source* analyzed.

These classifications are not mutually exclusive; for example, a research study classified by type of information sought might also be classified by objectives, application, presence of data, or data source. Some studies do not fit into all five perspectives. For example, a study classified as theoretical in the presence-of-data category essentially has no data, which means that it cannot be classified according to data source. Figure 1.1 provides a partial illustration of the various types of research.

Application: Pure and Applied Research

Research classified on the basis of application occupies a continuum ranging from pure to applied. **Pure research**, sometimes referred to as **basic research,** is undertaken to gain a better understanding of a theoretical concept, and it may be conducted without regard to a specific problem or issue. Its purpose may involve the development, examination, verification, or refinement of research methods, procedures, techniques, or tools that form the body of research methodology. One example would be a study aimed at developing a survey to assess the attendance motivation of sport consumers. **Applied research**, on the other hand, is carried out to solve a specific problem or provide a solution to a practical question. More specifically, various research methodologies (e.g., procedures, methods) are applied in order to collect information about various aspects of a specific problem, issue, phenomenon, or situation so that

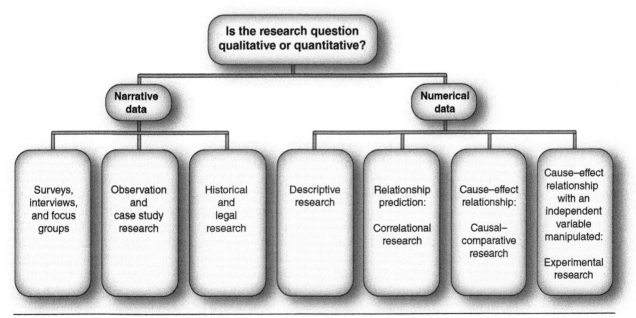

Figure 1.1 Types of research.

the gathered information can be used in a practical manner. Therefore, applied research can be particularly valuable to practitioners. As noted by Weese (1995), sport management scholars should continue to explore applied research opportunities in order to better serve practitioners in the field.

Objectives: Exploratory, Descriptive, Explanatory, and Predictive Research

Research may also be classified according to the researcher's objectives: exploratory, descriptive, explanatory, or predictive. **Exploratory research** is often used when the research question or problem is not particularly well defined; as a result, this type of research is often aimed at clarifying concepts, gathering explanations, gaining insight, refining problems and ideas, and forming hypotheses. Exploratory research methods include, but are not limited to, performing a literature review (see chapter 3), surveying individuals about their experiences (see chapter 7), conducting focus groups (see chapter 8), and developing case studies (see chapter 10). Exploratory research is very flexible and is used to develop hypotheses rather than test them.

Descriptive research focuses on what is happening rather than on why it happens. It typically describes characteristics of a population or phenomenon through the use of surveys, interviews, or observations. It can also be used to systematically describe a problem, situation, service, program, or attitude. Descriptive research is not as flexible as exploratory research because it specifically defines questions, the population surveyed, and the specific method of analysis prior to data collection.

Explanatory research moves beyond descriptive research in order to explain why something happens. In other words, explanatory research attempts to clarify why and how there is a relationship between two or more variables. Thus the goal of explanatory research is to assess causal relationships between variables, and it can be used to determine the accuracy of a theory, extend a theory to a new context, advance knowledge about an underlying process, or provide evidence to support or refute an explanation.

Finally, **predictive research** forecasts the likelihood that particular phenomena will occur in given circumstances. Predictive research often incorporates some form of quantitative regression analysis that allows researchers to predict a particular outcome by simultaneously addressing a number of independent predictor variables. Thus predictive research relies heavily upon the use of data to predict a future outcome, and it is inherently susceptible to changes in environment, consumers, or the market in general. For example, a sporting goods manufacturer may conduct predictive research to determine the potential success of a new product given the presence of viable competitors, resources dedicated to promotion of the product, and consumer attitudes in the target market.

Type of Information Sought: Qualitative, Quantitative, and Mixed-Methods Research

Research can also be labeled as quantitative, qualitative, or mixed-methods according to the type of information sought. This type of classification is generally based on three characteristics: purpose of the study, how variables are measured, and how information is analyzed. **Qualitative** studies usually attempt to describe a problem, issue, phenomenon, or situation without quantification. They tend to incorporate emerging methods, open-ended questions, data (in the form of an interview, observation, document, or audiovisual material), text or image analysis, and concluding themes, patterns, or interpretations. For example, a qualitative focus could be used to provide an account of varying opinions expressed by individuals concerning a certain issue (see chapter 8), to describe an observed situation (see chapter 9) or a unique context (see chapter 10), or to develop a historical analysis of events (see chapter 11).

Alternatively, if the researcher intentionally quantifies the variation in a problem, issue, phenomenon, or situation, then the information gathered will be primarily quantitative (i.e., numerical); furthermore, if the researcher is concerned with analyzing the magnitude of the variation, then the study is classified as **quantitative**. Quantitative studies generally employ the following tools: predetermined methods; instrument-based questions (primarily closed-ended or forced-choice items), data involving performance, attitude, observation, or census information; and statistical analysis and interpretation. Statistics are not required but are used in most quantitative research for purposes such as analyzing structure (see chapter 13), quantifying relationships between variables (see chapter 14), determining the significance of group differences (see chapter 15), and predicting group membership (see chapter 16).

Research that adopts both qualitative and quantitative approaches in a single study is classified as

mixed-methods research. This type of study often involves both predetermined and emerging methods, open- and closed-ended questions, multiple forms of data, statistical and textual analysis, and a final conclusion based upon findings obtained from both qualitative and quantitative perspectives. As noted by Rudd and Johnson (2010), the use of mixed-methods studies in the field of sport management is, unfortunately, still rare. Indeed, in an analysis of studies published in the *Journal of Sport Management,* the *International Journal of Sport Management,* and *Sport Management Review* from 2000 to 2007, these authors uncovered only 27 studies that could be classified as mixed-methods in nature. Similarly, Quarterman and colleagues (2006) reviewed 299 articles published in the *Journal of Sport Management* from 1987 to 2004 and uncovered only 6 mixed-methods studies. This dearth notwithstanding, given the fact that sport management research often addresses causal questions (i.e., whether one variable causes changes in another), sport management researchers could used mixed-methods designs to enhance causal inference (i.e., the links between two or more variables), thus strengthening the quality of their findings.

Presence of Data: Theoretical and Empirical Research

Studies are also classified according to whether or not data is presented to support the study. Studies that incorporate findings from past research in order to develop new ideas, theories, and explanations in the absence of data analysis are termed **theoretical research** studies. For example, Mahony, Hums, Andrew, and Dittmore (2010) published a review article on the topic of organizational justice (i.e., perceived fairness) in sport. A review article does not present and analyze its own data; rather, it examines published research on a given topic and synthesizes broad overall findings while identifying research gaps that need to be addressed. In their study, Mahony and colleagues (2010) first summarized the overall literature on organizational justice over the past 50 years, then reviewed 22 articles on organizational justice in the sport context. They identified a number of research gaps that enabled them to suggest seven broad areas for future research. **Empirical research**, which uses data to support the development of new ideas, accounts for the majority of articles published in sport management journals. Quarterman and colleagues' (2006) review of 299 articles classified two-thirds of them as empirical research. Thus the theoretical and

empirical research categories are indeed distinct, but they can also be complementary, and a theoretical study is often followed up by empirical study in order to provide support for the ideas and theories generated by the theoretical study.

Data Source: Primary and Secondary Research

Research can also be classified according to the type of data involved in the study. **Primary research** involves collecting original data specific to a particular research project. In sport management research, such original data are typically collected through the use of methods such as questionnaires and interviews. Studies that do not involve collecting original data are typically referred to as **secondary research**. In these studies, researchers rely on existing sources of data, such as census or tax information, for analysis. Although secondary research studies do not analyze original data, they can still be very useful in addressing research questions and hypotheses. For example, a meta-analysis uses the results of several studies to address a specific question, thus allowing the researcher to draw upon the data of a much larger overall sample than what might be feasible by other means.

A study by Aitchison (2005) is particularly useful for illustrating the difference between primary and secondary research because it incorporates both types. The purpose of the study was to develop a critical theory to advance feminist research in sport management, and the author analyzed empirical data that she collected in a national study of gender equity in leisure management from 1998 to 1999, as well as secondary data drawn from a number of comparative studies in Australia, New Zealand, Canada, and the United States (Aitchison, Brackenridge, & Jordan, 1999; Henderson & Bialeschki, 1993, 1995; McKay, 1996; Shinew & Arnold, 1998). Cumulatively, these data samples provided strong evidence to demonstrate that women's experiences of sport and leisure management were shaped by both material and cultural factors.

Research Traditions

A number of philosophical approaches to research exist, and these approaches are guided by ontology and epistemology. **Ontology** is the study of the philosophy of knowledge, and **epistemology** is the philosophical study of how such knowledge is acquired. Ontology deals with questions concerning what entities exist or can be said to exist and how such entities can be grouped, related within a hierarchy, and subdivided according to similarities and differences. In simpler terms, ontological approaches attempt to answer questions that begin with the phrase "What is . . . ?" (e.g., What is sport?). Epistemology, on the other hand, assumes that we know about the presence of a construct because of knowledge that we have about it. In other words, epistemological approaches assume knowledge about the presence of a construct because of existing related knowledge; thus epistemology answers questions that begin with "how" or "what" (e.g., How does sport influence us?). As researchers, we create epistemological theories to support the ontological theories we create. Creswell (2009) identifies a number of ontologies and epistemologies that often lead researchers to embrace **paradigms** that in turn lead to a qualitative, quantitative, or mixed-methods approach in their research.

Postpositivism

Postpositivist researchers stress the need to identify and assess causes that influence outcomes. In a typical postpositivist research project, an individual begins with a theory, collects data that either supports or appears to support the theory, and then makes necessary revisions before additional tests are made. Phillips and Burbules (2000) summarize the key assumptions of **postpositivism** as follows:

- Since knowledge is conjectural and absolute truth can never be found, evidence established in research is always imperfect and fallible. Therefore, researchers never "prove" hypotheses; rather, they indicate a failure to reject hypotheses.
- Research is the process of making claims, then refining them or abandoning them in favor of other claims that are more strongly supported.
- Knowledge is shaped by data, evidence, and rational considerations.
- Research seeks to develop relevant and true statements that can explain the situation of interest or describe causal relationships of concern.
- Objectivity is an essential aspect of competent inquiry, and researchers must examine methods and conclusions for the presence of bias.

Constructivism

Social **constructivism** is rooted in the assumption that individuals seek understanding of the world in

which they live and work and that they develop subjective meanings of their experiences. As a result, it is perhaps not surprising that constructivist researchers rely heavily upon qualitative methods in order to conduct research. Constructivist studies typically employ broad, *open-ended questions* posed by the researcher in order to elicit detailed responses from participants that highlight their views of the situation being studied. Crotty (1998) identified the following assumptions of constructivism:

- Meanings are constructed by individuals as they engage with the world they are interpreting.
- Individuals engage with and make sense of their world based on historical and social perspectives that are dictated by culture.
- Meaning is always generated by social influences on the basis of interaction with a community.

Advocacy/Participatory Paradigm

The **advocacy/participatory paradigm** insists that research inquiry is intertwined with politics and a political agenda and that it contains an action agenda for reform that may change the lives of participants and researchers and the institutions in which individuals work or live. In this approach, researchers may help design questions, collect data, analyze information, or reap the rewards of the research. While research associated with the advocacy/participatory paradigm is typically qualitative in nature, it can also serve as a foundation for quantitative research. Kemmis and Wilkinson (1998) summarized the key features of the advocacy/participatory paradigm as follows:

- Participatory action is recursive or dialectical and focused on bringing about change in practices and advancing an action agenda for change.
- This approach to research helps individuals free themselves from constraints in the media, language, work procedures, and power relationships in educational settings.
- The advocacy/participatory paradigm is emancipatory in that it helps individuals free themselves from the constraints of irrational and unjust structures that limit self-development and self-determination.
- This approach is practical and collaborative and allows researchers to engage the participants as active collaborators in their inquiries.

Pragmatism

Researchers who adopt the principles of **pragmatism** are primarily concerned with applications and solutions to problems (Patton, 1990). Rather than emphasizing methods, pragmatists focus on the research problem and on all available approaches to understanding it (Rossman & Wilson, 1985). As a result, they often rely on both qualitative and quantitative approaches to address research questions—that is, they often use a mixed-methods approach. Cherryholms (1992), Creswell (2009), and Morgan (2007) identified the following principles of pragmatism:

- Pragmatism is not committed to any one system of philosophy or reality and therefore often relies on a mixed-methods approach.
- Individual researchers are free to choose the methods, techniques, and procedures of research that best meet their needs and purposes.
- Pragmatist researchers need to establish a purpose articulating why qualitative and quantitative data are necessary to address the research question.
- Pragmatists concur that research always occurs in social, historical, political, and other contexts.

As mentioned previously, Creswell (2009) notes that ontologies and epistemologies often lead researchers to embrace a particular qualitative, quantitative, or mixed-methods approach in their research.

Table 1.1 describes how the four research paradigms—postpositivism, constructivism, the advocacy/participatory paradigm, and pragmatism—typically relate to the qualitative, quantitative, and mixed-methods approaches.

Table 1.1   Typical Philosophical Assumptions, Methods, and Research Practices of the Qualitative, Quantitative, and Mixed-Methods Approaches

	Qualitative	Quantitative	Mixed-methods
Philosophical assumptions	Constructivist or advocacy/participatory knowledge claims	Postpositivist knowledge claims	Pragmatic knowledge claims
Methods	Open-ended questions, emerging approaches, text and/or image data	Closed-ended questions, predetermined approaches, numeric data	Both open- and closed-ended questions, both emerging and predetermined approaches, and both qualitative and quantitative data analysis
Research practices	Positions researcher within the context	Tests or verifies theories or explanations	Collects both qualitative and quantitative data
	Collects participant-generated meanings	Identifies variables of interest	Develops a rationale for mixing methods
	Focuses on a single concept or phenomenon	Relates variables in questions or hypotheses	Integrates the data at various stages of inquiry
	Brings personal values into the study	Uses standards of reliability and validity	Presents visual pictures of the procedures in the study
	Studies the context or setting of participants	Observes and then measures information numerically	Employs practices of both qualitative and quantitative research
	Validates the accuracy of findings	Uses unbiased approaches	
	Interprets the data	Employs statistical procedures	
	Creates an agenda for change or reform		
	Involves researcher in collaborating with the participants		

The Evolution of Sport Management Research

Before reviewing the current state of sport management research, it is important to define the scope of sport management. DeSensi, Kelley, Blanton, and Beitel (1990, p.33) defined **sport management** in a broad sense as "any combination of skills related to planning, organizing, directing, controlling, budgeting, leading, and evaluating within the context of an organization or department whose primary product or service is related to sport and/or physical activity." Additionally, VanderZwaag (1998) identified other areas of sport to be included within the professional realm: recreational sport programs, industrial and military sport programs, corporate-sponsored sporting events, sporting goods, developmental sport programs, sport news media, and sport management academic programs. Refer back to the highlight box on pages 4 and 5 for a conceptualization of the various subdisciplines of sport management and their contexts.

The need for sport management was evident in 1957, when Walter O'Malley, owner of the Los Angeles Dodgers, wrote,

> *I ask the question, where would one go to find a person who by virtue of education has been trained to administer a marina, race track, ski resort, auditorium, stadium, theatre, convention or exhibit hall, a public camp complex, or a person to fill an executive position at a team or league level in junior athletics such as Little League baseball, football, scouting, CYO, and youth activities, etc. (Mason, Higgins, & Wilkinson, 1981, p. 44)*

O'Malley's question was posed to Dr. Clifford Brownell, a professor at Columbia University, and later conveyed by Dr. Brownell to his doctoral student, Dr. James Mason, who led the development of one of the first sport management programs in the United States at Ohio University in 1966 (evidence also exists of an earlier program at Florida Southern University from 1949 to 1959). About 20 years later, the North American Society for Sport Management was formed during the 1985–1986 academic year. The *Journal of Sport Management* was first published in 1987 to address sport management in the context of management theory and practice; it focused specifically on sport, exercise, dance, and play, since these activities are pursued by all sectors of the population (Parks & Olafson, 1987).

In the first issue of the *Journal of Sport Management*, Zeigler (1987) addressed the past, present, and future of sport management as a field of study. He concluded that the field still had an opportunity to relate significantly to the developing social science of management but that it needed to do so soon. Zeigler also emphasized that the vast enterprise that is sport must more effectively address the urgent need for qualified managers, and he highlighted the then-new North American Society for Sport Management as an entity that could make a significant contribution in this regard. Finally, Zeigler recommended that such developments should be carried out in full cooperation with the National Association for Sport and Physical Education within the American Alliance for Health, Physical Education, Recreation, and Dance and with the Canadian Association for Health, Physical Education, and Recreation (now known as Physical and Health Education Canada).

Zeigler (1987) recognized potential conflicts between practitioners and scientists early on, and this issue still affects the field of sport management today. Practitioners often claim that scientists are out of touch with reality while scientists charge that practitioners often fail to properly base decisions on research. Further, he criticized sport management scholars for their lack of significant contribution to research during the prior 20 years. When discussing the academic quality of sport management programs, he commented, "One can only speculate about the intellectual level of these programs when the professors and instructors have typically been such reluctant, unproductive scholars themselves (p. 10)." Such harsh yet realistic comments from one of the most respected scholars in sport management helped usher in a new era of productivity in the field.

Paton (1987) took the initiative to critically examine the progress of sport management research in the inaugural issue of the *Journal of Sport Management*. After an exhaustive literature review, Paton concluded that the bulk of the research was descriptive in design and directed toward postsecondary institutions. Furthermore, major research emphasis was placed on leaders and leadership behavior, yet few concrete conclusions had emerged from such research. Paton recommended that researchers work to improve the theoretical base and strive to make the knowledge sensible and useful. He also recommended that sport management researchers broaden their horizons to examine noneducational organizations: "[P]rojections suggest that we must turn our attention to other areas such as professional and amateur sport organizations and the increasingly diverse organizations in private enterprise" (p. 30). Although more research is available today on professional sport teams, a majority of research still focuses on collegiate teams, and only scant research has addressed amateur sport organizations.

Other sport management scholars have also voiced their concerns about the direction of research in the field. James Weese (1995) argued that in addition to enhancing the field of sport management from a theoretical perspective, sport management research should serve practitioners in professional and organizational sport settings and environments. He suggested that practical implications should be addressed in order to assist sport industry professionals in understanding the conclusions of research.

Trevor Slack (1996) expanded on Weese's (1995) idea that sport management research has not kept pace with the growth of the sport industry. Slack claimed that the bulk of sport management research has been geared toward issues involving physical education and athletic administration, whereas little attention has been given to enterprises such as athletic equipment and apparel and sport organizations. Slack suggested that sport management academicians must broaden their areas of research, as well as the theoretical basis for this research; if they do not, he cautioned, the field of sport management will remain limited and lack generalizability. Slack (1996) suggested steps by which sport management researchers could improve in these needed areas. It is essential, he said, for researchers to be familiar with current management concepts, theories, and strategies. Such information can be obtained by reading management books and journals outside the field of sport management. Slack also urged sport management academicians to present their research to a broader audience and sustain scrutiny from other academic fields. He suggested that credibility in the field of sport management can be earned if sport management academicians teach outside of their respective domains—for example, within business schools.

Slack (1996) also suggested areas of research that would help the field of sport management stay current—among them, organizational strategy, the impact of technology on the sport industry, organizational culture, and the power and politics found in the sport industry. There has been some growth in research addressing the topics suggested by Slack,

such as organizational culture, but many of the topics he suggested are still sparsely researched in the realm of sport.

In addition, Slack (1996) advocated other types of research—some that are not so heavily quantitative, such as the biographical approach (examining an organization's past, present, and future) and the use of secondary data to analyze and draw conclusions. Since Slack's suggestion, secondary data has indeed been used more often, primarily in sport finance and economic research. The biographical approach has yet to be used to its full potential.

Slack's (1998) suggestions for creating a unique aspect in the field of sport management from the overall management discipline include being reflective and critical of personal scholarly research and identifying voids in the field, especially as viewed from a theoretical or practical viewpoint. Also, he suggests that researchers must theorize their work and use sport organizations to test their own theories as well as more established theory. Finally, Slack suggests that sport management academicians must broaden the types of sport organizations they examine and expand upon the subdisciplinary areas of sport management education. Slack's insightful comments have challenged sport management programs to reconsider their approach to research. Even today, many of his research suggestions remain current and applicable.

The Status of Sport Management Research

Given the relative infancy of the field of sport management and the numerous commentaries offered by scholars on the status of sport management research in the 1980s and 1990s (Boucher, 1998; Chalip, 1997; Cuneen & Parks, 1997; Paton, 1987; Slack, 1996, 1998; Weese, 1995; Zeigler, 1987), Costa (2005) conducted a study of 17 prominent sport management scholars who responded to three iterations of a **Delphi questionnaire** (i.e., a series of increasingly probing questionnaires on an identified topic) concerning their views about the status and future of the sport management field. Costa was particularly interested in finding out whether gaps existed between the experts' perceptions of the importance of various facets of sport management research and the current success of those facets (see table 1.2). All 16 aspects of sport management research listed in table 1.2 were rated as less successfully attained than they were important, and the difference was significant for 13 of the 16

Table 1.2　**Importance and Current Success of Sport Management Research**

Item	IMPORTANCE Mean (Standard Deviation)	SUCCESS Mean (Standard Deviation)	Gap
Use of theory from parent disciplines	6.41 (0.62)	4.20 (0.94)	2.21*
Developing sport management theory	6.40 (0.83)	3.07 (1.10)	3.33*
Increasing the quality of research outlets in the field	6.33 (0.72)	3.73 (1.10)	2.60*
Developing overall sport management knowledge	6.33 (0.98)	4.27 (0.96)	2.06*
Recognition of sport management as a legitimate academic field of study	6.27 (0.80)	4.47 (0.99)	1.80*
Developing knowledge of sport ethics	6.13 (1.07)	3.47 (1.13)	2.66*
Establishing an infrastructure for sport management	6.07 (1.03)	5.53 (0.92)	0.54**
Increasing quality of analyses in sport management research	5.93 (1.03)	3.73 (0.96)	2.20*
Linking theory to practice	5.80 (1.70)	3.30 (1.29)	2.50*
Developing specific sport marketing knowledge	5.73 (1.62)	4.20 (1.01)	1.53*
Broadening sport management research to include both quantitative and qualitative methodologies	5.60 (1.68)	3.87 (1.55)	1.73*
Increasing quality of sport management research designs	5.47 (1.41)	3.53 (0.99)	1.94*
Developing knowledge about leadership in sport	5.33 (1.35)	3.33 (1.35)	2.00*
Developing knowledge about sport liability	5.29 (1.27)	4.07 (1.54)	1.22**
Diversifying sport management research settings	5.27 (1.53)	3.40 (1.45)	1.87*
Increasing the number of research outlets in the field	4.87 (1.55)	4.13 (1.25)	0.74**

*$p < .003$ (Bonferroni criterion); **$p \leq .05$.

Reprinted, by permission, from C.A. Costa, 2005, "The status and future of sport management: A Delphi Study," *Journal of Sport Management* 19(2): 117-142.

areas (significant differences below the Bonferroni criterion $p < .003$ are noted with a single asterisk in the table). Overall, the experts clearly felt that sport management research had not yet attained levels of success commensurate with the importance of many of its facets.

In general, the experts agreed that the following objectives were desirable: stronger research, additional cross-disciplinary research, a stronger link between theory and practice, enhanced infrastructure, and improved doctoral training. However, disagreement was noted about the appropriate academic home for sport management, what constitutes high-quality research, the roles of qualitative and quantitative research, and the relative value of basic versus applied research. Such disagreements are common in almost every academic discipline, but particularly in those as young as the field of sport management. Regular reflection and discourse on these issues in academic venues and in applied settings will help researchers further clarify significant issues in the field.

Summary

In order to become effective decision makers, sport managers must make decisions based on the best current knowledge, and doing so requires sport managers to become research consumers. Research is typically generated by a specific research question, hypothesis, or problem and is complemented by a specific plan or procedure, otherwise known as the research process. In addition, research is intended to increase understanding by interpreting facts and reaching conclusions based on facts and on reasoned argument. Research can be classified according to five perspectives: (1) the *application* of the research study (pure or applied research), (2) the researcher's *objectives* in undertaking the study (exploratory, descriptive, explanatory, or predictive research), (3) the *type of information sought* (qualitative, quantitative, or mixed-methods research), (4) the *presence of data* (theoretical or empirical research), and (5) the *data source* analyzed (primary or secondary research). A number of philosophical approaches to research exist, and these approaches are guided by ontology and epistemology. More specifically, certain ontological and epistemological assumptions—associated variously with the paradigms of postpositivism, constructivism, advocacy/participatory research, and pragmatism—often lead researchers to embrace a given qualitative, quantitative, or mixed-methods approach in their research. As with any relatively young discipline, sport management research has experienced growing pains, but regular reflection and discourse on disputed research issues will help researchers bring about effective growth in the field.

Research Methods and Design in Action
Journal of Sport Management

Selected text reprinted, by permission, from C.A. Costa, 2005, "The status and future of sport management: A Delphi Study," *Journal of Sport Management* 19(2): 117-142.

Access the full article online at www.humankinetics.com/products/all-products/Research-Methods-and-Design-in-Sport-Management.

ABSTRACT

Ongoing debates about appropriate foci and growth of sport management research, application, theory, and training are evidence of the field's growing pains. These growing pains also occur in other fields in which they function as a means to expand and elaborate the paradigms through which fields of inquiry grow and mature. In this study, a panel of 17 leading sport management scholars from around the globe responded to three iterations of a Delphi questionnaire probing their views about the status and future of the field. Panelists agreed that stronger research, additional cross-disciplinary research, a stronger link between theory and practice, enhanced infrastructure, and improved doctoral training are desirable objectives. They disagreed, however, about the appropriate academic home for sport management, what constitutes quality research, the roles of qualitative vs. quantitative research, and the relative value of basic vs. applied research. The results show that by actively engaging in debates over the issues identified in this study, sport management scholars can explore new ways of perceiving, thinking, and valuing that could enable proficient and constructive development of the field.

TEXT EXCERPTS

A paradigm, because it can be said to be a lens through which we see the world, has the power to shape, define, and dominate academic discourse through its deeply rooted assumptions and values.

．．．．．．．．．．．．．．．．．

Elliot (1999) observes, "appreciative inquiry creates a development pathway based on what is right rather than what is wrong" (p. vi). In the case of sport management, apprecia-tive inquiry can enable a more rapid advance of the field by identifying useful pathways for future work.

．．．．．．．．．．．．．．．．．

Because the Delphi technique requires that panelists be experts in the field about which they are being queried (Martino, 1983), it was necessary to identify scholars who could arguably be considered experts. In order to identify experts, a three-step process was used.

．．．．．．．．．．．．．．．．．

The first question asked panelists to indicate current successes in sport management research that should be sustained. Responses to the open-ended question in the first round yielded 14 themes that fully described the successes panelists identified.

. . . .

A panelist with editorial-board experience noted, "Some reviewers reject qualitative studies based on their own positivist biases rather than on knowledgeable assessment of research." On the other hand, some panelists felt that both qualitative and quantitative research are respected in the field, but are often poorly carried out.

. . . .

The related debate among panelists about the relative value of qualitative vs. quantitative research reflects a more subtle paradigmatic difference between those who feel that sport management research can be conducted in a strictly objective (i.e., positivist) manner and those who feel that the management of sport is socially constructed.

DISCUSSION QUESTIONS

1 The conceptual basis of this study involves scholarly debate about research. Referring to the literature review, identify two concerns that past scholars have raised about sport management research.

2 What research questions guided this study?

3 What is the current status of sport management research? More specifically, identify some of the successes achieved by sport management research.

4 Describe an ideal future for sport management research.

5 What can be done to build and enhance sport management research?

6 What areas of disputation exist in sport management research?

7 What paradigms and perspectives are likely to prove useful in moving research forward in the field?

8 Describe the three steps taken to select the participants for the study (i.e., the Delphi panel).

9 In terms of the type of information sought, should this study be classified as qualitative, quantitative, or mixed-methods research? Why?

10 What debates about qualitative versus quantitative research are highlighted in the discussion section?

11 What debates about basic (i.e., pure) versus applied research are highlighted in the discussion section?

Ethical Issues in Research

Learning Objectives

After studying this chapter, you should be able to do the following:

- Understand why human subjects need to be protected in research
- Discuss ethical principles and guidelines for research studies
- Describe the role and function of an institutional review board
- Identify the purposes of informed consent
- Describe areas in which scientific dishonesty might arise in a research study

Before embarking on any research project, researchers must ensure that their proposed study conforms to prevailing ethical standards. That is why we are addressing the topic of ethical research issues early on in this textbook. This chapter begins with a discussion of why human subjects need to be protected, then outlines ethical principles and guidelines for research. The chapter also discusses institutional review boards, guidelines for protecting human rights in sport management research, and issues of scientific dishonesty, including publication ethics.

Protection of Human Subjects

Unfortunately, the need for protection of **human subjects** is best illustrated by a number of studies in which the researchers used clearly unethical practices in their treatment of humans. Two of the most famous examples of unethical research are the Nuremberg medical studies and the Tuskegee syphilis study (Brandt, 1978). The unethical practices conducted in these two studies helped shape the formation of ethical guidelines and codes for modern research.

The Nuremberg medical studies were conducted in the 1940s on prisoners in German concentration camps, who participated involuntarily in numerous inhumane experiments conducted by German physicians. These inhumane experiments included placing prisoners in ice water to determine the length of time to death as a result of reduced core body temperature, infecting prisoners with the malaria virus to determine the treatment effectiveness of experimental drugs, and exposing prisoners to high altitude in order to determine how much pain one could endure before dying. After the war, many of the participating doctors were tried and convicted, and several were subsequently executed at the Nuremberg trials for their crimes. This study led to the publication of the Nuremberg Code (see highlight box).

The Nuremberg Code

The great weight of the evidence before us is to the effect that certain types of medical experiments on human beings, when kept within reasonably well-defined bounds, conform to the ethics of the medical profession generally. The protagonists of the practice of human experimentation justify their views on the basis that such experiments yield results for the good of society that are unprocurable by other methods or means of study. All agree, however, that certain basic principles must be observed in order to satisfy moral, ethical and legal concepts:

The voluntary consent of the human subject is absolutely essential. This means that the person involved should have legal capacity to give consent; should be so situated as to be able to exercise free power of choice, without the intervention of any element of force, fraud, deceit, duress, over-reaching, or other ulterior form of constraint or coercion; and should have sufficient knowledge and comprehension of the elements of the subject matter involved as to enable him to make an understanding and enlightened decision. This latter element requires that before the acceptance of an affirmative decision by the experimental subject there should be made known to him the nature, duration, and purpose of the experiment; the method and means by which it is to be conducted; all inconveniences and hazards reasonably to be expected; and the effects upon his health or person which may possibly come from his participation in the experiment. The duty and responsibility for ascertaining the quality of the consent rests upon each individual who initiates, directs or engages in the experiment. It is a personal duty and responsibility which may not be delegated to another with impunity.

The experiment should be such as to yield fruitful results for the good of society, unprocurable by other methods or means of study, and not random and unnecessary in nature.

The experiment should be so designed and based on the results of animal experimentation and a knowledge of the natural history of the disease or other problem under study that the anticipated results justify the performance of the experiment.

(continued)

Nuremberg Code   (continued)

The experiment should be so conducted as to avoid all unnecessary physical and mental suffering and injury.

No experiment should be conducted where there is an a priori reason to believe that death or disabling injury will occur; except, perhaps, in those experiments where the experimental physicians also serve as subjects.

The degree of risk to be taken should never exceed that determined by the humanitarian importance of the problem to be solved by the experiment.

Proper preparations should be made and adequate facilities provided to protect the experimental subject against even remote possibilities of injury, disability or death.

The experiment should be conducted only by scientifically qualified persons. The highest degree of skill and care should be required through all stages of the experiment of those who conduct or engage in the experiment.

During the course of the experiment the human subject should be at liberty to bring the experiment to an end if he has reached the physical or mental state where continuation of the experiment seems to him to be impossible.

During the course of the experiment the scientist in charge must be prepared to terminate the experiment at any stage, if he has probable cause to believe, in the exercise of the good faith, superior skill and careful judgment required of him that a continuation of the experiment is likely to result in injury, disability, or death to the experimental subject.

Source: Reprinted from *Trials of War Criminals Before the Nuremberg Military Tribunals Under Control Council Law No. 10*, Vol. 2, pp. 181–182. Washington, DC: U.S. Government Printing Office, 1949.

The Tuskegee syphilis study was a large-scale study of syphilis conducted on 399 rural African American males between 1932 and 1972. The study was conducted by the United States Public Health Service in order to determine the effectiveness of various syphilis treatments. The participants were not informed of their syphilis diagnosis and were enticed to participate in the study with promises of free medical treatment, rides to the clinic, meals, and burial insurance in case of death. Although penicillin had become the standard treatment for syphilis by 1947, researchers intentionally withheld penicillin from the study participants in order to continue studying the progression of the disease. Over 100 participants died from syphilis or complications of syphilis. The revelation of the researchers' unethical conduct led to the publication of the Belmont Report in 1979, a landmark document in medical ethics, the establishment of the National Human Investigation Board, and the requirement for establishing institutional review boards, the importance of which will be discussed later in this chapter.

Ethical Principles and Guidelines

The American Psychological Association (APA) provides ethical guidance for researchers in the form of five ethical principles:

- Beneficence and nonmaleficence
- Fidelity and responsibility
- Integrity
- Justice
- Respect for people's rights and dignity

These principles, as presented in the APA's (2002) *Ethical Principles of Psychologists and Code of Conduct,* are described in the highlight box.

Based on these five ethical principles, the APA provides a number of guidelines for ethical research:

- Using recognized standards of competence and ethics, psychologists plan research so as to minimize the possibility of misleading results. Any ethical problems are resolved before research is started. The welfare and confidentiality of all participants are to be protected.

- Psychologists are responsible for the dignity and welfare of participants. Psychologists are also responsible for all research they perform or that is performed by others under their supervision.

- Psychologists obey all state and federal laws and regulations, as well as professional standards governing research.

- Except for anonymous surveys, naturalistic observations, and similar research, psychologists reach an agreement regarding the rights and responsibilities of both participants and researcher(s) before research is started.

Principle A: Beneficence and Nonmaleficence

Psychologists strive to benefit those with whom they work and take care to do no harm. In their professional actions, psychologists seek to safeguard the welfare and rights of those with whom they interact professionally and other affected persons, and the welfare of animal subjects of research. When conflicts occur among psychologists' obligations or concerns, they attempt to resolve these conflicts in a responsible fashion that avoids or minimizes harm. Because psychologists' scientific and professional judgments and actions may affect the lives of others, they are alert to and guard against personal, financial, social, organizational, or political factors that might lead to misuse of their influence. Psychologists strive to be aware of the possible effect of their own physical and mental health on their ability to help those with whom they work.

Principle B: Fidelity and Responsibility

Psychologists establish relationships of trust with those with whom they work. They are aware of their professional and scientific responsibilities to society and to the specific communities in which they work. Psychologists uphold professional standards of conduct, clarify their professional roles and obligations, accept appropriate responsibility for their behavior, and seek to manage conflicts of interest that could lead to exploitation or harm. Psychologists consult with, refer to, or cooperate with other professionals and institutions to the extent needed to serve the best interests of those with whom they work. They are concerned about the ethical compliance of their colleagues' scientific and professional conduct. Psychologists strive to contribute a portion of their professional time for little or no compensation or personal advantage.

Principle C: Integrity

Psychologists seek to promote accuracy, honesty, and truthfulness in the science, teaching, and practice of psychology. In these activities psychologists do not steal, cheat, or engage in fraud, subterfuge, or intentional misrepresentation of fact. Psychologists strive to keep their promises and to avoid unwise or unclear commitments. In situations in which deception may be ethically justifiable to maximize benefits and minimize harm, psychologists have a serious obligation to consider the need for, the possible consequences of, and their responsibility to correct any resulting mistrust or other harmful effects that arise from the use of such techniques.

Principle D: Justice

Psychologists recognize that fairness and justice entitle all persons to access to and benefit from the contributions of psychology and to equal quality in the processes, procedures, and services being conducted by psychologists. Psychologists exercise reasonable judgment and take precautions to ensure that their potential biases, the boundaries of their competence, and the limitations of their expertise do not lead to or condone unjust practices.

Principle E: Respect for People's Rights and Dignity

Psychologists respect the dignity and worth of all people, and the rights of individuals to privacy, confidentiality, and self-determination. Psychologists are aware that special safeguards may be necessary to protect the rights and welfare of persons or communities whose vulnerabilities impair autonomous decision making. Psychologists are aware of and respect cultural, individual, and role differences, including those based on age, gender, gender identity, race, ethnicity, culture, national origin, religion, sexual orientation, disability, language, and socioeconomic status and consider these factors when working with members of such groups. Psychologists try to eliminate the effect on their work of biases based on those factors, and they do not knowingly participate in or condone activities of others based upon such prejudices.

Source: American Psychological Association (2002). *Ethical Principles of Psychologists and Code of Conduct.* www.apa.org/ethics/code/index.aspx.

- When consent is required, psychologists obtain a signed, informed consent before starting any research with a participant.

- Deception is used only if no better alternative is available. Under no condition is there deception about aspects that might influence a participant's willingness to participate.

- Psychologists make reasonable efforts to avoid offering excessive or inappropriate financial or other inducements for research participation when such inducements are likely to coerce participation.

- After research results are published, psychologists do not withhold the data on which their conclusions are based from other competent professionals who seek to verify the substantive claims through reanalysis and who intend to use such data only for that purpose, provided that the confidentiality of the participants can be protected and unless legal rights concerning proprietary data preclude their release. Psychologists who request data from other psychologists to verify the substantive claims through reanalysis may use shared data only for the declared purpose.

- Psychologists provide a prompt opportunity for participants to obtain appropriate information about the nature, results, and conclusions of the research, and they take reasonable steps to correct any misconceptions that participants may have of which the psychologists are aware.

More specific information about these guidelines can be found in the full text of the APA's (2002) *Ethical Principles of Psychologists and Code of Conduct.*

Institutional Review Board

Federal regulations require institutions (including all colleges and universities) to maintain an ***institutional review board*** (IRB) to oversee all research involving human subjects. An IRB is also commonly referred to as a human subjects committee or human subjects review board. According to the APA, researchers must inform participants about the following:

- The purpose of the research, expected duration, and procedures

- Their rights to decline to participate and to withdraw from the research after participation has begun

- The foreseeable consequences of declining or withdrawing

- Reasonably foreseeable factors that may be expected to influence their willingness to participate, such as potential risks, discomfort, or adverse effects

- Any prospective research benefits

- Limits to confidentiality

- Incentives for participation

- Who to contact with questions about the research and the research participant's rights

For more on informing participants about the details of a study, and on obtaining participants' consent, see this chapter's next section, which addresses informed consent.

IRB procedures differ from institution to institution; some core principles, however, can be found across institutions. Researchers must submit research plans to the IRB before collecting data on human subjects. IRB representatives or committees review the research plan with a focus on assuring the subjects' safety and privacy and their right to informed consent. IRBs typically recognize classifications or categories of review based upon the type of research being conducted, though classification names and procedures may differ slightly across institutions. Studies involving no risk to participants are typically designated as having exempt status, meaning that they are considered exempt from examination by the full IRB; instead, just one or two board members review and approve such a study prior to data collection. Much of the research conducted in the sport management discipline falls into this category—for example, sport marketing fan surveys conducted at baseball games and qualitative interviews conducted with athletic directors about leadership styles (unless the interviews are recorded).

Studies with minimal risk to subjects are typically classified as having expedited status (again, specific status terminology and procedures may differ across institutions). An expedited review does not require participation by an entire IRB board but is more rigorous in nature than an exempt review. This category includes, for example, studies involving exercise testing or the collection of blood, neither of which, of course, is common in the sport management discipline. Sport management examples could include recording an interview or surveying or interviewing children, since research involving children generally warrants more stringent review in order to assure their protection. Finally, studies involving more substantial risk to subjects are typically classified as warranting full review. Due to the nature of most sport management research, full reviews are rare in this discipline, since institutions typically use this category for projects involving collection of data from or about fetuses, pregnant women, and other vulnerable populations—groups not often examined in sport management literature. Regardless of the classification or type of review, researchers must obtain IRB approval before collecting data. Failure to do so could result in forfeiting data already collected or, in extreme cases, more severe penalties.

Informed Consent

In order to adhere to legal standards, researchers must provide research participants with all the facts about a study before participation is initiated. The legal principle that requires researchers to obtain voluntary consent is referred to as **informed consent.** Subjects should be presented with a consent form and asked to give their consent to participate prior to the study. A consent form often includes information about the purpose of the study, a brief identification of the primary researcher, an explanation of any risks or harm associated with study participation, an estimate of the time it will take to participate in the study, *a statement about confidentiality*, and a statement concerning the voluntary nature of participation in the study. Fischman (2000) suggests that a consent form include 12 components (see the highlight box).

The following is an example of an informed consent form included at the beginning of a survey instrument that was used to collect data from patrons at a college sporting event. The form has been altered for purposes of confidentiality. On the actual survey instrument, the researcher's name and contact information, as well as that of the employing institution, were provided as part of the informed consent form.

You must be at least 18 years of age to participate in this survey. Your participation in this study is voluntary. There are no penalties for choosing not to participate and you may withdraw at any time, without penalty. Data will be analyzed and reported using group demographics and at no time will an attempt be made to identify specific responses with names, minimizing risks of confidentiality. There are no direct benefits to you for participating in this study. If you have any ques-

tions or concerns about this study please contact the principal investigator and/or the institution's research ethics and compliance office.

Scientific Dishonesty

Researchers should avoid **scientific dishonesty** at all times. Shore (1991) describes seven areas in which scientific dishonesty might occur. First, researchers should avoid **plagiarism**—that is, using the ideas, writings, or drawings of others as your own (Thomas, Nelson, & Silverman, 2005). Second, researchers should not fabricate or falsify data. Third, researchers should avoid nonpublication of data, which occurs when a researcher does not report collected data that fails to support the hypothesis. Fourth, researchers should avoid faulty data gathering procedures (e.g., failing to conform to IRB guidelines). Fifth, researchers must ensure that data are stored and maintained in their original and unaltered form. Sixth, researchers should not participate in misleading authorship activities. The order of authorship for presentations and publications in sport management research is generally based on the researchers' specific contributions to the project. The first author is the primary contributor to the study and is usually responsible for developing the research idea and the plan for research. Subsequent authors are then listed in descending order based on their contributions to the research project. Finally, researchers should not participate in unacceptable publication practices—for example, dual publication, in which the same scientific paper is published in more than one journal.

Summary

It is imperative that researchers make every effort to conform to proper ethical standards in conducting their research. Failure to do so could result in tragic consequences, as exemplified in the horrifying examples of the Nuremberg medical studies and the Tuskegee syphilis study. The ethical standards discussed here provide a basic framework for assuring ethical research activity in the sport management discipline. Researchers must also adhere to IRB requirements and informed consent procedures in order to protect subjects' safety, privacy, and right to be fully informed about the purposes and procedures of a research study and to be free in choosing whether to participate.

Fischman's Twelve Components of the Consent Form

1. Invitation to Participate

This invitation makes it clear that the participant is volunteering for the role of research participant.

2. Purpose of the Research

The purpose states the overall reason for the research, including, when appropriate, research goals at the individual and group levels.

3. Selection Bias

Stating clearly why the participant is appropriate for the study allows prospective participants to exclude themselves if they do not believe they meet the criteria for inclusion.

4. Study Procedures

The study procedures should be clearly described to prospective study participants.

5. Descriptions of Risks and Discomforts

Making potential volunteers aware of possible risks and discomforts enables them to make informed decisions about whether to participate in the study.

6. Description of Benefits

In general, benefits can be summarized under the category of anticipated additions to a systematic body of knowledge.

7. Available Alternatives

Giving potential participants information about available alternatives is most relevant for therapeutic studies in which nonvalidated interventions are being examined.

8. Assurance of Confidentiality

It is impossible to guarantee absolute confidentiality, and the extent and limits of the confidentiality guarantee should be described as part of the informed consent process.

9. Financial Considerations

Any costs of participating in the research should be clearly described. Economic advantages might include money, merchandise vouchers, food, access to improved facilities, therapy, physical exams, or subsidized transportation.

10. Offer to Answer Questions

It is important that participants know who to contact if they have questions, encounter problems as participants, or incur an injury while participating.

11. Noncoercive Disclaimer

Participation in research should be voluntary, and a decision to not participate or to discontinue one's participation should not result in any penalty or loss of benefits.

12. Incomplete Disclosure

Although the researcher should provide sufficient information for each potential participant to make an informed decision about whether to participate in a specific study, there are times when some information may be withheld. Although generally not the first choice of researchers, this approach is sometimes necessary in order to protect the validity of the data collected. To the extent possible, the researcher should present information necessary to make an informed decision and should include a statement in the consent form indicating that some information is being withheld.

Source: Fischman, M.W. (2000). Informed consent. In B.D. Sales & S. Folkman (Eds.), *Ethics in research with human participants* (pp. 35-48). Washington, DC: American Psychological Association.

Research Methods and Design in Action
Journal of Sport Management

Selected text from L. Kihl, T. Richardson, C. Campisi, 2008, "Toward a grounded theory of student-athlete suffering and dealing with academic corruption," *Journal of Sport Management* 22(3): 273-302.

Access the full article online at www.humankinetics.com/products/all-products/Research-Methods-and-Design-in-Sport-Management.

ABSTRACT

The purpose of this grounded theory study was to explain how student-athletes are affected by an instance of academic corruption. Using a grounded theory approach (Glaser & Strauss, 1967; Strauss & Corbin, 1998), multiple sources of data were collected and analyzed using the constant comparison method leading to theory generation. Findings revealed that student-athletes suffer three main consequences (negative treatment, sanctions, and a sense of loss) that lead to various harmful outcomes (e.g., distrust, embarrassment, dysfunctional relationships, stakeholder separation, anger, stress, and conflict). However, the consequences also created a positive outcome displayed through a dual consciousness of corruption (resiliency and empowerment). The results are compared with existing theoretical concepts and previous research associated with the outcomes of corruption. This theory adds to our knowledge of the nature of suffering experienced by student-athletes as a result of corruption and provides direction for future research and practice.

TEXT EXCERPTS

A single case study and grounded theory approaches were employed as the aim of the research was to generate a substantive theory of student-athlete suffering and dealing with academic corruption within the context of an intercollegiate MBB program.

· · · · · · · · · · · · · · · · ·

While conceptual frameworks exist relating to intercollegiate athletic reform (e.g., Coalition on Intercollegiate Athletics, 2005; Gerdy, 1997; National Association of Academic Advisors for Athletes, 2004), these frameworks address prevention rather than provide detailed theoretical accounts of the influence that corruption has on organizational stakeholders. As a result the reform literature is less applicable to providing explanatory insights into postscandal experiences. Given that nominal theory exists about the impact of corruption on organizational stakeholders in an in intercollegiate athletic setting this combined approach was used to theorize about the consequences of academic corruption.

■■■■■■■■■■■■■■■■■

The first stage in data collection, coding, and analysis was negotiating access. One of the coauthors negotiated access with the University of Minnesota's MBB Head Coach to conduct the study. Negotiations lasted approximately three months and subsequently the lead author and one of the coauthors gained further permission from the athletic director. Institutional Review Board ethics approval was then obtained as all guidelines were suitably met. One of the assistant coaches served as an "ally" in acquiring the participation of the other assistants. Another assistant served as a separate ally in securing the partici-

pation of former student-athletes. The various kinds of support provided by the two assistant coaches were a crucial aspect of the access process. While the assistants did not serve as formal gatekeepers in the traditional sense, their help represented Morrill, Buller, Buller, and Larkey's (1999, p. 52) description of the different aspects of gatekeeping, where fieldworkers must "negotiate 'everyday access' to informal groups and individuals within organizations."

■■■■■■■■■■■■■■■■■

Confidentiality agreement between the researchers and participants entailed that since the University name was identified that the researchers would only identify the participants by general position (e.g., a coach, a student-athlete, or an administrator) and that no demographic information would be included in the findings.

DISCUSSION QUESTIONS

1 The authors used a case study design in order to examine the situation at a single school rather than study multiple schools. What reasons might they have had for making this choice?

2 The authors discuss at length their struggle to gain access to the subjects in the study, particularly the coaches. Why might the coaches have been hesitant to participate in the interviews and in the study overall?

3 It is likely that the school's institutional review board (IRB) examined the issue of confidentiality in this study. Subjects were identified by position rather than by name, but because the University of Minnesota was identified it would not be difficult to determine the identities of some of the subjects. How might the school's IRB have viewed this issue in light of Fischman's twelve components of consent as presented in this chapter?

part

II

The Research Process

The questions faced by sport managers vary widely, but the research process typically used to address them is stepwise and fairly standardized. In the interest of clarity, part II of this book presents the steps of the research process in a certain chronological order, but in practice researchers often move back and forth between steps in a quest to continually refine a research question. For example, if a researcher's literature review reveals that his or her selected topic has already been sufficiently addressed, the researcher may choose to change the topic. A researcher might also vary the steps in the research process for methodological reasons; for instance, a qualitative research project may dictate that the literature review and data collection stages be merged. Therefore, the steps presented in this part of the book should be viewed as essential elements of a high-quality research study, but they need not always be completed in the linear order presented here.

Given the volume of research conducted in the discipline of sport management in any given year, it is important that each project be presented in a standardized manner in order to produce a consistent body of research. Thus this section of the book not only covers the research process but also addresses considerations that each researcher must take into account when producing a research paper.

chapter 3

Creation
of Research Questions

Learning Objectives

After studying this chapter, you should be able to do the following:

- Discuss methods commonly used in selecting a research problem
- Identify potential sources for conducting a literature review
- Understand criteria for writing a high-quality literature review
- Describe the five steps in developing a conceptual framework
- Discuss issues to consider in creating research questions
- Understand the types of variables used in research
- List the four important characteristics of high-quality hypotheses

The initial steps of the research process are also some of most important and difficult ones. The researcher must define a research problem of interest, conduct a thorough literature review on that problem or topic, create a well-structured theoretical or conceptual framework aligned with the research problem, delineate specific and measureable research questions flowing from these previous steps to address weaknesses in the literature, identify variables, and establish hypotheses to use in answering the research questions. If any of these steps is not done effectively, it may be too late to salvage a solid and valid research study no matter how well the remaining steps are done. Figure 3.1 illustrates the steps involved in creating research questions.

Problem Selection

For a sport manager, one of the most challenging stages of the research process is the initial selection of a problem or topic to explore. This stage can be particularly daunting for novice researchers, who may feel that they do not possess enough knowledge about particular sport management topics that need further exploration. It may be encouraging for new researchers to know that this concern can

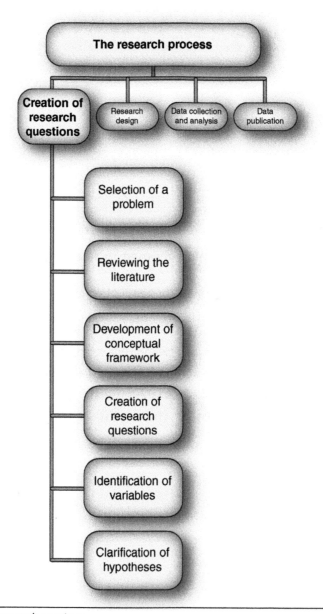

Figure 3.1 Steps for creating research questions.

affect any sport management researcher, regardless of how much experience he or she has with a given topic or problem area, because the more educated one becomes the more one realizes how much one does *not* know about various problems both within and beyond the realm of sport. To help you address this challenge, we provide (in chapter 1, page 4) a list of research topic areas as a starting point for considering sport management subdisciplines and their context areas. Once you choose a general topic of interest, you can identify potential research problems by examining existing literature, considering social concerns and popular issues, exploring your personal background, brainstorming ideas, and talking with professors and practitioners. Figure 3.2 illustrates a personalized approach to selecting a research problem.

▪ Existing literature. This is perhaps the most obvious source of potential research problems or topics, and you can scan the literature in various ways. For example, if you are comfortable with the general area into which your specific topic falls, you might begin by conducting searches by means of electronic databases with specific search terms already in mind. As your search for more specific information progresses, you might narrow or broaden the original search terms depending on the number and quality of sources you find. Alternatively, if you are struggling to select a problem, you might begin your search by perusing printed sources, such as recent editions of peer-reviewed journals; specifically, you might scan the table of contents in various journals until you have identified a number of potential areas of interest. You can then explore these problem areas in order to narrow your focus. Using existing literature to generate research ideas also enables you to become familiar with previous attempts to address your selected problem, as well as the various approaches that have been used. Remember, too, that many well-written journal articles conclude by identifying

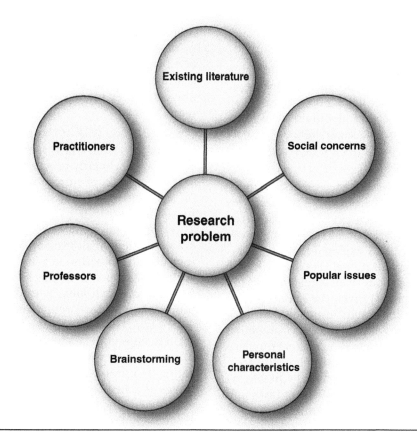

Figure 3.2 A personalized approach to selecting a research problem. Here are some questions to ask: What issues are emerging in the literature? What research problems could be answered to benefit society (e.g., what are the effects of large-scale sporting events on local economies?)? What contemporary topics are being discussed in the media (e.g., the Olympics)? What experiences from your background might lead to a research study (e.g., are you a recreational skier? A sport-marketing student?)? Who can you collaborate with to develop a research problem? What issues are faculty researching, teaching, and discussing? What issues are industry professionals facing in the field?

avenues for further research about the problem. This is a service to the field and offers you ideas for work that you might choose to do.

- Social concerns. Research ideas rooted in contemporary social concerns include problems such as the integration of individuals with disabilities into sport and society (Andrew & Grady, 2005; Grady & Andrew, 2003, 2006, 2007; Hums, Moorman, & Wolff, 2003), the impact of diversity in the workplace (Cunningham, 2007; Cunningham & Sagas, 2007; Fink & Cunningham, 2005), and gambling in sport (Thrasher, Andrew, & Mahony, 2007a, 2007b). Researchers who select their topics on the basis of social concerns may also enjoy an additional benefit insofar as their research may be viewed as a vehicle for social reform.

- Popular issues. Research ideas may also be found in the wide range of popular contemporary issues discussed on Web sites and in newspapers and magazines. If you take this approach, it is crucial to choose a high-quality Web site or print publication in order to locate a thorough review of problems of that may be of interest. One disadvantage of using popular issues to generate a research problem is that these issues are often so contemporary that it may be challenging to identify a research base within the academic literature to support such a novel topic or problem. On the other hand, popular issues can serve as valuable sources for identifying new areas for discovery, and certain subdisciplines of sport management (e.g., sport law) are more reliant on popular issues than others.

- Your own personal characteristics. Sport management researchers hail from a variety of cultures and backgrounds, and their experiences can serve as a platform for research problems. For instance, Todd and Andrew (2006) explored the role of satisfying tasks and organizational support in the job attitudes of sporting goods retail employees. As the researchers explained, "[g]iven the importance of satisfaction and commitment outcomes to sales force turnover, the possibility that environmental factors in sporting goods retail could alter employee attitudes, and the absence of research in the area, we purposed to extend the literature by highlighting the impact of intrinsically satisfying tasks and perceived organisational support on the job satisfaction and commitment of sporting goods retail employees" (p. 380). Ultimately, the researchers discovered that intrinsically satisfying tasks and perceived organizational support contributed significantly to the prediction of job satisfaction and affective organizational commitment. In other words, sporting goods retail employees who were given more intrinsically satisfying tasks (e.g., a tennis-playing employee who is assigned to work in the store's tennis department) and who perceived organizational support (e.g., an employee who believes that the organization keeps her best interest in mind, supports her, and writes policies that will benefit her) are more satisfied with their jobs and are more likely to want to continue working for that organization. The idea for this particular study was generated through Todd and Andrew's cumulative work experiences, some of which involved managerial responsibility in the sporting goods retail setting. As they discuss in their article, these work experiences impressed upon them the importance of controlling turnover, as well as the uniqueness of the context of sport, in the retail setting.

- Brainstorming. Generally speaking, brainstorming is a group activity with the expressed purposed of generating a large number of potential solutions to a problem. It can also be a good way to generate research ideas. Discussing ideas with others often helps a researcher develop and refine possible research questions, which is a key benefit of collaborative research. As ideas and terms emerge during brainstorming, key phrases are often written down and then related to each other in generative ways.

- Professors. One of the many duties typically assigned to professors is the publication or presentation of scholarly research. As a result, professors typically concentrate on a modest number of research topics and design research projects to facilitate further exploration of these topics. Therefore, while professors typically receive their academic credentials from an overall field of study, they develop expertise in a few concentrated areas within that field. With this in mind, one way to generate research ideas is to open dialogue with professors who hold research interests similar to your own. For students, establishing mentoring relationships with faculty members can be integral in getting their own research started, and participating in a professor's research project commonly serves as a first foray into becoming a researcher. Others may find a research problem idea in a conversation with a professor or in something a professor discusses in a classroom lecture.

- Practitioners. Another potentially valuable source for research ideas is sport management practitioners, who can often identify applied problems within the field that they have encountered through their work experiences. In a critique of the existing sport management research at the time, Weese (1995) lamented that sport management scholars were not serving the needs of practitioners, and, unfortunately, much of his critique remains valid today. By involving practitioners in topic selection, you can help ensure that your study will be pertinent to those working in the field. In one example, McEvoy and Morse (2007) examined how game attendance for an NCAA Division I men's basketball program was affected by whether or not the game was televised. The study originated in a conversation McEvoy had with the athletic director of a NCAA Division I school, who said that he believed televising games would cause potential spectators to stay home and watch games on television rather than purchase tickets and attend games in person. McEvoy, in contrast, hypothesized that televising the school's games would expose potential spectators to the product, serve as a 2-hour advertisement of sorts for the school and its athletic teams, and potentially add a layer of excitement to the game itself due to the presence of television. McEvoy and Morse designed a study to test the relationship between game attendance and the televising of games while controlling for other variables that might affect this relationship, such as strength of opponent and day of the week. They found that attendance increased by 6.3 percent when games were televised, thus illustrating how involving practitioners in the process of generating research problems can lead to research that is practical and actionable in the industry. In this example, practitioners considering whether to televise their games may be able to rely on data-based research in addition to their own thoughts and instincts in making such a decision.

After assimilating a number of sources regarding a potential research topic, researchers sometimes find that a past study has already addressed their original research idea. Such a discovery, however, does not necessarily indicate that further research is moot in the chosen area. Veal (1997) suggested some ways in which researchers can build upon prior research in the field. First, the results of any study may vary according to the geographic background of the sample; for example, an analysis of cricket fans' attitudes in Australia is not particularly generalizable to cricket fans in Canada. Indeed, several sport management studies have focused on cross-national differences found in samples from two different countries on topics ranging from leadership behavior (Chelladurai, Imamura, Yamaguchi, Oinuma, & Miyauchi, 1988) to the consumption motivations of mixed martial arts fans (Kim, Andrew, & Greenwell, 2009). Therefore, a researcher can consider conducting a new study using fans from a different targeted geographic area. Second, past studies in a particular problem area may have devoted less attention to some social groups than to others. The impetus for analyzing neglected social groups may be a desire to highlight an underrepresented social group or to respond to changing societal demographics. For example, an increasing Latino population in the United States has recently generated a stream of sport marketing research about patterns of sport consumption by Latinos (Harrolle & Trail, 2007; Mercado, 2008). Furthermore, determining the applicability of past research (or the lack thereof) to particular social groups can often lead to the advancement of theory in the field.

Another way to complement past research is to provide a temporal update to a prior research project. This approach allows a researcher not only to provide an up-to-date snapshot of current trends in the area but also to initiate data comparisons between past and present research. Significant events in history can also provide a supportive rationale for a modern treatment of past research. For example, a researcher interested in the perceived security of spectators at sporting events might not feel comfortable relying on results reported prior to the tragic events of September 11, 2001, in the United States, since that event has ramped up the need for security at major events held throughout the world.

Fourth, researchers may identify existing theories outside the realm of sport and propose to test them in the unique context of sport. Such a contextual approach can also be used to revisit existing research under modern theoretical paradigms to determine whether the new theoretical approaches provide greater explanatory power.

A final approach whereby researchers can build on prior research involves adapting a novel method of analysis to explore a phenomenon. For example, a researcher might follow up a previously published qualitative study with a quantitative approach that focuses on testing theory with a larger sample. Researchers can also help confirm findings from past research by using alternative designs (e.g., using a survey to follow up on findings from in-depth interview data).

Literature Review

Once you have selected a research problem or topic, the next step is to review the relevant literature. A *literature review* involves critically reading, evaluating, and organizing existing literature on a problem in order to assess the state of knowledge in the chosen area. During this phase, you will learn more about the problem you selected and become able to make a judgment, based on this new information, regarding the viability of the chosen problem. For instance, a thorough literature review might uncover several sources that have already explored your original research problem, thus forcing you to modify the problem in order to add new knowledge to the field. On the other hand, a literature review might also reveal an insufficient research base to support your original problem, and this finding would also prompt you to modify your problem. Thus literature review serves an important role in the research process while also allowing you to refine your problem.

Gratton and Jones (2004) delineate a number of purposes that a literature review can serve in a research project:

- To demonstrate the researcher's familiarity with and knowledge of the subject
- To provide an outline of theories and concepts important to the researcher's project
- To focus the research question
- To determine the extent of past research into the subject matter
- To develop a hypothesis (i.e., an educated guess regarding the study's outcome)
- To identify methodologies and methods that have been utilized in the past
- To help ensure that all relevant variables are identified
- To allow comparison of the researcher's findings with the findings of others

Each of these purposes deals with the generation of an appropriate basis and context for a study; in other words, the literature review serves as the foundation for any research project.

Sources of Literature

The researcher has a number of potential sources available for any research project: peer-reviewed journals, books and textbooks, conference papers, Web sites, theses and dissertations, newspapers and magazines, and trade journals. These sources vary in terms of academic rigor depending on the intended audience. In general, articles published in peer-reviewed journals will be of higher academic quality than material found in other sources, but the peer-review system is not perfect, and articles published in peer-reviewed journals can still contain erroneous information. Therefore, it is important to use sound judgment in assessing any source's quality.

When assessing the quality of a source, whether print or electronic, consider the following factors:

- Source itself: Does it include primary data (self-collected) or secondary data (already collected by others)? Has the content undergone any form of refereeing process?
- Authors: What are their qualifications? Are they experts in the subject area?
- Source's popularity as a reference work: Is the source often referred to in other articles in the subject area?
- Producers of the source: What was the purpose for producing the source (e.g., academic knowledge, product promotion, sales)? Who was the intended audience?
- Date of publication: When was the source published or last updated?
- Source's perceived accuracy and quality: Given your background and experience, what is your judgment of the source's quality? Does it take into account all of the relevant factors?

With the rise of the Internet, information is more accessible than ever for many people; however, given the relative ease with which individuals can publish information via outlets such as personal Web sites, it is important that researchers understand the importance of selecting high-quality sources in their literature reviews. Indeed, the quality of sources cited by a researcher in the literature review can also be viewed as an indicator of the overall quality of the current research project.

- Electronic databases. Once a researcher has identified potential sources, it is time to locate them, and modern sport management researchers enjoy the convenience of electronic databases to aid them in this quest. Electronic databases can be conceptualized as specialized search engines on specific academic topics. For example, at the time of publication of this text, the SPORTDiscus electronic database included more than 700,000 qualified references from thousands of international periodicals, books, e-journals, conference proceedings, theses, dissertations, and Web sites, as well as direct links to full-text articles covering all aspects of sport. These aspects include sport science and medicine, exercise physiology, fitness, physical education, recreation and leisure studies, kinesiology, biomechanics, coaching, athletic training, physical therapy, occupational therapy, psychology, sociology, history, sport management, facilities and equipment, and other related disciplines. Remember, however, that databases are only as good as the sources they search—SPORTDiscus, for example, does not search all available sport management journals—and they are also limited to some extent by the skill of the database operator. Also note that other search engines or databases may be valuable in finding articles related to a research problem, even if the articles found are not sport-related. Indeed, it is common in sport management literature for authors to develop theoretical frameworks for their research that rely on scholarship from other disciplines, such as business, sociology, psychology, and education. Electronic databases and search engines that may be useful in this regard include, for example, PsycINFO and ERIC (Education Resource Information Center).

■ Library catalogs. Now available online, library catalogs allow an individual to search for sources that are immediately available within a particular library. They can be used in conjunction with electronic database searches when the electronic database output includes citations for sources that were not available in full-text form through the electronic database. Many of the same techniques used for electronic databases are also applicable when using library catalogs, such as Boolean operators like *and* and *or*.

■ Internet searches. Online search engines can help you uncover valuable sources. In fact, the recent development of specialized search engines, such as Google Scholar (http://scholar.google.com/), has allowed researchers to search for peer-reviewed sources in an accessible environment. Google Scholar was released in November 2004, and it includes most peer-reviewed online journals of the world's largest scientific publishers. Like subscription-based electronic databases, Internet search engines are limited by the number and quality of sources they search.

■ Publisher's Web pages. These pages often include summary information about a book, or perhaps information about the scope of a particular journal, that can help a researcher determine whether a source will be helpful in addressing a chosen problem. Often, they also provide information (e.g., an ISBN number) that is helpful in locating the sources, and some offer the option of purchasing the source online.

■ Review articles. Often found in peer-reviewed journals, review articles are similar to book chapters in that they summarize key information about a particular problem, but they often provide more in-depth information, and they offer the added benefit of having been peer-reviewed. While the popularity of review articles often varies by discipline, a number of review articles have been published in the field of sport management. For example, Chelladurai (1990) published a review article on leadership behavior in sport that summarized research efforts on the problem through its publication date.

Writing the Literature Review

After the potential sources are located and critically evaluated, the researcher is ready to begin writing the literature review. Well-written literature reviews begin with an introduction that identifies the problem under investigation and provides a context for the review. The introduction should highlight the need for additional research, and this justification can often be strengthened by focusing on the practical application of the selected research problem (e.g., the financial and nonfinancial impact of enhanced customer satisfaction). The introduction should clearly convey the importance of the problem to the reader.

After introducing the problem, the researcher should begin writing the body of the literature review. This section should take a broad-to-narrow approach in which background information is presented first and the issues most pertinent to the research problem should be addressed last. Information should be presented in the form of an essay rather than an annotated list. In other words, in discussing past research, the writer should discuss relevant articles collectively, rather than individually, so that the materials in question can be grouped on the basis of issues such as research problem, methodology, and conclusions. The literature review should emphasize not just the research methodologies and variables in question but also the findings of previous research. In addition, the review should point out trends, themes, and gaps in the literature. Direct quotations should be used sparingly in literature reviews since they often do not convey their full meaning when quoted out of context; they may also disrupt the flow of the review due to variance in the writing styles of different authors. Since a literature review should serve as a critical analysis of available research about a chosen problem, the writer may elect to insert his or her opinions about the quality and importance of the research being cited.

As the literature review moves from a broad discussion of applicable theory to a narrower discussion of the specific problem at hand, the researcher should point out how the current study differs from previous studies. A primary purpose of the literature review is to build the researcher's hypothesis by the end of the review, which typically concludes with a purpose statement or a series of hypotheses that have been conceptually justified throughout the review. If this type of literature review is well written, the reader will be able to anticipate the statement of purpose prior to its formal introduction in the review. If the reader can correctly guess the problem statement by reading the previous portions of the literature review, then the writer has done an excellent job of scaffolding the purpose statement by identifying gaps in the literature and providing justifications for research on the problem.

Upon completing a draft of the literature review, the researcher should take a step back to critically evaluate its content and presentation, then revise as appropriate to strengthen the review. Here are some questions to ask:

- Is the literature included related to the research problem?
- How reasonable are the parameters of the literature (i.e., neither too broad nor too narrow)?
- Are all of the seminal, or most important, studies in this area of the literature covered?
- Are the most recent studies included?
- Is the review logically organized?
- Have gaps or weaknesses in the literature been addressed?
- Does the review contain a brief introduction and conclusion?
- Does the review lead to research questions and provide a rationale for those questions?

Development of a Conceptual Framework

The third step in the research process is to develop a theoretical or conceptual framework. In reality,

however, this step is accomplished in conjunction with writing the literature review since theoretical and conceptual frameworks are based in the literature. Defining theory can be quite challenging for novice researchers; indeed, even seasoned scholars can struggle with the components of theory (Sutton & Staw, 1995). Brief and Dukerich (1991) define theory as a set of logically related propositions that describe and explain a set of observations. Theories help researchers explain or understand a phenomenon of interest by addressing the question of why particular relationships occur.

Theoretical and conceptual frameworks involve the application of one or more theories to describe the variables in a study, their relationship to one another, and how they will be measured. Although the terms conceptual framework and theoretical framework are often used interchangeably, the term **conceptual framework** technically refers to a novel framework developed by a researcher that links concepts from the literature, whereas the term **theoretical framework** refers to a framework previously established in the literature. Regardless of whether a researcher develops a novel framework (i.e., a conceptual framework) or cites a popular framework that was developed by someone else (i.e., a theoretical framework), the proposition of a framework is an important component of the research process.

In order to develop a novel conceptual framework for a particular study, a researcher must address a number of considerations. Gratton and Jones (2004) describe five steps for developing a conceptual framework. First, the researcher must identify the relevant concepts in the study. For example, Andrew and Kent (2007) explored the effect of perceived leadership on the satisfaction, commitment, and motivation of college tennis players. These researchers adopted Chelladurai's (1978, 1990) Multidimensional Model of Leadership (MML) as a theoretical framework to explain the relationship between leadership and satisfaction, but since the relationships between leadership and commitment and motivation were not defined within the MML, they developed a conceptual framework to establish these links via an expansion of the outcomes typically associated with the MML. The relevant concepts in this particular study were identified as leadership, satisfaction, commitment, and motivation.

Next, the relevant concepts must be defined. In Andrew & Kent's (2007) study, leadership was acknowledged as having three aspects via the Multidimensional Model of Leadership: required (behavior required for a particular situation), preferred (behavior preferred by athletes in their coach), and actual or perceived (the coach's behavior as perceived by the athletes). In this particular study, Andrew and Kent (2007) explored only perceived leadership behaviors, which are determined in part by characteristics of the leader (e.g., personality, ability, and experience) and in part by preferences regarding leader behavior (e.g., the leader may conform his or her behavior to the requirements of the situation and to the preferences of the members). Athlete satisfaction was defined as a positive affective state resulting from a complex evaluation of the structures, processes, and outcomes associated with the athletic experience (Chelladurai & Riemer, 1997). Motivation was defined as the direction and intensity of effort (Sage, 1977), and it was further categorized into intrinsic motivation (engaging in activity purely for pleasure and satisfaction derived from doing so), extrinsic motivation (engaging in activity as a means to an end and not for its own sake), and amotivation (perceiving no contingencies between actions and outcomes, which often results in feelings of incompetence and lack of control) via Deci and Ryan's (1985) Self-Determination Theory. In the context of sport participation, commitment was defined as a psychological state representing the desire to resolve or continue sport participation (Scanlan, Carpenter, Schmidt, Simons, & Keeler, 1993). Clearly defining the important concepts within the framework helps prevent confusion should others decide to adopt your framework.

Third, after defining all relevant concepts in the study, the variables must be operationalized. In other words, the researcher needs to clearly delineate how each variable will be measured. Andrew and Kent (2007) adopted a number of previously published scales to measure the central concepts in their study. Leadership behavior was measured via Zhang, Jensen, and Mann's (1997) Revised Leadership Scale for Sports; athlete satisfaction was assessed via four subscales of Riemer and Chelladurai's (1998) Athlete Satisfaction Questionnaire; various components of intrinsic motivation and extrinsic motivation, as well as amotivation toward sport, were measured by the Sport Motivation Scale (Pelletier, Fortier, Vallerand, Tuson, Briere, & Blais, 1995), and determinants of sport commitment were assessed by means of the Sport Commitment Model Scale (Scanlan, Simons, Carpenter, Schmidt, & Keeler, 1993). It is crucial to identify how each construct will be measured because the quality of results relates directly to the quality of the measurement tools.

Fourth, researchers should identify moderating and mediating variables in the study. Moderating variables change the relationship between two other variables. For example, Chelladurai's (1978, 1990) Multidimensional Model of Leadership stipulates that a coach's leadership behavior has an influence on group performance. However, team performance can also be affected by other variables, such as the weather, the quality of the opposing team, injuries to key players, the influence of the crowd, the performance of the referee, and even luck. These influences can operate as moderating variables, then, because they can alter the relationship between the coach's leadership and the team's resulting performance. On the other hand, mediating variables explain the relationship between two other variables. For instance, Gratton and Jones (2004) identify self-efficacy as a mediating variable between leadership behavior and team performance. In other words, they propose that leadership behavior does not directly influence team performance but that it directly influences self-efficacy, or belief in one's abilities, which in turn influences team performance. In this case, self-efficacy is a mediating variable because it explains or accounts for the relationship between leadership behavior and team performance.

Finally, after identifying any moderating or mediating variables, the researcher must identify the proposed relationship between each of the variables. Such relationships are typically defined as being either positive, negative, or neutral. If a relationship between two variables is proposed to be positive, both variables are thought to move in the same direction. In other words, as the first variable increases, the second variable increases—or as the first variable decreases, the second variable decreases. In a negative relationship, the variables move in opposite directions (i.e., the first variable increases while the second variable decreases, or vice versa). A neutral relationship is proposed when two variables are seemingly unrelated. Note that variables are discussed in further detail a bit later in this chapter.

Focusing of Research Questions

At this point in the process, the researcher has selected a problem or topic to investigate and explored the literature. Upon completing a thorough literature review, the researcher should be able to identify gaps or weaknesses and develop a conceptual framework for the study. The next step is to narrow the overarching research problem or topic to one or more specific **research questions** that will lead the researcher to the remaining aspects of designing the study: variable selection, hypotheses, sampling, and statistical methodology (the latter two of these are discussed in subsequent chapters). Here are several issues to consider when creating a research question:

- Does the question address gaps or weaknesses in the existing literature?
- Is the question clear and concise?
- Is the question too broad, too narrow, or adequately in the middle?
- Can the question be answered, logistically, in a reasonable manner?
- Can I access the subjects or information necessary to answer the research question?
- Are the potential answers for the question important and interesting?

For example, let's assume that a researcher wants to study the impact of coaching leadership on sport team performance. This topic is fairly broad and has been addressed substantially in the literature, so the researcher considers narrowing the study to the leadership behavior of elite coaches in the National Football League. However, though this may seem to be a promising avenue for study, the necessary data collection would be highly dependent on the cooperation of several busy coaches who might not have or be willing to give the necessary time. As a result, barring some sort of special access to NFL coaches, the question may be an ill-advised one for most researchers. Similarly, if a researcher based in the United States created a research question regarding coaching characteristics common among successful coaches in English Premier League soccer, it might not be reasonable or feasible for the researcher to gain access to the subjects. At the same time, it is ineffective to simply revert to a general formulation such as how coaches affect the performance of athletes, which is far too broad to be answered in a single research study. The researcher must narrow or focus the research question in a way that enables him or her to design a study that is feasible to undertake.

Identification of Variables

Variables are the factors measured in a research study. For example, in an investigation of the effect

of day of the week on attendance at Major League Baseball games, two variables are examined: day of the week and attendance. One way to differentiate between types of variables is to determine whether they are serving as dependent or independent variables. *Independent variables* are the various factors controlled or manipulated in the study. *Dependent variables*, on the other hand, are the outcome variables of the investigation, often described as the variables of interest in a given study; they depend upon the independent variables that the researcher controls or manipulates. In the baseball attendance example, day of the week is the independent variable, and attendance is the dependent variable—the outcome of the study. In short, the researcher wants to see how variations in the independent variable (day of the week) affect the outcome, or dependent variable, which is game attendance.

Another distinction to make between types of variables involves how they are measured. Variables with a definite, or limited, number of possible values are called categorical variables, in that their finite possible values can be labeled as categories. Day of the week is a perfect example of a categorical variable: there are seven, and only seven, possible values (i.e., Monday, Tuesday, and so on through Sunday). Categorical variables that allow just two possible values are referred to as dichotomous variables. If the baseball attendance example was altered so that the researcher instead wanted to study the effect on attendance of whether a game was played during the day or at night, the game time would be a dichotomous variable (either day or night, depending upon start time). In contrast, variables with unlimited, or nearly unlimited, possible values are called continuous variables. In the examples used in this section of the chapter, Major League Baseball game attendance is a continuous variable because the value for attendance at a baseball game could be any of tens of thousands of possibilities, from mere hundreds (or, theoretically, even fewer) up to forty or fifty thousand or more. Technically, of course, this range isn't unlimited, since a stadium can hold only so many spectators, but it is close enough to unlimited that it is better defined as continuous rather than as categorical.

Clarification of Hypotheses

The next step in the research process is to clarify research questions and hypotheses. This step may also be completed in conjunction with the literature review since many research questions and hypotheses will be based in the literature. The process of clarifying research questions and hypotheses often allows a researcher to refocus on the specific objectives of the study.

A **hypothesis** is a suggested relationship between concepts based on prior research. Gratton and Jones (2004) note four important characteristics of good hypotheses. First, hypotheses should be adequate in the sense that they must be able to explain findings or relationships that are determined by subsequent data collection. Second, hypotheses must admit empirical testing by means of data analysis. Third, hypotheses should require relatively few assumptions, as it should be valid under multiple sets of conditions rather than be true only in very few circumstances. Finally, good hypotheses possess better explanatory power than their alternatives.

Summary

The initial steps in the research process—wherein the researcher goes about creating the research study—are vital. These beginning steps include formulating a research problem or topic, reviewing the relevant literature, developing a conceptual framework, defining specific research questions, identifying variables, and outlining hypotheses. If these steps are done poorly, it will be very difficult to salvage a solid study, no matter how well the remaining steps in the research process are performed. If, on the other hand, these initial steps are done well, they can form the backbone of a good research study that provides valuable insight into both the literature and the profession.

Selected text from M. Walker and A. Kent, 2009, "Do fans care? Assessing the influence of corporate social responsibility on consumer attitudes in the sport industry," *Journal of Sport Management* 23(6): 743-769.

Access the full article online at www.humankinetics.com/products/all-products/Research-Methods-and-Design-in-Sport-Management.

ABSTRACT

Organizations within the sport industry are facing increasing pressure to both maintain profitability and behave in socially acceptable ways, yet researchers have provided little information on how consumers perceive and react to corporate social responsibility (CSR). This mixed-design study examined the relationship between CSR activities and fans' assessments of reputation and patronage intentions. In addition, the study sought to determine the role of team identification in the aforementioned relationship. Fans of two NFL teams were sampled ($N = 297$), with quantitative results suggesting that CSR is an important predictor of reputation, and that two types of patronage could be significantly impacted as well. The moderating effect of team identification was significant yet influenced the outcomes in different ways. Qualitative findings reinforced the quantitative discussion by providing support for the general conclusions that CSR was viewed favorably by most fans, and is an important aspect of the overall business strategy of a sport organization.

TEXT EXCERPTS

A review of the existing CSR literature reveals three distinct categories of writing: (1) conceptual/theoretical work, (2) motives-oriented work, and (3) outcomes-oriented work. Overwhelmingly, the articles related to the conceptual (i.e., definitional) understanding of the construct dominated the review (see Carroll, 1999), perhaps due to the relative infancy of CSR scholarship and the general ambiguity of the term. Articles focusing on the motives (e.g., managerial and corporate) have generally sought to reveal the motivations and characteristics of corporate giving managers engaging in CSR activities (cf. Bucholtz, Amason, & Rutherford, 1999; Fitzpatrick, 2000; Quazi, 2003; Thomas & Simerly, 1994).

. . . .

Based on our content analysis results and previous literature suggesting that additional consumer-oriented CSR work needed to be done (Mohr et al., 2001), the conceptual model is presented in Figure 1. The propositions in the figure suggest that the (independent variable) CSR with four domains (i.e., philanthropy, community involvement, and youth programs in both education and health) will impact the five dependent variables of corporate reputation and the four dimensions of patronage intentions (i.e., repeat purchase, merchandise consumption, media consumption, and word of mouth). Since the study is focused on team-level analyses, the (dependent variables) are suggested to be moderated by a psychological connection variable (i.e., team identification). To support testing of the model, several (hypotheses) were developed, which are elucidated below.

DISCUSSION QUESTIONS

1 What research problem or topic area do the researchers address in this article?

2 On page 748, the authors use a figure to present the conceptual framework model they are testing in the study. In brief, how would you describe this model to someone unfamiliar with it?

3 How many hypotheses and research questions did the authors test in this study? Briefly describe the results of each hypothesis and research question.

4 What dependent and independent variables are investigated in the study?

Research Design

Learning Objectives

After studying this chapter, you should be able to do the following:

- Discuss the three major research designs, or modes of inquiry, and their strengths and weaknesses
- Understand the relationship and differences between a population and a sample
- Discuss the different types of probability and nonprobability sampling techniques
- Describe how to select an appropriate sample size
- Discuss the concept of reliability and its types
- Discuss the concept of validity and its types

The next step in the research process is to establish the research design—that is, the structural component. In this step, the researcher designs a study to answer the questions created in the earlier steps. To do so, the researcher chooses a type of research design (qualitative, quantitative, or mixed-methods); performs *sampling*, which means selecting subjects to be used in the study; and assures that the study's findings will be both reliable and valid.

Types of Research Design

Research designs, or modes of inquiry, can be divided into two main categories: qualitative and quantitative. Qualitative research uses nonquantitative or nonstatistical techniques to gain an in-depth understanding of a research problem, typically one involving a limited number of subjects. Results are presented in narrative form. Quantitative research, on the other hand, uses statistical techniques to explain phenomena, and results are presented in the form of statistics. A third type—mixed-methods research—uses both qualitative and quantitative techniques. All three of these modes are characterized by strengths and weaknesses, and the researcher must choose the mode that will best answer the research question(s).

Qualitative Research

The qualitative research process involves emerging questions and procedures, data typically collected in the participant's setting, data analysis that builds inductively (from particulars to general themes), and interpretations of the meaning of the data (Creswell, 2009). Qualitative research aims to develop theory and promote description, understanding, and meaning primarily through nonnumerical analysis. **Qualitative research** is typified by rich and subjective data (often collected via open-ended questions) and, accordingly, relatively small sample sizes. Whereas quantitative research may use, for example, a survey with multiple-choice or scaled questions, thus reaching thousands of subjects and generating large amounts of statistical data, qualitative research uses techniques such as 1- to 2-hour interviews, which would be difficult or impossible to conduct with thousands of subjects. As a result, qualitative research studies typically involve far fewer subjects than do quantitative ones. Strengths of qualitative methodologies include the following:

- Depth and richness of results
- Opportunity to ask follow-up questions that are not feasible when using a data collection instrument such as a survey
- Flexibility
- Ability to address complex why questions

If, for example, a researcher wants to understand why spectators attend college football games, one way to answer the question would be to develop a survey instrument asking spectators about their motivations for attendance. This method would be limited, however, by the inability to ask spectators follow-up questions and thus probe deeply into their reasons for attending. Qualitative interviews, on the other hand, would enable the researcher to address such questions.

Qualitative studies employ numerous approaches and procedures, and specific approaches that are often used in sport management research are thoroughly detailed in part II of this textbook. For now, here is a brief introduction to qualitative strategies. Ethnography is a strategy of inquiry in which the researcher studies an intact cultural group in a natural setting over a prolonged period of time by collecting observational and interview data (Creswell, 2007). In grounded theory designs, the researcher derives a general abstract theory of a process, action, or interaction grounded in the views of participants (Creswell, 2009). A case study approach is often used when the researcher wants to explore, in detail, a singular entity, such as a program, event, activity, process, or individual. Phenomenological research is a strategy of inquiry wherein the researcher identifies the essence of human experiences about a certain phenomenon as described by participants in terms of their lived experiences (Creswell, 2009). In narrative research, a researcher studies the lives of individuals and retells the story in a narrative chronology. Although this is not an exhaustive list, it does provide representative examples of qualitative approaches commonly employed in research activities.

Quantitative Research

At the other end of the research design spectrum lies **quantitative research,** which typically tests theories by examining the relationships between variables. Therefore, quantitative research is generally deductive; in other words, it is typically used to test a theory statistically rather than to build theory (as is commonly the case with qualitative research).

Variables in quantitative studies are usually measured by means of instruments that produce numerical data for statistical analysis. Quantitative research is often aimed at using data from a sample (often collected via closed-ended questions) to generalize to a larger population, and it often stresses objectivity and replicability. Other strengths of quantitative research include precise measurement of variables, the ability to statistically test research questions and hypotheses, and the opportunity to longitudinally measure subjects' subsequent performance.

Quantitative designs can be experimental, quasi-experimental, or nonexperimental. True experimental designs randomly assign subjects to either an experimental group or a control group. Examples include the pretest/post-test control group design, the post-test-only control group design, and the Solomon four-group design. In the pretest/post-test control group design, both the experimental and control groups are given a pretest, but only the experimental group receives the treatment. After the treatment has been administered, a post-test is given to both groups, and any resulting differences between the experimental and control groups are attributed to the treatment. For example, two groups of randomly assigned subjects are given a strength test (e.g., the bench press). The experimental group is taught a new conditioning technique, whereas members of the control group work out as they normally do. If the experimental group performs better on the post-test after 6 weeks of the new workout regimen, the researcher could conclude that there is evidence to support the effectiveness of the new conditioning technique. The post-test-only control group design works in similar fashion except that no pretest is administered.

Another group of designs, termed preexperimental designs, do not assign subjects randomly to groups and are therefore considered weaker than true experimental designs. Types of preexperimental design include the one-shot case study, the one-group pretest/post-test, and static group comparison designs. In one-shot case studies, subjects in a single group are introduced to a treatment or condition, then observed for changes that are attributed to the treatment. In a one-group pretest/post-test design, subjects are given a pretest, then exposed to a treatment, and finally given a post-test. In a static group comparison, experimental and control groups undergo the testing procedure, but only the control group is exposed to the treatment.

Due to practical constraints, quasi-experimental designs do not randomly select subjects or assign subjects to groups. These approaches include the time series design, multiple-time-series design, and nonequivalent control group design. The time series design expands the one-group pretest/post-test design by adding multiple pretests and post-tests to provide greater control over extraneous variables by minimizing the history effect (i.e., the potential impact of major events that occur between testing periods distorting the relationship between independent and dependent variables). The multiple-time-series design merely adds a control group to the time-series design. The nonequivalent control group design mimics the pretest/post-test control group design except that subjects are not randomly assigned to the two groups. This and other quasi-experimental designs are commonly used in sport management and related disciplines because sport management research often involves intact groups of subjects, thus eliminating the opportunity to randomly assign subjects.

Mixed-Methods Research

While qualitative and quantitative research projects pursue different goals and objectives, the two approaches should be thought of as complementary research designs with the common goal of generating new knowledge. Qualitative research allows the researcher to generate theory, usually by means of small samples, and quantitative research tests and refines theory by means of larger samples in order to generalize findings. Thus the two forms rely upon each other. Given the importance of both qualitative and quantitative approaches to research, it is not surprising that mixed-methods research—which combines the qualitative and the quantitative approaches—has recently gained in prominence. If well executed, **mixed-methods research** can capitalize on the strengths of both qualitative and quantitative research, using techniques from both approaches to triangulate research results (i.e., reach the same conclusion through the use of multiple methods).

Types of mixed-methods strategy include sequential mixed-methods, concurrent mixed-methods, and transformative mixed-methods. In sequential mixed-methods, the researcher begins with either a qualitative or quantitative method, then uses the alternative method in order to elaborate on or expand the findings produced with the original method. In the concurrent mixed-methods procedure, the researcher converges or merges quantitative and qualitative data in order to provide

Choosing a Research Design Style

Settling on a research design is one of the most challenging steps of the research process, particularly for inexperienced researchers. Consider a research question that involves determining the relationship between the success of a college football team and fundraising donations to the university. The researcher could use a qualitative study in which he or she interviewed university donors, either individually or in focus groups, to determine whether the football team's level of success affects how much they give. The researcher could also choose a quantitative design wherein he or she statistically tested whether significant differences appeared in fundraising totals depending upon the football team's winning percentage. Another alternative would be to incorporate both qualitative and quantitative

techniques. None of these choices is "the" right or wrong answer to the question of which design to use; each method has its strengths and weaknesses. Inexperienced researchers should take some comfort in knowing that multiple options are available and that no given option is necessarily wrong. Remember, too, that this decision is not made in isolation but is one of many steps in the research process. You can reflect on your research questions in order to examine which design might best answer your question(s). You might also examine previous studies identified in the literature review to see what methodologies are common and accepted in the area—or perhaps uncommon and therefore warranted in order to help fill a gap in the literature.

a comprehensive analysis of the research problem (Creswell, 2009). Thus the investigator collects both qualitative and quantitative data simultaneously, then integrates the information into overall results. In transformative mixed-methods work, the researcher uses a theoretical lens or perspective (e.g., a feminist perspective or critical theory) as an overarching viewpoint within a design that contains both quantitative and qualitative data (Creswell, 2009).

Sampling

The next step in the research process is sampling, which is the process by which the researcher chooses subjects for inclusion in the study. It is from these subjects that data will be collected through methods such as surveys and interviews.

 In order to select a **sample,** the researcher must first define the *population*—that is, the group of cases, meeting particular criteria, to which the researcher intends to generalize the study's results. For example, in a recent study of job satisfaction among college coaches, Dixon and Warner (2010) defined their population as coaches at NCAA Division III institutions. For obvious reasons, it was infeasible for the authors to interview all of the thousands of NCAA Division III coaches. This is where sampling comes in. Instead of collecting data

from vast numbers of subjects, sampling techniques provide ways to select smaller, more manageable numbers of subjects. If sampling is done effectively, the results of a study involving a fairly small sample can be generalized to members of the entire population, meaning that assumptions can be made about the whole population, or group, based upon the results from the smaller sample.

Sampling strategies can be divided into two groups: probability and nonprobability. In probability sampling, each unit within a population has an equal probability of being chosen. Probability sampling methods include random sampling, stratified random sampling, cluster sampling, and systematic sampling. Nonprobability sampling, in contrast, does not involve random selection; it includes convenience sampling and specific methods of purposive sampling, such as modal instance (or typical cases) sampling, expert sampling, quota sampling, heterogeneity sampling, and snowball sampling.

Probability Sampling

In a random sample, every member of the population has an equal probability of being selected. This technique is considered the best way to obtain a representative sample, but it requires the researcher to specifically define the population and ensure that each member has an equal chance of being selected. Stratified random sampling involves random sampling of particular subgroups within a population. For example, a sport marketing researcher might divide the consumer population into two groups—those who hold season tickets and those who do not—based on the percentage of fans at a particular sporting event who are currently season ticket holders. If, for a particular event, 45 percent of consumers are season ticket holders and 55 percent of consumers are individual game ticket purchasers, the researcher would then randomly select 45 percent of the sample from season ticket holders and 55 percent of the sample from buyers of tickets for an individual game. The stratified random sampling method ensures that the initial sample is reflective of the subgroups present in the population. Another approach, known as cluster sampling, randomly selects groups rather than individuals. For example, sport marketers could randomly select various seating areas within a stadium and survey all consumers within those sections. A third approach, systematic sampling, involves selecting every n^{th} case. In other words, the researcher might survey every seventh person entering a particular gate of a sport facility or every fifth sponsor on a comprehensive list of event sponsors. Systematic sampling is most effective when the list from which the names are taken is randomly ordered.

Nonprobability Sampling

In cases where **probability sampling** is cost-prohibitive or otherwise infeasible, researchers can use a nonprobability sampling technique. One widely used **nonprobability sampling** technique in sport management is convenience sampling, in which, as the name suggests, the researcher selects a sample based on convenience of access. For example, a number of published sport marketing studies sample college students and, in particular, students enrolled in sport marketing classes. One weakness of convenience samples is that they may not be representative of the target population (e.g., college football fans who are students of the target institution may have different attitudes than college football fans outside that particular demographic).

A related nonprobability approach is purposive sampling, which involves sampling with a specific purpose in mind. A researcher who uses a purposive sample is more likely to get the opinions of the target population; however, he or she is also likely to overweight subgroups in the population that are more readily accessible. Modal instance sampling involves sampling the most frequent (or typical) case. Expert sampling involves targeting a sample of persons with known or demonstrable experience and expertise in a given area. For example, a researcher wishing to determine the specific effect of the Americans with Disabilities Act on the day-to-day operations of a facility might survey facility managers who are responsible for implementing such policies. In quota sampling, individuals are selected nonrandomly according to a predetermined quota. Consider the ticket holder example discussed earlier. The researcher might set out to capture a sample in which 45 percent are season ticket holders and 55 percent hold tickets to an individual game. In nonrandom quota sampling, the researcher might contact fans until the percentage for one or the other category for the sample is met. If, for instance, the researcher desires to collect a sample of 1,000 fans and, of the first 600 fans sampled, 450 were season ticket holders, the researcher might then continue by surveying only single-event ticket holders until the final sample of 1,000 is reached. In contrast, researchers who want to include all opinions or views, even at the expense of losing proportionality, can turn to heterogeneity sampling. In essence, heterogeneity sampling, or diversity sampling, is almost the opposite of modal instance sampling, because the goal is to obtain all opinions rather than just the most popular, or typical, opinion. Finally, snowball sampling is particularly useful when a researcher is trying to reach a population that is inaccessible or hard to find. In snowball sampling, the researcher identifies an individual who meets the criteria for inclusion in the study, then asks him or her to recommend others who also meet the criteria. For example, a sport management researcher who wishes to analyze the experiences of sport managers in their first year after graduation might contact recent graduates of a particular sport management program who are new employees in a sport organization and ask them to distribute surveys to similar individuals in their new organizations.

Determination of Sample Size

The researcher's goal should be to collect a sample that is large enough to be representative of the population but not so large as to incur unnecessary cost. Several strategies are available: census data, the literature in the field, published tables, and formulas.

A **census**, sometimes referred to as population sampling, can be used for small populations. In this approach, every member of the target population is included as a subject in the study. For example, Dittmore, Mahony, Andrew, and Hums (2009) incorporated a census in their analysis of fairness perceptions of financial resource allocations in United States Olympic sport. The population in their study included the presidents and executive directors of all national governing bodies (NGBs) governed by the United States Olympic Committee. Given that only 37 NGBs existed at the time of data collection, Dittmore and colleagues sampled the entire population, thus eliminating the possibility of sampling error and obtaining data on all individuals within the population who responded. In cases where the population is particularly small, a census

sample may even be necessary in order to achieve the desired level of precision.

Second, the researcher can consult the literature in the field. Since acceptable sample sizes vary by discipline, a researcher can review the literature to search for studies similar to the proposed study in order to receive guidance about typical sample sizes in the subject area. However, if the researcher fails to review the procedures employed in these studies to determine sample size, he or she runs the risk of repeating any errors made by his or her predecessors.

Third, researchers can consult published tables, such as table 4.1. Such tables require the researcher to specify a given set of criteria, namely the preci-

Table 4.1 Sample Size for Three Precision Levels

Size of population	SAMPLE SIZE (N) FOR PRECISION (E) OF:		
	±5%	±7%	±10%
100	81	67	51
125	96	78	56
150	110	86	61
175	122	94	64
200	134	101	67
225	144	107	70
250	154	112	72
275	163	117	74
300	172	121	76
325	180	125	77
350	187	129	78
375	194	132	80
400	201	135	81
425	207	138	82
450	212	140	82
500	222	145	83
1,000	286	169	91
5,000	370	196	98
10,000	385	200	99

Precision levels where confidence level = 95% and P = .5.

sion (i.e., sampling error), confidence level (i.e., extent to which the sampled attribute is reflective of the true population value), and degree of variability (i.e., distribution of attributes in the population). With respect to variability, a proportion of .5 indicates the maximum variability in a population; therefore, it is often used in determining the most conservative sample size. For example, if a researcher desired a precision level of ± 5 percent with a confidence level of 95 percent and a degree of variability of .5 in a population size of 300, the appropriate minimum sample size would be 172 participants. When using tables to project sample sizes, it is important to remember that the recommended values in the table reflect the number of obtained responses—not necessarily the number of subjects who should be contacted to participate. Researchers typically contact a higher number of potential participants in order to compensate for the predicted estimate of nonresponses.

Finally, formulas can be used to calculate a sample size given a specific combination of levels of precision, confidence, and variability. When searching for a formula, researchers should take great care to use the appropriate one. Although some formulas assume that a large population is available, it may be possible to apply corrections in cases involving a smaller population (Cochran, 1963). In quantitative research, some statistical designs carry recommended formulas for sample size. In the case of multiple linear regression analysis, for example, two formulas are often used for determining the minimum number of subjects needed. One commonly accepted formula for conducting a multiple linear regression calls for a minimum of 10 subjects for each independent variable being examined. Another formula for multiple linear regression requires a minimum number of subjects equal to eight times the number of independent variables—plus 50. Recall that these figures refer to the number of obtained responses, and the researcher must design the study to account for the prospect of nonparticipation by some subjects in the sample.

Reliability

Reliability refers to the consistency of the results obtained. It is an integral component of high-quality research, and it concerns the extent to which the instrument yields the same results on repeated trials. For a researcher to have confidence in her or his data, the instrument must produce consistent results when presented with the same stimulus.

If test results vary considerably from one trial to another, the test may not be reliable, thus bringing into question the results of a research study relying upon that test instrument. Types of reliability include interobserver reliability, test–retest reliability, equivalence or parallel forms reliability, and internal consistency reliability.

Interobserver reliability assesses the extent to which different observers would give similar scores to the same phenomenon. It is especially important when a number of researchers are involved in collecting data for a project. For example, Dittmore, Mahony, Andrew, and Phelps (2007) examined recent doctoral dissertation topics in sport management to determine the breadth of content areas being examined and to identify any gender differences in the focus areas. Each researcher independently coded 144 dissertations from 1999 to 2003 into one of ten doctoral areas of specialization as identified by the Sport Management Program Review Council: sport marketing, organizational theory in sport, sport governance, sport finance, sport venue and event management, sport public relations, sport law, sport economics, human resource management in sport, and "other." The researchers then compared their data and determined that their initial interobserver reliability was 86.1 percent, meaning that 86.1 percent of the time, one reviewer would assign, or code, a dissertation to the same category as another reviewer. Through consultation of dissertation abstracts, the researchers acquired additional information to help them code the remaining dissertations, thus increasing the final interobserver reliability to 100 percent.

Test–retest reliability assesses the extent to which the instrument would provide the same measurements if repeated at a different time. An instrument with high test–retest reliability reports the same score consistently as long as the stimulus does not change. For example, in a room with constant temperature over various time intervals, a thermometer with high test–retest reliability would provide identical temperature readings in each measurement.

Equivalence reliability, or parallel forms reliability, involves using multiple but equivalent versions of the same instrument. To test parallel forms reliability, the researcher creates multiple forms or versions of an instrument by dividing a large set of items into two sets of smaller instruments. The two instruments are then administered to the same group of subjects. The correlation between subjects' two sets of scores provides an estimate of reliability.

Internal consistency reliability refers to the extent to which each question consistently measures the same variable—that is, whether the items in a scale are consistent with one another in that they represent only one dimension, construct, or area of interest throughout the scale. For example, Wann's (2002) Sport Fandom Questionnaire is a five-item measure of the degree of one's identification with the social role of a sport fan. The items relate to the importance one attaches to being a sport fan, attending sporting events, watching or listening to sporting events, and discussing sporting events with others. If these items are nonbiased measures of sport fandom, then respondents should report similar responses for each of the items. Such a response pattern would be indicative of high internal consistency reliability. One common examination of internal consistency reliability is split-half reliability, which involves dividing the items on an instrument (e.g., a survey) into two halves and checking for consistency between subjects' scores on the two halves.

Reliability is a vital part of the process for research studies that rely upon various instruments, such as surveys, for data collection. Studies that fail to discuss how the authors assured the reliability of their instruments should be interpreted with caution.

Validity

Validity is the extent to which an instrument accurately measures what it was designed to measure—in other words, whether it accurately addresses its designed purpose. It is possible for an instrument to be valid but not reliable; for example, an intelligence test might accurately measure intelligence but fail to yield consistent results. It is also possible for an instrument to be reliable but not valid, as in the case of an intelligence test that produces consistent results but is ineffective at accurately measuring the construct of intelligence. The researcher's goal, of course, is to create or adopt an instrument that is both reliable and valid.

Types of validity include **content validity, criterion validity,** and **construct validity.** Content validity, also called *face validity,* can be measured by experts in the content area or by prospective study participants. It addresses whether or not the instrument appears to measure what it was designed to measure from another person's point of view. Typically, the perspective of study participants is valuable to ensure that the instrument is comprehensible to the target audience, whereas experts in the topic area can critically assess more subtle issues. For example, a researcher who develops a survey instrument to examine the well-being of college athletes might have experts identify the instrument's strengths, weaknesses, and omissions. Such experts might include current or former college athletes, coaches, administrators, and scholars who have studied the topic. The limitation on content validity is that it is not testable or measurable and therefore not as precise or credible as other forms of test validity.

Criterion validity is measured by comparing the instrument with current or future criteria. There are two types of criterion validity: predictive validity and concurrent validity. Predictive validity involves a comparison between the instrument and some later behavior that it predicts. Concurrent validity compares scores on an instrument with performance on some other measure(s), such as previously established instruments in the chosen area of research. The purpose of an instrument dictates whether the measurement of predictive or concurrent validity is warranted.

Construct validity refers to whether a scale measures or correlates with a theorized psychological construct. The two types are discriminant validity and convergent validity. An instrument with high discriminant validity does not correlate significantly with variables from which it should differ. Conversely, an instrument with high convergent validity correlates highly with other variables with which it *should* theoretically correlate. For example, an instrument for measuring intelligence would be expected to relate to findings for similar constructs (convergent validity) but produce results very different from unrelated constructs (discriminant validity).

As with reliability, it is imperative that researchers using instruments establish their validity. Failure to do so brings into question the overall validity of the research study.

Summary

Research study design is vitally important. The researcher is charged with designing a study that effectively answers the research questions in a manner that enhances the credibility of the study's results. Steps in the designing the research study include choosing the type of research design or mode of inquiry (qualitative, quantitative, or mixed-methods), using proper sampling methods to select subjects for inclusion in the study's data collection, and assuring the reliability and validity of the instruments used for data collection. Data collection techniques are discussed further in chapter 5.

Research Methods and Design in Action
Journal of Sport Management

Selected text from H.J. Gibson, C.X. Qi, and J.J. Zhang, 2008, "Destination image and the intent to visit China and the 2008 Beijing Olympic Games," *Journal of Sport Management* 22(4): 427–450.

Access the full article online at www.humankinetics.com/products/all-products/Research-Methods-and-Design-in-Sport-Management.

ABSTRACT

Although there is growing awareness of the relationship between hosting megasporting events and destination image, there is little empirical evidence documenting what images people hold before an event. The purpose of this study was to investigate the images young Americans hold of China both as a tourist destination and as the host of the 2008 Olympic Games. Specifically, the relationships among destination image, travel intentions, and tourist characteristics were explored. A total of 350 college students were surveyed before the close of the Athens Olympic Games. Overall, the respondents perceived China and the Beijing Olympic Games positively. Destination image was significantly ($p \leq .05$) predictive of the intention to travel to China and the Olympic Games. Hierarchical regression analyses revealed that destination image partially mediated the relationship between past international travel experience and intention to travel. The theoretical and practical implications of these findings are discussed with a view to promoting China as a tourist destination and the host of the Olympic Games.

TEXT EXCERPTS

Because previous studies found that life stage, nationality, and education level can influence destination image and travel intentions (Baloglu & McCleary, 1999; Lepp & Gibson, 2003), this study was designed to control for these three variables by focusing on a homogenous population, students below 30 years of age, U.S. born and raised, and enrolled at a large southeastern university in the U.S.

. . . .

A test of content validity of the questionnaire was conducted by a panel of experts in sport tourism and sport management. The panel members focused on the relevance, representativeness, and clarity of items in each measurement area. Based on their input, improvements were made, primarily in the areas of item clarity.

. . . .

A combination of spatial-location sampling and systematic random sampling was used. Spatial-location sampling was used to identify four high foot traffic areas on campus. Data were collected at each site during different times of the day and different days of the week. Participants were selected using a systematic sampling procedure with a sampling interval of every 10th person and a random entry point. Potential participants were asked two screening questions before they were deemed eligible to participate. Only those who were born and raised in the U.S. and those aged between 18 and 30 years old were selected to participate in the study.

. . . .

For the factor analysis, the following four criteria were applied: (a) only those factors (domains) with an eigenvalue equal to or greater than 1.0 were extracted (Hair, Anderson, Tatham, & Black, 2004), (b) items with loadings of at least .40 and without double loading were retained (Hair et al., 2004; Stevens, 1996), (c) each domain was subjected to a reliability testing, and domains with alpha coefficient equal to or greater than .50 were deemed acceptable (Baumgartner & Jackson, 1999), and (d) items that reduced the reliability of a factor were eliminated from further analysis (Chen & Kerstetter, 1999).

DISCUSSION QUESTIONS

1 Did the authors use a qualitative, quantitative, or mixed-methods research design? What clues led you to that conclusion?

2 What type of validity analysis was conducted for the questionnaire instrument that was used to collect data? Are there any potential weaknesses of using only this type of validity analysis?

3 How did the authors define membership in the population of the study? Would the results of this study be generalizable to college students at other institutions? To people in other age ranges?

4 How was sampling conducted in choosing subjects for inclusion in the study? Describe the authors' sampling methods in detail.

Data Collection and Analysis

Learning Objectives

After studying this chapter, you should be able to do the following:

- Explain the concept of nonresponse bias in data collection
- Describe strategies for increasing survey response rates
- Understand the process of data coding
- Discuss the four scales of measurement and provide examples of variables belonging in each of the four scales
- Understand the four types of descriptive statistics
- Describe the inferential statistics concepts of statistical significance, error, power, and effect size
- List the factors used to select an appropriate statistical design
- Identify the components of drawing conclusions at the end of the research process

After selecting the research design and identifying the sample, the next step in the research process is to initiate data collection. Assuming the researcher has received permission to collect data from the targeted population (see chapter 2 for a discussion of ethical issues in research), the challenge for the researcher is simply to implement the selected research design. The researcher must also, however, keep in mind a few other considerations during the data collection phase: controlling for nonresponse bias, implementing strategies to increase response rate, and choosing the right statistical design based upon the chosen research questions and research design. At this stage, researchers must confront issues including statistical significance levels, error, power, and effect size. Upon finishing the statistical analysis, the researcher completes the research process by drawing conclusions based on the findings.

Nonresponse Bias

In survey research, **nonresponse bias** occurs when there is a systematic difference between respondents and non-respondents. One way to test for potential non-response bias is to examine various characteristics of the sample in order to see whether all applicable demographics responded. In addition, if the information is available, you might compare the characteristics of the respondents with those of the population under investigation to see if differences exist. Researchers can also test for non-response bias by sending a follow-up letter and survey to those who did not respond in the initial data collection wave. If any additional responses are obtained, characteristics of those who responded to the second appeal can be compared with characteristics of the original respondents in order to determine whether the groups are similar or different. If the groups are systematically different, then some degree of non-response bias is likely present.

Researchers hope to avoid low response rates because they may indicate bias in the data and could alter the researcher's preferred data analysis technique if the number of respondents falls below the minimum for using a particular statistical technique. Frankfort-Nachimas and Nachimas (1996) list several techniques that might be used in order to increase response rates. *Follow-up reminders* have been shown to increase response rates, and researchers can also offer inducements (i.e., objects of value to the respondent) to individuals who agree to participate in a study. Research has shown, however, that studies using incentives to increase response rates likely attract a different sample than studies that do not rely on inducements to attract participants. For example, offering gift cards for a digital music service (e.g., Apple's iTunes) may result in a higher response rate among participants under the age of 40 while failing to attract the same level of response among senior citizens in the sample, thus skewing responses toward a younger demographic profile. Researchers can also enhance response rates through the use of a sponsor, or an individual who personally knows the potential respondent and encourages him or her to participate in the study.

Another way to increase response rates is to use an altruistic introductory or prenotification letter (Kent & Turner, 2002). Such letters typically focus on the positive aspects of participating in the study and notify the recipient that an opportunity to do so is forthcoming. Researchers should also critically analyze their method of return; not surprisingly, methods that are more convenient for the survey recipient tend to elicit higher response rates. It also helps to use an enticing format with an aesthetically pleasing cover, an attractive page format, an interesting title. Finally, the selection of respondents in itself can affect response rate. For instance, researchers who wish to collect data via written questionnaires should ensure that their sample population possesses the requisite reading and writing skills to complete the questionnaire. Research has also shown that people who are interested in the topic, who are highly educated, and who are professional white-collar workers are more likely to respond to surveys than are their respective counterparts (Frankfort-Nachimas & Nachimas, 1996).

Preparation of Data for Analysis

The next step in the research process is data analysis. In all instances, the selected analysis should address the research questions or hypotheses. However, before the data can be subjected to analysis, researchers should ensure that it is properly prepared, which entails detecting data anomalies and correctly coding data.

Detecting Data Anomalies

A data analysis is only as good as the quality of the data analyzed, and researchers must be alert to **data**

anomalies, which are unusual or unexpected data points. Green and Tull (1978) detail a number of ways to detect anomalies in a data set:

- Legibility: All data should be clear and legible.
- Completeness: All responses should be checked for completeness.
- Consistency: Responses should not conflict with each other.
- Accuracy: Respondents who selected more than one answer or did not respond to an item may have done so for one of several reasons (Huisman & van der Zouwen, 1999; McDaniel & Gates, 1991).

Regarding this last point, one example would be a completed survey in which a respondent indicated being a college student on one question and selected the "75 years old and above" grouping on another question. This pairing of responses doesn't necessarily mean that the responses were incorrect, since a number of senior citizens do enroll in college classes, but the researcher might choose to look more closely at other responses on that particular survey to verify that they are likely correct and sincere. Depending on what the researcher finds, he or she might choose either to include that particular survey in the data set or to exclude it.

Coding Data

The next step is to code the data, which involves grouping and assigning numeric codes to the various responses to a particular question (McDaniel & Gates, 1991). For closed-ended questions, which give the respondent a set of predetermined response options, the coding process involves assigning a number for each respective possible response. For example, if a respondent is asked about her or his overall job satisfaction on a 7-point scale (1 = very dissatisfied and 7 = very satisfied) and circles the number 6, the researcher can input the number 6 into the data set pertaining to that item for that respondent. With some questions—such as indicating one's gender—the researcher might choose to assign a code of 1 for female and a code of 2 for male (or perhaps 0 and 1 instead). However, as noted by McDaniel and Gates, the process for coding open-ended questions is slightly more complicated. First, all responses on a particular item are listed. Second, responses that have the same meaning are consolidated. Third, a numeric code is assigned to each of the remaining categories. Finally, the

researcher enters that specific code into the data set, making sure to note the response associated with each numeric code.

Scales of Measurement

Before selecting which statistical analysis to employ, the researcher must determine the scale, or level, of measurement for each variable or factor. In other words, the selection of statistical procedure depends upon how the variables are measured quantitatively. Possible scales of measurement include nominal, ordinal, interval, and ratio scales.

- Nominal scales have no order and simply give a name or label to various categories. For instance, depending on the context, sport consumers can be labeled as season ticket holders or single-game buyers, and baseball players can be labeled according to their playing position (e.g., pitcher, catcher). If the researcher chooses to code baseball players using a system such as 1 for pitcher, 2 for catcher, and so on, the number codes serve simply as a way to record the data; they have no mathematical purpose (e.g., stating that a catcher carries double the value of a pitcher). Again, nominal scales simply involve providing a name or classification to each category. Nominally scaled variables are also referred to as categorical variables.

- As the name suggests, ordinal scales involve order, and examples include the order of finish in a horse race and the tennis rankings at a sport club where members are ranked based on their performance against each other. The interval between measurements, however, is not meaningful. In other words, knowing the order of finish in the horse race allows one to rank horses based on order of finish in that particular race, but it gives no indication of how much faster the winning horse ran as compared with the competing horses.

- In addition to the qualities of ordinal scales, interval scales possess equivalent intervals between measurements. Interval scales can feature negative numbers, and though they may have the number zero within a scale, the inclusion of zero is arbitrary since negative values can be used. One example of an interval scale is temperature, whether measured in degrees Celsius or degrees Fahrenheit. Most *Likert scales*, which offer a numerically ranked set of response options, are also interval scales—for instance, an item that asks a respondent to rank overall customer satisfaction on a scale of 1 to 7 (1 = very dissatisfied and 7 = very satisfied).

▪ Ratio scales are based on order and possess equal intervals of measurement, but they are also proportional. They also have a nonarbitrary zero and therefore cannot include negative numbers. Temperature, if measured in degrees Celsius or Fahrenheit, does not qualify as a ratio scale (due to the presence of negative numbers), but it does qualify as a ratio scale variable if it is measured in Kelvin, which does not feature negative numbers. Other examples include an individual's age and the number of times the individual attended class in a given term. In the Statistical Package for Social Sciences (SPSS) software, nominal and ordinal scales are separately coded, but interval and ratio scales are consolidated into one descriptor. Interval and ratio variables are also collectively referred to as continuous variables. The importance of classifying variables based on how they are measured quantitatively will become evident when the researcher wishes to select an appropriate statistical test for analyzing the data.

Descriptive Statistics

Descriptive statistics include a number of data analysis options with the expressed purpose of describing or summarizing the data, collected on a set of subjects, that constitute the sample of interest. In some studies (e.g., basic demographic studies and customer satisfaction studies), descriptive statistics may be the only analyses employed, but for the most part researchers incorporate descriptive statistics in a study to summarize information about a sample and then move on to more advanced techniques for addressing more complex research questions. These advanced statistical techniques are addressed in part IV of this book. The four main types of descriptive statistics include measures of central tendency, variability, relative position, and relationship.

Measures of Central Tendency

These measures permit the researcher to describe a set of data with a single numerical value that represents the average or typical value associated with that data set. The most common measures of central tendency are the mean, median, and mode. The *mean* is simply the arithmetic average of a set of scores. It offers the advantage of taking into account the actual values of all scores in a distribution, but this also means that it can be unduly influenced if extreme scores, or outliers, are present in the distribution. For example, if all of the numbers in a data set range between one and ten but the last

data point is one thousand, this final data point will cause a dramatic increase in the data set's mean. In such cases, a more appropriate measure of central tendency is the median—the score that divides the upper 50 percent from the lower 50 percent of scores in the distribution. In this approach, extreme values at the upper or lower end of the distribution have little effect on the median, which is particularly useful for ordinally scaled variables. Finally, the mode is the most frequently occurring score in a distribution, and it can be useful to know when dealing with nominally scaled variables, but it is otherwise a fairly crude measure of central tendency since, unlike the mean and median, it does not account for the value or order of scores in the data set.

Measures of Variability

These measures give an indication of how scores are spread around the mean or another measure of central tendency. The three most common measures of **variability** are range, standard deviation, and variance. The range is the difference between the highest score and lowest score in a distribution, and it provides a rough estimate of the overall variability in a set of scores. The *standard deviation* is an appropriate measure of variability for variables that are interval- and ratio-scaled; it measures the average distance of scores from the mean. Standard deviation is calculated by first subtracting the mean from each score, then squaring the resulting differences, summing the squared differences, and finding the average of that summed value. A large standard deviation indicates that the scores in a distribution are relatively spread out, and a small standard deviation indicates the scores in a distribution are clustered closer together. Another measure of variability is called variance, which is calculated simply by squaring the value of the standard deviation. The standard deviation measure of variability is more popular and is often paired with the mean—a measure of central tendency—to describe a set of scores.

Measures of Relative Position

These measures indicate where a specific score is located in relation to the rest of the scores in a distribution. The most common measures of relative position are percentile ranks and standard scores. A percentile rank indicates the percentage of scores that fall at or below a given score. For example, if a student takes a test and receives a score of 70, which is in the 75th percentile, then 75 percent of the scores in the distribution were equal to or less than the student's raw score of 70. Percentile

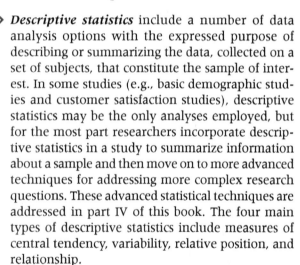

ranks are most appropriate for ordinal measures, but they are often used for interval measures as well. A standard score is a manipulation of a raw score that indicates how far away from the mean a given score is located. Standard scores are usually expressed in standard deviation units, and the two most popular types of standard scores are z-scores and T-scores. A z-score indicates a score's distance from the mean in terms of standard deviation units. It is calculated by subtracting the mean from the raw score, then dividing that value by the standard deviation. For example, a z-score of +1.50 indicates that the raw score is 1.5 standard deviations above the mean. A T-score is merely a z-score expressed on a different scale, and it is calculated by multiplying the z-score by 10 and adding 50. The use of standard scores is appropriate when the data are measured at an interval or ratio level.

Measures of Relationship

These measures indicate the degree to which two quantifiable variables are related to each other. They verify only that a relationship exists between two variables; they do not imply a causal relationship; that is, they verify that variable X is related to variable Y but not that variable X causes variable Y (or vice versa). The degree of relationship between two variables is expressed quantitatively as a correlation coefficient, which can range from -1.00 to +1.00. Correlation coefficients close to zero indicate little or no relationship between the two variables, whereas correlation coefficients closer to -1.00 or +1.00 indicate strong relationship between the two variables. A positive correlation coefficient indicates that the two variables move in unison with each other (whether up or down), whereas a negative correlation coefficient means that the two variables move in opposition to one another (e.g., as one variable increases, the other decreases). For example, if the relationship between a fan's loyalty to a sport team and the number of home games attended was +.85, then a strong positive relationship exists between those two variables. That is, the more loyal the fan is, the more games he or she attended. On the other hand, if the relationship between those variables was -.10, then a weak negative relationship exists, suggesting that loyalty has little relationship to games attended but that what little relationship does exist involves a decreased number of games attended when loyalty increases (or vice versa). The two most common measures of relationship are the Spearman rho and the Pearson r. The Spearman rho is used in cases of one variable or both variables being ordinal (i.e., the Spearman rho is a nonparametric statistic), and the

Pearson r is used when the data for both variables are interval- or ratio-leveled (i.e., the Pearson r is a parametric statistic).

Inferential Statistics

Inferential statistics involve collecting and analyzing information from samples in order to draw conclusions about the larger population. Sport management researchers often look for results that apply to an entire population of people, but it is not always cost-feasible or even possible to gain access to every member in the population. Therefore, researchers often collect data from a small subset or sample of the population and use these data to make inferences about the whole. By definition, choosing not to sample every member of a population introduces error, but inferential statistics allow researchers to use data from samples to make reasonable inferences about a larger population. Of course, since large samples contain a higher percentage of the population than do small samples, larger samples allow researchers to be more confident in their inferences about the overall population. Inferential statistics are discussed in further detail in part IV of this book.

Statistical Significance

Researchers who incorporate inferential statistics in their studies use significance levels to report their findings. In common language, the term *significant* typically means *important*, but in statistical jargon it means *probably true* or *not due to chance*. Significance levels are used with inferential statistics to make judgments about whether to accept or reject the null hypothesis, which is a statement of no difference. The null hypothesis is tested because it is easier to disprove the null hypothesis than to prove the alternative. For example, if a researcher is testing whether a **statistically significant** relationship exists between the number of football games won and fundraising donation levels at universities, the null hypothesis would be that no significant relationship exists between those two variables. That assumption would be made unless the Pearson r test revealed that a statistically significant relationship did exist between the variables.

Before conducting statistical testing, the researcher sets a significance level or alpha (α) level, which represents the odds of something (e.g., a relationship between football games won and donation levels) occurring by chance rather than by purpose. This significance level is then compared to the p-value, which is produced as a result of conducting most statistical tests. Traditionally in sport management, researchers set their significance level at .05, which means that for significant results (i.e., $p < .05$), researchers can infer that a true difference exists in the population based on the sample results and be incorrect less than 5 percent of the time. In other words, a p-value of .02, for instance, means that two times out of one hundred, or two percent of the time, we would be incorrect, or committing an error, in rejecting the null hypothesis. Significance levels are somewhat arbitrarily set, and the lower the significance level, the more the data must diverge from the null hypothesis to be significant (i.e., a .01 significance level would be more conservative than a .05 significance level). Lower significance levels decrease the chance of a probability error, but they also decrease the odds of discovering statistically significant results.

Type I and Type II Errors

Given that inferential statistics test the null hypothesis and that the researcher can never know with 100 percent certainty whether the statistical decision is correct, statistical decisions have four possible outcomes. The first two outcomes are correct and are as follows:

1. The null hypothesis is actually true (i.e., there is no difference), and the researcher concludes that it is true (i.e., the researcher fails to reject the null hypothesis).

2. The null hypothesis is actually false (i.e., a real difference exists), and the researcher concludes that it is false (i.e., the researcher rejects the null hypothesis).

The last two outcomes are incorrect:

3. The null hypothesis is actually true, and the researcher concludes that it is false (i.e., the researcher rejects the null hypothesis). This is a Type I error.

4. The null hypothesis is actually false, and the researcher concludes that it is true (i.e., the researcher fails to reject the null hypothesis). This is a Type II error.

The probability of committing a Type I error and the probability of committing a Type II error have a complimentary relationship; in other words, as one reduces the possibility of a Type I error (i.e., being too statistically liberal), he or she increases the possibility of a Type II error (i.e., being too statistically conservative). Above all, researchers strive to avoid Type I errors, since claiming that a significance difference exists when it does not is especially undesirable.

Statistical Power

The power of a statistical test lies in the probability of rejecting the null hypothesis when the null hypothesis is, in fact, false (i.e., making correct decision number 2 in the preceding discussion). In other words, power is the essence of every researcher's goal in that it means the ability to detect a difference when it truly exists. The factors that affect **statistical power** include the following:

- Type I error: As Type I error increases, power increases.
- Directionality of the alternative (research) hypothesis: Directional (one-tailed) hypotheses increase power.
- Size of the actual difference between the means of the treatment groups (otherwise known as effect size): As the actual difference between the means increases, power increases
- Amount of error variance: As error variance (i.e., standard deviation) increases, power decreases.
- Sample size: Larger sample sizes increase power.

Power is measured on a scale of 0 to 1, where 0 indicates no power and 1 indicates very high power. Cohen (1988, 1992) recommends that researchers strive for a power level of .8. In other words, researchers should strive to develop an 80 percent chance of detecting an effect if an effect genuinely exists.

Effect Size

Effect size is an objective and standardized measure of the magnitude of the observed effect (Field, 2005); it is also referred to in the literature as ES and partial $\eta 2$. The most common measures of effect size are Cohen's d and Pearson's correlation coefficient r (Field, 2001). Just because a particular test is statistically significant does not mean that the effect it measures is meaningful or important, but effect sizes allow researchers to make comparisons across different studies that have measured different variables or even used different scales of measurement. As a result, the American Psychological Association now recommends that researchers report effect sizes in the results of their published work. Effect sizes are measured on a scale of 0 to 1, wherein 0 indicates no effect size and 1 indicates a very high effect size. Cohen (1988, 1992) has made widely accepted suggestions about what constitutes a small or large effect in terms of Pearson's r:

- r = .10 (small effect): The effect explains 1 percent of the total variance.
- r = .30 (medium effect): The effect explains 9 percent of the total variance.
- r = .50 (large effect): The effect explains 25 percent of the total variance.

Effect sizes are calculated for a particular sample, not for a population, but the effect size in the sample can be used to estimate the likely effect size in the population (Field, 2001).

Statistical Design

When making decisions about which statistical test to use for an analysis, the researcher must be aware of several factors: the general purpose of the research question, the number and type of dependent variables, the number and type of independent variables, the presence of covariates, and the specific goal of the analysis.

The general purposes of research questions in relationship to statistical tests include the following:

- Degree of relationship: Proposes that one or more (independent) variables have a positive or negative effect on one or more (dependent) variables
- Group differences: Proposes that differences exist between groups on one or more (dependent) variables on the basis of one or more (independent) variables
- Prediction of group membership: Proposes that membership in groups (the dependent variable) can be predicted by two or more (independent) predictor variables
- Structure: Proposes that an underlying structure can explain a set of variables

The number and type of dependent and independent variables refer to the specific quantity of each type of variable and whether or not the variable in question is categorical (i.e., nominally scaled) or quantitative (i.e., interval- or ratio-scaled). The presence of a covariate is determined by identifying how many, if any, covariates exist. Finally, the specific goal of the analysis includes a number of possibilities that are reflected in table 5.1. Note that the statistical designs included in this table are explained in further detail in Part IV of this text.

In summary, when using a decision-making tree, as depicted in table 5.1, follow the following steps:

1. Identify the variables in the research question.
2. Indicate which variables are the independent and dependent variables and covariates.
3. Determine the type (categorical or quantitative) of all variables. If a variable is categorical, determine the number of categories.
4. Determine the purpose of the research question: degree of relationship, group differences, prediction of group membership, or structure.
5. Apply the information from the preceding steps to the decision-making tree to arrive at the appropriate test.

Drawing Conclusions

One of the final steps in the research process is that of drawing conclusions, which are typically presented in the discussion section of a research paper or presentation. This step includes several aspects. First, the researcher should summarize and explain the results of the study, and this discussion should address whether the results were expected and present thorough explanations of the study's results. Second, the researcher should compare the results with results from previous research in the area as identified in the literature review earlier in the research process. Did the results of the study confirm or refute previous research? Third, the researcher should present implications of the study, both theoretical and practical. What do the results of the study mean for research in this area? What can sport industry professionals learn from the results? Finally, the discussion and conclusion sections of the research process typically provide suggestions for future research in the topic area.

Summary

Final major steps in the research process include collecting and analyzing data and drawing conclusions based upon that analysis. In doing these steps, the researcher must address issues including nonresponse bias, response rate, data coding, measurement, statistical design, and aspects of statistical analysis (e.g., statistical significance, error, power, and effect size). Finally, the research must draw conclusions based upon the results of the statistical or qualitative data analysis. The last remaining step in the research process is the dissemination or sharing of findings from the research project, which is the focus of chapter 6.

Table 5.1 Statistical Test Decision-Making Tree

Step 1: Purpose of the research question	Degree of relationship			Group differences									Prediction of group membership		Structure	
Step 2: Dependent variables?	1 quantitative	1 quantitative	1+ quantitative	1 quantitative	1 quantitative	1 quantitative	1 quantitative	1 quantitative	2+ quantitative	2+ quantitative	2+ quantitative	2+ quantitative	1 categorical*	1 categorical**	3+ quantitative	3+ quantitative
Step 3: Independent variables?	1 quantitative	2+ quantitative	2+ quantitative	1 categorical*	1 categorical**	1 categorical**	2+ categorical	2+ categorical	1 categorical	1 categorical	2+ categorical	2+ categorical	2+ mixed	2+ quantitative	Theoretical	Empirical
Step 4: Covariates?	n/a	n/a	n/a	n/a	No	Yes	No	Yes	No	Yes	No	Yes	n/a	n/a		
Step 5: Test =	Bivariate correlation, regression	Multiple regression	Path analysis	t-test	One-way ANOVA	One-way ANCOVA	Factorial ANOVA	Factorial ANCOVA	One-way MANOVA	One-way MANCOVA	Factorial MANOVA	Factorial MANCOVA	Logistic regression	Discriminant analysis	Factor analysis	Principal components

* indicates 2 categories; ** indicates more than 2 categories

Adapted from Daft 1995

Selected text reprinted, by permission, from D.F. Mahony et al., 2006, "Recruiting and retaining sport management faculty: Factors affecting job choice," *Journal of Sport Management* 20(3): 414-430.

Access the full article online at www.humankinetics.com/products/all-products/Research-Methods-and-Design-in-Sport-Management.

ABSTRACT

The growth of sport management has led to concerns about the quantity and quality of candidates for faculty positions. In addition to trying to recruit recent doctoral graduates, many programs focus on recruiting established faculty members. This study examines factors affecting the willingness of sport management faculty to accept new positions, and the likelihood of leaving their current positions. While the likelihood of leaving was not high, objective factors such as salary and location were important to those willing to take a new position. Subjective factors such as fit within the program and quality of faculty in the program were also important, whereas several factors were less important (e.g., recruiter description, recruiter approach, and leadership opportunities). Results confirm that attracting faculty in sport management is challenging and universities must consider a combination of strategies to attract them.

TEXT EXCERPTS

In order to address recruitment and retention issues, the authors surveyed 427 faculty members in North America currently teaching in sport management programs. The address list came from two sources: the North American Society for Sport Management membership list (for 2003) and college and university sport management Web pages. Participants had the option of completing a hard copy of the survey by mail or going to a Web site and completing the survey there. Follow-up e-mail reminders were sent to the participants every month for 3 months, with the survey attached and a link to the Web site.

....

The survey had three parts. Part A collected basic demographic information (e.g., tenure status, gender, year of birth). The participants were then asked (on a 5-point Likert scale, 1 = much lower and 5 = much higher) to evaluate their workloads (the research, teaching, and service expectations of their positions versus typical faculty positions in the field) and rewards (the comparison of their salary versus the typical faculty salaries in the field). They were also asked, "Would you ever consider leaving your current institution for a sport management faculty position at another institution?" If they responded yes, they were then asked the likelihood they would leave for a new position (on a 5-point Likert scale, 1 = highly unlikely and 5 = highly likely).

■■■■■■■■■■■■■■■■

Descriptive statistics were generated for the items in Part A. In order to do a preliminary analysis on relationships among the items within each factor in Part C, the authors then computed Cronbach's alpha coefficients for each factor. In addition, the authors used a multiple regression analysis to examine the impact of various factors on the likelihood of leaving.

■■■■■■■■■■■■■■■■

Using responses from Part A of the survey, Tables 1 through 3 present the means, standard deviations, frequencies, and percentages by rank. Several results are worth noting. First, there was little variability by rank except where expected (e.g., age, years of teaching, years at institution, salary, tenure, administration, would consider leaving). Second, although approximately 91% were untenured, over a third of the assistant professors had some administrative title. This has implications for the difficulty that some sport management faculty members may face when trying to meet tenure requirements.

DISCUSSION QUESTIONS

1 What strategies did the article authors use in attempting to increase their survey's response rate?

2 On page 417 of the article, the authors discuss using Likert scale items (both five-point and seven-point scales) in asking many survey questions of respondents. Which of the four scales of measurement discussed in chapter 5 of the textbook would apply to these Likert-scaled questions?

3 What statistical techniques or methods did the authors use in analyzing their data?

4 Briefly, what are some of the major conclusions that the researchers drew from their findings?

chapter 6

Dissemination of Findings

Learning Objectives

After studying this chapter, you should be able to do the following:

- Describe the process of presenting research at an academic conference
- Understand how to select a journal to target for submission of a manuscript
- Identify the major structural components of a research article or manuscript
- Describe the process for submitting a manuscript to a journal for review
- Discuss the criteria for evaluating research articles

Once the research process is complete, researchers have several options for disseminating their research: giving a presentation at an academic conference, publishing a manuscript in an academic journal, or doing both. Often, sport management researchers elect to present their research at an academic conference in order to receive feedback from their peers before submitting a manuscript to a refereed (i.e. peer-reviewed) journal. It is worth the time it takes to become familiar with the various research dissemination options because doing so allows you to share your study's findings in the most appropriate medium that will maximize the effect of your work.

Academic Conference Presentation

In its infancy, the field of sport management offered very few **research dissemination** options. Indeed, many early scholars in the field were forced to disseminate their research by means of scholarly conferences and academic journals in related disciplines. Today, however, sport management researchers enjoy a large variety of scholarly conferences and academic journals to choose from. Table 6.1 lists many of the annual scholarly conferences staged in the field of sport management; though not inclusive, the table highlights the vast array of presentation options available to sport management researchers.

Academic conferences generally publish a call for papers several months prior to the submission deadline. The call includes specific submission requirements, which can range from something as brief as a 100-word abstract to a full 30-page manuscript. In addition, academic conferences generally require prospective presenters to select a presentation category at the time of submission. Typical presentation categories include oral presentation (15 to 25 minutes), oral symposium (45 to 90 minutes), and poster presentation.

Most oral presentations at academic conferences in sport management are accompanied by a PowerPoint presentation to help the presenter remain focused and organized while also providing a visual platform for sharing details of the study. PowerPoint slides should be designed with the audience in mind; they should be concise and focused only on the major points of discussion. Oral presentations are typically organized similarly to written papers and proceed in the same logical manner. Thus they include an introduction, literature review (concluding with research questions), description of methods, results, conclusions, and discussion. Many conferences allot at least 5 minutes for questions at the end of the presentation, and presenters should always keep the presentation time limits in mind when designing their presentations. The question session at the end of an oral presentation is often the most beneficial aspect for the presenter because it provides valuable feedback that he or she can incorporate into a subsequent manuscript submission.

Oral symposiums typically feature a number of presenters, and they are typically organized in

Table 6.1 Presentation Outlets for Sport Management Studies

American Alliance for Health, Physical Education, Recreation and Dance	North American Society for Sport Management
Asian American Association for Sport Management	North American Society for the Sociology of Sport
The Drake Group	North American Society for Sport History
European Association for Sport Management	Scholarly Conference on College Sport
Florida State University Sport Management Conference	Southern Sport Management Association Conference
International Association of Assembly Managers	Sport and Entertainment Venues Tomorrow Conference
International Association of Sports Economists	Sport and Recreation Law Association
Latin American Organization in Sport Management	Sport Lawyers Association
National Association for Kinesiology & Physical Education in Higher Education	Sport Management Association of Australia & New Zealand
National Association of Academic Advisors for Athletics	Sport Marketing Association
National Intramural-Recreational Sports Association	

one of two ways. First, an oral symposium could consist of a collection of individual presentations on the same general topic. Symposiums organized in this manner typically allow for 3 to 5 individual research presentations that last 10 to 15 minutes each. Another popular way to structure an oral symposium is to arrange a panel discussion that is usually directed by a moderator with a list of predetermined questions. This method is typically used when the symposium features a number of established experts discussing a popular or controversial topic. Such sessions often conclude with a question session that allows the audience to learn more about the varying opinions of the expert panelists.

Many conferences also allow for poster presentations. Posters are display boards on which researchers illustrate their data and describe their studies. The size and organization of each poster is usually dictated by regulations set forth in the call for papers. Posters should be self-explanatory and allow viewers to proceed at their own pace. Most posters include an introduction, sections addressing methods and results, and a discussion. An abstract is sometimes included to give the viewer a general overview of the study. The introduction should succinctly present the problem and clearly state the study's purpose. The methods section is typically quite brief—long enough only to sufficiently describe the type of approach used. The results of the study generally occupy most of the available poster space. Finally, the discussion section highlights the conclusions of the study, notes findings that were similar to or different from previous research, indicates the limitations of the study, and offers directions for future research. Poster presentations can attract viewers who share specific research interests with the presenter, and the one-on-one dialogue that often ensues between the researcher and the viewer can often be very insightful.

Academic Journal Selection

A researcher faces a number of issues when submitting a research manuscript to an academic journal. First, the researcher must decide where to submit the manuscript. This process is made easier by scanning journal Web sites, author instructions, and recent issue contents, which allows the researcher to become familiar with journals that might be interested in publishing their work. Table 6.2 lists

Table 6.2 **Publication Outlets for Sport Management Studies**

Academic Athletic Journal	Journal of Sport Management
Annals of Leisure Research	Journal of Sports Economics
Applied Research in Coaching and Athletics Annual	Journal of Sports Law & Contemporary Problems
Australian and New Zealand Sports Law Journal	Journal of Sports Media
Chronicle of Kinesiology and Physical Education in Higher Education	Journal of Sports Sciences
Coach and Athletic Director	Journal of the Philosophy of Sport
Entertainment and Sports Law Journal	Journal of Vacation Marketing
Entertainment and Sports Lawyer	Journal of Venue & Event Management
Entertainment Law Review	Korean Journal of Sport Science
European Journal for Sport and Society	Legal Issues in College Athletics
European Journal of Sport Science	Leisure Sciences
European Sport Management Quarterly	Leisure Studies
Fordham Sports Law Forum	Managing Leisure
ICHPER•SD Journal of Research	Marquette Sports Law Review
International Gambling Studies	Journal of Sport History

(continued)

Table 6.2 *(continued)*

International Journal of Applied Sports Science	Measurement in Physical Education and Exercise Science
International Journal of Coaching Science	Michigan State Entertainment and Sports Law Journal
International Journal of Sport and Exercise Psychology	NISR Journal of Sport Reform
International Journal of Sport Communication	Physical Education and Sport Pedagogy
International Journal of Sport Finance	Physical Educator
International Journal of Sport Management	Psychology of Sport and Exercise
International Journal of Sport Management and Marketing	Quest
International Journal of Sport Management, Recreation & Tourism	Recreational Sports Journal
International Journal of Sport Policy	Research Quarterly for Exercise and Sport
International Journal of Sport Psychology	Seton Hall Journal of Sport Law
International Journal of Sports Marketing & Sponsorship	Sociology of Sport Journal
International Journal of Sports Science & Coaching	Sport, Business and Management
International Journal of Sports Science and Physical Education	Sport, Education and Society
International Journal of the History of Sport	Sport History Review
International Review for the Sociology of Sport	Sporting Traditions
International Sports Law Review	Sport in History
International Sports Studies	Sport in Society
Journal for the Study of Sports and Athletes in Education	Sport Journal
Journal of Applied Sport Psychology	Sport Management Education Journal
Journal of Contemporary Athletics	Sport Management Review
Journal of Hospitality, Leisure, Sport & Tourism Education	Sport Marketing Quarterly
Journal of ICHPER·SD	Sport Psychologist
Journal of Issues in Intercollegiate Athletics	Sports and Entertainment Litigation Reporter
Journal of Legal Aspects of Sport	Sports Engineering
Journal of Leisure Research	Sports Lawyers Journal
Journal of Park and Recreation Administration	Sports, Parks and Recreation Law Reporter
Journal of Physical Education, Recreation & Dance	Texas Review of Entertainment & Sports Law
Journal of Quantitative Analysis in Sports	University of Miami Entertainment and Sports Law Review
Journal of Sponsorship	Villanova Sports and Entertainment Law Journal
Journal of Sport Administration & Supervision	Virginia Sports and Entertainment Law Journal
Journal of Sport & Exercise Psychology	Willamette Sports Law Journal
Journal of Sport and Social Issues	Women in Sport and Physical Activity Journal
Journal of Sport & Tourism	World Leisure Journal
Journal of Sport Behavior	YouthFirst: The Journal of Youth Sports

What Are the Best Journals in Sport Management?

Though many sport management academics could offer opinions in answer to this question, the field of sport management is presently devoid of a ranking system for its journals. Researchers have attempted, however, to rank journals on the basis of their perceived prestige by scholars. Shilbury and Rentschler (2007) published an assessment of sport management journals in *Sport Management Review*. Their methodology included identifying 13 journals "determined through the input of sport management academics at the institution undertaking the research [Deakin University], plus input from the professional association representing sport management academics in Australia and New Zealand" (p. 36). Based on a sample of academics in Australia, New Zealand, Europe, and North America, 64 individuals were invited to participate by evaluating the journals on four criteria. Based on the response rate of 70 percent (n = 45), the data were analyzed through cluster analysis,

and the 13 journals were ranked on the basis of perceived quality.

Although his study represented an important first step in quality assessment of sport management journals, the inherent limitations of the study prevent a broad application of the results. Perhaps the most obvious limitation is the small number (13) of journals selected for analysis—far less than the number of journals presented in table 6.2. Other limitations include the low number of respondents and the biased selection of journals for evaluation, as only researchers from Australia and New Zealand selected the journals. Given this ongoing lack of a clear prestige ranking for journals in the field, the most prudent course of action for a sport management researcher wishing to publish a manuscript is to select an outlet whose scope includes the topic of interest and whose readership promises maximum influence for the study.

almost 100 publication outlets for sport management research. Authors generally base their final manuscript submission decisions on congruency between the topic of the study and the publication scope of the journal, as well as the journal's perceived prestige and influence.

After choosing a potential publication outlet, the researcher should ensure that the manuscript conforms to the publication's guidelines for potential authors. These guidelines are typically published on the journal's Web site or within the printed journal itself, and they indicate such requirements as specific sections to include in the manuscript and the journal's reference style.

Manuscript Structure

Manuscripts published in sport management journals generally follow a similar basic structure. Granted, some differences do exist—for example, variation across journals and variation in authors' individual writing styles—but almost all studies published in academic journals include a specific title, an abstract, a literature review, a research

methods section, a results section, and a discussion section. The title for an academic manuscript is typically brief by design and commonly refers to the population of interest and the variables studied. Next, an abstract, or brief summary of the research (usually 100 to 250 words long), is often included to help readers quickly identify research reports of interest to them. Even though the abstract is featured early on in the written report, it is often not written until the remainder of the study has been prepared. Abstracts commonly address the study's purpose, research questions or hypotheses, associated theories, methods, results, and perhaps a brief description of the implications of the study.

As discussed in chapter 3, literature reviews typically feature a broad-to-narrow focus and make liberal use of subheadings to guide the reader. The literature review provides a critical review of previous research; it identifies trends, themes, and gaps in the literature and ultimately generates a justification for the study at hand. It also formally states research questions and hypotheses. The section on research methods often includes three main subsections: participants, instrumentation, and data analysis. The subsection on participants

Writing for Practitioners Instead of Academic Journals

While most research writing by sport management scholars is related to academic research, scholars are sometimes presented with an opportunity to conduct research specifically for sport organizations. This type of research may take the form of a fan behavior survey, a sponsorship effectiveness evaluation, or an economic impact study, and possible audiences include organizations such as major and minor league sport teams, intercollegiate athletic departments, sport governing bodies, and corporations that invest in sport sponsorships. When writing research reports for practitio-ners, it is important to consider the needs of your target audience. Practitioners depend on research in order to make informed deci-sions in applied settings, and they are most interested in studies that address the specific issues they face on a daily basis in their orga-nization. They will likely be less concerned than academics are about extensive literature reviews or theoretical frameworks, and sport management researchers should ensure that their written reports for practitioners focus on presenting problems and data-driven solu-tions.

describes the identification and selection process of the participants in the study, the subsection on instrumentation describes the tools used to collect data (e.g., specific surveys), and the data analysis section describes the specific analysis procedure employed in the study.

The results section reports the findings associated with the data analysis and often includes visual aids (e.g., tables); these findings are often reported in order according to the specific research question or hypothesis they address. The section typically begins with descriptive statistics about the sample. It also often addresses whether or not each specific research hypothesis was supported. Tables are com-monly included in the results section to present quantitative findings in a visually informative and easy-to-read manner. Detailed commentary about the findings is reserved for the discussion section, which assesses whether or not the results of the current study are consistent with those from past research. This section also interprets the results of the study and presents possible explanations for the results. The discussion section typically con-cludes with an outline of the specific strengths and limitations of the study, as well as treatment of any potential practical implications. Some researchers also thoughtfully include recommendations for future research, which help illustrate how the pres-ent study might serve as a basis for future work.

References

Since research builds on prior work by others, it is only natural that scholars need to reference the work of others at some point during their studies,

and academics use a variety of reference styles. The most popular reference style in sport management research is that of the American Psychological Association, but others are also used, including the Harvard system, MLA style, and *Bluebook* style (for legal research). Given the popularity of the APA reference style in sport management journals, we provide here the guidelines for in-text citations (see table 6.3) and reference lists (see the highlight box).

In the information age, sport management researchers can make use of a relatively new tool called reference management software. Although several reference management programs are avail-able, the most commonly used programs are End-Note and Reference Manager. This type of program can serve as a database for storing and retrieving bibliographic references. These programs are used to search and retrieve references from online biblio-graphic databases, organize references and images, and create bibliographies instantly in a Microsoft Word document. Additional features allow the user to automatically add sets of references from biblio-graphic databases to their own library and instantly create reference lists that conform to one of more than 1,000 different reference styles (e.g., APA, MLA, Harvard, *Bluebook*). The most recent versions interface seamlessly with a number of electronic databases and are quite user friendly.

Journal Publication Process

Once the manuscript conforms to the submis-sion requirements of the targeted journal, the researcher typically constructs a cover letter

Table 6.3 APA Reference List Examples

Source	APA format
Book	Author, A. A., & Author, B. B. (2009). *Title of book.* Location: Publisher.
Book chapter	Author, A. A. (2009). Title of chapter. In A. Editor, B. Editor, & C. Editor (Eds.), *Title of book* (p./ pp. nn/nn–nn). Location: Publisher.
Journal article	Author, A. A., Author, B. B., & Author. C. C. (2009). Title of article. *Title of Journal, volume,* page numbers.
Magazine article	Author, A. A. [if named, or Article title if no author.] (2009, Month day). Title of article if not given before [useful descriptive information]. *Title of Magazine, volume if given,* page numbers.
Newspaper article	Author, A. A. [if named, or Article title if no author.] (2009, Month day). Title of article if not given before [useful descriptive information]. *Title of Newspaper,* p/pp. nn/nn–nn.
Review article	Review author, A. A. (2009, Month day [as needed]). Review title [Review of the medium *Title of item reviewed: Subtitle*]. *Title of Periodical,* publication information following appropriate format above.
Online article in periodical	Author, A. A., Author B. B., & Author C. C. (2009). Title of article. *Title of Periodical,* volume, page numbers. Retrieved Month day, year, from source.
Online book	Author, A. A., & Author, B. B. (2009). *Title of book.* Retrieved Month day, year, from source.
Web site	Author. (2009). Title of Web site: Subtitle if needed. Retrieved Month day, year, from source.

APA Style Rules Governing Textual and Parenthetical Citations

- At the appropriate point in your text, insert a brief parenthetical reference consisting usually of the last name(s) of the author(s), a comma, and the year of publication. Your reader can use your reference list to obtain the full reference.

- Do not include suffixes such as Jr. or qualifiers such as Ed. Do not include months or days even if they are included in the reference list entry.

- For quotations and references to a specific part of a work, follow the year of publication with a comma and provide the page number(s) or identify the section you refer to. Precede the page numbers with p. or pp. or para. or sect. as appropriate. For Web pages without page numbers, be as specific as possible in order to help your reader find what you are referring to.

- For an anonymously authored work, use the first few words of the first element in the reference list entry for the work, followed by the date and other specifics needed.

- If your reference list includes more than one work by authors with the same last name, provide initials (before the last name, not inverted order) for each author in the textual and parenthetical citations.

- For undated works, include n.d. for "no date."

- For works by two authors, provide the last names of both every time the work is cited in the text. For three to five authors, provide the last names of all authors the first time the work is referred to in the text, and in subsequent references provide only the last name of the first author followed by et al. For more than six authors, provide only the last name of the first author and shorten the rest to et al. beginning with the first citation of the work.

- **General**. List the elements that identify the work's author, title, publication date, and publisher. For online publications, add elements stating where and when you retrieved the document.

  - Your reference list should be alphabetized by the last name of the author (or first title word, if no author) so that your reader can find the complete citation belong to each of your citations.

  - APA style suggests that the reference list be titled as such and views the term Bibliography as a broader designation to be used if your list of references includes more than just the works referred to in your paper.

- **Punctuation**. Periods are generally used to end elements in references. Commas are generally used to separate items within an element, except for the colon between a book's place of publication and the publisher's name and except for parentheses around year of publication, the Eds. notation for an edited book, and page numbers for book chapters. If there are two or more authors, separate them with commas and precede the last named author named with an ampersand rather than the word *and*.

- **Capitalization**. Capitalize only the first letter (and any proper nouns) in titles and subtitles of articles, books, chapters, and unpublished periodicals. Capitalize the first letter of all significant words in titles of published periodicals.

- **Italics**. Italicize titles of books and periodicals (e.g., journals, newspapers, magazines). Italicize the volume number only of periodicals.

- **Authors**. All authors' last names are inverted (last name first), and first names are abbreviated to the authors' initials. For one to six authors, list all. For seven or more, list the first six followed by a comma and et al.

- Corporate names as authors are written out; capitalize the first letter of significant words. A parent body precedes a subdivision within an organization.

- For an edited book without a named author, treat the editors as authors (inverted order), and include (Ed.) or (Eds.) in parentheses after the last editor's name. Editors' names and other names not in the author position (e.g., translators) are not inverted and are followed by an abbreviated designation in parentheses.

- If there is no named author or editor, move the title to the author position before the date.

- **Publication date**. The year of publication is enclosed in parentheses, precedes the title, and generally follows the authors' names. For works with no author or editor, put the title first and follow it by the year of publication. For magazines, newsletters, and newspapers, provide the month, month and day, or quarter of the issue if following the year format (YYYY, Month dd) or (YYYY, Season). If no date is available, enter (n.d.).

- **Volume, issue, and page numbers**. For periodicals with continuous pagination throughout a volume, provide only the volume number (italicized), a comma, and then the inclusive page numbers. If and only if each issue begins with page 1, give the issue number in parentheses immediately after the volume: *38*(2), 12–17. Precede page numbers with p. or pp. only for chapters in books, newspaper articles, and when unavoidably required for clarity.

- **Publishers and place of publication**. For publishers, give the city and state (or country, if the city is not well known for publishing or is ambiguous). Omit superfluous terms such as "Publishers,"

(continued)

Reference Lists   (continued)

"Co.," and "Inc." but include "Press" or "Books." Use 2-letter abbreviations for states if needed. Do not abbreviate "University." If two or more publisher locations are listed, give the first or the home office location if it is known.

- **Reviews.** The review author is listed first. Review title follows publication date in the format appropriate for the type of periodical. In brackets provide a statement identifying the article as a review, the medium being reviewed, and its title: [Review of the book/motion picture/television program/etc. Title of reviewed item]. Finish by providing the rest of the periodical citation. If a review is untitled or lacks an author, use the material in brackets as the title; retain the brackets.

- **Electronic publications.** For online publications, follow the rules for print publications as far as this is possible.

- Page numbers may be irrelevant.

- After the body of the reference, provide a "Retrieved" statement telling the date retrieved and source. The source may be the URL or the name of an indexing service or journal database where the article was located. Do not provide the URL for well known providers of journal articles or books such as a library database.

- Omit the final period if a citation ends with a URL.

- If an online journal is an exact reproduction of the print publication (e.g., JSTOR, NetLibrary, and most PDF documents) and you did not consult the print version, cite the item as if it were a print source (with page numbers) and include [Electronic version] as the last element of the article title.

to introduce the manuscript submission. The cover letter is addressed to the journal editor and includes information about the manuscript's author(s) and title and how to contact the writer of the letter. Cover letters also typically include a statement that the manuscript has never been previously published and is not under consideration for publication elsewhere. Many journals have moved to an online submission process, but a fair number still require manuscripts to be submitted through the postal service or another physical delivery service.

Once a manuscript and cover letter have been received by the journal's editor, the **peer review** process begins. The editor forwards a blind copy of the manuscript to a group of (typically) anonymous reviewers who judge the quality of the manuscript and its suitability for publication in that particular journal. Although editors often strive for a 4- to 6-week review process, it can take several months to complete the initial review of the manuscript. At that point, a decision is made to accept the manuscript as is, accept it after minor revisions are completed, request a revision and resubmission, or reject the manuscript outright. One way for researchers to limit the possibility of outright

rejection is to ensure that the manuscript conforms to the article review checklist published by Campion (1993). Manuscripts are rejected for a number of reasons, the most common of which, as noted by Daft (1995), are featured in table 6.4. Manuscripts are rarely accepted without modification of the original submission, so authors who do not receive outright rejections are often faced with the challenge of responding to reviewers' comments and suggestions. Though it is often difficult to review constructive criticism of one's work, it is important for the author(s) to remove emotion from the process and consider each comment and suggestion objectively. All reviewer comments should be addressed, and in cases where they are not addressed the author(s) should provide a logical rationale for choosing not to do so. Once each comment and suggestion is clearly addressed, the manuscript is ready for resubmission to the editor. If all the reviewers' suggestions are addressed adequately, the manuscript will then be accepted after an additional review period.

Once the manuscript has been accepted for publication, it is considered "in press" and is added to the publication queue. The length of time between the acceptance of the manuscript for publication

| Table 6.4 | **Common Reasons for Manuscript Rejections** |

Problem	Explanation
No theory	Not explaining what the variables mean and why they are related to one another
Concepts and operationalization not in alignment	Operational base of the research does not reflect the variables or model under study (i.e., the variables measured do not precisely match the variables as explained in the model)
Insufficient definition: theory	No explanation of the meaning of the concepts or variables
Insufficient rationale: design	No explanation of study procedures
Macrostructure: organization and flow	Parts of the paper do not fit together to form a coherent whole
Amateur style and tone	Taking a nonprofessional approach to the writing process
Inadequate research design	Design issues that typically constitute fatal flaws because the research has already been executed in an invalid manner
Not relevant to the field	No fit within the field
Overengineering	An overemphasis on methodology that obscures the true purpose of the study
Conclusions not in alignment	Not using the conclusions section to fully develop the theoretical contribution and point out new understandings from the study
Cutting up the data	Attempting to improperly multiply publications from a single database (i.e., intentionally splitting up the study into smaller parts than necessary and, consequently, engaging in the practice of "salami publishing")

R. Daft, 1995, Why I recommended that your manuscript be rejected and what you can do about it. In *Publishing in the organizational sciences*, 2nd ed., edited by L.L. Cummings and P. J Frost (London: Sage Publishing), 164-182.

and its actual publication varies by journal, but the process can take up to a year or even longer. As the manuscript nears publication, the editor or publisher often forwards a publication proof to the corresponding author for analysis. The proof allows one last opportunity for the author(s) to check for typographical errors. Once these proofs are approved by the author(s), they are returned to the editor or publisher for final printing.

Some manuscripts, of course, are not accepted for publication; indeed, some sport management journals maintain acceptance rates at or below 20 percent. Upon receiving notification of a manuscript rejection, the author(s) must evaluate the reviewers' comments and determine whether the reviewers have uncovered a critical flaw that cannot be corrected or whether their concerns can ultimately be addressed. If these comments can be addressed, the author(s) can reevaluate publication outlet options and begin the manuscript submission process again.

Evaluation of Journal Articles

One of the most challenging tasks for beginning researchers is that of identifying high-quality research, both as readers or consumers of research and in attempting to conduct their own initial research projects. The materials presented in this part of the textbook (chapters 3 through 6) have outlined many characteristics of good research in a step-by-step examination of the research process. Viewing this topic through a different lens, Pyrczak (2008) presents a thorough discussion of criteria for evaluating high-quality research by means of a section-by-section analysis of a journal article. While Pyrczak's work itself is recommended for further detail, the highlight box contains a partial list of criteria to consider when reading or writing research articles (many of these criteria also apply to research presentations).

Criteria for Journal Article Evaluation

Titles and Abstracts

- Is the title sufficiently specific yet concise?
- Does the title identify the types of individuals who participated in the study?
- Does the abstract state the purpose of the study?
- Does the abstract highlight the research methodology?

Introductions and Literature Reviews

- Does the researcher begin by identifying a specific research problem area?
- Does the researcher establish the importance of or need for the study?
- Does the review cite the most important and current related studies?
- Is the conceptual framework clearly linked to the research problem?
- Are the research questions and hypotheses stated?

Methods

- Has the researcher used sound sampling techniques?
- Where appropriate, have items or questions been provided?
- Has the researcher provided evidence of the instruments' validity and reliability?

Results

- Have appropriate descriptive statistics been provided?
- Does the researcher refer back to the research questions and hypotheses posed previously in the study?
- Are the tables appropriate and adequately explained in the results section?

Discussions

- Are the results discussed in terms of the literature cited previously in the study?
- Do the researchers acknowledge specific methodological limitations?
- Are specific implications provided for both practical and scholarly purposes?
- Are specific suggestions made for future research?

Overall Issues

- Have the researchers selected an important problem for investigation?
- Is the report cohesive?
- Does the study extend the boundaries of knowledge in the topic area?

Reprinted, by permission, from F. Pyrczak, 2008, *Evaluating research in academic journals: A practical guide to realistic evaluation*, 4th ed. (Glendale, CA: Pyrczak Publishing).

A research study does not have to perfectly meet each and every one of these criteria in order to be considered a strong study with valid results, but the list provides a starting point for identifying high-quality work.

Summary

The very last step of the research process is to disseminate or share the study's findings. Without this step, good research projects would simply gather dust on the researcher's bookshelf, failing to benefit either the scholarly community or the professional field. The two major ways to disseminate research are to present it at a conference and to publish it in a scholarly journal. Beginning researchers need to understand the proper processes and guidelines to follow in order to enjoy success in sharing the results of their research.

Selected text reprinted, by permission, from J.S. Fink et al., 2009, "Off-field behavior of athletes and team identification: Using social identity theory to explain fan reactions," *Journal of Sport Management* **23(3): 142-155.**

Access the full article online at www.humankinetics.com/products/all-products/Research-Methods-and-Design-in-Sport-Management.

ABSTRACT

In the current article, we extend the literature on fan identification and social identity theory by examining the effects of unscrupulous off-field behaviors of athletes. In doing so, we drew from both social identity theory and Heider's balance theory to hypothesize a significant interaction between fan identification level and leadership response on fans' subsequent levels of identification. An experimental study was performed and a 2 (high, low identification) × 2 (weak, strong leadership response) ANOVA was conducted with the pre to post difference score in team identification as the dependent variable. There was a significant interaction effect ($F_{(2, 80)} = 23.71$, $p < .001$) which explained 23% of the variance in the difference between pre and post test scores. The results provide evidence that unscrupulous acts by athletes off the field of play can impact levels of team identification, particularly for highly identified fans exposed to a weak leadership response. The results are discussed relative to appropriate theory. Practical implications and suggestions for future research are also forwarded.

DISCUSSION QUESTIONS

1 Given the content of this study, use the list provided in table 6.1 in the chapter to identify at least two academic conferences that would offer appropriate presentation outlets for this study. Why did you choose those conferences?

2 Identify the pages where the following sections begin and end in this study:

a. Title, b. Abstract, c. Introduction, d. Review of Literature, e. Methodology, f. Results, and g. Discussion.

3 Use the criteria for evaluating journal articles provided near the end of chapter 6 in the text to identify at least three criteria that this study meets. Does the study fail to meet any of the criteria? Briefly explain your answers.

part III

Research Design in Sport Management

Research in sport management is used for a variety of purposes, ranging from the theoretical to the practical. In fact, the founding editor of the *Sport Marketing Quarterly*, Dallas Branch, started the journal to serve individuals in both categories: "The academician could use it, obviously, for publication," whereas practitioners (professionals in the field) "could use it to enhance what it is they do, to grow their business" (2000, p. 62). Even as sport management scholars use their research to build the body of knowledge in the field, they also conduct research to assist practitioners in their various endeavors. Practitioners and sport organizations, in turn, often use research and findings produced by the academic community. They also conduct their own research studies. Take, for instance, Dan Derian, who serves as senior director of research for Major League Baseball. His employees gather and evaluate research data concerning professional baseball and how fans experience the game. Regardless of the methodology used to secure and assess their data, Derian (2008) explains that his research department works "to both understand the minds of our consumers to make sure we are providing them with the best possible fan experience . . . [and] to help sell the game to sponsors and other business partners" (p. 5). In addition to tracking demographics and other numbers related to baseball's television and radio audience, Derian's research department analyzes and manages information about fans in the ballparks and about the various ways (e.g., Internet, merchandise, video games) in which fans connect with professional baseball. Derian notes that information "enables good decision making no matter what part of the business you are in" (p. 5).

Whereas the first two sections of this textbook introduce the process of sport management research, this third part examines research designs used by sport management students, scholars, researchers, and practitioners. Whether sport industry research is used by practitioners to make better decisions or by academicians to develop new theories, the investigations conducted in sport management involve securing and assessing data through quantitative, qualitative, or mixed methodological approaches. Researchers use many methods of designing studies and collecting data, and the following six chapters focus on the most common approaches: surveys, interviews and focus groups, observation approaches, case studies, and historical and legal analyses. Because the sport management field relies so heavily on survey research, we examine that approach first, in chapter 7, which focuses on how surveys are developed and used by sport management researchers.

The remaining five chapters are devoted to the most common qualitative methodologies, which at times have been viewed as secondary to the more quantitative methodologies employed in sport management research. Costa (2005) used the Delphi technique (described in chapter 8) to elicit views on sport management research issues from a panel of scholarly experts. She found "a sense among some panelists that there is a negative perception of qualitative research among some sport management researchers" (p. 129). Panelist comments included the following (p. 129): "Qualitative method is underutilized and underappreciated in sport management." "Many still look at qualitative as 'fluffy' research." "Some reviewers reject qualitative studies based on their own positivist biases rather than on knowledgeable assessment of research." Regardless of such perceptions, however, Costa notes that both quantitative and qualitative methodologies in sport management have produced "a substantial volume of useful research and theory" (p. 133). Indeed, both quantitative and qualitative approaches are used quite frequently in sport management studies. Specifically, Pedersen and Pitts (2001) found that just over half (51 percent) of the articles published in the *Sport Marketing Quarterly* were qualitative; the methodologies used in these

qualitative articles ranged from descriptive and theoretical to observational and historical.

Chapter 8 examines interviews and focus groups, exploring the process and techniques of interviewing, gaining access, establishing rapport, and collecting and coding data. Chapter 9 address observation research, in which sport management researchers conduct their investigations by entering a sport setting in order to observe and spend time with the participants. Chapter 10 explores the value and components of case study research, which is a social science approach employing a variety of methodologies (e.g., interviewing, observing, analyzing documents). Chapter 11 focuses on historical research—specifically, what is involved in researching, analyzing, interpreting, and writing about sport management topics. Issues addressed in this chapter include the importance and relevance of historical research in sport management, the tools and materials needed to conduct such research, topic selection, and the process of distinguishing and analyzing primary and secondary source material. The chapter concludes with a discussion of types of historical writing in sport management. Chapter 12 completes this section with an overview of legal research in sport management. This chapter illustrates how legal research is used to investigate various phenomena, policies, and practices in the sport industry. Specific areas examined in this chapter include sources, design strategies, and writing techniques.

Surveys

Learning Objectives

After studying this chapter, you should be able to do the following:

- Comment on the purpose of survey research
- Discuss technical differences between a survey and a questionnaire
- Describe various interview types and their strengths and weaknesses
- Describe various questionnaire types and their strengths and weaknesses
- List the types of questions available to researchers who design their own questionnaires
- Describe the need and general procedure for a pilot study
- Discuss methods for increasing survey response rates
- Compare types of error in survey research

The field of sport management is more reliant on survey research than are many other sport disciplines. In particular, sport management subdisciplines such as organizational behavior and sport marketing rely on surveys to reach mass target populations of sport firm employees and sport team fans, respectively. Surveys allow sport management researchers to gain desired information about a characteristic, attitude, or behavior within a selected sample or population. Surveys are particularly useful in describing the characteristics of a large population, and they make it feasible to collect data from large samples. Surveys require standardization, which strengthens measurement quality by asking exactly the same questions of all subjects and allowing for a particular response. Standardization ensures that the survey's content remains consistent throughout the process of data collection. This quality, however, can make surveys an unattractive option for those who are investigating new phenomena and want to use probing questions based on a respondent's previous response to an item. As a result, researchers who use surveys must often develop their items to represent the lowest common denominator among the targeted sample or population when assessing people's attitudes, orientations, circumstances, and experiences.

It is important to note the difference between a survey and a questionnaire. Although the terms are often used interchangeably in sport management research (and, accordingly, within this textbook), the term **survey** technically refers to the action of collecting information, whereas a **questionnaire** is only one method of collecting data that involves asking a set of questions. As this distinction implies, survey research options involve much more than a standard questionnaire.

Interviews

Whether conducted in person or by telephone, interviews allow researchers to incorporate a human element into the data collection process. This human element is magnified in face-to-face interviews, which may allow the interviewer to gain rapport with the interviewee—a particularly useful factor when exploring sensitive topics. However, the interviewer must be careful not to influence the respondent to answer in a particular way, either consciously or unconsciously. Furthermore, given the necessity of training interviewers appropriately, the process of interviewing can be very expensive

and time consuming. In addition, even though face-to-face interviews may help researchers gain rapport with interviewees, respondents may still be untruthful about sensitive or potentially embarrassing information (e.g., recreational drug use); this issue is further complicated by the phenomenon of **social desirability**, which involves the tendency of individuals to respond in a manner that makes them appear better than they are. Overall, even though face-to-face interviews offer tangible advantages to researchers in certain situations, their expense and practical limitations (e.g., time required) limit their broad use in sport management research.

To reduce the participant withdrawal rate, telephone interviews are often much shorter than face-to-face interviews. Successful telephone interviews typically last no more than 10 minutes, which of course may limit the interviewer's ability to ask probing and complex questions. The major advantage is that the interviewer need not be in the same location as the interviewee, which in some scenarios significantly reduces the overall cost of administering the survey. However, telephone interviews are subject to selection bias because some members of a specified population may not have a telephone listing, either because they lack a personal telephone or because they request an unlisted number. The issue has been complicated by the advent of answering machines and telephones with caller ID (i.e., call display) capabilities, since some potential participants may decide not to answer calls from an unfamiliar source. Despite these disadvantages, telephone surveys allow researchers to contact potential respondents over large geographical areas and are quite useful in some research settings (e.g., projects with an international focus).

Questionnaires

Questionnaires can be administered in several ways: distributed in person to potential respondents individually or as a group, mailed to potential respondents, or conducted via the Internet. Regardless of how they are distributed, questionnaires require that the participant have at least minimal literacy proficiency in order to complete the survey. For this reason, researchers should consider the typical literacy level of the target population and make their questionnaires as clear and direct as possible.

If the research question can be addressed via a questionnaire, then it is likely to be the researcher's most efficient and cost-effective option. Direct distribution of paper surveys is particularly effective when participants are grouped together, as in a classroom full of students or an arena full of sport consumers. On the other hand, as with face-to-face interviews, direct distribution of paper surveys requires that the researcher (or a trained representative) be in the same place as the potential respondents. Nonetheless, direct distribution of paper surveys is a popular method of data collection in sport management, both because questionnaires give respondents a stronger feeling of anonymity and because a large number of questionnaires can be administered simultaneously.

As with telephone interviews, a mailed questionnaire offers an economical way to reach a large number of individuals over a broad geographic region; it also offers efficiency, in that a large number of questionnaires can be distributed simultaneously. However, mailed questionnaires have historically received low *response rates*—often in the range of 10 to 20 percent—and thus can increase the cost of data collection by requiring researchers to send many more surveys than the desired sample size. For example, assuming a response rate of 20 percent, a researcher who wants a sample of 100 respondents would need to send 500 surveys to valid potential respondents. In addition, respondents may not be representative of the entire sample, because those who respond to questionnaires are likely to be people who find the survey to be of particular interest or have strong opinions about the topic, whereas those who know or care very little about the topic may disregard the survey even if they fall within the sample focus.

Internet Surveys

The rise of the Internet has given researchers yet another option for collecting data. Internet surveys are often used as a way to administer the survey instrument to a large number of subjects over a broad geographical area. According to Reips (2000), Internet surveys offer several specific advantages and disadvantages when compared with their traditional "paper and pencil" counterparts. Advantages include the following:

1. Ease of access to a large number of demographically and culturally diverse participants

2. Ease of access to very rare, specific participant populations

3. A stronger justification for generalizing findings of Internet experiments to the general population compared to laboratory experiments if convenience samples are avoided

4. Generalizability of findings to more settings and situations, since external validity is considered to be high in Internet experiments compared to laboratory experiments (due to familiarity with the physical environment)

5. Avoidance of time constraints

6. Avoidance of organizational problems (e.g., less scheduling difficulties, since thousands of participants may participate simultaneously)

7. Completely voluntary participation

8. Ease of acquiring just the optimal number of participants for achieving high statistical power while being able to draw meaningful conclusions

9. Detectability of **motivational confounding**

10. Reduction of **experimenter effects**

11. Reduction of **demand characteristics**

12. Cost savings in terms of lab space, person hours, equipment, and administration

13. Greater openness of the research process assuming the project remains openly accessible indefinitely on the Internet for documentation purposes

14. Ability to assess the number of nonparticipants via comparison of total webpage viewers to participants

15. Ease of comparing results with results from a locally tested sample

16. Greater external validity through greater **technical variance** (i.e., equipment malfunctions are likely to be confined to individual users rather than impacting the entire experiment)

17. Ease of access for participants (through bringing the experiment to participants instead of vice versa)

18. Public control of ethical standards (participants, peers or other members of the academic community might look at an experiment and communicate any objections to the researchers)

Disadvantages (and some suggested solutions) include the following:

1. Multiple submissions can be avoided or minimized by collecting personal identification items (e.g., birthdates), checking internal consistency (see chapter 4) as well as date and time consistency of answers, and using techniques such as subsampling (i.e., analyzing a selected sample of a larger sample), participant pools, and provision of passwords.

2. Experimental control may be an issue in some experimental designs but is less problematic when using a between-subjects design with random distribution of participants to experimental conditions.

3. Self-selection can be controlled by using the multiple-site entry technique.

4. Dropout is high in Internet experiments, especially if no financial incentives are given for participation.

5. The reduction or absence of interaction with participants during an Internet experiment creates problems if instructions are misunderstood.

6. The comparative basis for the Internet experiment method is low.

7. External validity of Internet experiments may be limited by their dependence on computers and networks.

As with the limitations of telephone interviews, researchers who use Web-based questionnaires must understand that not everyone is connected to the Internet, and that, as a result, online surveys can be particularly ineffective with certain populations known to have little or no access to the Internet (e.g., people in some rural locations). Furthermore, even if they are connected to the Internet, some respondents are less computer literate than others, and researchers need to ensure that the questionnaire, as presented on the screen, remains consistent across multiple computer platforms and Web browsers. In addition, the development of spam filters may prevent a researcher's request for participation from reaching its intended audience in the first place. Finally, since e-mail addresses are not necessarily as standardized as telephone numbers are, the sampling of e-mail addresses is challenging. For example, some potential participants have multiple e-mail addresses and thus may potentially be able to respond to the questionnaire several times, which of course could skew the results of the study.

Questionnaire Development and Design

If a researcher decides to use a questionnaire to collect data, it is important that he or she first determine whether a suitable questionnaire already exists. By conducting a thorough literature review on the selected topic, the researcher may uncover several existing questionnaires that measure the concepts of interest. Another advantage is that existing questionnaires typically have already been assessed for reliability and validity and therefore provide the researcher with a benchmark for future studies using the instrument. Given the considerable time and effort required to develop valid and reliable questionnaires, researchers can save considerable time by selecting an existing questionnaire—with appropriate citations, of course, to recognize the questionnaire's original author(s).

If an existing questionnaire is not available, the researcher should consider the types of questions typically asked in questionnaires and develop items for the new study to coincide with its purpose and hypotheses. First, the researcher should consider whether to use open questions, closed questions, or a combination of the two. An **open question** allows the participant to respond in an unrestricted manner. Open questions are often associated with qualitative studies and are most useful when the researcher is unsure of the likely responses, when the responses have the potential to be quite complex, or when it is important to know the respondent's own words. Here is an example of an open-ended question: "What are the important aspects of a successful sport camp experience?" Such a question is likely to elicit a wide range of detailed responses, and the resulting data may be qualitatively analyzed or coded and converted into numerical data.

A **closed question**, on the other hand, requires the respondent to choose from a number of predetermined responses. Consequently, closed questions are associated with quantitative studies and are typically used when the researcher has a clear idea of the available responses, when the responses are likely to be simple, or when it is otherwise important that respondents answer using a predetermined set of responses. For example, a simple demographic question such as, "Are you a season ticket holder?" can be most easily addressed with a closed response set consisting of yes and no. If the researcher is not entirely certain of all of the available responses, the question may be structured to include closed responses but end with an opportunity for open response that allows further explanation. Here is an example: "Other: _____."

When designing closed questions, the researcher has a number of options from which to select. One of the most popular question types in sport management involves the Likert scale, which is commonly used to assess attitudes. A **Likert scale** allows the respondent to indicate the extent to which she or he agrees with a particular statement, usually along a five-, seven-, or nine-point scale. For example, a Likert scale that corresponds to the question, "To what extent are you satisfied with your job?" might consist of a seven-point scale anchored by end responses of "very dissatisfied" and "very satisfied." In this example, respondents are allowed to select the point on the scale that most closely matches their opinion, which, in the case of job satisfaction, allows them to give an answer that is far more representative of reality than allowing them only to indicate that they are simply satisfied or dissatisfied. Such attitudes are complex and likely range along a continuum from extreme dissatisfaction to extreme satisfaction. A slight variation of the Likert scale involves the **semantic differential** format, which measures the respondent's reaction along a scale with contrasting adjectives at each end. For example, an attendee of a sporting event could be presented with an architectural rending of a new proposed arena and asked to rate it on a seven-point scale anchored by "contemporary" at one end and "traditional" on the other end.

Researchers can also choose from a number of other closed question formats. A **list question** allows the respondent to select more than one response. For example, sport spectators could be asked after an event whether they recall the official sponsors of the event. The response list would include a number of correct response options and a number of similar but incorrect options, and participants would be asked to check all that apply. A **ranking question** asks the respondent to place responses in order of importance. For instance, respondents might be asked to rank a list of sporting events according to which ones they are most likely to attend. Finally, a **filter question** is often used to allow respondents to skip a series of questions that may not apply to them. For example, a questionnaire that asks respondents about the perceived quality and value of food purchases made at a sport event would probably include an option for those who answered "no" to the first question—"Did you purchase food at this event?"—to skip subsequent items related to the first question (e.g., "If no food

purchases were made, please skip ahead to question 7.").

Regardless of whether the study's design calls for open or closed questions, researchers must take great care when designing items in order to avoid a number of common pitfalls. According to Gratton and Jones (2004), potential problems in item development include ambiguous or complex wording; incorrect precoding of closed questions; the presence of leading questions, double-barreled questions, or threatening questions; and incorrect operationalization of constructs. In order to avoid ambiguous or complex wording, researchers should develop items at a level of language that can be understood by a diverse audience. For example, questionnaires targeted to young children should not include words that exceed the typical vocabulary of the expected child participants. To avoid errors associated with incorrect precoding of closed questions, researchers must conduct a thorough review of the predetermined responses. Consider the following demographic item:

What is your annual household income?

☐ Less than $19,000 ☐ $20,000-$29,999 ☐ $30,000-$39,999
☐ $40,000-$49,999 ☐ $50,000-$59,999 ☐ $60,000-$69,999
☐ $70,000-$79,999 ☐ $80,000-$89,999 ☐ $90,000-$99,999
☐ $100,000-$109,999 ☐ $110,000-$119,000 ☐ $120,000+

At first glance, the item seems to identify a number of obvious response categories, but closer inspection reveals that a respondent with an annual household income of, say, $19,500 or $119,500 would have trouble answering the item, because an appropriate category is not defined in either case. Thus, two precoded responses (the 1st and the 11th) are incorrect. The same question could also be hampered by the following response set:

☐ Less than $20,000 ☐ $20,000-$30,000 ☐ $30,000-$40,000
☐ $40,000-$50,000 ☐ $50,000-$60,000 ☐ $60,000-$70,000
☐ $70,000-$80,000 ☐ $80,000-$90,000 ☐ $90,000-$100,000
☐ $100,000-$110,000 ☐ $110,000-$120,000 ☐ $120,000+

In this set, individuals with an annual household income equal to a multiple of $10,000 (from $20,000 to $120,000) each have two responses they could choose. Researchers can eliminate precoded response errors like those presented here by thoroughly editing their questions before distributing the questionnaire.

A **leading question** influences responses by pressuring the respondent to respond in a certain manner. Here is an example of a leading question asked of a baseball fan: "Do you think the greedy team owner should cap the salaries of the unappreciated baseball players on the team?" Descriptors such as "greedy" and "unappreciated" can sway one's response to the question.

A **double-barreled question** requests respondents' views on two separate issues within the same item. For example, asking a stakeholder the question, "How satisfied are owners and players with the most recent version of the collective bargaining agreement?" actually asks the respondent to answer two questions: How satisfied are owners, and how satisfied are players? Since owners and players likely hold various opinions about the collective bargaining agreement, the question should be split into two separate questions.

A **threatening question** is one where the respondent may have a vested interest in concealing the information requested. For example, an item that queries National Collegiate Athletic Association (NCAA) athletes about gambling on their own sports is potentially threatening since NCAA regulations strictly limit such behavior. Questions asked about such sensitive topics are likely to convince the respondent to underreport or even deny the behavior in question, even if they often engaged in the behavior. Researchers can minimize this problem by wording potentially threatening items as neutrally as possible.

Finally, a researcher who equates a professional sport fan's commitment to a certain sport with the number of games that he or she attends in a particular season has failed to correctly **operationalize** the concept (i.e., failed to measure the concept appropriately). Specifically, since attendance at a particular event can be influenced by work, family, or volunteer commitments, it is problematic to equate one's psychological commitment to a particular team with one's attendance at team events.

Once a researcher has developed a questionnaire, he or she must ensure that it is properly ordered. Preferably, the questionnaire should begin with relatively simple, interesting, and straightforward closed questions that entice the respondent to become immersed in the questionnaire. More complex items that require extensive thought or more complex responses should be included later in the questionnaire. Items that assess a similar theme (e.g., job satisfaction, organizational commitment) should be grouped together to prevent responders from having to refocus their perspective extensively. Finally, personal or potentially threatening questions, including demographic questions (e.g., annual household income), should be placed at the end of the questionnaire. Asking such sensitive items at the beginning of a questionnaire could decrease the response rate.

When administering a newly developed questionnaire, it is wise to pilot the questionnaire before administering it in full. A **pilot study** involves a small-scale administration of the survey prior to the main administration and is often conducted by using a similar sample (Gratton & Jones, 2004). In addition to having the respondents in the pilot study complete the questionnaire in order to ensure that it is clear and unambiguous, researchers can share the purpose of the questionnaire with the pilot study participants and ask them the following questions:

1. Given the purpose of this survey, do you think the questions in the survey collect the information needed? Why or why not?

2. Are the phrasing and terminology clear and easy to understand?

3. Are the directions easy to follow?

4. Is the survey attractive and neat?

5. Is the survey too long to be comfortably completed in one sitting? Approximately how long would it take you to complete it?

6. Is any important background information missing?

7. Should any statements or categories be added or deleted? If so, please explain.

8. Please include any other comments relevant to improving this survey.

Incorporating the resulting feedback from pilot study participants can help the researcher increase the reliability and validity of the questionnaire. Pilot-testing a questionnaire also allows the researcher to test the questionnaire's administration procedures (from initial distribution to receipt of completed questionnaires) and the planned data analysis procedures—both of which can be particularly important when using a questionnaire. Table 7.1 presents an example of a well-designed questionnaire involving a motivation scale for online sport consumption (Seo & Green, 2008).

Table 7.1 Motivation Scale for Online Sport Consumption

Subscale	Consumption statement	Rating*
Information	It provides quick and easy access to large volumes of sport information.	1 2 3 4 5 6 7
	I use the team's Web site because I am able to obtain a wide range of football information.	1 2 3 4 5 6 7
	I use the team's Web site because I can learn about things happening in the football world.	1 2 3 4 5 6 7
Entertainment	I use the team's Web site because it is exciting.	1 2 3 4 5 6 7
	I use the team's Web site because it is cool.	1 2 3 4 5 6 7
	I use the team's Web site because it is amusing.	1 2 3 4 5 6 7
Interpersonal communication	I use the team's Web site because it shows me how to get along with others.	1 2 3 4 5 6 7
	I use the team's Web site because I won't be alone.	1 2 3 4 5 6 7
	I use the team's Web site because it allows me to meet others, which helps me cope with personal problems.	1 2 3 4 5 6 7
Escape	I use the team's Web site because I can escape from reality.	1 2 3 4 5 6 7
	I use the team's Web site because it allows me to enter a nonthinking, relaxing period.	1 2 3 4 5 6 7
	I use the team's Web site because I can forget about work.	1 2 3 4 5 6 7
Pass time	I use the team's Web site because it gives me something to do to occupy my time.	1 2 3 4 5 6 7
	I use the team's Web site because it passes the time away, particularly when I'm bored.	1 2 3 4 5 6 7
	I use the team's Web site during my free time.	1 2 3 4 5 6 7
Fanship	One of the main reasons I use the team's Web site is that I consider myself a fan of football.	1 2 3 4 5 6 7
	One of the main reasons I use the team's Web site is that I am a huge fan of football in general.	1 2 3 4 5 6 7
	One of the main reasons I use the team's Web site is that I consider myself to be a big fan of my favorite football team.	1 2 3 4 5 6 7
Team support	One of the main reasons I use the team's Web site is because of a particular team I am interested in following.	1 2 3 4 5 6 7
	I use the team's Web site because I believe it is important to support my favorite team.	1 2 3 4 5 6 7
	Using the team's Web site demonstrates my support for football in general.	1 2 3 4 5 6 7
Fan expression	I use the team's Web site because I can express myself through communication contents (message board, chat,...).	1 2 3 4 5 6 7
	I use the team's Web site because I can form my own opinion through communication contents (message board, chat,...).	1 2 3 4 5 6 7
	I use the team's Web site because I enjoy interacting with other fans on the Web.	1 2 3 4 5 6 7

(continued)

Table 7.1 *(continued)*

Subscale	Consumption statement	Rating*
Economic	I use the team's Web site because I am able to make purchases on the team's Web site.	1 2 3 4 5 6 7
	When I want to buy a big-ticket item, I use the team's Web site to search for bargain prices.	1 2 3 4 5 6 7
	I use the team's Web site because it is a great place to buy gifts.	1 2 3 4 5 6 7
Technical knowledge	I use the team's Web site because I want to know the technical aspects of football.	1 2 3 4 5 6 7
	I use the team's Web site because I want to know the rules of football.	1 2 3 4 5 6 7
	I use the team's Web site because I want to know football strategy.	1 2 3 4 5 6 7

*Respondents were asked to rate the degree to which they agreed or disagreed with each item on a 7-point Likert scale ranging from 1 (strongly disagree) to 7 (strongly agree).

Adapted, by permission, from W.J. Seo and B.C. Green, 2008, "Development of the motivation scale for online sport consumption," *Journal of Sport Management* 22(1): 82-109.

Implementing an Internet Questionnaire

In order to minimize some of the problems inherent in Internet questionnaires, Dillman (2000) has proposed the following best practice guidelines for Web-based surveys:

1. Use a multiple-contact strategy much like that used for regular mail surveys. If a researcher has access to complete contact information for a potential participant, he or she may be able to positively affect the overall response rate by notifying the potential participant via mail or telephone of the importance of the upcoming survey.

2. Personalize contacts through e-mail if possible. Survey invitations that include the recipient's name have been shown to be more effective in eliciting responses than general greetings such as "Dear Sir or Madam."

3. Keep the invitation brief. It should highlight the purpose and importance of the survey, but including too many details may decrease the overall response rate.

4. Begin with a question that is interesting but easy to answer. First impressions are important, and if the first question presented to potential respondents is complex, participation in the survey may be diminished. A caveat: Although demographic questions are generally considered easy for participants to answer, they should be included at the end of the questionnaire because questionnaires that begin by asking personal information (e.g., annual household income) have been shown to elicit lower response rates.

5. Introduce a Web survey with a welcome screen that is motivational, emphasizes the ease of response, and instructs potential respondents to proceed to the survey. Given that the introduction screen is entirely within the researcher's control, he or she should invest a great deal of time and thought into the design of an aesthetically pleasing welcome screen that could encourage participation.

6. Present each question in a conventional format similar to that normally used for self-administered surveys presented on paper. Since potential participants have likely encountered conventional survey formats in the past, it is best to capitalize on their familiarity with that format by mimicking it in the online environment.

7. Do not require respondents to provide an answer to each question before answering subsequent questions. As with conventional surveys and assessments, respondents may not necessarily desire to answer the items in the order presented by the researcher. Unless order of response is important (e.g., if the answer to a given item will dictate

which additional items are asked of the respondent), it is best to give the potential respondent as much freedom as possible in answering the questionnaire.

8. Make each question and any corresponding potential responses to that question visible on the screen all at the same time. Items that require a respondent to scroll excessively or return to a previous screen may be frustrating to the participant. It is also helpful to present each item in its entirety in order to minimize potential confusion in a participant's mind.

Increasing Response Rate

As mentioned in Dillman's (2000) first recommendation, researchers can use multiple-contact strategies to increase response rates for Web-based surveys (Mehta & Sivadas, 1995; Smith, 1997). One such strategy involves sending a **prenotification** e-mail message a few days before administering the survey. Prenotification messages have been shown to increase response rate in a sample of intercollegiate head coaches (Kent & Turner, 2002). In their study, Kent and Turner compared response rates of three groups of full-time NCAA head coaches. The first group ($n = 340$) was not sent a prenotification message, the second group ($n = 340$) was sent a prenotification message by standard mail 10 days prior to the mailing of the questionnaire, and the third group ($n = 340$) was sent a prenotification message by electronic mail 7 days before the mailing of the questionnaire (the timing difference between groups two and three was based on the delivery time required for standard mail versus electronic mail). The response rate increased progressively from group one (36.2 percent) to group two (44.1 percent) to group three (51.5 percent). Chi-square analyses revealed a significant difference between the *control group* (group one) and the two treatment groups (groups 2 and 3), but there was no significant difference between the two treatment groups, thus highlighting the positive effects of sending prenotification messages in surveys of full-time NCAA head coaches.

A **follow-up reminder** can also be an effective way to enhance response rate. In general, follow-up reminders should be sent first via e-mail and then through progressively more expensive methods such as paper mail (Schaeffer & Dillman, 1998). A review of the sport management literature reveals that most researchers use three follow-up reminders in their studies. Another way to enhance response rate is to use an inducement—that is, a reward given to the participant in return for completing the questionnaire. Inducements in sport management research include direct monetary rewards, free merchandise, and participation in drawings for high-priced merchandise. If a researcher chooses to use an inducement, he or she should disclose this practice when disseminating results of the study, since it could alter the participation motives of the study's participants.

Response rate can also be affected by several other practices, such as **sponsorship**, in which an individual who is held in high regard by potential respondents endorses or directly encourages them to participate in the study. If potential respondents invest a high level of trust in the sponsor, they are more likely to participate in the study. Another option is to send an **introductory letter**. Effective introductory letters highlight the purpose and importance of the study, include an altruistic appeal to the potential respondent, and are relatively brief. Method of return is another important factor in determining response rate. Researchers who make it easy for respondents to return the questionnaire are most likely to enjoy higher response rates. For example, a researcher who uses a mailed questionnaire and expects the respondent to pay for postage or manually address the return envelope will likely be stuck with a lower response rate; instead, the researcher should provide a preaddressed, postage-paid envelope. Response rate has also been shown to be affected by a questionnaire's format. Researchers should aim for an aesthetically pleasing cover and an attractive flow of information within the questionnaire in order to reduce confusion among participants. Finally, response rate is also affected by the selection of respondents. Studies have shown that higher-educated professionals with an interest in the topic at hand are the most likely people to respond; thus, researchers who sample potential respondents outside of this demographic should expect lower response rates.

Types of Error

All survey research is subject to error, which, in general, relates to two issues: (1) how closely the responding sample is representative of the population (i.e., error associated with who answers), and (2) how well the questionnaire answers measure the characteristics to be described (i.e., error associated with the answers themselves).

When a sample is not representative of a population, the sample is said to be biased. The types of error associated with who answers are generally confined to sampling error and frame error. **Sampling error** occurs when the sample drawn from the population is not representative of the entire population. In other words, sampling error results from measuring a characteristic in some but not all kinds of members of a population. For example, if a researcher wants to assess attitudes of spectators at a college football event about the quality of stadium amenities but for reasons of convenience sampled only spectators who were seated in luxury boxes, the sample would not be representative of the entire population. The extent of a sampling error depends on the variability of the population (more homogeneous samples help reduce sampling error) and on the size of the sample (larger samples help to reduce sampling error by increasing the probability that all kinds of members of a population are sampled). **Frame error**, also referred to as coverage error, occurs when the list from which the sample is drawn fails to contain all members of the population. For example, a researcher who decides to implement an Internet-based survey may exclude certain portions of the population who either do not have access to the Internet or are computer illiterate.

The extent to which questionnaire answers measure the characteristics to be described are limited by two types of error: response error and nonresponse error. **Response error** occurs when, as a result of the communication process, the respondent is unable or unwilling to respond to all items in a survey (see chapter 5 for discussion of nonresponse bias). A respondent's inability to respond to certain items could be due to ignorance, forgetfulness, or inability to articulate a response. Furthermore, a respondent may be unwilling to respond to some items in a survey as a result of privacy concerns or time pressure. For example, a researcher who distributes questionnaires to spectators at a sport event immediately after the event may encounter respondents who are being rushed by family members or friends. As a result, items that are more challenging or that appear near the end of the questionnaire may not receive full attention from the respondent. **Nonresponse error** refers to the extent to which subjects included in the sample fail to provide usable responses and are systematically different from those who respond to the survey. For example, a researcher who wants to survey all collegiate coaches in an athletic conference at the same time may encounter a lower response rate from coaches whose sport is currently in season and a higher response rate from coaches whose sport is not in season. Nonresponse error can be measured by comparing early respondents with late respondents, using "days to respond" as a progression variable, comparing respondents to nonrespondents, or comparing respondents on characteristics known a priori (Dooley & Linder, 2003).

Summary

Surveys allow sport management researchers to gain desired information about a characteristic, attitude, or behavior within a selected sample or population. Surveys are typically conducted via an interview (face to face or by telephone) or a questionnaire (mailed or administered online). Each of these survey methods offers distinct advantages and disadvantages. It is always preferable to use an existing survey that meets the researcher's needs, if one is available, but studies of novel constructs or settings may require the researcher to develop a new instrument. This chapter presents a number of question options and design considerations, as well as strategies for increasing survey response rate. Finally, all survey research is subject to error relating to two issues: (1) how closely the responding sample is representative of the population (i.e., error associated with who answers), and (2) how well the questionnaire answers measure the characteristics to be described (i.e., error associated with the answers themselves).

Selected text reprinted, by permission, from A. Kent and B. Turner, 2002, "Increasing response rates among coaches: The role of prenotification methods," *Journal of Sport Management* 16(3): 230-238.

Access the full article online at www.humankinetics.com/products/all-products/Research-Methods-and-Design-in-Sport-Management.

ABSTRACT

This study determined whether, in a population of intercollegiate head coaches. Prenotification had a significant influence on the return rate of mailed questionnaires. Acknowledging the growing use of e-mail and the Internet for survey distribution, the current study evaluated the effectiveness of e-mail as a prenotification technique. Response rates of Intercollegiate Head Coaches to mailed questionnaires from two separate samples were analyzed. Comparisons were made based upon the categorization of coaches into groups of prenotification by e-mail, formal letter, and a non-prenotified control group. Results indicated that prenotification of the survey recipients significantly increased response rates, with the group receiving e-mail prenotification having the highest response rate among the three groups. In addition to being cost effective for researchers, e-mail prenotification was an effective way to increase both the number and variety of contacts with survey recipients.

TEXT EXCERPTS

While this trend has not been noted in the sport management literature, the importance of continued attention to survey response rates remains. As noted by Krosnick (1999), "these are exciting times for survey research. The literature is bursting with new insights that demand dramatic revisions in the conventional wisdom that has guided this research method for decades" (p. 538). Much of this optimism comes from advances in technology, through which researchers have realized the prospect of reducing the cost of research, increasing the speed of data collection, and allowing for larger and more diverse samples to be accessed (e.g., Dillman, 2000; Opperman, 1995; Parker, 1992; Schaefer & Dillman, 1998).

. . . .

Prenotification usually takes the form of a formal letter or a post card, although more rarely, it occurs as a telephone call or personal contact. The intention of establishing this initial contact is threefold: (a) to identify the researchers to the potential respondents, (b) to present the purpose of the study, and (c) to request the recipient's cooperation and participation in the research endeavor (Dillman, 2000). The fundamental assumption of prenotification is that "if the respondents know something about the researcher and the study, they may be more likely to complete the questionnaire."

■■■■■■■■■■■■■■■■

Of primary concern to all studies using survey research is non-response error. Non-response bias is the potential difference between those who respond to a survey and those who do not (King et al., 2001). One method to help control non-response error is to compare early to late respondents (Miller & Smith, 1983).

■■■■■■■■■■■■■■■■

Response rate statistics for the two prenotification treatment groups and the control group are presented in Table 1. Prior to pooling the data, the samples were independently compared to one another and were found to have similar distributions with no significant differences in overall response rate ($\chi^2 = .893$, Cramer's V = .030, p =.345), letter prenotification response rate ($\chi^2 = .291$, Cramer's V = .029, p=.590), e-mail prenotification response rate (($\chi^2 = .933$, Cramer's V = .052, p =. 334), nor control group response rate ($\chi^2 = 3.030$, Cramer's V = .094, p =. 082). To determine the effect of prenotification on response rates on the pooled data sent, the two treatment groups were combined and compared to the control group.

■■■■■■■■■■■■■■■■

A limitation of this study is that although there were an equal number of coaches in each of the three conditions, not all coaches in the sample had valid e-mail addresses.

DISCUSSION QUESTIONS

1 What are some of the advantages of survey research methods?

2 What are the three purposes of prenotification?

3 What potential limitations of e-mail surveys are noted by the authors?

4 How did the authors control for non-response bias? Did the results indicate that a nonresponse bias was present?

5 Do the results of the study support the notion that prenotification methods can affect survey response rate?

6 What potential explanations do the authors offer for the +7.4 percent response rate advantage that e-mail prenotification produced over the formal letter prenotification?

Interviews

Stephen W. Dittmore, PhD ▪ University of Arkansas

Learning Objectives

After studying this chapter, you should be able to do the following:

- Effectively and objectively enter the field to conduct research interviews
- Identify the appropriate interview technique for your particular research question
- Understand the benefits of various interview techniques
- Describe the process of breaking down interview transcripts into similar codes and themes
- Discuss the importance of validating interview data

Regardless of what form a researcher's qualitative study takes (case study, ethnography, or historical study), chances are that he or she will conduct an **interview**. Denzin and Lincoln (1998, p. 36) called the interview "the favorite methodological tool of the qualitative researcher," and Gubrium and Holstein (2002, p. 4) noted that the interview "has become a commonplace feature of everyday life" for a researcher. The process of interviewing involves asymmetrical communication in which the interviewer facilitates a conversation with an interviewee with the intent of obtaining desired information. The interviewer makes the initial contact, schedules the interview, and initiates the questions (Gubrium & Holstein, 2002).

The interview is not, however, as one-sided as it appears. Denzin and Lincoln (2005, p. 643) stress that the interview is not neutral, because "at least two people create the reality of the interview situation." They contend that the method is influenced by personal characteristics of the interviewer, such as race, class, ethnicity, and gender. Similarly, Fontana and Frey (2005, p. 698) encourage researchers to recognize that "interviews are not neutral tools of data gathering but rather active interactions between two (or more) people leading to negotiated, contextually based results."

The interviewee responds to the questioning, providing information from his or her personal knowledge or experience. The logistics of the exchange may involve a public opinion poll, demographic questionnaire, consumption survey, conversation, or other form. To that end, the interview may be viewed as a foundational aspect of research, whether qualitative or quantitative.

Interviews date back as far ancient Egypt and population censuses but began gaining in utility and popularity in clinical diagnosis and counseling, as well as psychological testing and measurement, during World War I. In 1935, George Gallup formed the American Institute of Public Opinion, which ushered in a movement toward the study and measurement of attitudes (Fontana & Frey, 2005). Additional survey organizations formed shortly thereafter, including the National Opinion Research Center and the Survey Research Center, the latter of which was formed in 1946 by Rensis Likert at the University of Michigan. Likert would create a measurement scale that is now used frequently in social science research to construct indexes from questionnaire data (Babbie, 1986). Likert scales are discussed in more detail in chapter 7.

According to some qualitative researchers (e.g., Platt, 2002), academics initially resisted numbers-based social science research, preferring instead to focus on theoretical concerns in social science. Platt noted that since the interview encompasses so many different practices, it is hard to generalize about it. She further explained that changes over time were driven partly by methodological concerns and partly by sociopolitical motives.

Today, the interview is used widely in sport marketing, politics, communication, and many other disciplines. Indeed, the ubiquity and significance of the interview in contemporary society prompted Silverman (1997) to suggest that we live in an "interview society"—a statement elaborated on in more recent research by Fontana and Frey (2005) and by Gubrium and Holstein, who noted that the interview society "is flourishing as a leading context for addressing the subjective contours of daily living" (2002, p. 10).

Researchers can use the current societal prevalence of the interview to their advantage as they seek to understand not just the traditional "what" of everyday life but also the "how" of people's lives (Fontana & Frey, 2005). This rest of this chapter explores interview processes and techniques in sport management research; it also addresses the processes of assembling and analyzing interview data.

Interview Process

Qualitative researchers refer to the process of collecting data as being "in the field" (Rossman & Rallis, 2003), and researchers must adequately prepare themselves for what they will encounter in the field before they begin the data collection process.

Some traditional and commonly accepted "how-to" steps do exist for conducting interviews in the field, though many postmodern researchers hold that interviewing cannot be distilled into a certain process but varies from person to person and from context to context. The following subsections address several aspects of interviewing as viewed traditionally: accessing the setting, understanding the language and culture of respondents, deciding how to present oneself, locating an informant, gaining trust, establishing rapport, and collecting data (Fontana & Frey, 2005). Although the presentation of these approaches implies some form of sequence, it is not necessary for them to occur sequentially.

Accessing the Setting

This step involves actually getting into the field. In ethnographic research, the researcher becomes a part of the setting. Fontana and Frey (2005) noted that ways of getting into a setting may vary but that they all share the same goal of gaining access. For example, in Shaw's (2006) study of social processes of gender relations in British national governing bodies (NGBs) for sport, she sought to gain access to influential members of several NGBs and encountered different processes for doing so.

Two NGBs responded enthusiastically to her request to conduct research by inviting her to board meetings, encouraging her to volunteer at organization events, and providing access to documents and interviews with members. The third NGB was more "resistant to the research, in part because of a perception [that] it conflicted with their work time" (Shaw, p. 517). In the end, Shaw did gain access to the third NGB, though she interviewed only 5 members of that organization as compared with 15 members of the other two NGBs. Her experiences underscore the challenges associated with gaining access to organizations, especially when the research involves controversial subject matter. Silk and Amis (2000) used an ethnographic approach in studying the 1998 Commonwealth Games in Kuala Lumpur, Malaysia. To gain access, the researchers contacted a broadcaster 2 years in advance of the games and developed a rapport with the network and the host broadcaster. These relationships led to one author becoming an accredited crewmember with the network, staying in the same hotel as the network crew, eating with the broadcasters, and socializing and working with the crew.

Understanding the Language and Culture of the Respondents

When researchers conduct international research, they must frequently confront potential barriers based on language and cultural differences. Even if an interviewer is fluent in the respondents' language, he or she may be unaware of all the culturally specific ways of saying or not saying various things (Fontana & Frey, 2005).

In Silk and Amis' (2000) study of the 1998 Commonwealth Games, they became involved with the host broadcaster of the Games to study what, if any, pressures existed for the organizers of the Games to represent the nation of Malaysia in a particular fashion. In becoming part of the organization, the researchers needed to acknowledge their difference in cultural perspective: "We were concerned with the dual crises of representation and legitimation in the actual write-up of this paper in respect to the issues surrounding the author's place in the text, of voice, of who speaks, who is excluded, how they are given weight, how they are interpreted, along with questions of priority and juxtaposition, all deserving attention in any adequately written ethnographic text" (p. 274).

Locating an Informant

Interviewing requires human subjects who have knowledge of a particular phenomenon being investigated and are willing to discuss that phenomenon in detail, making the identification of a sample of subjects critical to the success of the research project. Whereas a quantitative researcher may be concerned with a completely random sample of individuals, a qualitative researcher is often looking for a more specific sample to study a specific research question; however, the process of identifying that sample for interviews can be similar to other sampling techniques. This process often involves identifying an insider—a member of the group being studied—who is willing to serve as an **informant** about the group and act as a guide (Fontana & Frey, 2005).

For example, in their study of motive among individuals who go abroad to volunteer for the Olympics Games, Fairley, Kellett, and Green (2007) used a member of the Sydney Olympic Volunteer social club to identify a group of 32 persons planning to travel to Athens to volunteer for the Games. After contacting the group organizer and fully disclosing the intent of the research project, the researchers were approved to attend group meetings in order to collect data.

Parent and Foreman (2007, p. 22) used a combination of theoretical and snowball sampling techniques to identify persons to interview in their two-setting case study of organizational image and identity of major Canadian sport events. After interviewing the initial individuals, the researchers selected certain interviewees as their study unfolded "to shed light on the processes of image and identity management and their relationships with other, previous interviewees."

Deciding How to Present Oneself

A researcher's self-presentation can be critical to breaking down—or erecting—barriers to data collection. For example, when studying intercollegiate athletes, should a graduate student in sport management present herself as a representative of academia or as a peer in age and experience? If the graduate student is closely identified as a peer, she may have an easier time getting intercollegiate athletes to openly discuss issues, providing richer data. Conversely, if she presents herself as a member of academia, the interviewees may not be as forthcoming with detailed responses. Further suggestions for gaining trust of interview subjects is discussed in the section which follows this one

It is helpful, if not required, for a researcher to gain informed consent from a participant in a research study. Informed consent is the process of informing each participant about the nature of the study and how the data obtained will be used. When Shaw (2006) studied social processes as an integral part of gender relations in British NGBs, she conducted semistructured and unstructured interviews about this sensitive topic with 35 individuals, and she obtained informed consent from each interviewee prior to beginning the interview.

Gaining Trust and Establishing Rapport

Because an interview involves a conversation between a researcher and an interviewee, it is essential for interviewers to establish and maintain trust and rapport between themselves and respondents. Interviews are used to develop meaning and understanding, and researchers must be able to move beyond their own preconceptions in order to see situations and contexts from a respondent's point of view (Fontana & Frey, 2005).

Amis (2005) stressed another aspect of rapport— the impression that the interviewer makes on interviewees, particularly during face-to-face contact. Amis emphasized the importance of projecting an air of professionalism at all times.

Hopwood (2005, p. 178) interviewed persons affiliated with two cricket clubs in the United Kingdom for a study about the use of communication strategies. To aid in gaining trust and establishing rapport with her participants, she chose to interview them face-to-face, sent her questions to them before the interview, and allowed participants to decline to answer certain questions. She hoped "this approach would generate a more detailed response and would help put interviewees at ease." By emailing questions to her participants in advance, Hopwood found the interviewees are more secure in allowing her record the interview as well as more likely to elaborate on their answers because they know she is not trying set a trap for them. In addition, by allowing interviewees to withdraw from the interview at any time, Hopwood found that it gives the participants a sense of control of the situation (Hopwood, M., personal communication, July 14, 2010).

Collecting Data

While it is desirable for a researcher to audio- or video-record interviews, it may not always be possible to do so. Thus it is crucial for a researcher to be effective at taking field notes, both when conducting interviews and when observing interaction among participants. Beyond focusing on the content of what is said, researchers can create richer replications if they also make observations about nonverbal communication, posturing, and the ambiance of the setting.

Occasionally, the environment in which data is collected adversely affects the researcher's ability to take accurate notes. Imagine, for example, interviewing spectators at a sporting event, where crowd noise may obstruct the recording or render a key statement inaudible. In such cases, even if the researcher is taping an interview, it is advisable to take field notes as well.

Babiak (2007, p. 345) described her method of collecting data from observations made at meetings of Canadian nonprofit organizations: "Notes were taken documenting observations, interactions, and discussions among partners such as exchanges relating to resource acquisition, organizational and partnership planning, or approaches regarding what organizations to target for [interorganizational relationships]."

Note that the researcher made observations not only about what meeting participants said but also about the interaction between the subjects. By observing and subsequently replicating the context in which a conversation takes place, researchers position themselves more strongly to accurately represent what happened.

Interview Techniques

Several interview techniques are common in qualitative research. Each offers advantages and disadvantages in terms of time commitment, ease of use, and data gathering. Researchers are advised to choose the technique that will best help them extrapolate the data they are seeking in order to pursue their research questions and objectives. The most commonly employed interview techniques are structured interviewing, unstructured or in-depth interviewing, phenomenological interviewing, and group interviewing.

Structured Interviewing

According to Riddick and Russell (2008, p.194) a **structured interview** contains "a set of pre-established questions that follow strict administration and scoring rules." Little room is allowed for open questions or variation. The interviewer records responses according to a coding scheme (explained in more detail later in the chapter) and controls the entire experience, including the environment, question order, and wording of questions.

This interview technique would be effective if, for example, a minor league baseball team wished to gain information about customers' satisfaction with the ballpark experience. The interviewer could approach random spectators as they left the game and ask a series of predetermined questions about the spectator's experience. Thus each person interviewed would be approached in the same fashion and in the same environment.

One advantage of this interview type is that it allows the researcher to obtain a large amount of data in a short time. A team of interviewers spread out around the ballpark could interview dozens of spectators in one evening, and because the questions are predetermined the researchers can be assured of finding answers to specific research questions.

Disadvantages, as noted by Gratton and Jones (2010), include resource constraints, data analysis requirements, and interviewee behavior. The nature of interviews often requires the researcher to travel to meet with subjects, then transcribe the interviews and code the data—all of which require considerable time and resources. In addition, persons responding to this type of interview may deliberately try to please the interviewer or prevent the interviewer from gaining personal information. Because the interview is initiated (whether face-to-face or via telephone) without prior notification, individuals may not be comfortable answering questions on the spot or may be preoccupied with something else. Imagine, for example, a phone call from a marketing company that interrupts a family dinner.

Finally, the interaction between researcher and interview may in itself pose challenges. For one thing, it is always possible that the interviewer will misspeak or change the wording of a question from one interviewee to the next. In addition, although research on interviewer effects has shown that age and gender have little effect on responses, some research suggests that an interviewer's race makes a difference on questions related to race.

Unstructured Interviewing

As its name would suggest, the **unstructured interview** (or in-depth interview) involves open-ended questions aimed at eliciting richer responses

▪ ▪ ▪ ▪ ▪ Choosing the Best Interview Technique ▪ ▪ ▪ ▪ ▪

Interview technique	Advantages	Disadvantages	Uses
Structured	Is similar to quantitative survey (rigid questions); obtains large amount of data in short time.	Allows no room for follow-up questions.	To gain perspective from different persons on the same topic
Unstructured	Permits flexibility in questions and follow-up; seeks deep understanding.	Is time consuming; may not lead directly to themes or outcomes.	For case study or historical research
Phenomenological	Offers advantages similar to those of the unstructured interview.	Time consuming	For theory building
Group	Allows participants to guide the discussion rather than have the researcher lead questioning.	Risks having conversation dominated by one or two voices.	For market research, policy building

from interviewees in a less formal approach. Many similarities exist between unstructured interviewing and phenomenological interviewing, which is explained in the next section. In fact, Rossman and Rallis (2003, p. 97) refer to a phenomenological study as one "through which the lived experience of a small number of people is investigated. Extensive and prolonged engagement with individuals typifies this work, often through a series of in-depth, intensive, and iterative interviews."

Both unstructured interviewing and phenomenological interviewing are grounded in the interpretivist view of research, which emphasizes observation and analysis. (Chapter 9 focuses in detail on observation research in sport management—particularly ethnographic research, where the researcher becomes immersed in the setting, and other forms of observation, such as participant observation, natural observation, and content analysis.) However, as Fontana and Frey (2005, p. 705) note, "many qualitative researchers differentiate between in-depth (ethnographic) interviewing and participant observation." This section focuses on understanding the meanings of in-depth interviewing.

Rossman and Rallis (2003, p. 180) view generic in-depth interviewing as "the hallmark of qualitative research." They noted that an in-depth interview may serve as an overall approach to a study (as may be the case in a phenomenological study) or as one of several techniques (as may occur in a case study or historical research project).

Most researchers agree on the purpose of an unstructured or in-depth interview. Johnson (2002, p. 106) suggested that "in-depth interviewing seeks 'deep' information and understanding" and noted four meanings of the word "deep": First, the interviewer is seeking to achieve the same level of knowledge and understanding as the participants. In this sense, the interviewee functions as a teacher, and the interviewer functions as a student. Second, deep understandings go beyond commonsense explanations by exploring contextual boundaries of a particular experience or perception. Third, deep understandings "reveal how our commonsense assumptions, practices, and ways of talking partly constitute our interests and how we understand them" (Johnson, p. 106). Finally, deep understandings allow the researcher to articulate multiple perspectives and meanings because interviewees on a given subject may provide different points of view.

In this sense, unstructured or in-depth interviews are particularly effective at identifying themes or trends that have not previously been identified or explored in the literature. This benefit is also a hallmark of the phenomenological interview. In either case, the researcher is taught new knowledge by the interviewees. Indeed, one advantage offered by unstructured or in-depth interviewing is the chance for the researcher to learn rich details about an interviewee or a segment of society without suggesting any a priori categorization that would limit the research (Fontana & Frey, 2005).

Richelieu and Pons (2005) conducted an in-depth interview about strategic vision with a National Hockey League franchise's vice president of marketing. The researchers compared the themes of that interview with the results of a survey questionnaire administered to fans of the team. They learned that the team's management vision was not aligned with the profile of its fans and that the team's marketing efforts did little to connect emotionally with the community. Without having a clear, in-depth understanding of the team's vision, it would not have been possible for the researchers to draw the conclusions they did.

Alternatively, researchers might employ a hybrid approach known as a semi-structured interview. In this approach, the researcher uses the rigidity of the structured interview but leaves some flexibility in the protocol to alter the sequence of questions or probe for more in-depth responses by means of follow-up questions (Gratton & Jones, 2010). For example, Cleland (2009) conducted 47 semi-structured interviews with officials and executives associated with four football clubs in the United Kingdom to analyze the relationships between the clubs and the media. Each interview focused on two themes central to the research objectives of identifying an organizational structure and clarifying who in the organization was responsible for dealing with outside media.

Phenomenological Interviewing

The purpose of a *phenomenological analysis* is to understand how the subjective world or social reality that we live in is constituted. Schwandt (2003, p. 297) describes the aim of phenomenology as learning "how we come to interpret our own and others' action as meaningful." To understand how this social reality is constructed, researchers must be concerned with the conversation they are having with the interviewee and how that interacts with the data.

Rossman and Rallis (2003) emphasize that it is crucial for the researcher to approach a phenomenological analysis with an open mind. They suggest four strategies for analyzing phenomenological interview data, all focusing on theme development.

The first strategy is meaning condensation, in which long interview passages are distilled into shorter meanings or statements. The second strategy involves *categorizing* these meanings. In this approach, the categorization forms an organizational structure for a narrative of the phenomenon, and the third strategy is to structure the narrative to reveal a story. The final strategy involves interpreting the meaning of the phenomenon (Rossman & Rallis, 2003). This approach closely aligns with the detailed description of interview data analysis explained later in this chapter.

Fairley et al. (2007) used unstructured interviews in their study of volunteer motives at the 2004 Athens Olympics. Their questioning of 14 individuals provided data pertaining to travel planning, motives for traveling to volunteer, and previous travel experience. After analyzing their interview responses and field notes and coding the responses, the researchers concluded that four themes embodied the individuals' motivation to volunteer: nostalgia, camaraderie, Olympic connection, and sharing and acknowledgment of expertise. One of these motives—nostalgia—had not been previously identified in the literature on volunteering. Fairley et al. (p. 53) suggested that "the lack of any previous findings regarding nostalgia's significance may be a result of the limited number of studies that have focused on volunteering pursuits that are of a repeat nature with considerable time between each event."

Thus these researchers' use of unstructured interviews and their subsequent analysis allowed for new knowledge about volunteer motivation to emerge. Based on their understanding of previous research on the topic, the researchers were able to make a substantive contribution to their field.

Group Interviewing

Group interviewing "relies on the systematic questioning of several individuals simultaneously in a formal or informal setting" (Fontana & Frey, 2005, p. 703). In marketing research, group interviews are commonly known as focus groups, the purpose of which is to gauge consumers' attitudes toward a product or service. The technique has also gained popularity among political parties and candidates interested in understanding public reactions to issues and policies. The *Delphi procedure* is an emerging group technique that focuses on interviewing experts.

Focus Groups

A typical focus group involves 8 to 12 subjects who are addressed in a controlled environment. The subjects may be chosen randomly or on another basis depending on the nature of the research question. It is a common practice in marketing research for a business to assemble a focus group when it is seeking input about a particular product or service. Table 8.1 presents the American Marketing Association's seven reasons to use—and seven reasons

Table 8.1   **When and When Not to Use a Focus Group**

When to use a focus group	When not to use a focus group
To test new concepts	To make a final decision
To evaluate advertising copy	To explore extremely sensitive or personal topics
To evaluate promotions	To answer "How many?" or "How much?"
To develop questionnaires	To conduct research for an audience that doesn't understand the purpose of qualitative research
To generate ideas or support brainstorming	To evaluate a product, advertisement, or other item to which revisions will not be made despite the results of the study
To position a product or service	To save money or time required for quantitative research
To assess product usability	To set prices for a product or service

Adapted, by permission, from H. Edmunds, 1999, *The focus group research handbook* (Lincolnwood, IL: American Marketing Association), 5 and 7.

not to use—a focus group in marketing research (Edmunds, 1999).

Note that focus groups in marketing research are most effective when the business or researcher is seeking to identify new ideas or solicit feedback on proposed messages, products, or services. The focus group is an effective technique for gathering information to enhance or alter an organization's decision-making process—but not to make the final decision.

Focus group research can also be used as an antecedent to quantitative research (Krueger & Casey, 2000). It is particularly useful to marketers, for example, to define customer satisfaction with a product or service. "Armed with this information, survey researchers can then design instruments that can quantify satisfaction by region, type of use, customer demographics, or other relevant variables" (p. 15).

Focus groups apply to other aspects of sport management research beyond marketing. Professional and college teams might, for example, use a focus group to test reactions to a new logo or mascot, and a community that is interested in building a new stadium may wish to gather public feedback before asking taxpayers to fund the construction.

Regardless of why a focus group is used, the sport management researcher must answer the critical question of how she or he will identify the participants. Here, the same concepts apply that were discussed in chapter 4 regarding types of sampling. A researcher may have a theoretical framework that dictates how participants are to be purposefully chosen. Alternatively, the researcher may want to use a random cross section of participants and thus may employ a random sampling technique.

Berg (2004, p. 139) advised that the sampling technique should be part of a larger triangulation strategy in qualitative research: "Standard sampling procedures can improve the validity of group interview results." Krueger and Casey (2000) suggested that a marketing focus group should have some homogenous characteristics, such as occupation, age, gender, family characteristics, or past use of a product or service. Amis (2005) noted that a homogenous group of participants is especially important in focus groups that deal with sensitive information such as race or gender, since a degree of homogeneity is likely to raise participant's confidence in the focus group process.

The researcher's role in a focus group often resembles that of a moderator or facilitator rather than an inquisitor. Focus groups typically address a series of structured interview questions, each of which is followed by discussion among the group members. Data that emerge from the focus group are, of course, group data, reflecting "collective notions shared and negotiated by the group" (Berg, 2004, p. 138). Researchers should expect data from focus groups to be different than data from individual interviews because of the possibility of interaction with other interview subjects.

This moderating role is one of the most crucial aspects of focus group interviewing. Morgan (2002) suggested that it offers both pros and cons. In the more structured approach, used frequently in marketing research, the moderator directs the discussion by setting an agenda and keeping the answers relevant to the predetermined questions. This approach is particularly useful in answering research questions. Alternatively, Morgan points out, a less structured approach is more useful in understanding participants' thinking. In this approach, the moderator facilitates interaction by allowing participants to talk to each other. Questions guide the discussion rather than set the agenda.

Dixon and Breuning (2007) used a series of focus groups administered through an online discussion board in their study of work–family conflict in collegiate coaching. On average, the researchers posted a new question to the Web site each week. Participants responded either to their particular group or to all participants in the nine focus groups. The researchers posted selected responses for all participants to view, thus stimulating further discussion among the participants.

Because the moderator's attention should be focused on the discussion and the interaction of the participants, it is essential for the researcher to arrange for additional assistance when conducting a focus group. Research assistants, perhaps in the form of classmates or undergraduate students, should be present to take notes and monitor nonverbal interactions between the focus group participants. As in all interviews, the conversation should be recorded and transcribed later, but observation as the event transpires is also essential to accurately reporting it later on.

A final consideration when conducting a focus group involves creating a comfortable environment for the participants. This process may include arranging chairs so that the participants can see one another, blocking out background noise, providing notebooks and pens or pencils so that participants can jot down ideas, and arranging refreshments or snacks (Krueger & Casey, 2000).

Delphi Procedure

Sometimes a researcher is interested in learning the opinions not of a consumer group but of a group of experts on a given research topic. Rossman and Rallis (2003, p. 192) noted that special considerations should be afforded when interviewing "elites" who are selected based on their expertise in areas relevant to the research: "In working with elites, great demands are placed on the ability of the interviewer, who must establish competence by displaying a thorough knowledge of the topic or, [if] lacking such knowledge, by projecting an accurate conceptualization of the problem through shrewd questioning." Knowledge can be solicited from such experts by means of the Delphi procedure, which was originally developed for this purpose at the Rand Corporation (Martino, 1993).

The Delphi procedure differs from focus group interaction in that it allows for anonymity, iteration with controlled feedback, and statistical response. During a Delphi sequence, participants may not know other participants and they certainly do not know which participant contributed a particular statement or opinion. Interaction occurs through the use of written questionnaires. As Martino (1993, p. 18) explains, this process is beneficial because it avoids the possibility that one panel member might be influenced by the reputation of another panel member and thus allows each panel member to change opinions or statements without fear of "losing face."

In a Delphi procedure, the researcher acts in much the same manner as a focus group moderator. He or she extracts information provided in response to an initial question and presents it to the group. The individual panel members receive only the current collective opinion and arguments for or against a point of view. This approach prevents the group from taking on its own goals and objectives and thus allows the group to concentrate on its original objectives (Martino, 1993).

Finally, the Delphi procedure presents a statistical response that includes opinions of the entire group. Group responses regarding a particular issue are presented in the form of statistics that describe the degree of spread away from the center of the group opinion (Martino, 1993).

Costa (2005) used a full Delphi procedure to assess the status and future of sport management. She began with a panel of 3 sport management faculty members, who identified the 5 most established and active researchers in the field. When Costa contacted these 5, she received responses from 4 of them, who responded to Costa's queries and named 38 additional persons. The 10 who were mentioned most often were selected for the study. Then, because the literature in the field indicated that accuracy increases as more panelists are assembled, Costa asked the initial 3-member panel to review the 28 individuals who had not been selected. The panel chose on 7 additional recommended participants, bringing the total to 17, all of whom agreed to participate.

Costa (2005) used three rounds of survey questions in which each round built on the preceding round. Findings from each round were returned to the panelists for response. The first round was designed to elicit views about the current status of sport management research. Using a content analysis procedure, 11 to 16 themes were identified for each question. Round 2 consisted of developing survey items based on the themes identified in the first round; the survey was then administered to the 17 participants who were encouraged to provide qualitative comments. Round 3 involved the same items from round 2, and modes and frequencies were added for each item. The panelists were asked to rate each item again and respond to panelists' comments from round 2. The resulting combination of quantitative survey data and qualitative interview responses was processed by means of content analysis to determine 16 final themes or successes in sport management research.

Data Analysis

One of the biggest challenges faced by qualitative researchers is the process of making sense out of interview transcripts and data. Indeed, it is an intimidating task to convert stacks of paper into a few cogent themes. And, as Fontana and Frey (2005, p. 712) point out, "the researcher has a great deal of influence over what part of the data will be reported and how the data will be reported."

The process of deconstructing interview transcripts into meaningful data should be connected to the researcher's established concerns and theoretical framework. Grounded theory is a useful and flexible method for analyzing interview data. Grounded theory consists of "simultaneous data collection and analysis, with each informing and focusing the other throughout the research process" (Charmaz, 2005, p. 508). In this sense, grounded theory guidelines enable researchers to focus their data collection through a series of successive levels of data analysis and conceptual development (Charmaz, 2002, 2005).

The researcher who employs grounded theory methods must be prepared to compare data with data, data with categories, and categories with categories throughout the analytic process (Charmaz, 2005). This feat is accomplished through memos, data coding, identification of themes, and data validation.

Memos

Researchers may find it useful to write themselves notes, or memos, as they begin managing their data. Memos help researchers move easily from raw data to a conceptual level. Ideally, the researcher begins keeping memos as soon as he or she begins to analyze the data; in the beginning, they may be notations in the margins of raw transcribed data. As analysis continues, the researcher may write memos that are longer and more complex. Such memos assist in the creation of codes (Riddick & Russell, 2008).

Coding Data

As Auerbach and Silverstein (2003, p. 35) suggested, the process of **coding** is simply the act of moving "from raw text to research concerns in small steps, each building on the previous one. . . . You can think of the steps of coding as a staircase, moving you from a lower to a higher (more abstract) level of understanding. The lowest level is the raw text, and the highest level is your research concerns."

Charmaz (2002) offers a two-step process in which the researcher initially codes the data. This first stage forces the researcher to begin making analytic decisions about the data, or deciding which text is relevant to the research. The second stage focuses the coding by sorting, synthesizing, and conceptualizing the data into the most frequently appearing codes. This process, known as developing themes, distills events and meanings without losing essential properties. It is explained in more detail in the next section.

Codes used by researchers are often based on a review of scholarly literature and on the researcher's theoretical framework or research concerns, but they leave room for a previously unexamined phenomenon to emerge. For example, in their study of sponsorship decision making in the athletic department at a Canadian university, Long, Thibault, and Wolfe (2004, p. 141) coded transcripts of interviews with 15 administrators by "using concepts derived from the literature on power and influence . . . and

concepts that emerged from the interviews." Thus, the researchers entered their data analysis phase with a preexisting framework (the use of power and influence in organizations) but also allowed for new themes to emerge.

Similarly, Kihl's (2007, p. 288) study of morality in NCAA compliance officers began with inductive and deductive development and operationalization of codes. From there, the data were

> openly coded into categories and respective sub-categories that were representative of participants' understanding of morality and how their moral thoughts manifested in performing their professional work. For example, major categorical codes included "conception of morality," "ethical problem," and "professional ethics." Subcategories included "conception of morality—right vs. wrong," "ethical problem—conflict," and "professional ethics—substantive."

Auerbach and Silverstein (2003, p. 44) describe this stage as a way of "making the text manageable" by reducing the data into smaller, related, and relevant chunks. However, they stress the importance of keeping the process focused on the research concerns: "As you begin to read the text, everything seems important, and it seems impossible to omit anything a participant has said. On the other hand, if you include everything, the amount of data will become unwieldy. With your statement of research concerns in front of you, you can check a portion of the text against your statements."

Identifying Themes

Once the data have been coded, the researcher must further reduce it into more manageable pieces. Auerbach and Silverstein (2003, p. 54) suggest focusing on similar words or phrases used to identify the same phenomenon. These repeating ideas are often expressed within the relevant text by two or more participants. There is no minimum or maximum number of repeating ideas in a research study, but Auerbach and Silverstein suggest "something in the neighborhood of 60 is a workable number (of repeating ideas), with a minimum of 40 and a maximum of 80" (p. 60).

From there, the researcher uses a similar process to inductively develop a **theme,** or implicit topic that organizes a group of repeating ideas. Again, there is no minimum or maximum number of themes, though Auerbach and Silverstein (2003, p. 65) offer a guideline for further reducing the data: "Although there is no hard and fast rule, we suggest reducing the number of repeating ideas by a factor of 3 or 4, resulting in from 10 to 20 themes, with an average of 15."

Grounded theory requires the researcher to make comparisons at each level of analysis. Thus, grounded theory coding might lead a researcher in unanticipated directions (Charmaz, 2002). Based on the themes that emerge, the researcher may need to ask follow-up questions of interviewees, add new participants to increase sample size, or reexamine the scholarly literature for potentially overlooked phenomena.

For example, Long et al. (2004, p. 142) initially began their analysis with a code they called "displays of emotion." However, as their analysis continued, "participant responses regarding the use of displays of emotion as a method of influence revealed both positive and negative perceptions of its effectiveness." Therefore, the researchers developed two separate codes, one for effective displays and one for ineffective displays, in order to differentiate the data.

Validating the Data

When a researcher conducts qualitative research, particularly via interview methodology, he or she faces a challenge regarding the reliability and validity of the data reported. Specifically, the challenge for the researcher is to convince the reader that he or she has accurately reflected what was said and placed it into the proper context within the research study.

Quantitative researchers are concerned with establishing reliability and validity of their data, a concept discussed in more detail in chapter 4. Qualitative researchers often consider whether their data are validated—that is, whether their data adequately represent what they saw or heard.

In addressing the accuracy of interview transcripts, researchers often employ a tactic called **member checking**, a process wherein the researcher provides participants with transcripts of their interviews to ensure that what the researcher recorded is, in fact, what the participant was saying. This process is also appropriate for researchers who want to confirm their interpretations of what was said or of the conclusions they drew from the data.

Amis (2005) acknowledged the usefulness of member checks despite the problems inherent in representing precisely everything that was said: "While it will be impossible for the individual to accurately remember all that transpired, this [process] should still help ensure that what was said

forms an accurate reflection of her/his [i.e., the participant's] thoughts and feelings at the time, [which is] important for the credibility and veracity of the study" (p. 125).

Gratton and Jones (2010, p. 119) have offered a definition of the process of validating data, frequently referred to as *triangulation*. In their view, triangulation "refers to the use of multiple means of data collection to explore a single phenomenon." Miles and Huberman (1994, p. 267) extend this thinking by conceiving of triangulation in several ways—by data source (which can include a person), by method (which can include an interview or observation), by researcher, by theory, and by data type (qualitative and quantitative).

Amis (2005, p. 126) addressed the "considerable debate" regarding how qualitative researchers establish that their findings have credibility and legitimacy while simultaneously rejecting the quantitatively based notions of validity and reliability. He offered two steps for enhancing the credibility of interview-based research. The first step involves developing an audit trail that allows a researcher who is unfamiliar with the project to follow the research process from its development through its implementation and analysis. The second step draws upon Lincoln and Guba's (1985, p. 308) concept of "peer debriefing." In this step, the researcher provides a colleague who has no direct involvement in the research with an explanation of the data collection process. "This 'disinterested peer' tries to uncover the interpreter's biases and clarify interpretations, and generally plays the role of 'devil's advocate'" (Amis, p. 127).

The issues of researcher bias and data validation in qualitative research must be major concerns for anyone conducting interview research. Researchers who present their data in a way that is deemed reliable and valid stand a greater chance of having their research taken seriously. As Auerbach and Silverstein (2003, p. 83) noted, the inherent biases of a researcher must not show through in the data. "We think it is justifiable, even inevitable, for a researcher to use his [or her] subjectivity in analyzing and interpreting data. However, it is not justifiable . . . to impose . . . [one's] own subjectivity in an arbitrary manner, that is, in a way that is not grounded in the data."

Summary

Sport management researchers frequently use interview techniques to gain knowledge about marketing, interorganizational relationships, and behaviors of individuals. The process of interviewing research participants in qualitative research is different than it is in quantitative research and involves careful consideration on the part of the researcher in gaining access to a particular setting, establishing rapport with the interviewee, and collecting data. Interview techniques vary from a rigid structured interview to an informal unstructured technique. Whatever approach is used, a researcher must develop sound practices for coding and justifying the data that she or he is interpreting.

Research Methods and Design in Action
Journal of Sport Management

Selected text reprinted, by permission, from S. Uhrich and M. Benkenstein, 2010, "Sport stadium atmosphere: Formative and reflective indicators for operationalizing the construct," *Journal of Sport Management* 24(2): 211-237.

Access the full article online at www.humankinetics.com/products/all-products/Research-Methods-and-Design-in-Sport-Management.

ABSTRACT

This article reports the findings of an investigation into the atmosphere in stadium during live team sports. Experiencing this special atmosphere represents an essential part of the total service provided by the organizers of sport events. However, existing research into the concept of atmosphere focuses on the retail environment. Our first step was therefore to define sport stadium atmosphere as a theoretical construct, drawing on theories from environmental psychology. We then developed a mimic (multiple indicator-multiple cause) model to measure the construct. To specify the mimic model, we generated and selected formative measures by means of a delphi study ($N = 20$), qualitative expert interviews ($N = 44$), and an indicator sort task ($N = 34$). The results indicate that various physical and social aspects of the stadium environment are causal indicators of sport stadium atmosphere. Following this, we conducted phenomenological interviews with spectators at sport events ($N = 5$) to identify typical affective responses to stadium environment (representing the reflective indicators of the mimic model). These interviews revealed that fans' experience of stadium environment is characterized by high levels of arousal and pleasure. In addition to our findings, the mimic model developed in this study represents a useful tool for future research into sport stadium atmosphere.

TEXT EXCERPTS

The concept of atmosphere includes the notion that environments or places have specific affect-inducing qualities. It is therefore closely related to the environmental psychology construct of the *affective quality* of a place (Darden & Babin, 1994; Russell & Pratt, 1980).

．．．．．．．．．．．．．．．．．．

The construct of sport stadium atmosphere can thus be defined as a preferential affective state that spectators attribute to the idiosyncratic environmental features of a sport stadium.

．．．．．．．．．．．．．．．．．．

To generate formative indicators, a multistage expert survey was conducted based on the delphi method. The delphi method is considered a suitable approach for identifying the opinions of an expert group about a diffuse and unclear issue (Haeder, 2002).

Using a heuristic technique for categorizing qualitative data (Kleining 1995), the 77 indicators were grouped into seven preliminary dimensions. These seven dimensions represent the conceptual content of the formative part of sport stadium atmosphere.

In the interviews, a phenomenological approach was followed: We asked the respondents to describe the feelings and sensations they typically experience at the stadium. Depending on the interviewees' level of understanding of the question and their ability to verbalize their feelings, the question could be rephrased or made more precise. Throughout the interviews, participants were reminded to report their emotional experiences relating to the stadium environment, as opposed to their affective attachment to a particular team.

We analyzed the qualitative data gathered in the interviews using content analysis (Kassarjian, 1977). In two readings, the authors of this study identified and marked all statements representing fans' emotional states. Subsequently the authors independently classified each statement using the dimensions high versus low arousal and high versus low pleasure. Disagreements were resolved by discussion.

DISCUSSION QUESTIONS

1 The goal of this study was to develop a construct for assessing the effect of sport stadium atmospherics for marketing purposes. Why is interview methodology appropriate for this project? What role did expert interviews play in the methodology?

2 How did the researchers in this study go about reducing their data into themes or dimensions?

3 How did the researchers manipulate the environment in study 4? Why would doing so be important in producing reliable and valid data?

4 Critique the researchers' process for resolving differences in their theme (or dimension) development in study 4. Was this an appropriate methodological way to create agreement?

Observation Research

Learning Objectives

After studying this chapter, you should be able to do the following:

- Provide a definition of ethnography and describe the various types of observation research
- Understand how observation research can be conducted by sport management researchers and applied to the practice of sport management
- Compare the major elements and methods involved in observation research
- Categorize the advantages, disadvantages, and steps of observation methodology
- Comment on the various observation site issues related to ethnographic research
- List the observer roles involved in observation research in sport management
- Provide a general description of the ways in which observation research can be used in examining new media
- Discuss the processes, procedures, and types of data collection used in observation research
- Understand how content analysis can be conducted in sport management research

The term *observation research* is used to describe the research methodology covered in this chapter. The term generally indicates a qualitative research approach grounded in traditional ethnography, which is a methodology that John Hughson and Chris Hallinan (2001) "hope will be a developing area of research within sports scholarship" (p. 6). Before we examine observation research as applied to sport management, we must first explore its association with ethnography, which involves efforts to explain a people and their way of life. Ethnography is a naturalistic methodological process through which social scientists use field research to investigate social phenomena in order to understand human culture, communities, and institutions, as well as people's lives, interactions, and experiences (O'Reilly, 2005). When practicing ethnography, researchers enter the field—the natural or real setting—to conduct research. Angrosino (2007) notes that in a traditional ethnography, the researcher stays in a new place, watches and listens to the inhabitants' behaviors and interactions in order to understand their culture, engages with the subjects by talking with and interviewing them about certain issues, takes field notes and records (e.g., on paper or video) their lives, and then writes an academic article or scholarly book about the research findings. Ethnographers' observations of real life in their fieldwork—which stands in contrast to the work done by other social scientists in laboratories or other research settings—help them develop explanatory theories (Angrosino, 2007).

Ethnographic research study involving sport is relatively new, although a few ethnographers touched on the subject in passing in the later decades of the 1800s (Sands, 2002). A few sport ethnographies were published in the 1900s, including seminal pieces examining games (Roberts, Arth, & Bush, 1959) and baseball (Fox, 1961). By contrast, ethnographic investigations have a long and rich history in other fields of study and among other researchers—for instance, anthropologists functioning as anthropological ethnographers. Other scholars, however, have produced a myriad of perspectives regarding the definition and application of ethnographic research; some, for example, have defined *ethnography* as simply the process of describing culture or conducting research in a natural setting, whereas others have defined it as writing one's observations or providing detailed and accurate descriptions of a natural setting. Over the past few decades, researchers have used many names for ethnographic research and practiced many offshoots of it. Some scholars use traditional types of ethnography that they refer to as *participant observation, field observation, direct observation,* or *natural observation* (Bernard, 2006). For instance, **participant observation**—similar to ethnography—can involve various methodologies (e.g., interviews, focus groups, observation) and is aimed at understanding human social phenomena and answering research questions in a field setting. The methodology could be summarized as a procedure in which a researcher joins (e.g., lives with, participates in) and spends considerable time in a society (e.g., a running club or high school rowing team), becomes very familiar with it, observes the interactions within that society, asks questions (e.g., via survey or interview), interprets the observations and answers, and records the findings (Spradley, 1980). As Fetterman (1989) describes it, "participant observation combines participation in the lives of the people under study with maintenance of a professional distance that allows adequate observation and recording of data." He adds that the "residence helps the researcher internalize the basic beliefs, fears, hopes, and expectations of the people under study" (p. 45). Therefore, the method of participation observation shares similar procedural characteristics with ethnography—such as immersing oneself in a natural environment; listening and observing; asking questions; and seeking to understand culture, patterns, experiences, and behaviors—and embodies both the philosophical and naturalistic foundations of ethnography.

It is somewhat difficult to make clear distinctions between terms such as *ethnography, participant observation, natural observation,* and *observation.* "The important point about the concept of ethnography, regardless of one's language and terminological preference, is that the practice places researchers in the midst of whatever it is they study," explains Berg (2007). "From this vantage, researchers can examine various phenomena as perceived by participants and represent these observations as accounts" (p. 172). Whether one views participant observation or natural observation as synonymous with ethnography or as constituting the main observation technique or fieldwork method used in ethnography, the various terms are very similar and share the fact of referring to observation research in the field or natural environment. This chapter presents ethnography as defined by Warren and Karner (2005), who provide a succinct definition by equating ethnography—the written accounts offered by ethnographic observers—with participant observation. Consistent with their explanation, this chapter explains the process of observation in sport management research. Therefore, the term *observation research* is used in this textbook to

As future leaders and researchers in the sport industry, students should develop some understanding of the observation research technique regardless of their future aspiration or anticipated position in sport management or any of the field's various subdisciplines. As noted by Hatch (2002), "observation is a cornerstone of qualitative data collection. No matter what the paradigm, if the researcher is interested in participant perspectives, observing those participants in action provides avenues into their understandings that are unavailable any other way" (p. 90). Because those involved in sport management are concerned with perspectives of participants (e.g., employees, spectators, consumers), observation research is a valuable tool in sport management research. Researchers hoping to understand the dispositions, behaviors, decision-making tendencies, perspectives, activities, and interactions of certain stakeholders or groups in the sport industry can use observation techniques to gather data by, for example, watching sport managers in the front office of the WNBA's Indiana Fever, participating with fans at a tailgate party at NASCAR's Daytona 500, or listening to reactions at a shareholders meeting of the Green Bay Packers.

Observation research allows the researcher to gain more and better insight into the behaviors and interactions of individuals and helps the researcher develop a more complete understanding of how these individuals and their associated groups function and how they engage in activities and make decisions (Whyte, 1997). This method is used in sport because it is unobtrusive and allows researchers to collect both qualitative and quantitative information. Wilkinson and Birmingham (2003) discuss a variety of reasons that researchers do traditional observation research, and it is used for similar reasons in sport management. It is often used when researchers want to investigate behaviors, social phenomena, activities, and interactions of people in or related to a particular sport setting (e.g., basketball arena, fishing tournament, sports bar). Investigators in sport management engage in this research process by establishing and holding a relationship (and then examining the action) with an individual or group of people in their natural environment (e.g., observing participants' use of certain machines in a health or fitness center). Though it can be conducted electronically (e.g., examining Internet activities and relationships associated with a sport Web site), such research is usually performed in a physical setting. For example, an investigator interested in understanding New England fans' consumption patterns regarding Major League Lacrosse (MLL) would attend matches involving the Boston Cannons and observe activities at Harvard Stadium. Observation is often used when researchers—wanting to conduct their research in a natural setting—go into a sport-related site (e.g., party for season ticket holders, online discussion forum, clothing section of a sporting goods store) to clearly understand the context of or circumstances surrounding a sport gathering, group, event, or situation.

When researchers go to a sport site or setting and use proper and rigorous observation research techniques, they can often produce the richest, most useful, and largest amounts of data (Bryman & Bell, 2007). Thus observation can be an excellent tool in sport management research. For instance, a researcher could join a fantasy baseball league or participate as a player on a club team in order to experience (and observe) the subjects of the study. Sport marketers often use observation methodology in their quest to collect accurate information in order to make educated decisions and gain a competitive edge in the crowded sport marketplace. They research various aspects of their consumers (e.g., how fans navigate a team's Web site), products (e.g., how players respond to a new softball glove design), competitors (e.g., how viewers respond to a business rival's television promotion), and industry segment (e.g., how consumers of music concerts compare to sport spectators in their approach to purchasing walk-up tickets). Such marketing research can be used to determine sport consumer needs and wants in order to serve them better, to discover untapped market segments for a just-released sport product, or to uncover unique opportunities for a sport product that has been on the market (O'Reilly & Seguin, 2009).

describe participant observation, direct observation, and ethnography in sport management, and this chapter focuses on how observation has been applied in sport management research and on ways in which it can be applied in future research associated with the sport industry. Keep in mind, however, that observation research involves much more than just watching behavior or interactions in a sport management setting. While observing is the primary methodological skill, other skills involved include preparing, listening, interacting, participating, taking field notes, soliciting additional information, interviewing, analyzing, describing, and a host of other activities that require skill, time, and preparation (Bernard, 2006).

Just as observation research has been used in the fields of management, marketing, and business (Rosen, 1991), professors and practitioners in sport management should have at least some basic knowledge of how to read, interpret, and conduct observation research. This is true whether they use observation methods for applied research (i.e., to solve a problem in a sport organization) or for basic or pure research (i.e., to improve understanding and contribute to the body of knowledge in sport management). For example, in applied research, consultants who use observation methodologies can "fix mismanaged businesses" by "describing a company's cultural reality" and covering topics that range from consumer behavior and marketing strategies to "organizational dynamics, change management, organizational behavior, [and] group facilitation" (Sands, 2002, p. 139). Sands provides three examples of this type of applied research in his sport consultant work with Wilson Sporting Goods, Heineken Beer, and a fantasy sport Web site and notes that the labels used to identify observation consultants include "cultural researcher, cultural consultant, cognitive designer, information specialist, [and] analyst" (p. 141). See the sidebar on the previous page for more information.

In addition to the applied and pure research settings, Skinner and Edwards (2005) argue for "sport management researchers to embrace ethnographic research designs underpinned by critical and postmodern thought in order to advance our understanding of sport management practice and organizations" (p. 405). Observation research that embraces postmodernism addresses methodological issues such as

> acknowledgement of the researchers' values, interests, interactions, and interpretations in the research process; acknowledgement of the reasons for undertaking research; recognition of research as a mutu-

ally participative, creative process wherein the voice of the participants is valued and recognized in the research process; acknowledgment of the authorial self as intrusive but indispensable to the research process; and encouragement of individuals in order to facilitate and allow them to tell their own stories, identify their own issues, and find their own solutions beyond the activities of the researcher. (p. 416)

Sport management researchers who approach observation methodology from a critical or postmodern perspective can use this research tool in order to understand the social interactions, political processes, power structures, and historical forces that help shape social reality (Edwards, Skinner, & Gilbert, 2005; Skinner & Edwards).

As Skinner and Edwards (2005) state,

> although qualitative research has not been universally embraced in the general discipline of management, it is gradually evolving into a more accepted practice in the specific discipline of sport management. (pp. 404–405)

Indeed, it is not difficult to find observation research publications within any subdiscipline in sport management.

As detailed in table 9.1, numerous ethnographic studies have been conducted in sport management, including organizational ethnographies (observation studies) wherein the researcher examines a sport-related company in order to determine how to better manage it. Overall, sport management academicians frequently use observation research to build the body of knowledge, whereas sport management practitioners can use this method as a best practice technique for examining current activities, competitors, and consumption patterns, in addition to analyzing trends and future directions for research in the field.

Methodological Foundations

Sport management research generally has an exploratory, descriptive, analytical, or predictive purpose. Whereas predictive (causal) research is used to examine cause and effect and thus often involves some type of experiment technique, exploratory research is used to gain greater insight, familiarity, or clarification regarding an issue. Deeper understanding of an issue usually rests on

Table 9.1 Selected Ethnographies in Various Segments of Sport Management

Topic	Citation
Sport communication	Battenfield & Kent, 2007 Silk & Amis, 2000 Strathmann, 2001
Sport tourism and events	Fairley, 2003 Seaton, 2002 Xing & Chalip, 2009
Sport entrepreneurship	Rehman & Frisby, 2000 Sugden, 2007
Sport marketing	Choi, Stotlar, & Park, 2006 Lai, 1999 Martin, 1990
Sport facilities	Eckstein & Delaney, 2002
Sporting goods	Kahle, Boush, & Phelps, 2000
Organizational issues	Hoeber, 2007 Mitrano, 1999 Skinner, Stewart, & Edwards, 1999
Extreme sport	Donnelly, 2006
Managerial roles	Bechtol, 2002 Bennett & Hardin, 2002
Professional sport	Forsyth & Thompson, 2007 Hanis-Martin, 2006
Amateur and community sport	Caza, 2000 Chalip & Scott, 2005 Hill & Green, 2008 Misener & Doherty, 2009

exploratory inquiries and can be situated in research that is descriptive (providing answers to the who, what, when, and where questions) and analytical (providing explanatory answers to the why and how questions). Sport management scholars and practitioners often use observation for exploratory and descriptive purposes, but they also use it for analytical or explanatory research purposes. They do so in order to study how people in the sport industry behave, interrelate, are influenced, communicate, make purchasing decisions, interact, and engage in other related activities. Observation research is a versatile methodology that goes beyond what can be obtained through interviews and surveys by allowing the researcher to explore the multifaceted natural setting and gain unique and rich insight into how those in the sport industry

see and understand their surroundings (Bernard, 2006).

Certain philosophical assumptions are associated with observation research in sport management. While much of the research work in the sport industry relies strictly on the positivist perspective, observation research in sport management is a tool used mainly to collect and analyze data from the interpretive perspective. Keep in mind, however, that researchers often use positivist data from procedures such as questionnaires that are more quantitative and objective as supplemental findings in observation research. But for the most part, observation research reconstructs reality through a self-reflective approach. As illustrated by Angrosino (2007), in observation methodology the interpretive perspective—with its roots in inductive reasoning and postmodernism—accepts that there is no single reality. Whereas positivist researchers hold to the idea of a single objective reality (one that is shared between all observers and that is not influenced by being observed), interpretative researchers emphasize both the observer's influence on what he or she observes and the subjective nature of reality more generally. In the interpretive approach, it is emphasized that the researcher helps to create the reality that he or she observes and that this reality would not have existed without these observations.

Some investigators have tried to take a more positivist approach to observation studies. For instance, in Hill and Green's (2008) study of the management of youth sport, the researchers used both an embedded participant and a nonaffiliated academic. As the researchers noted, "the dual roles enabled the researchers to obtain an insider's insight tempered with the objectivity of an outsider" (p. 191). Even with this strategy, however, the observation research still involves an interpretive approach because, as noted by Hughson and Hallinan (2001), though the researcher "might attempt to be true to the particular group under study, the final account provided in the form of a written document (thesis, research report or book) is necessarily the product of the [researcher's] individual perspective" (p. 3). Keep these epistemological assumptions in mind as you study, read, and conduct observation research in sport management.

Although each study involves unique research questions and objectives, the overarching goal of observation research in sport management is to explore contexts (e.g., physical, social, cultural, economic), intercorrelation among variables (e.g., people, norms, events, behaviors), and the general flow of (e.g., activities of, interactions among) certain individuals or groups (Wilkinson & Birmingham, 2003). Depending on the research questions and objectives, observation research in sport management is often used as supplemental to or in conjunction with other methodologies (e.g., questionnaires, case studies) to form a mixed-methods or multimethod research study—for example, interviewing and then observing participants (or observing and then interviewing them) in a sport setting. In Fairley's (2003) study of the role that nostalgia plays in sport fans' travel behaviors, she used observation methodology as well as unstructured interviews with two trip-organizer stakeholders before the trip and semi-structured interviews with 20 participants during the trip.

As this and most observation studies reveal, researchers can use a combination of methodologies associated with observation research to fully address a study's aims. These methods include in-depth or informal interviewing, direct observation, self-analysis, participation in activities or events with subjects, examination of life histories, analysis of narratives or subjects' documents and materials, collective discussions, and audio or video recording. Such conjoint methodology provides assorted and varied data or explanations that can be used to further develop, explore, corroborate, and strengthen the overall research study, results, and analysis (Angrosino, 2007). Silk and Amis (2000) used both observation and interviews in their study of the production and processes involved with broadcasting the Commonwealth Games in Kuala Lumpur, Malaysia. They noted that "interviews may have allowed observations to be interpreted differently, and observations allowed responses to questions to be more fully understood as well as aiding in question formation for further interviews. . . . The key point is that the study used two types of data collection in an attempt to [have them] illuminate each other" (p. 275).

Researchers obtain observation data through watching and recording. Therefore, the research instruments that you must develop in observational methodology are your own skills at observing participants, collecting data, and interpreting and reporting the results. Good observational researchers become proficient by developing methodological skills, and observational skills can be learned and developed through training and pilot studies. O'Reilly (2005) and Bernard (2006) illustrate and explain key skills that observational researchers should develop: ascertaining the language of the participants, strengthening your explicit awareness, developing memorization skills, developing writing proficiency, learning how to develop rapport with participants, and becoming an effective and efficient notetaker. First, ascertaining the language of participants involves understanding the culture by becoming familiar with the particular language practices (e.g., words, usage, context) of the participants (e.g., players, fans, sport company employees, sport journalists). Second, strengthening your explicit awareness involves paying attention to details as they relate to the objectives of the study. Third, it is essential to become skilled at memorizing because various (and important) details can be forgotten when it is not possible to take detailed notes immediately. Fourth, writing proficiency involves being able to describe (in both your field notes and your final manuscript) what you have observed in detail and with clarity, concision, and good organization;

all of these elements require practice and repetition. Fifth, developing rapport requires the ability to hang out and interact naturally with participants. You need to develop this skill because participants will not act freely or open up if they do not trust you or are uncomfortable with you. Sixth, you must become an effective and efficient notetaker because your field notes provide the data you need in order to be thorough and accurate in analyzing and writing up your observations.

Observational Skill Development

Here are some ways to develop your observational skills:

- Strengthen your explicit awareness. For instance, if you were comparing the ambience of two basketball arenas (e.g., the Los Angeles Lakers' Staples Center and the Washington Wizards' Verizon Center), you would need to look for particular differences related to the aims of the study (e.g., lighting, decor, quality and variety of concession stands, seating comfort, service quality).

- Practice memorizing. One way to develop this research skill is to walk around and then leave a specific department in a sporting goods store. After leaving the department or establishment, write about the various items and their locations within the department or store. When you have exhausted your memory, reenter the store and evaluate your results. Your short-term memory will improve as you go from store to store.

Observation methodology offers numerous advantages for sport management researchers. As noted by Mack, Woodsong, MacQueen, Guest, and Namey (2005) and DeWalt and DeWalt (2002), these advantages include the methodology's flexibility, use of a natural setting, reliance on empathy, and uniqueness in providing foundational and comparative information. First, in terms of flexibility, the observation researcher can modify, adjust, and change the research plan according to the prog-

ress of the analysis. For example, someone who is initially studying the relationship between sport team fans and their consumption of media coverage can—as deemed necessary and appropriate via the analytic process—adjust the study to examine the sport fans' team identification or team merchandise consumption habits. Second, in terms of natural setting, ecological validity is increased because observation research is conducted in a real (natural, field) environment. For instance, Caza (2000) used observation research to examine innovations in a sport organization. He was able to get inside the setting for his study of the Amateur Boxing Association (ABA) because he was "an active member of the ABA, and thus in routine contact with many members of the organization, privy to and participating in various sport-related interactions" (p. 232). Because of his involvement in the natural setting, his study examined a real-life situation and thus had strong ecological validity. Third, in terms of the methodology's reliance on empathy, observation researchers become familiar with the subjects and are thus able to empathize with them more easily and completely. This empathy helps the investigator gain insight into the subjects' lives, interactions, behaviors, culture, relationships, and overall context. Fourth, observation research can provide researchers with foundational and comparative information that they can use as a basis for building other methodologies and comparing, triangulating, and understanding other data and results.

Along with these advantages, Mack et al. (2005) and DeWalt and DeWalt (2002) also point out some disadvantages of using observation methodology. Shortcomings include a long data collection process, difficulties in documenting data and selecting what should be recorded, the researcher's inability to be always present and observing, and the challenge of objectivity. Observation methodology can also be quite time-consuming, since it is often quite challenging for researchers to collect data quickly (e.g., because of limited access to the observation site) or analyze it in a prompt manner (e.g., because there is an overwhelming amount of data to analyze). It is also difficult to take field or mental notes about everything that one observes during the research study; therefore, some data (observations) are lost. Additional data are missed when the researcher or observer cannot be present for all incidents that need to be recorded; sometimes things happen when the researcher is not around or is not expecting them to occur. Given that validity and reliability are strengthened by objective recording of results, the subjectivity that sometimes exists in the recording of observations can be a disadvantage. For example, in Bechtol's (2002) observation study of the managerial roles and activities of athletic directors, he noted that "the researcher's interest in this type of study grew out of professional experience in education, athletics, and business sales and marketing. This influenced the data collection and analysis of all facets of the work as a researcher" (p. 31). Whereas the interpretation of results is often more subjective, the recording of observations should be as objective as possible. Overall, these disadvantages of using observation methodology in sport management research are outweighed by the advantages if the research technique is required and is performed systematically and properly.

The process of observation research involves numerous steps (Sommer & Sommer, 2002). One preliminary step involves discovering a research problem that can be examined through observation research. In other words, before you decide to conduct observation research, it is best to form specific research aims and determine whether observation methodology is the best way to address the research issue or problem at hand. Make sure that no other methodology (e.g., questionnaire, experiment) would be more applicable, effective, and efficient. For instance, Chalip and Scott (2005) determined that a 5-year observation methodology (in addition to document analyses and interviews) offered the best way to fully study and understand the social forces operating in a summer swimming league. Once you have determined that the observation approach is appropriate for your research problem, here are some initial steps to take:

1. Select a general research topic
2. Develop a proposed research design (e.g., possible observation times and locations)
3. Perform casual observations (observing what is happening in the sport setting of interest without any definitive plans or approaches in mind)

These steps are followed by deciding what you will ask or observe (this step involves developing the research questions) and specifying the data collection tools you will use.

If more than one investigator is involved, the next step is to train research observers. Not all observation research is conducted by a solo investigator. For instance, two or more (or even a team of) researchers can work together in observational research if the study involves a large or complex setting that presents formidable barriers for a single researcher (Mack et al., 2005). Once any training has been done, the next step involves conducting a pilot study to test procedures, reliability, and validity and then changing the research design if indicated by the pilot study. Now it is time to collect the data and test qualitative trustworthiness (e.g., reliability, validity). For instance, in Choi, Stotlar, and Park's (2006) study of what consumers visualized in terms of sport sponsorship at an action sport championship, the investigators examined the trustworthiness of their findings through triangulation. This process commenced, "in a methodological sense, utilizing interviews, observation, and physical artifacts that confirmed the emerging findings" (p. 74). The investigators further strengthened their study's validity by means of other data sources (e.g., interview transcripts, photos), peer examinations (by methodology experts), and their own professional backgrounds in sport marketing. In another example of how investigators worked to strengthen a study's validity, Skinner, Stewart, and Edwards (1999) addressed temporal issues of validity in their examination of the Queensland Rugby Union (QRU): "This meant that the research needed to span a sufficient period of time to account for the inferences drawn from it, and that valid inferences required generalization. Consequently, the research comprised of 240 hours of interaction within the QRU over a 20 month period" (p. 181).

The final steps in observation methodology involve coding and analyzing the data and writing the final report or manuscript. Because many of these research steps are detailed throughout this textbook (e.g., developing research aims and questions, arriving at a definitive research topic, conducting pilot study activities), we will highlight here only the steps that are specific and unique to observation methodology.

While the research problem in observation studies often surfaces through conduits such as casual observations and unresolved dilemmas, observation research questions—which often relate to behavior activities, cultural processes, or organizational intercorrelations—should be developed through reading the academic literature, understanding the associated research theories, and developing some knowledge of the subjects and setting that will be involved in the research study (DeWalt & DeWalt, 2002). For example, Hanis-Martin's (2006) observation of ownership and ground-level processes in professional women's basketball was developed through both sociological literature and theories and her own involvement in the research setting.

With a background in the theory and her participation in the research site, she was able to focus on the owners' interactions, their management and marketing decisions, and the effects of their activities on the teams and stakeholders (e.g., athletes). The research problem upon which she focused her observations addressed patterns of domination, and she observed behavior and interactions in order to understand social change in women's sport. Thus, she sought to "identify how women's professional basketball, arguably a success story of liberal feminist efforts, was constituted on the ground through social interactions" (p. 270). Regardless of the literature, theory, or setting upon which an observation study is based, fundamental research questions can surface through queries such as wondering why an incentive program is working well in one sport company, what makes a certain segment of fans unique, or how certain management leaders operate. If the research questions require an in-depth understanding of a sport management issue, then observation research, which allows one to go into much greater detail than other research methods, is an excellent (and most likely preferred) methodological choice.

The observation research design—built to address the research questions—involves two key considerations (Bernard, 2006). First, the research design should illustrate how the research questions will be solved. Second, the design should resemble traditional observation research plans but remain open to modification in accordance with the data collection procedures and the systematic analysis. In developing the research design, the researcher will need to address issues including site selection, how the subjects define the setting in which they are situated, management plans (e.g., researcher's role, plan, timeline, access, ethics), research strategies, how to collect data, management and recording of data, and data analysis (Spradley, 1980). Many of these issues are covered in detailed in the remaining pages of this chapter.

Observation Site

An observation researcher must select a sport management site that will enable him or her to collect data to address the targeted research issues. The **observation research site**—which can be chosen based on an organizational variable, a demographic makeup, or any other characteristic that fits the research agenda of the study—is also known as the setting, environment, or field for observation work.

Therefore, many people refer to the activities of observation research as field work or field research. The field or site in sport management observation research is any location—from a Canadian athletic department (Hoeber, 2007) to a shoe factory and apparel company (Kahle, Boush, & Phelps, 2000) to an online discussion group about professional hockey (Mitrano, 1999)—where the researcher can watch people interact with each other in a natural setting and participate in some way in the activity being examined in the research. Take, for example, Lai's (1999) examination of the marketing and managerial implications of sport globalization. She sought to examine the penetration of the Swedish sport known as floorball into Australia. She chose a local floorball club as the site (field or setting) for her observation research.

In some cases, a site may be optimal for certain aspects of a research study yet not conducive for conducting the complete study. For example, in a study on team ownership, one optimal site might be a National Football League owners meeting; most likely, however, it would not be a practical site. As Hoeber (2007) noted in her study of one intercollegiate athletic department with more than 500 students and 30 competitive sport teams, "it was not feasible to study gender equity within the context of 30 different teams" (p. 366). Therefore, she chose to narrow the site selection process to 4 teams (basketball, ice hockey, rugby, and swimming) by using 4 institutional criteria. One must also determine whether a potential site is available (in terms of scheduling), economical, appropriate (e.g., does it provide a large enough sample?), ethical (e.g., would doing observation there raise human rights concerns?), and acceptable in terms of risk.

A given site may be selected for any of numerous reasons in observation research (Wilkinson & Birmingham, 2003). It might be selected because the researcher is interested in a theory regarding behavior or activities that typically occur in that setting. For example, Skinner et al. (1999) sought to examine the phenomenon of organizational change by choosing an observation site within the Queensland Rugby Union (QRU). While within the QRU, they observed over 250 hours of interactions, including internal and external meetings between managers, representative, and volunteers. A site might also be selected because it is associated with another research endeavor that has been completed or is already in progress. In such cases, the site can enable linkage with other research studies or methodologies. Green (2001) linked three separate sporting events (a flag football tournament, a marathon, and a motorcycle race) through her observation research into how organizations can promote and increase consumption of their events by leveraging their fans' identification with the subculture of the sport. A third reason for selecting a site involves its connection with a sport policy or with legal issues that the researcher wants to examine. A site might also be selected because a public or private funding agency commissions or provides a grant or contract for the researcher to conduct a study at that location.

Gaining entrance into a site is, of course, a prerequisite for completing observation research. Simply put, if you cannot enter the field, you cannot complete your field work. Therefore, the site must be accessible for the observation researcher. Generally, there is no problem with access to public sites (e.g., city-owned walking paths leading to a stadium), and the researcher generally does not need to secure special permission or access to such sites because they are open to the general public. However, private sites (e.g., sports bar, sporting goods warehouse, fitness center, locker room, sport industry organization) can sometimes be difficult to enter since permission is needed and can be quite problematic to obtain. For instance, trying to perform an observation study about some aspect of golf fans or golf management at the Masters Tournament at Augusta National Golf Club would be nearly impossible because of the intense restrictions on access enforced at the club.

Once a setting has been chosen for addressing the study's research problem, researchers should pursue any lead that might provide access to the research site. Researchers should use any connections—personal friends, relatives, colleagues, or other relevant relationships—to help them secure access to the site (Angrosino, 2007). For instance, in an observation study of managerial activities and leadership decisions, Bennett and Hardin (2002) gained intimate access and complete observation opportunities through a relationship with the study's subject. Often, however, the researcher will have no personal connections to the site; as a result, the research will need to go through someone—a gatekeeper—who makes access decisions for the organization or setting. As noted by O'Reilly (2005), gatekeepers can be formal or informal. Researchers go through formal gatekeepers when they have to secure access by asking for permission to conduct a study or submitting a formal request to an organization or research setting. As Fairley (2003) notes in her study of sport tourism, "the trip organizer was contacted by phone and informed of the research plan in order to gain access to the group with the

purpose of becoming a full participant in the travel experience. The trip organizer responded favorably" (p. 290). Sometimes, however, it can be challenging to negotiate and secure access through formal gatekeepers. For example, a professional soccer team's director of media relations might be hesitant to give (or ask the team's senior management to give) a researcher access to her team.

In contrast, it is often much easier to obtain access through informal gatekeepers, who are so named because they can provide access through informal processes (e.g., a friend introducing the researcher to the participants; a former colleague vouching for the research project; a relative assuring participants about the proposed study's legitimacy and the researcher's promises of confidentiality). Optimally, the researcher has a source or contact who already functions in the chosen research setting and thus can help the researcher gain access; an informal gatekeeper may also be able to help with the research. For example, Silk and Amis (2000) explain that in their study of sport television production, "contact was made with a client broadcaster and a meeting set up with the then executive producer for that network. The communications and meetings that followed led to access being granted by a client and the host broadcaster into the closed world of televised sport production" (p. 274).

It is important for researchers to maintain their relationship with gatekeepers. While the importance of this may seem obvious, it important for young researchers to remember that they should not use a gatekeeper to secure access and subsequently go on to avoid or ignore this person. In many cases, the researcher may need to contact the gatekeeper for more access during later stages of the study or during follow-up studies.

In addition to the gatekeepers, as Bernard (2006) explains, researchers can benefit from interaction with guides and key informants who provide valuable knowledge about the setting and the participants and assist researchers in gaining access, securing inside information, clarifying issues not readily understood by the outside researcher, and connecting with certain people (e.g., additional gatekeepers, key participants). Researchers should learn to recognize these insiders, decision makers, and informants and work to develop and maintain relationships with them because they can help the researcher more clearly understand the research setting, culture, participants, and interactions. These relationships may develop by accident or through the researcher's ability to recognize decision makers, opinion leaders, and key informants.

In their engagement with observation methodology, researchers have to decide whether they will make themselves known or keep themselves unknown to the participants. In overt observation, the researcher makes full disclosure by informing participants that he or she is a researcher conducting a study. However, because participants can be influenced by the presence of an observer, some investigators decide to veil their identity (O'Reilly, 2005) and gain access to the site by means of covert observation—that is, they observe participants without the explicit awareness, approval, and access of the participants or their organization (Bryman & Bell, 2007). This sort of access is generally quite simple to achieve, but even though the researcher does not disclose his or her role as researcher to each person who will be observed, he or she does need to secure approval from the appropriate gatekeeper within the site or organization. Although covert observation offers easy access to the site and minimizes the researcher's influence on participants, it also carries some disadvantages, among them difficulties in recording data, challenges regarding reliability and validity, and ethical issues (Bernard, 2006).

Unless the research involves some type of covert observation, the researcher should—before access to the field is secured through formal or informal gatekeepers—fully disclose the study's purpose, how data will be collected, any possible risks or disadvantages as a result of participation, each researcher's role, and how confidentiality will be maintained. As Angrosino (2007) further explains, the ethics of observation research require that researchers follow universal research standards (e.g., comply with their university's institutional review board), defend the confidentiality of the study's participants, avoid disturbing the normal activities of those being observed, and respect—and not try to interfere or manipulate—the subjects' decisions, values, culture, lifestyle, and interactions.

Observer Roles

Observation research in sport management involves several roles, which are similar to the major observation research methods (Angrosino, 2007): nonreactive (researcher observes action with minimal interference), reactive (researcher observes but is allowed to intervene), and participatory (researcher observes and can be active in the study itself). The first role involves complete observation, where the researcher simply watches, listens, and records the findings. For example, an investigator might sit in a fitness center, far enough away from participants that the investigator is not part of the setting, and passively record the behavior of fitness center members and trainers. "Observation typically requires no interaction between the researcher and the subject," note sport marketing scholars O'Reilly and Seguin (2009), "yet the qualitative and quantitative data can easily be acquired by the observer" (p. 65). The complete observer role can also involve covert observation. For instance, Martin's (1990) research team used covert observation techniques in their examination of customer relations in the bowling industry. "The mystery patron audits, conducted unobtrusively," notes Martin, "enabled the research team to systematically and objectively record observations of the employee/customer interface" (pp. 6–7). As O'Reilly (2005) notes, however, one of the disadvantages of complete observation is that the investigator may not be able to completely understand the situation or the activities or decisions of the participants.

The second role involves a combination of observer and participant. One way to structure this role is to have the observer act as a participant; in other words, the investigator enters the site and participates with the subjects but does so specifically for the purpose of conducting research and making observations. For example, in Battenfield and Kent's (2007) study of the communication culture in the office of a sports information director (SID) in intercollegiate athletics, the researchers note that, "following the start of the observations . . . efforts were made to solidify relationships and to earn the trust of those who work in the SID office" (p. 243). The other combination role involves a regular participant acting as an observer; in this case, the investigator is already involved with the subjects or is a member of the organization being studied and thus simply steps back from the native setting and records her or his observations. Smith (2005) states that native participant-observers "contribute to change for the benefit of communities, to ensure that science listens to, acknowledges, and benefits indigenous communities" (p. 96). Researchers can play a combination of roles based on the study's objectives. For example, the two investigators in the Hill and Green (2008) study took on separate roles. "Neither of us was involved in the soccer program as a coach or administrator," they note. "Hill obtained entry into the setting as the parent of a player. He made his research plans known and embedded himself in the weekly operations of the club, its team, and its games. Green was responsible for debriefing the coauthor" (p. 191).

The third role involves complete participation, where the investigator is fully involved in the organization or fully engages with the participants of the study. An investigator who takes on this role has the advantage of being an insider. Furthermore, if the investigator works to be as complete and unobtrusive a participant as possible, the study's subjects will be less likely to modify their behavior, and the researcher will be more likely to secure more in-depth and accurate observations (data). Such was the case in Caza's (2000) research, where the investigator held a variety of executive positions in the Amateur Boxing Association (ABA) during the observation process. "While the ABA was informed of and consented to this research, the study was effectively based on covert observation due to the author's (role as a complete participant). Such a means of observation is generally considered to increase the ecological validity of the ethnographic data by reducing subject reactivity" (p. 232). This role offers distinct advantages but also poses a challenge insofar as it is sometimes difficult for observers to record observations while they are participating (DeWalt & DeWalt, 2002).

Participant Observation in New Media

Observation often involves watching or listening in the field, but sport management investigators can also conduct virtual or online observation. Kozinets (1997) coined the phrase **netnography**, and Puri (2007) called it *webnography*. Regardless of the terminology (other labels include *cyberethnography* and *digital ethnography*), this form of online observation methodology can be used in forums such as e-mail lists, message boards, discussion boards, chat rooms, Web logs (blogs), and online journals. In the dozen years since Kozinets' publication, numerous studies have utilized netnography, and even though the term *netnography* has not been widely used in sport management, an increasing number of studies involve online observation methodologies. For example, in their analysis of the public funding debate regarding a new stadium, Mondello, Schwester, and Humphreys (2009) examined the online blog postings of various stakeholders. Sanderson (2009) examined the phenomenon of "audience labor," wherein sport organizations can monitor and benefit from the information that fans publish via social media sites (e.g., Twitter, Facebook). In December 2010, an entire issue of the *International Journal of Sport Communication* was dedicated to new media research, and many of the articles could be considered netnography.

Sport management netnographers do their unobtrusive research by observing the interactions of their subjects in a virtual community. If the netnographer becomes engaged at all in the computer-mediated communication, they do so only on the periphery and not as full participants. O'Reilly, Rahinel, Foster, and Patterson (2007) explore the merits of this form of ethnography, and their reasons for using it to understand online cultures include its value in assessing interactions in large groups, its convenience, and the fact that it provides access to "data-rich online forums to provide incremental insight for commercial marketers" (p. 71).

Online observation methodology in sport management simply adapts traditional observation research in the field to the investigation of computer-mediated communication. For example, Mitrano (1999) used this methodology to observe the "social psychological effects of [sport franchise] relocation on the fans from cities being abandoned" (p. 134). He did so by observing fan interactions based on their postings on two popular Internet discussion groups associated with the Hartford Whalers. Similarly, in Heinonen's (2002) study of the behavior, culture, and social aspects of World Cup soccer fans, the investigator observed fans at a World Cup match and in the "debates and travel reports" (p. 34) of participants in an Internet discussion group. In addition to examining social interactions, the online form of observation research helps those in the sport industry develop better understanding of how a sport organization and its products are viewed and how they can better target participants in online communities. Such research can provide insight into consumption habits, promotion effectiveness, and a host of other important areas of concern for sport managers. O'Reilly and Seguin (2009) explain the use of this methodology: "Netnography offers sport market researchers a way to gauge reactions to elements of the marketing mix" (p. 69). For example, they explain that researchers can gauge reactions when they read message postings related to

- sport product (e.g., "How come my soccer ball doesn't stay inflated?")
- place (e.g., "Where do I get tickets to the game, and how come they're not even posted on the team Web site?"),
- price (e.g., "Why don't you shop around a bit more?"), and

- promotion (e.g., "Did you see the commercial they just aired? I could have taken better shots with my cell phone.").

They add that online observation research can also assist researchers in understanding the general culture and consumption patterns.

The process of netnography, as O'Reilly and Seguin (2009) explain, begins by focusing your objectives through a list of good research questions. These questions should be based on the research initiative—for example, "to find out what functionalities or benefits are sought after in the next product line, what fans thought about your last acquisition, or what the current perception of your brand is compared to those of your regional competitors" (p. 67). The next step is to find a research site, which means any online forum where participants or consumers gather and interact. In selecting online community resources to observe, sport management and marketing researchers should consider four variables (Kozinets, 1997):

1. Is the source relevant to the research question?

2. Is there a wide variety of traffic (or just lurkers)?

3. Are the data detailed and rich (e.g., not just Q&A, but expressions of feelings, influence, sharing)?

4. How much interaction takes place between posters?

Data sources in online observation research may include verbatim message postings by participants, field notes by the observer, and interviews with online participants. These interviews can be conducted through traditional e-mailing, private messaging, or instant messaging (Edwards & Skinner, 2009; O'Reilly & Seguin).

Data Collection

Various types of qualitative data can be collected in observation research. Generally, gathering information in the research setting—that is, conducting the study—involves primary data collection by means of taking field notes (about interactions and behavior observed directly or via Internet activity or audio or video recording), participating in the setting, or conducting interviews or focus groups. For example, Silk and Amis (2000) used "interviews, observations, verbal descriptions, and explanations" (p. 273). Observation research also

often involves secondary data collection through processes such as searching through archives and analyzing documents and materials (e.g., photographs). Caza's (2000) study of innovation in sport organizations, for example, relied on observations, organizational minutes and memos, and personal conversations. Regardless of the observation approach, investigators who use this methodology generally work to collect a mixture of primary and secondary data that achieves the study's aims and focuses on the study's target population (Bernard, 2006). Therefore, the researcher's data collection activities should be guided by the study's purpose and research questions. As Merriam (1998) notes, "where to begin looking depends on the research questions" (p. 97). Keep in mind, however, that adjustments will often be made as the investigator advances through the study. Silk and Amis, for example, note that "this research developed as the first author became immersed within the setting itself. That is, what to observe, when and how, to some degree developed from the actual research setting and process itself" (p. 274).

Observation Process

Direct observation is the primary method of collecting data in observation research. In the observation process, the researcher collects data through field visits and direct witnessing (observing) of the event or site and of the activities and behaviors of the participants. The investigator does this in order to determine how those being studied act, react, or interact and what they feel or perceive (Angrosino, 2002). The choice of observation approach should be based on the desired observer role—complete observer, observer-participant, participant-observer, or complete participant. Regardless of the role, good and reliable data can be collected if the observer remains as unobtrusive as possible, becomes familiar with the site before data collection begins, keeps observations short and not too technical or detailed, and is honest in all interactions with participants and in recording results (Taylor & Bogdan, 1984).

Participant-observers may engage in numerous activities. The researcher systematically records each observation as a field note—that is, a note that the researcher writes down during or after a site visit in order to record what was observed and heard in the natural setting. In short, field notes (addressed in detail in the next section of this chapter) record what the researcher sees and hears through observations and eavesdropping. All of these observations should be grounded in the study's purpose and research questions. For example, in Hoeber's (2007) study of athletic departments and teams, "observation practices and competitions were conducted in order to gain an appreciation of the culture and institutional conditions of the sport programmes and to witness firsthand if and how gender equity was enacted in organisational practices" (p. 367). Therefore, the question of what should be observed or listened for is answered by determining the study's research aims—what the researcher wants to learn or investigate (Wolcott, 2001). Researchers should observe, track, and listen for many things in their data collection activities in the field. Observations can include demographics (e.g., age, ethnicity, gender), other personal characteristics (e.g., occupation, position, role, skills), groupings of the participants (e.g., informal groups, subgroups, power bases), and the patterns and frequency of activities and interactions in the research setting (Lofland, Snow, Anderson, & Lofland, 2006). In seeking out new insights and observations, as DeWalt and DeWalt (2002) further explain, the researcher should look for interactions (e.g., who is making decisions, who is talking to whom, whose opinions are accepted). They add that counting activities, incidents, and participants is helpful, as is listening to conversations and observing nonverbal expressions. Observations usually center on specific questions. Based on suggestions by Kawulich (2005), here are some possible questions: What is happening during the activity or in the sport setting? Who are the participants? Who is initiating—and how is the subject initiating—the activity? What are the other participants' reactions (verbal or nonverbal) to the activity or setting? What conversations are taking place? How is the one activity or setting unique or similar to other observed activities, settings, and participant behaviors?

While covert (unknown, veiled) observers do not have to worry about how they get along with the subjects, known observers must decide how to behave, present themselves, and acquire information. Lofland et al. (2006) note that the observer can often acquire data and sustain information flow by appearing to be nonthreatening (coming across as no threat to the setting or participants) and acceptably incompetent (appearing ignorant and needing to be taught by the participants).

While it can be difficult to know exactly when to stop the observations, observers often reach a saturation point where they realize that it is time to end data collection and exit the field. The saturation point, according to Angrosino (2007), arrives when current observations consistently overlap other observations that have already been noted. Observers may also realize that they have reached a saturation point if they become bored with recording results. At that point, the observers should plan their departure from the setting. An observer can use various exit strategies, ranging from departing by degrees to simply abruptly departing. Regardless of the approach used, the observer should inform the subjects (if not conducting a covert observation) and leave in a professional way (e.g., giving thank you notes to staff for their cooperation) that leaves the door open for future research or visits by the investigator or other researchers (Buchanan, Boddy, & McCalman, 1988).

Mixed Methods and Multimethod Designs

Observation studies often use either a mixed-methods or a multimethod research design. A mixed-methods research design involves a single study that uses both qualitative and quantitative data, whereas a multimethod research design in qualitative research involves a single study that uses multiple qualitative methodologies (Creswell & Clark, 2007). An observation study that uses a mixed-methods research design could use any combination of observation and quantitative data collection (e.g., a survey instrument). For example, in Martin's (1990) study of the bowling industry, the investigator used observation research and mixed-methods research: "literature surveys of sports, leisure, marketing, and management fields," "fourteen experience interviews including customer relations consultants as well as sports managers and proprietors," "three focus groups of bowlers and bowling center customer contact employees," and "surveys of 82 league and casual bowlers" (p. 5). Another example of mixed-methods design in observation research can be found in Kay and Laberge's (2002) study of participation by corporate managers in adventure racing (AR). These investigators "chose to rely on multiple modes of data generation" (p. 19), including observation, interviews, and "some quantitative data, statistics, and competitor information that rounded out our knowledge of sociodemographic characteristics and sport experiences of AR participants" (p. 20).

When an observation study uses a multimethod design, two of the most common qualitative methodologies employed are interviewing and document analysis. Interviewing and focus groups—and the transcriptions that result from these activities—provide additional sources of data in observation research. Observations can provide the foundation upon which interview questions are based. For example, in a study by Skinner et al. (1999), "data collection was based initially on observation and further supported by interviews" (p. 181). However, as Angrosino (2007) and Bernard (2006) explain, researchers can either ask questions first and then observe, or observe before asking questions. That is, you can observe first and then ask questions based on your observations, or you can ask questions and use the responses to guide your observation strategy. Interviews—which can be either informal (e.g., brief dialogue with participant) or formal (e.g., structured, open-ended, or questionnaire-based)—can provide context and substantial insights from participants and thus help the researcher complete the observation study; interview methodology is covered in detail in chapter 8. Interviews are commonly used as supplementary data sources in observation methodology. Other frequently used data sources include documents, archives, and artifacts (e.g., clothing, objects, accessories).

A study by Battenfield and Kent (2007) provides an example of the use of multiple data sources. The investigators triangulated their observation findings by including "field notes, transcripts of audiorecorded interviews, reviews of press releases, media guides, promotional materials, website updates, daily e-mails, official documents, memorandums, and the use of symbolic material like the school logo" (p. 243). Archives can provide data including public records, statistics, census data, personal letters, organizational records, photographs, sales records, and computer databases. For example, in Lai's (1999) study of the Australian Floorball Association (AFA), "documents pertaining to floorball governance and development in Australia were obtained from the AFA national office. . . . In addition, marketing materials (catalogues and fliers about floorball clinics in the schools) were obtained" (p. 138) from a company that supplied floorball equipment. Indeed, the use of archival sources is common in observation research. For example, in an observation study of a sales department, the investigator could examine the organization's archives to gain information such as the number of members in a fitness center or various demographic data regarding a team's season ticket holders.

Regarding document analysis, the sources for this data generally come from organizational communication, people such as key stakeholders and informants, review articles and bibliographies, and online databases (Angrosino, 2002; Bernard, 2006). The document analysis of organizational communication can include everything from business minutes and stakeholder meeting transcripts to office memos and corporate filings. People can also serve as document sources because investigators can ask knowledgeable informants for suggestions about, for example, documents, books, and articles to seek out. Indeed, reviewing articles and bibliographies is an important aspect of observation research, since investigators can obtain substantial background material and insight from academic journals (e.g., *Journal of Sport Management, Sport Management Review, International Journal of Sport Management, Sport Marketing Quarterly, International Journal of Sport Communication*), newspaper clippings, practitioner publications (e.g., *SportsBusiness Journal, SportsBusiness International, Stadium and Arena Management*), sport industry newsletters (e.g., *Team Marketing Report, Revenues from Sports Venues, SportsBusiness Daily, Migala Report*) and even unpublished manuscripts. In addition to hard (paper) copies, many online databases can serve as excellent sources of documentary evidence to support observation research. For example, information about sporting goods can be obtained at the Web sites of the Sporting Goods Manufacturers Association (www.sgma.com) and SportsOneSource (www.sportsonesource.com). Keep in mind, however, that while archival and documentary sources in observation research offer distinct advantages (e.g., nonreactive and unobtrusive, sometimes easily obtained, relatively inexpensive), Bernard notes that they can also carry disadvantages, which include the need to corroborate (triangulate) with other data and the investigator's lack of control over or knowledge of what has been saved and what has been excluded (e.g., because of selective deposits by the individual or organization collecting the data).

Content Analysis

Content analysis is "the generic name for a variety of means of textual analysis that involve comparing, contrasting, and categorizing a corpus of data in order to test hypotheses" (Schwandt, 2007, p. 41). Scholars use a variety of names to describe this research methodology (e.g., document analysis, textual analysis, discourse analysis, narrative analysis, thematic analysis). Content analysis in sport management is simply the unobtrusive and nonreactive examination of communication in the field. The content analytic method has been applied to virtually every form of communication in sport management (e.g., books, newspapers, magazines, journals, diaries, company documents, letters, television shows, Internet message boards, Web sites). In the *Journal of Sport Management* (JSM) alone, the content analytic method has been used to examine myriad aspects of communication in the sport industry related to golf controversies (Daddario & Wigley, 2006), media advertisements (Cuneen & Sidwell, 1998; Kelley & Turley, 2004; Lynn, Hardin, & Walsdorf, 2004), gender portrayals and issues (Kane, 1988; Lovett & Lowry, 1995), interscholastic athletics (Conn, 1991; Pedersen, Whisenant, & Schneider, 2003), and academic and research issues in sport management (Li & Cotton, 1996; Olafson, 1990; Snyder & Kane, 1990).

Content analyses have frequently been conducted on the sport management literature published by both academicians and practitioners. For example, content analysis has focused much attention on popular publications such as *Sports Illustrated* (e.g., Bishop, 2003; Byrd & Utsler, 2007; Jones & Schumann, 2000), *ESPN The Magazine* (e.g., Clavio & Pedersen, 2007), and *Sports Illustrated for Kids* (e.g., Cuneen & Sidwell, 1998; McNary & Pedersen, 2008). Numerous other content analytic studies have focused on sport management dissertations (e.g., Dittmore, Mahony, Andrew, & Phelps, 2007), textbooks (Pitts & Danylchuk, 2007), scholarly articles (e.g., Barber, Parkhouse, & Tedrick, 2001; Mondello & Pedersen, 2003; Pedersen & Pitts, 2001; Pitts & Pedersen, 2005; Quarterman, Jackson, et al., 2006; Quarterman, Pitts, Jackson, Kim, & Kim, 2005), and professorial positions (e.g., Pedersen, Fielding, & Vincent, 2007; Pedersen & Schneider, 2003; Pedersen, Whisenant, & Schneider, 2005). For instance, Choi and Park (2007) used this methodology to examine trends in the publication patterns of the *Journal of Sport Management* (JSM) and the *Korean Journal of Sport Management* (KJSM). The researchers classified articles based on 15 categories: communication, economics, ethics, finance, governance, legal aspects, management/leadership, marketing, organizational theory, professional preparation, research, sociocultural aspects, teaching, tourism, and other. Their study found that JSM published most often on organizational theory (18 percent of articles) and marketing (14 percent). In KJSM, however, marketing accounted for 52 percent of publications, followed by management and leadership at 7 percent.

In addition to academic journals and popular publications, sport management researchers use content analysis to deconstruct company documents, industry literature, media commentary, and most any other form of communication. In postmodernist content analysis, content such as texts and dominant discourses are frequently deconstructed in sport management in order to reveal power structures and ideologies. For instance, many researchers have studied media portrayal of athletes. This topic is important for sport managers who want to understand the power of the media in shaping public opinion about issues, persons, events, groups, and organizations. This work entails examining newspapers, Web sites, and other forms of media, and it helps people understand how an organization can interact with the media.

Researchers in the field use content analyses to examine words, texts, and discourses in systematic and replicable ways, and they conduct both qualitative and quantitative content analyses. Whereas quantitative content analysis typically involves tabulating manifest data, qualitative content analysis usually uncovers the meaning of more latent (beneath-the-surface) data through such efforts as document analysis, narrative analysis (e.g., Chalip, 1992), and discourse analysis. There is even an associated communication methodology called *reception analysis*, which was used in one study to examine how young female volleyball players used media images from health and sport magazines to construct their own physical self-concepts (Thomsen, Bower, & Barnes, 2004). Regardless of terminology, qualitative research—which works through content analysis to probe descriptions and meanings in communication—promotes further understanding of language (or data) (Gratton & Jones, 2004).

Document analysis is probably the most prominent form of qualitative content analysis in sport management research. Document analyses are conventionally conducted by only one coder because the process is unique to each coder because, as Altheide (1996) notes, the coder is immersed in developing the protocol and collecting the data. When more than one coder is used, certain processes are typically followed. In multiple-coder document analysis, coders typically first read the material (e.g., letter, column, article, report) individually while looking for general themes related to the study's objectives and research questions. Because document analysis is considered to be an emerging research approach (and has a flexible approach to data collection, as illustrated by Gratton and Jones [2004]), correct methodology will guide the research on the basis of initial categories (Altheide), but new themes should emerge through the reading and analysis of the various documents. The coders then individually read the material again, refining the original general themes and providing more detailed coding overall. They then come together for discussion, during which themes that are common among the coders are examined, refined, connected to each other and to the study's theoretical framework, and accepted as part of the study's findings.

Because the objective of qualitative content analysis research is to develop meanings, processes, and definitions, this methodological approach depends on descriptions, texts, and narratives (Altheide, 1996). It offers an effective way to disclose the potency of discourse and primary sources (e.g., the results of qualitative analysis of coverage devoted to the Wimbledon Championships [Vincent, Pedersen, Whisenant, & Massey, 2007]). Understanding the nuances of documents affords a deeper connection to culture and to the implications for sport and its key players. Regarding the sample selection process in qualitative content analysis work, Gratton and Jones (2004) note that sample size should not be determined at the beginning of the study. Rather, they explain, the investigator should "aim to achieve what is referred to as 'saturation'" (p. 153), the point after which gathering additional data will not provide new or different information.

Quantitative content analysis, as distinguished from qualitative content analysis, involves the systematic, objective, and replicable examination of symbols of communication that been assigned numeric values, as well as the analysis of relationships involving those values, in order to describe the communication and draw inferences about its meaning (Riffe, Lacy, & Fico, 2005). Thus, rather than examining latent content in order to uncover hidden meaning (as in qualitative content analysis), the quantitative approach systematically and objectively examines manifest data. "The focus on manifest communication content is essential to producing scientifically valid results," note Poindexter and McCombs (2000). "By analyzing the obvious meaning, the researcher can produce objective results" (p. 188). Therefore, researchers use a systematic approach to the various stages of quantitative content analysis work. These procedures involve deciding on the units of analysis, developing measures, determining the sampling frame, selecting and training coders, engaging in a precoding process, and then coding and analyzing the findings.

For example, a study of newspapers might include a descriptive analysis of written elements (e.g., columns, articles, feature stories, editorials) and photographic elements (e.g., mug shots, still shots, action shots). If this is the case, then the units of analysis would be the article (for the written material) and the photograph (for the photographic material). After deciding on the unit of analysis, the researcher must develop the measures (e.g., size, length, location) that will be coded for the study. These measures are based on the study's objectives and hypotheses or research questions.

The determination of the sampling frame should be based on several factors. With most content analyses, a reduced sample size is enforced by the location of the researcher (many researchers will not have easy access to every source) and the requirement that all the information be measured and recorded manually. Therefore, due to financial and time constraints, sport management studies are typically limited in some way (e.g., via random sampling). The sampling frame differs depending on whether the study is conducted to look at coverage patterns over time or to analyze a current trend. Take, for instance, content analysis of daily newspapers (e.g., the examination of basketball coverage by Pedersen, Miloch, Fielding, and Clavio [2007]). Precautions must be taken in the selection of newspapers because the content of these publications varies by day of the week due to advertising and the regular scheduling of events. Therefore, it is preferable to use a stratified sampling method to construct 2 weeks from the year (randomly selecting two Mondays, two Tuesdays, and so on). As stated by Riffe, Aust, and Lacy (1993), "two constructed weeks would allow reliable estimates of local stories in a year's worth of newspaper entire issues" (p. 139). For example, Pedersen, Whisenant, and Schneider (2003) examined the coverage given to interscholastic sport by content-analyzing 2 constructed weeks of the 43 daily newspapers in Florida.

Coders are used in content analysis work to examine the measures and record the findings of the study. Depending on time and financial constraints, published content analyses have used any number of coders (from single coder to many coders). The training and evaluation of coders must address the concept of reliability, which examines how consistently the coders make decisions. This measurement in content analysis determines whether the coders, working independently of each other, are measuring the variables consistently. Content analysis reliability involves

1. operationalizing concepts in a study protocol,

2. training coders to apply the operationalized concepts, and

3. evaluating the coders' application through intercoder reliability testing (Riffe et al., 2005).

Therefore, operationalizing the study's concepts is the first step in establishing reliability, and it is accomplished through the development of a study protocol. "The protocol's importance cannot be overstated," notes Riffe et al. (2005). "It is the documentary record that defines the study in general and the coding rules applied to content in particular" (p. 127). In addition to the protocol, the investigator should create both a study codebook and precise coding sheets. The second step in establishing reliability is to train the study's coders. This precoding process typically involves a pilot study that helps test the coding system, train the study's coders, and determine (and, if necessary, clarify) any problematic areas in the study design (e.g., measures, protocol, codebook, coding sheets). The third step involves testing how consistently the coders are applying the study's operationalized concepts through intercoder reliability testing, in which the coders independently code a specific percentage (usually a minimum of 10 percent) of the selected sample. Their recordings are then compared.

In the first stage of reliability testing, the researcher is looking for simple percentage agreement, which is determined by tabulating the number of times the coders agree. This percentage, however, may result from accurate coding or simply from agreeing by chance alone. Therefore, the second stage of reliability assessment removes the factor of agreement by chance alone by turning the percentage of agreement into a reliability coefficient. A reasonable standard number for acceptable simple agreement is at least 80 percent, and the minimum coefficient related to corrections for chance agreement is .70. Acceptable and high intercoder reliability percentages and numbers confirm that the coders are thoroughly familiar with the coding protocol and codebook by the time the study is conducted.

Researchers doing content analysis work must also establish validity because a certain measure might be reliable in its application yet still wrong in what the researcher assumes it is measuring (Riffe et al., 2005). Thus, reliability is a necessary and vital condition for arriving at valid inferences from content analysis, but it is not in itself sufficient. Validity is necessary to determine whether a study's methods produce the desired information. The most commonly accepted form of validity assessment in content analysis is direct or face validity, which is based upon the assumption that self-evident, clear, logical, and consistent coding measurements will simply record what they are supposed to record (Riffe et al., 2005). This type of assessment involves examining the content analysis methodology to determine whether the measurement categories are clearly defined and the coding scheme is logical and consistent (Folger, Hewes, & Poole, 1984). Face validity is simply a matter of a particular measure

making sense on its face. In other words, on the face of it, the measure works, and the adequacy of the measure is obvious to all (Pedersen, 2002). In addition to face validity, Krippendorf (2004) notes that semantical and sampling validity are also applicable to content analysis. Semantical validity involves a method's sensitivity to the symbolism within a particular context. It is similar to the traditional question of whether researchers are measuring what they think they are measuring. Sampling validity is the degree to which the data used in a study constitute an unbiased sample and are statistically representative of the population from which the sample is drawn. A study can conform to this assessment by virtue of its sampling frame and sample size.

Field Notes

Taking notes—or recording observations—is the primary source of data in sport management observation research; therefore, writing these notes is the most important research method in observation studies. **Field notes** are taken about various aspects of interactions and behaviors, but the major part of observation research is talk (e.g., conversations, statements, speeches, directives), as "distinguished from interviewing by the fact that it is embedded in the accomplishment of episodes other than interviews" (Lindlof & Taylor, 2002, p. 135). Investigators also use field notes to record their observations about participants, settings, gestures, attitudes, environment, behaviors, ambience, interactions, expressions, and activities in the research setting. For example, as Hill and Green (2008) note in their study of the management of youth soccer programs, "Hill attended practices twice per week and games each weekend for two seasons. Field notes were kept throughout the observation period" (p. 191). Field notes are used and recorded as soon as possible, because with the passing of time it becomes more and more difficult to accurately and completely remember activities and interactions (Gummessen, 1991). There is no required time in which field notes must be taken; they should simply be recorded as close as possible to the time of observation. In Hanis-Martin's (2006) study of ownership and management activities in women's professional basketball, she "typed up detailed field notes the same day or, in a few cases where that was not possible, the following day" (p. 270). Throughout the process of taking field notes, keep in mind that the notes provide documentary and objective evidence not of the investigator's expectations or interpretations but of what occurred and was observed.

Field notes come in various types, including scratch notes, detailed descriptions, and analytic notes. With scratch notes, also known as cryptic jottings or fly notes, the investigator writes brief statements about various activities, interactions, behaviors, or anything related to the research aims during the observation process. Usually, scratch notes or field jottings are simply handwritten observations and comments on loose pieces of paper or in some type of notebook. For example, Gallmeier (1989), who studied how workers in sport react to failure (e.g., turnover, job loss) in their occupations, noted that "to increase the accuracy and completeness of the field notes and to claim some statements as verbatim, numerous notes were taken while in the field in a small, pocket sized notebook. . . . These notes consisted of key words indicating specific incidents, their nature or sequence, and verbatim phrases jotted down within 5 to 10 minutes after they occurred" (p. 27). Scratch notes are most often handwritten—perhaps on small pieces of paper that can be quickly slipped into the researcher's pocket, unobserved by the subjects—but they can also be recorded on a laptop computer. Perhaps the best way to take field notes is with a palmtop computer. Some palmtops use a keyboard, whereas others, sometimes called *hand-held computers* or *personal digital assistants* (PDAs), use a pen for data entry.

Whatever form they take, scratch notes are used later in the process (e.g., at the end of the day, during the analysis period) to trigger the investigator's recollections (Bernard, 2006). They should be vivid and obvious to the investigator but written briefly and quickly in the research setting (Wilkinson & Birmingham, 2003)—small on-site notes without lengthy explanations, since more detailed information (e.g., who, what, when, where) and arrangement of the data can be done at a later time in the investigator's daily notes or research journal. Thus suggestions for writing scratch notes include using shorthand, abbreviations, acronyms, keywords, and phrases rather than detailed information (Mack et al., 2005). Additional suggestions, offered by Schensul, Schensul, and LeCompte (1999), include quoting as precisely as possible, using pseudonyms to protect participants' confidentiality, recording activities and events in the correct order, and sustaining objectivity. When possible, in order to save time while in the field, the paper on which field notes will be written should include preprinted information (e.g., date,

time, place). Finally, Merriam (1998) suggests that these field notes should include moving from the overall situation or view to a narrower (e.g., single-participant) perspective and that the investigator should write down keywords that will trigger accurate recollections later on, concentrate on initial and concluding remarks in conversations, and mentally replay comments and scenes during breaks in the observations or action.

Another type of field note is the detailed (thick) description, in which the investigator writes more complete observations, impressions, conversations, and information. In observation research, investigators can gain a better understanding of the findings by recording (in as much detail as possible) what is happening and why and by looking for regular patterns, variations, exceptions, and irregular behaviors (DeWalt & DeWalt, 2002). These detailed descriptive narratives—which provide the major source of data for observation research—should be written as close as possible to the time when activity or interaction was observed in order for the information to be as complete, detailed, reliable, and accurate as it can be (Angrosino, 2007). For instance, Fairley (2003) says, "I participated fully in all group activities and was treated as one of the group. Field notes were taken after each group activity" (p. 291). As noted by DeWalt and DeWalt, the observer should listen carefully and try to remember verbatim conversations and interactions as much as possible. They suggest observers should keep a running observation record and develop their various jottings into detailed field notes that may even include interaction and spatial maps. Therefore, the investigator expands the field notes and includes as many details as can be observed and recollected. These detailed descriptions can then be categorized into files based on the purpose of the study and the chosen research questions (Lofland et al., 2006).

When taking analytic notes, investigators articulate their comments and ideas about what they observed. These are the data analysis, interpretation, and brainstorming notes where investigators explain what their various scratch notes and detailed descriptions may mean. Bernard (2006) states that as these analytic notes are developed and organized, they provide the framework for understanding and the foundation for the final research paper.

In addition—but similar—to analytic notes, other approaches to recording observations, including personal reflections and opinions, include the observation log and the observation diary, both of

Analytical Field Notes

Newman's (2007) study—which looked at the political, religious, and spectatorial activities within the culture of NASCAR—involved "more than 300 hours spent at eight races during NASCAR's 2006 season" (p. 291), and the resulting journal article about the study includes several in-depth and analytical field notes. One example begins with Newman stating that "[t]he presence of corporate logos, corporate hospitality tents, and corporate merchandise—ranging from Skoal to Crown Royal to the latest HDTV technologies—is staggering" (p. 295). Newman's analytic note continues for several more sentences before ending with this: "In a procession of the commodified corporeal, these spectators parade toward the NASCAR spectacle and its mesmerizing qualities. (Fieldnotes, 26 August 2006)" (p. 296).

which are detailed by Angrosino (2002) and Bernard (2006). The log involves the systematic and daily planning of how the investigator will spend her or his time in the field (as well as a recording of how much time was actually spent) and of the various activities and expenses involved in the observation research. The diary is a personal and private account of what the investigator encountered (e.g., resistance, openness, challenges), felt, and perceived throughout the observation process. These are subjective reflections, comments on personal matters, explorations and evaluations of the researcher's position, and overall reflective notes on the process.

As noted by Bryman and Bell (2007), the technique of taking field notes carries both advantages and disadvantages. Advantages include the fact that—depending on the observer's expertise—the note taking can be flexible (done at any time) and discrete (unobtrusive). Gallmeier (1989), for example, explains that his field notes

> were made in private places; toilets appeared particularly handy for such activities, as well as the press box where reporters and broadcasters were in the habit of taking notes or writing something down while watching the action on the ice. Notes were never taken in the subjects' presence. (p. 27)

Disadvantages include the fact that fields notes can be challenging to arrange, unwieldy for locating specific desired content in a timely manner, time-consuming to take, and difficult to record immediately and thus requiring reliance on memory. May (2001) described his field notes for a study of youth sport participation in this way:

> I routinely recorded my observations immediately following practices and games, although our late-night returns from games occasionally made it difficult for me to record notes that evening. In such instances, I recalled my observations from memory the next morning and recorded them. (p. 374)

In addition to field notes, data can also be gathered during on-site observation through such recording methods as photography and audio or video recording, as detailed in the work of Angrosino (2007). Photography can be used to aid the investigator's memory and provide graphic detail of various scenes, interactions, and artifacts. Audio recording can be used to record comments and conversations that provide insight into participants' perspectives and actions. Often done with a digital recorder, it can also be used by an investigator to record field notes rather than writing or typing them out; such recordings can require much time to transcribe, but they can be very helpful in providing a complete observation. Video recording can be used to watch interactions and activities over and over. As Silk (2005) reflects in regard to his observation work during 1998 Kuala Lumpur Commonwealth Games,

> in addition [to written field notes], I used a video recorder while in the field to record the settings, the work routines of the crews and some of the decisions being made. . . . I blended in with the crew as I started to take video footage of the labor process involved in the recreation of the Games. (p. 88)

Data Analysis

Researchers analyze observation findings through an inductive reasoning process in which codes, themes, and patterns emerge. In contrast to the deductive process used in much sport management research, generalizations in observation methodology are made based on what has been observed or heard during the field research. The *analysis* is not a step-by-step or mechanical sequence but an emergent, open-ended, and creative process in which the investigator serves as the main agent and is guided by the information (data) collected and the research aims of the study (Lofland et al., 2006). This approach is illustrated by Bricknell (2001), who notes that "as a social agent I interacted with the data, both in the field, and at the level of social analysis" (p. 7). As the main agent or instrument, the investigator's involvement in the study and analysis of the findings are informed, according to Charmaz (1983), by her or his personal history, interests, commitments, expertise, knowledge of the topic, and skill in addressing the study's research aims.

The analysis—the discovery of what the data mean—involves a coding process. The codes are simply ways in which the investigator organizes the data, and the coding process often begins by visually scanning and physically filing the various field notes that have been collected. As Bernard (2006) notes, this process can be initiated by literally placing the various notes on a desk or floor in order to visualize and more clearly comprehend the available contents. This strategy gives the investigator a sense of the data available and guides him or her in effectively and accurately analyzing the data. The physical filing of the notes, as described by Lofland et al. (2006), involves either systematically separating the various notes into file folders or using database software (e.g., even something as simple as Microsoft Word) or a qualitative data analysis software program.

Popular software includes Ethnograph, Hyper-Research, and NVivo. These programs can help researchers organize data and develop themes and subthemes. For instance, Frisby, Reid, Millar, and Hoeber (2005) used ATLAS.ti to transcribe and code their data. Another example is a study by Rehman and Frisby (2000), who used the NUD*IST (nonnumerical unstructured data indexing, searching, and theorizing) software in their examination of the work experiences of women fitness and sport consultants. They note that "all data from the interviews and field notes were transcribed and transferred into a qualitative data analysis program Q.S.R. NUD.IST." With the help of this software, "there were five main themes and a number of sub-themes that were developed through the data analysis process to represent the liberation and marginality perspectives of self-employment" (p. 50). Bricknell (2001) provides a detailed description of how one sport researcher used NUD*IST in her coding, arranging, and analysis of data. Remember, however, that while such software programs can help with organizing, storing, and retrieving

qualitative data, "they cannot do the hard work of data analysis, which requires certain intellectual and creative skills that, to date, only the analyst can bring to the enterprise" (Lofland et al., 2006, p. 204).

Regardless of the physical filing system used to systematically organize field notes, the investigator must work to identify themes, topics, and issues. Therefore, in the initial coding or categorizing stage, "researchers look for what they can define and discover in the data" (Charmaz, 1983, p. 113). As Hesse-Biber and Leavy (2006) suggest, one way to do this is by simply asking questions such as, "What is going on in the setting?" (p. 263). They further note that the same questions one might ask when looking at puzzle pieces should be asked by an investigator looking at field notes: "What is this piece? What does it mean? Are there other pieces like this? What makes piece 'A' different from/same as piece 'B'?" (p. 264). Other questions might address the distribution and frequency of certain phenomena (Chambliss & Schutt, 2006). For example, the investigator could review her or his notes and ask how often certain subjects (e.g., sport managers, fans) engaged in a particular activity, or how many of the subjects made a particular decision or offered a similar comment. The answers to such questions will help in the coding process. Once the notes are categorized in this thematic coding process, the investigator performs an initial reading, followed by several additional readings and further organizing and categorizing. As the investigator moves through the coding process and the arrangement of the data, he or she will discover that certain codes are being used more than others and that certain themes and patterns are becoming more and more relevant (Lofland et al., 2006).

Fairley (2003) describes this type of process in her study of sport tourism: "Reading through the interview transcripts and field notes, the researcher first coded all phrases and opinions from the transcript. This was repeated on three separate occasions, with the researcher working dialectically between the data and the literature to further develop, compare, and contrast the codes and themes identified" (pp. 291–292). In the end, data analysis in observation research leads to the investigator's interpretation, which answers Hesse-Biber and Leavy's (2006) question, "What does the puzzle mean?" (p. 263). The result of observation research, as noted by Wilkinson and Birmingham (2003), is that it helps scholars and practitioners detect and understand meaningful tendencies, patterns, categories, prototypes, and impressions in the practice of sport management. As Hatch (2002) explains, "observation is a cornerstone of qualitative data collection. No matter what the paradigm, if the researcher is interested in participant perspectives, observing those participants in action provides avenues into their understandings that are unavailable any other way" (p. 90).

Once the data analysis is complete, the investigator organizes and writes the final report or manuscript. The investigator simply tells the reader what she or he saw and how those observations were interpreted. Results are reported in observation research in a manner that is similar to how they are reported in other research studies in sport management. Based on the study's purpose and research questions, the investigator provides a title, abstract, introduction, review of literature, methodology (e.g., setting, procedures, data collection, and analysis), results of the data collection from the observation process and any conjoint findings (e.g., interviews, document analysis), discussion of the results and emergent themes, limitations of the study, and suggestions for future research.

Summary

Observation research is the third of six research designs detailed in this section of the textbook. This methodological approach to studying sport management phenomena is considered to be a qualitative data collection strategy and is often referred to as *ethnography*. Sport management researchers who use the ethnographic or observation approach conduct their investigations by entering the field (e.g., sport setting) and observing (e.g., listening, watching, asking questions) and spending time with the inhabitants (e.g., fans, sport employees). This chapter examines the observation research approach by first detailing the ways in which sport management researchers and practitioners can apply and benefit from this methodology. Next, the chapter explains the foundational elements, philosophical assumptions, and goals of observation research. The advantages, disadvantages, and steps associated with this methodology are then detailed, followed by an examination of observation sites and observer roles. The chapter then provides an overview of how individuals can use this methodology (e.g., netnography) in examining new media (e.g., blogs, message boards, microblogs) and details the various data collection techniques associated with observation research. After an overview of mixed-methods approaches and the content analysis methodology, the chapter concludes with information about data analysis techniques associated with observation research.

Research Methods and Design in Action
Journal of Sport Management

Selected text reprinted, by permission, from K. Misener and A. Doherty, 2009, "A case study of organizational capacity in nonprofit community sport," *Journal of Sport Management* 23(4): 457-482.

Access the full article online at www.humankinetics.com/products/all-products/Research-Methods-and-Design-in-Sport-Management.

ABSTRACT

As a pivotal part of the nonprofit and voluntary sector, community sport organizations provide opportunities for active participation, social engagement, and community cohesion. This study examined the nature and impact of organizational capacity in one nonprofit community sport club to identify factors that affect the ability of this organization to fulfill its mandate and provide sport opportunities in the community. Hall et al.'s (2003) multidimensional framework of human resources, financial, relationships/networks, infrastructure and process, and planning and development capacity was used. The study incorporated interviews with board members and coaches as well as active-member researcher observations (Adler & Adler, 1987). Key strengths and challenges of each capacity dimension were uncovered, and connections among the dimensions were revealed. The relatively greater importance of human resources and planning and development capacity for goal achievement was identified. The findings support the use of a multidimensional approach for generating a comprehensive understanding of organizational capacity in community sport, and for identifying where and how capacity may be enhanced.

TEXT EXCERPTS

The use of case studies is advocated as an effective means of organizational analysis in sport management (e.g., Caza, 2000, Sharpe, 2006; Stevens & Slack, 1998). This study follows an instrumental case study methodology (Stake, 2003) as a means of better understanding organizational capacity.

The second form of data collection was active-member researcher observations (Adler & Adler, 1987). The observations took place at monthly board meetings and other events (registration evenings, end of session galas). According to Adler and Adler (1987, p. 50), "with active membership, the researcher moves clearly away from the marginally involved role of the traditional participant observer and assumes a more central position in the setting."

. . . .

Extensive field notes collected during all observations were typed and further expanded upon after returning from the "field."

. . . .

Interview data were transcribed verbatim and analyzed in a multistep process. Hall et al.'s (2003) model of organizational capacity provided a priori categories by which to analyze the data (Patton, 2002). The observation data were coded and analyzed simultaneously with the interview transcripts. Both researchers independently read through the transcripts of each interview participant as well as the active-member researcher observations. This generated an understanding of each participant's perspectives on capacity (Patton, 2002). An emergent coding scheme was then developed based on the themes of organizational capacity referred to most often by the board members, coaches, and the active-member researcher. The analysis followed Guba and Lincoln's (1989) criteria for authenticity, which is consistent with constructivist epistemology (Schwandt, 2001). That is, methods of triangulation, including member-checking by sending the transcripts back to participants for verification and clarification as well as multiple data sources, were used to clarify meaning and ensure fairness of interpretation (Guba & Lincoln, 1989; Harrison et al., 2001) while providing converging lines of inquiry within the case (Yin, 2003).

DISCUSSION QUESTIONS

1 The goal of this study was to examine the influence of multiple organizational capacity dimensions on the goal achievement of community sport organizations. Why is observation research an appropriate methodology for this project? Would another methodology be more appropriate or secure more insightful or different results?

2 Within this case study, the researchers used a mixed-methodology approach. What forms of data collection were used in this study?

3 What type of observation research did the researchers conduct?

4 What observer role did one of the researchers take on in order to collect data?

5 What were the challenges facing the researcher in her role as observer?

6 How did the researchers use field notes?

7 How did the researchers analyze the data?

Case Study Research

Learning Objectives

After studying this chapter, you should be able to do the following:

- Define case study methodology and explain the three types (purposes) of this research
- Discuss how case study research is used by sport management practitioners and researchers
- Understand the difference between research and teaching case studies
- Explain the four key tasks in developing a case study research design in sport management
- Describe the two major case study designs or approaches
- Discuss the importance of evaluating a case study's reliability and validity
- Categorize the five case study preparation topics as applied to a sport management researcher
- Comment on the main evidence sources (data sources) used in case study research
- List the general analytic strategies involved in the data analysis step in case study research
- Provide a general description of how a case study report is formatted and presented

The case study is one of the most commonly used qualitative methodological approaches in sport management research. It is true that case study research can contain some quantitative aspects (e.g., surveying, census data, tabular evidence); for example, Amis, Slack, and Hinings (2004) used quantitative data about three organizational structural dimensions (specialization, formalization, centralization) as the foundation of their case study of change in sport organizations. This chapter, however, approaches case study methodology primarily from a qualitative perspective. As George and Bennett (2005) explain in their textbook *Case Studies and Theory Development in the Social Sciences*, "guidelines for case studies must take into account the special characteristics of qualitative methodology" (p. 106).

Case study research is a social science methodology used in real-life settings (outside the laboratory) and generally drawing information from other methodologies such as interviewing, observation, and historical research. While this chapter introduces students to the value and elements (e.g., design, protocol, collection and analysis of evidence) of case study methods used in the sport industry, other chapters in this section examine qualitative research in sport management as it pertains to interviews and focus groups (chapter 8), observation (chapter 9), history (chapter 11), and the law (chapter 12).

This chapter employs a five-phase model of creating and completing case study research in sport management. The first and second phases involve designing the case study and becoming prepared to conduct it. The third phase entails collecting the evidence, the fourth phase involves analyzing the findings, and the fifth phase consists of composing the case study report. This chapter—which relies heavily on the work of Robert K. Yin—focuses on the application of case study methodology to the sport industry. For detailed information about any aspect of case study research discussed in this chapter, we encourage you to examine Yin's *Case Study Research: Design and Methods* (2003). This is the definitive work on the subject and may be the only complete work that specifically examines all elements and techniques of case study research from a research-oriented, rather than a teaching-oriented, perspective.

Applied Research Advantages

Case study research—which involves intensive examination of a single-case study or multiple-case study—is an important tool in sport management research since it allows researchers to study specific events, activities, settings, and phenomena (e.g., personnel, organizations, issues, processes). Sport management research often focuses on applied (practitioner-based) research, which makes case study research particularly useful. It is true that some case study projects address more basic or pure research and that their results build the body of knowledge in the field. But while research case studies involve rigorous methodological processes and strong theoretical foundations, the end result of most case study inquiries is to help sport management practitioners in their quest to operate more effectively and efficiently. Thus, those working in academia or in the sport management industry should learn to become proficient in reading, interpreting, and conducting case study research.

Case studies can help practitioners develop theories and best practices in any area of sport management—for example, consumer behavior, sport leagues, sport retailers, gambling, governing bodies, sport events, facilities, cities, sporting goods, teams, clubs, and online activities. Indeed, case study research has been—or can be—applied to all types of issues, areas, and institutions within the field of sport management. For instance, the *Journal of Sport Management*—one of many academic journals in sport—has published numerous case studies, and some of the issues covered in this scholarly outlet are listed in table 10.1. Case study methodology can even be applied to examining education in the field (e.g., Drayer and Rascher, 2007).

In addition to their general usefulness to both practitioners and scholars, case studies offer several advantages. One key advantage is that case study research allows the researcher to secure insight through a variety of perspectives (Velde, Jansen, & Anderson, 2004) and sources of evidence and then triangulate the data. For example, the multiple perspectives and sources involved in conducting a case study of a sport organization's marketing plan could provide a variety of data (e.g., interviews, trends, historical background, projections, opinions, reports) from a variety of departments, levels, and stakeholders (e.g., sales, marketing, human resources, senior management). The case study approach also allows the investigator to study an organization or phenomenon in depth while paying meticulous attention to detail (Ghauri & Gronhaug, 2005); to study the order of events; and to identify the relationships between functions, individuals, and entities (Zikmund, 1991).

Table 10.1 Selected Case Studies in Various Segments of Sport Management

Topic	Citation
Sport or event policy and development	Boshoff, 1997 Girginov, 2001 Green, 2005 Misener & Mason, 2009 Sam & Jackson, 2006
Sport marketing	Amis, Pant, & Slack, 1997 Berrett & Slack, 1999 Long, Thibault, & Wolfe, 2004 Parent & Seguin, 2008 Shaw & Amis, 2001
Decision making in sport	Hill & Kikulis, 1999 Kikulis, Slack, & Hinings, 1995a Mason, Thibault, & Misener, 2006 Parent, 2010
Sport and organizational economics	Chalip & Leyns, 2002 Cousens & Barnes, 2009 Mason & Slack, 2001 Mason & Slack, 2003 Sack & Johnson, 1996 Weight, 2010
Strategic management	Babiak, 2007 Fielding, Miller, & Brown, 1999 Sack & Nadim, 2002 Smart & Wolfe, 2000
Sport participation	Frisby, Crawford, & Dorer, 1997
Organizational change	Amis, Slack, & Hinings, 2004 Cousens, 1997 Kikulis, Slack, & Hinings, 1995b Parent, 2008 Slack & Hinings, 1992 Stevens, 2006 Thibault & Harvey, 1997
Sport communication	Wenner, 2004
Fitness management	Hata & Umezawa, 1995
Sport behavior	Mitchell, Crosset, & Barr, 1999
Amateur and professional sport	Kihl & Richardson, 2009 Kihl, Richardson, & Campisi, 2008 O'Brien & Slack, 2003 O'Brien & Slack, 2004
Image management	Parent & Foreman, 2007
Gender issues	Shaw, 2006 Shaw & Hoeber, 2003 Sibson, 2010

Defining Sport Management Case Study Research

Sport management scholars, students, and practitioners can turn to the case study as a research tool when they want to gain a deeper understanding of an actual (real-life) sport industry phenomenon or issue (e.g., decision-making processes used by athletic directors, the effects of team relocation, a sport merchandise company's approach to expanding globally). Investigators can use case study methodology to verify a theory in the real world (e.g., examining the validity of a theory in a particular sport organization or situation), to study the precise characteristics of a unique situation in order to make comparisons to other situations, or to research a phenomenon that has not been studied in order to discover new features (Ghauri & Gronhaug, 2005). Therefore, in addition to examining and solving practical issues in the sport industry, case study research in sport management can also involve testing existing theoretical concepts or even creating new theories (Maylor & Blackmon, 2005). In case study theory-testing work, the investigator can examine a case in order to evaluate, strengthen, or challenge a theoretical proposition (Edwards, 1998).

Case studies typically explore, describe, illustrate, or explain a selected phenomenon in sport management. Case study research comes in three types (i.e., serves three purposes) that often overlap in sport management: explanatory, exploratory, and descriptive (Maylor & Blackmon, 2005). As detailed by Yin (2003), exploratory and descriptive case studies often answer research questions that address who, what, when, and where. In explanatory case studies, however, the investigator seeks to answer questions about how and why. For example, you could use an explanatory study to gain understanding of how sport marketing professionals have used a particular promotion to sustain consistently high attendance regardless of their team's wins and losses. You could also use an explanatory case study if you wanted to understand why baseball ownership and management failed to adequately address the issue of steroids in the 1990s. Most case studies in sport management are focused on answering the how and why research questions.

Communication studies pioneer Wilbur Schramm (1971) illustrates the use of these questions in his definition of a case study: "The essence of a case study is that it tries to illuminate a decision or set of decisions: why they were taken, how they were implemented, and with what results" (p. 21). Denizen and Lincoln (1998b) explain that the term case study is used "because it draws attention to the question of what specifically can be learned from a single case" (p. 86). The most widely accepted definition is offered by Yin (2003): "A case study is an empirical inquiry that investigates a contemporary phenomenon within its real-life context, especially when the boundaries between phenomenon and context are not clearly evident" (p. 13). Yin continues by noting that a case study "relies on multiple sources of evidence, with data needing to converge in a triangulating fashion, and . . . benefits from the prior development of theoretical propositions to guide data collection and analysis" (p. 14). Thus, a sport management case study is a research strategy built on theory and involving multiple sources of data collection (e.g., interviews, observations, documents).

Moving forward from these general definitions, a researcher can find numerous ways to frame sport management research in relation to popular definitions of case study. For instance, in applying Zikmund's (1991) definition to sport management, we would define a **case study** as an exploratory research technique used in sport management to intensively investigate a situation. Kirk's (1995) definition is also excellent when applied to sport management: A case study is examining (e.g., observing, exploring) certain factors of a sport management subject (e.g., people, company, organization, system) for some period of time.

A sport management investigator using case study methodology focuses on a specific, actual phenomenon in a practical, natural, or real context. For example, Amis et al. (2004) examined radical change in organizations by looking at the influence of various factors (e.g., organizational capacity, power, interest) in six uniquely designed Canadian national sport organizations. The typical case study—which involves little (and usually no) intervention, manipulation of behavior, or control over the events being studied by the investigator (Velde et al., 2004)—is facilitated through the use of several research strategies—for example, content analysis, use of a survey instrument, and archival procedures. In the study by Amis et al. (2004), their two primary research strategies involved conducting interviews and performing documentary analyses of governmental reports and newspaper articles. Because a case study uses several research methodologies, it should not be viewed as synonymous with an observation study or a historical treatise. For instance, although a contemporary case study researcher in sport management functions in a fashion similar to that of a sport historian in examining documents, artifacts, and archives, he or she also tends to use other sources of evidence (e.g., observations) not typically used by historians.

A case study generally entails in-depth examination of a single case (e.g., a certain sport industry phenomenon, group, situation, team, event, organization, or process). Even though a case study involves only one unit (N=1), the research process engages many variables and requires data collection and integrative interpretation (Ghauri & Gronhaug, 2005) of information from multiple sources, such as interviews with sport management personnel, observations of fans, *archival data* from organizational files, historical information, surveys of sport event participants, and analyses of documents (e.g., sport marketing plans, team budget and financial reports, newspaper articles, advertisements). As explained by Velde et al. (2004), case study research addresses the "degree to which the results and conclusions of the various data collection methods point in the same direction" (p. 79). In addition to the single-case approach (e.g., examining one sport organization), case study research can also involve studying multiple cases (e.g., performing a comparative case study of several sport organizations). Therefore, in the next section we examine both the single-case and the multiple-case study designs associated with this qualitative methodological approach.

Research Versus Teaching Case Studies

One important distinction should be made before we examine the background and phases of the case study research process. There is a difference between a research case study and a teaching case study. A research case study contains many features (e.g., primary source materials, evidence, data analysis, conclusions) that a teaching case study is not required to have. "For teaching purposes," Yin (2003) explains, "a case study need not contain a complete or accurate rendition of actual events; rather, its purpose is to establish a framework for discussion and debate among students" (p. 2). Just as in the disciplines of business and law, numerous case studies for teaching—as opposed to case studies for research—are available in sport management. Many of these studies can be found in books, such

as *Case Studies in Sport Law* (Pittman, Spengler, & Young, 2008), *International Cases in the Business of Sport* (Chadwick & Arthur, 2007), *Case Studies in Sport Communication* (Brown & O'Rourke, 2003), *Cases in Sport Marketing* (McDonald & Milne, 1999), and *Case Studies in Sport Marketing* (Pitts, 1998).

Journals also frequently publish nonresearch case studies for classroom discussion. The *International Journal of Sport Communication* (IJSC) presents a teaching case study in each issue, and recent cases have examined topics including fan and athlete interactions through social media (Kassing & Sanderson, 2010), commercial programming at a single-sport cable television channel (Carroll, 2009), challenges and opportunities facing professional soccer in China (Huang & Brewer, 2008), and image repair strategies of professional athletes (Sanderson, 2008). The *Sport Marketing Quarterly* (SMQ) and the *Sport Management Review* (SMR) also present teaching case studies in nearly every published issue. As Crow and Bradish (2002) note, "the case study section unquestionably satisfies the SMQ mission statement by being meaningful to both the academic and practitioner." They conclude that SMQ teaching case studies are well written and significant yet are lacking in "full data collection and analysis . . . lacking in empirical data" (p. 77). Examples of recent SMQ case studies for the classroom are descriptions and examinations of topics including market consumer analysis (Branch, 2008) and brand management techniques in sporting goods (Kraft & Lee, 2009) and in professional basketball (Apostolopoulou, 2005); brand equity (Bruening & Lee, 2007) and ambush marketing (Kent & Campbell, 2007) in intercollegiate athletics; sponsorship strategies related to a synchronized swimming governing body (Doherty & Murray, 2007); cause-related marketing in sporting goods (McGlone & Martin, 2006); and business and marketing operations in minor league sport (Friedman & Mason, 2007; Lachowetz, Dees, Todd, & Ryan, 2009). Examples of teaching case studies published in SMR include analyses of a range of subjects, including, for example, governance changes in professional football (Shilbury & Kellett, 2006), consumer behavior (Kellett & Fielding, 2001), volunteer management in tennis (Daprano, Costa, & Titlebaum, 2007), the growth of amateur hockey (Duquette & Mason, 2004), and the ways in which individuals and organizations balance work and family issues (Dixon & Bruening, 2006).

Teaching and practitioner case studies can also be found online at MarketingSherpa (www. marketingsherpa.com) and numerous other Web sites. MarketingProfs (www.marketingprofs.com), for example, publishes weekly case studies, some of which are focused on how specific sport marketing challenges and issues were encountered and handled (e.g., "How Major League Baseball doubled fan research without increasing costs").

Some of the best teaching case studies are published by the Harvard Business School (HBS). These often in-depth case studies cover a range of topics. Here are some examples: how baseball general managers perform effective player evaluations (Frei & Campbell, 2006; Roberto, 2005); leadership in intercollegiate athletics (Snook, Perlow, & Delacey, 2005) and professional football (Wells & Haglock, 2005); business operations in professional soccer (Quelch, Nueno, & Knoop, 2005); negotiations involved in collective bargaining agreements in hockey (Malhotra & Hout, 2006); and trends and operating strategies in professional basketball (Delong, Cheek-Clayton, & Reed, 2005), professional football (Beaulieu & Zimmerman, 2005), health clubs (Wells, 2005), and the Olympics (Bowen, 2006). All of the HBS articles address teaching, rather than research, case studies. As the first page of each of the publications notes, "HBS cases are developed solely as the basis for class discussion."

A sport management case study constructed as a teaching tool is quite valuable for pedagogical purposes, and they are popular in textbooks, Web sites, journal articles, and the classroom. They are, however, different from research case studies. As Yin (2003) explains, "[while] teaching case studies need not be concerned with the rigorous and fair presentation of empirical data; research case studies need to do exactly that" (p. 2). Therefore, the remaining pages of this chapter detail the latter (research) type of sport management case study— that is, a case study constructed and facilitated through rigorous research methodology.

Design and Implementation

The sport management student, scholar, or practitioner first needs to examine and evaluate the various methodological options available for a particular research endeavor. If the researcher decides that the case study is the best approach for the project, she or he then needs to develop a research strategy and outline the research process. These preliminary activities involve formulating a solid research design, which is the prerequisite for putting together a quality case study. The research design of a sport management case study is the chart that the investigator follows in order to connect the study's theoretical propositions and research questions with its findings and conclusions. With the research design—which constitutes the first phase of case study work in sport management—the investigator formulates the structure of the study by determining what questions to ask, how to collect data, and what approach to take in analyzing the study's findings. Although there has been no codification (e.g., step-by-step plan) of research designs for case studies, some basic rules (or tasks, as noted below) have been posited for researchers to follow in developing a case study that is both rigorous and sound in its methodology (Yin, 2003).

Process Steps

The basic rules of the sport management case study research process involve several steps. Maylor and Blackmon (2005) explain that these steps begin with defining the research problem, selecting the case (or cases, for a multiple-case study), and developing data collection instruments and protocols (i.e., preparing to collect date from multiple sources). These steps are followed by the acts of collecting and analyzing the data, building the evidence, constructing the explanation, comparing the findings with the theory and literature, and completing the study. All of these steps can be synthesized into and considered as the four key tasks that must be completed in developing a case study research design in sport management: formulating the study's (a) objectives, (b) research propositions, (c) unit or units of analysis, and (d) data analysis procedures. Let us now discuss these four design tasks in light of the work of Yin (2003).

The first key task in research design is to specify the research objectives, a step that includes illustrating the study's research problem and scope. Of particular importance, the researcher must develop the study's questions—the who, what, when, and where questions for exploratory and descriptive case studies and the how and why questions for explanatory case studies. For example, Chalip and Leyns (2002) examined how local businesses leveraged (or failed to leverage) sporting events in order to incentivize sport tourists to purchase their products and services. Based on the literature the scholars reviewed, they developed five general questions upon which to base their case study: "To what degree do local businesses seek to leverage a sport event in their community? When leveraging is attempted, what tactics are applied? To what effect? What special opportunities or needs for small business leveraging can be identified? What are the views of small business leaders about those opportunities and needs?" (p. 134).

While a case study's questions should be detailed enough to reveal the study's unit of analysis (this aspect is detailed in following paragraphs), they often are not specific enough to direct the researcher as to what to study. This potential problem can be alleviated through the study's propositions. Therefore, the second key task of the research design process is to develop **research propositions**, which direct, limit, and focus the researcher's thoughts about what should be studied. The propositions reflect the study's *theoretical framework* and tell the researcher where to look (and where not to look) for evidence. Let us return to Chalip and Leyns (2002), who used leveraging as the theoretical framework for their study. Within this frame, and using the questions they had developed, the researchers directed their attention and data collection efforts through their propositions for exploring local merchants' leveraging of the Gold Coast Honda Indy car race—studying where leveraging had occurred, reasons businesses failed to leverage, more detailed instances of leveraging, suggestions by experts regarding ways to cultivate leveraging, and the degree to which local businesses accepted the experts' suggestions. In another example, Kikulis, Slack, and Hinings (1995a) devote an entire section of their paper to explaining the propositions of their study of decision making in Canadian national sport organizations. Their four propositions were as follows:

- "Design archetypes will show differences in their decision making structures across decision topics" (p. 280)

- "In the Executive Office archetype, there will be a low level of concentration of decision making in the hands of volunteers" (p. 280)

- "Patterns of change toward a new design archetype (e.g., revolutionary patterns) will demonstrate the greatest change in the high-impact system of decision making" (p. 281)

- "Revolutionary patterns of change to the Executive Office archetype will show a shift in the concentration of decision making to professional staff" (p. 281)

The third key task in research design is to select the unit(s) of analysis—that is, the case(s) to study. For example, the specific case or unit of analysis examined by Smart and Wolfe (2000) was the Penn State football program. As the authors explain, "our unit of analysis, therefore, was 'the athletic program,' which refers to specific programs (e.g.,

the football program, the softball program, the gymnastics program) within an athletic department" (p. 137). This primary unit of analysis—or **case**—could be an individual (e.g., a sport management pioneer), an issue, an event, an entity, an organization, a decision, a segment, a policy, or any phenomenon in the sport industry. For instance, when Babiak (2007) studied organizational partnerships (interorganizational relationships) in sport, she could have selected any number of possible cases or units of analysis. Even when she limited the possibilities to nonprofit Canadian sport centers (CSCs), she still had nine options from which to choose. If she had chosen a multiple-case study design, she could have studied several or even all nine centers. On a side note, if a case study involves several particular and separate individuals or events or organizations, then each person, event, or organization is considered to be a case, and thus the researcher is doing a multiple-case study (as covered a bit later in this chapter). For her study, Babiak chose to use a single-case design, and she referred to this case in many ways—for example, "CSC," "focal organization," "center," and "research site." Regardless of terminology, her rationale for selecting this unit of analysis hinged on the fact that the organization had established operations, focused on high performance, and developed extensive partnerships (which is related to the theory [interorganizational relationships {IORs}, partnership formation]) on which the study was based). One other note about unit of analysis: With any case study, the researcher should examine the literature in sport management and related fields when developing the unit of analysis.

In the case selection process, the unit of analysis can range from the more tangible (e.g., specific sport management personnel, organizations, groups) to the more conceptual (e.g., sport management processes, sport marketing decisions, sport industry relationships). Choosing the unit of analysis involves considering your theoretical framework, research questions, time requirements, financial limitations, and ability to receive access. Therefore, you need to select a target population, determine accessibility, and then select the case or cases within that population (Ghauri & Gronhaug, 2005). For example, in Long, Thibault, and Wolfe's (2004) single-case study of sponsorship and funding in university athletics, the researchers selected a large university (referred to as WCU) for the case: "WCU is an appropriate research site for this study for several reasons. . . . First, WCU has one of the largest athletic departments in Canada. Second, the wide range of men's and women's sports offered increased the politicality and complexity of the decision process. . . . Third, one of the researchers had developed trusting relationships with athletic department administrators and coaches; access to necessary information was, therefore, substantially facilitated" (pp. 139–140). Although this study involved a large university, questions of time, resources, and accessibility often require that sport management researchers focus on a small or local sport organization.

When conducting a multiple-case study, the investigator needs to be particularly careful in his or her strategy for case selection. Comparison across cases, as illustrated by Velde et al. (2004), involves selecting the best cases in terms of variance, variables, and the study's research objectives. If the investigator is looking to minimize the variance between cases, she would select cases that are as similar as possible. She could look to see whether the results were similar across similar cases (e.g., whether the marketing plans were similar among the teams in a professional league). She could also determine which factors were similar across the similar cases (e.g., what the key determinants of success were among one conference's college athletic directors). If, on the other hand, an investigator wanted to maximize variance, he would look to select cases as different as possible. He could look to determine whether different or similar results could be found across the different cases (e.g., what the results are of similar incentives to increase minority representation in management positions in the National Football League and the National Basketball League). He could also look at whether similar factors could be found across the different cases (e.g., what the similar characteristics are of a profitable semiprofessional football team and a profitable professional football team).

After selecting a unit of analysis, the researcher clarifies and defines it by determining the beginning and ending of the case and what or who is going to be included (or not included) in it. For example, regarding the timeline, Babiak (2007) notes that her "research focused primarily on the period between 2000 and 2002. This time frame was selected because a number of changes were occurring in Canadian sport" (p. 345). Overall, taking a careful and methodical approach to selecting the unit of analysis helps the researcher clarify the research design steps and limit the data collection procedure.

The fourth key task of the research design process is to specify data analysis procedures. The data analysis element of case study research design involves how the researcher connects the findings of the study to the study's propositions. This connection is often made through pattern matching, in which the researcher matches certain aspects of the case study findings to the study's propositions, theoretical propositions, or rival propositions. Although data analysis procedures are specified during the research design process, the data analysis procedures that are commonly used in sport management case study work are examined near the end of this chapter.

Theory Development

As Yin (2003) explains, the development of theory is a part of the research design phase. Thus, "the complete research design embodies a 'theory' of what is being studied" (p. 29). Because the development of a theory (theoretical propositions) helps the investigator decide how to collect data and conduct analysis, it should be done before the investigator collects case study data. Although some case studies have no theoretical framework (e.g., some exploratory studies) and others use theories that are descriptive in nature or developed as the study progresses, for the most part the conceptual base for sport management case studies can be found in previously published theories. For instance, for a case study on culture in sport businesses, the researcher might choose to rely on organizational theories from relevant academic literature, as in Girginov's (2001) study of the key actors, strategies, and relations involved in the formation of sport policy. Girginov based his study on a conceptual framework that used strategic relations (a theory developed in the literature in the early 1990s) and critical theory of crisis (developed in the literature in the early 1970s).

Regardless of the source (e.g., academic fields such as business, economics, communication) or type (e.g., individualistic, group, organizational), an appropriate theory guides the researcher in developing his or her research design and data collection strategy. For instance, Hill and Kikulis (1999) note in their study of university athletics that an already established decision-making conceptual framework or theoretical model "was used as a guide for the data collection and analysis. The model . . . was used to formulate interview questions (and) as a starting point for coding and analysis" (p. 26).

In addition to helping with these developmental stages, theory is also used by case study researchers to improve the generalizability of a study's results. This process is called analytic—as opposed to statistical) generalization. Because a case study examines a single case (or, in a multiple-case study, several cases), case study methodology does not enable scientific generalization; that is, the results of the study cannot be statistically generalized to other cases. For example, if an investigator conducts a case study of the sales department of a National Football League (NFL) team, he or she cannot make an inference from the study's results about a larger population, such as other departments in the organization or other teams in the NFL. This limitation could be considered a disadvantage of case study research, since the results are valid only for the specific situation or phenomenon studied (Velde et al., 2004). In fact, as Chalip (1997) notes, "case studies have had a troubled history in social science, as their scientific merit has been contested. The point at issue has been whether it is possible to distinguish idiographic (e.g., case-specific) knowledge from nomothetic (e.g., general) knowledge in case research" (p. 4). Chalip explains that more general knowledge can be secured through replication or applying analytic induction. Thus the absence of statistical generalizability is not a serious limitation of case study research, because the goal of this methodological approach is to provide analytic generalizations—that is, to expand and generalize a theory. As Yin (2003) states, "case studies, like experiments, are generalizable to theoretical propositions and not to populations or universes" (p. 10). Through analytic generalization, "a previously developed theory is used as a template with which to compare the empirical results of the case study" (p. 32). Therefore, theory development is instrumental in each step of case study research; it occurs throughout the research process. Theoretical development involves reviewing related literature, identifying a conceptual framework, and analyzing the study's findings to determine whether they support, refute, or require a revision of the theory.

Design Types

The two major types of case study design in sport management are single-case and multiple-case. Researchers choose a single-case study design if they want to be inductive and specific in their methodological approach, as in Fielding, Miller, and Brown's (1999) study of Harlem Globetrotters International, Inc. Researchers select a multiple-case study design if they want to be inductive and general in their research approach, as in Berrett and Slack's (1999) examination of the pressures and actions surrounding sport sponsorship decisions in 28 major corporations. After determining a study's

boundaries (i.e., single-case or multiple-case), the researcher decides on various design aspects within these two categories that make the case either holistic or embedded in nature. Therefore, the two major types of case study research can be broken into four unique case study designs: holistic single-case, embedded single-case, holistic multiple-case, and embedded multiple-case (Yin, 2003).

Before we examine the difference between holistic and embedded case study research designs, let us first look at the two major types (single-case and multiple-case) of case studies in sport management. A **single-case study** involves in-depth study of one case, such as an analysis of a unique sport management example (e.g., a best practice in sport finance) or phenomenon (e.g., high turnover in a sport setting). In sport management case studies, the methodology often involves a single-case study design focused on a specific organization; common areas examined in these organizational studies include the organizational chart, degree of centralization and formalization, workflow, linkages between management and labor, technical structure (e.g., processes, activities, implementation), support staff, type and size of the organization, growth or shrinkage over the years, demographic developments, trends, and benchmarking activities (i.e., comparing the organization with competitors or other similar sport organizations) (Velde et al., 2004). The Fielding et al. (1999) study is an excellent example of single-case study design because it provides an in-depth analysis of the history, development, vision, objectives, competitive strategy, brand management tactics, strengths, weaknesses, opportunities, and threats associated with one sport organization: the Harlem Globetrotters. Because a single-case study involves, of course, only one case, it is crucial to select a good case. As Yin (2003) notes, "a major step in designing and conducting a single case is defining the unit of analysis (or the case itself)" (p. 46). The examination of a single case (N = 1) is useful in confirming and disconfirming theory, presenting complex phenomena, examining an extreme or unique case, studying a case to reveal something new or as an example of something common or typical, examining something to which the researcher has secured uncommon or privileged access, and in conducting a pilot study or a study over time (Ghauri & Gronhaug, 2005; McCormick, 1996; Yin, 2003).

A **multiple-case study** examines (or compares or replicates) several individual cases. It focuses on finding common factors or patterns among a variety of cases (Maylor & Blackmon, 2005). Whereas a single-case study involves more in-depth data collection and analysis of one specific case, a multiple-case study does not require the researcher to invest as much time and effort per case, since many cases are examined (Maylor & Blackmon, 2005). Even so, a multiple-case study research design is often quite time consuming, exhaustive, and expensive. However, Yin (2003) notes that when compared with the single-case study, the multiple-case study design is most likely stronger and will often produce more compelling evidence and more robust implications. A multiple-case study is useful in testing theory and enables more powerful analytic generalization than does a single case (Maylor & Blackmon, 2005). The number of cases used in a multiple-case study can range from two to six or even more. The rationale for selecting cases is based on the researcher's judgment and the research objectives of the study. For example, in Amis, Pant, and Slack's (1997) study of the resource-based approach to sport sponsorship, the scholars conducted a multiple-case study by examining two cases: one company's successful sponsorship agreement with the Canadian skiing team and one company's unsuccessful sponsorship agreements with many amateur and professional organizations and athletes.

Even after beginning the study, the researcher could determine that too many cases were being examined or that additional cases need to be included in the study. Therefore, the methodological design work in case study research allows for flexibility. The design can be "modified by new information or discovery during data collection. Such revelations can be enormously important, leading to your altering or modifying your original design" (Yin, 2003, p. 55). For instance, Amis et al. (1997) initially gathered data on 31 companies involved in sport sponsorship. After conducting the interviews and analyzing the data, however, "it was decided that because of the limitations of space, just two case studies would be included in this paper" (p. 88). A researcher would add cases only if she determined that the additional cases would somehow further assist her in fulfilling the research aims of the study or could reveal a different aspect or strengthen a similar factor already revealed in the cases initially selected (Ghauri & Gronhaug, 2005). The use of multiple-case study designs in sport management involves applying replication logic (as opposed to sampling logic, which should not be used in case studies). The replication logic used in selecting the multiple-case design holds that "each case must be carefully selected so that it either (a) predicts similar results (a literal replication) or

(b) predicts contrasting results but for predictable reasons (a theoretical replication)" (Yin, 2003, p. 47). Therefore, a case study researcher would predict at the beginning of his study that the literal replications will produce similar results while the theoretical replications will produce contrasting results. Literal replications will generally result in less complicated case study research designs than will theoretical replications, since the former can be much more similar to the original study. Generally, as compared with theoretical replication, literal replication results in less complicated case study research design. Cousens' (1997) study of contextual changes in minor league baseball provides an example of using replication logic in multiple-case study research. Cousens selected five franchises (competing in the same league) and used replication logic in conducting interviews and analyzing documents across the five cases. She did so "in order to gain insight into the structure and operations of these organizations and the values and beliefs that underpin them" (p. 325). Through the use of the archetype theoretical construct, her study revealed similar and different organizational structures (i.e., sport-centered, business-centered, and indeterminate or transitional).

Once the researcher has established the study's boundaries (single-case or multiple-case), he or she needs to determine the phenomenon and context (Maylor & Blackmon, 2005). This is done by determining whether the study (single-case or multiple-case) will involve a holistic or embedded approach. A holistic case study design involves examining an overall organization, group, situation, or phenomenon. One example of a single-case study with one unit of analysis (thus a holistic single-case study) would be an examination of a Major League Soccer (MLS) team (e.g., Columbus Crew); an example of a multiple-case study with one unit of analysis (thus a holistic multiple-case study) would be an examination of several MLS teams (e.g., Chicago Fire, Real Salt Lake, Los Angeles Galaxy). A more complex case study research design involves the development of an embedded approach, in which the case study addresses several units of analysis. One example of a single-case study with several units of analysis (thus an embedded single-case study) would be an examination of one MLS team and its various departments and levels. A multiple-case study with several units of analysis (thus an embedded multiple-case study) would be an examination of several MLS teams and their various departments and levels. Thus, an embedded case study design involves examining an organization (or organizations), as well as various subunits, substructures, or sublevels. It is optimal to develop a research study that involves an embedded design, because the presence of several subunits means that the entire case study does not rest on one overall finding or analysis, but instead allows for specific findings to be made about specific subunits.

Evaluating Validity and Reliability

Validity and reliability are key aspects of quality control in case study research design. More specifically, as detailed by Smith (1998) and Yin (2003), the credibility or trustworthiness of a case study design can be evaluated according to four key criteria: construct validity, internal validity, external validity, and reliability. Construct validity, which helps reduce subjectivity, involves determining whether the case study design measures what it is supposed to measure according to the research aims and objectives of the study. Supported both empirically and theoretically, construct validity—which differs from face validity, in which the case study design simply appears to measure what it is supposed to measure—is increased when the researcher clearly defines and operationalizes what will be measured, uses multiple sources of evidence, and establishes a clear chain of evidence. In Slack and Hinings' (1992) case study of the phenomenon known as organizational change, the scholars provide a detailed explanation of how they operationalized and measured each concept (e.g., specialization, standardization, centralization, environment, resources) in their study. Their description of resources, for instance, explains that "all organizations need resources to operate, whether financial, human, or physical. To determine the type of resources available to each NSO [national sport organization], we collected data about such areas as sources of income, number of members, facility availability, and so on" (p. 120). Construct validity can also be enhanced by having others (e.g., subjects, scholars) review interview transcripts, study findings, and investigator analyses. For example, in Parent's (2008) study of operational evolution and other issues in sport organizing committees, she had interview transcripts "returned to interviewees so that they could add, modify, or delete any passage, thus increasing validity of the data" (p. 144).

Internal validity in case study research typically involves testing to determine whether correct inferences are being made; therefore, it tests whether findings can be attributed to another reason (another possibility or explanation). Internal valid-ity can be affected by history, maturation, testing, instrumentation, selection of variables, mortality, interaction, ambiguity, and a host of other influences. Researchers can increase internal validity by conducting repeated assessments, providing support from the literature, offering explanation building, doing pattern matching, using logic models, and conducting time series analyses. Parent and Foreman (2007) illustrate how these procedures can be used in their study of how sport organizations manage their identity, reputation, and image. The scholars made extensive use of tables in their data analysis "to help identify trends, highlight emerging patterns, and make comparisons across categories" (p. 25).

External validity involves determining whether the results can be generalized. As with any research endeavor, caution must be exercised when making generalizations. In their multiple-case study of sponsorship agreements in women's sport, for example, Shaw and Amis (2001) explain,

> While it is obviously problematic to generalize our findings beyond these immediate instances (cases), the rich data that we were able to gather did provide a very useful, and we believe not atypical, insight into the way in which these women's sport sponsorship agreements were conceived and utilized. (p. 230)

As noted earlier in this chapter, generalizing in case study research involves analytical generalization (e.g., comparing the results with theory). External validity can be supported by focusing on relationships between cases, using rival theories for single cases, using replications, and determining consistent patterns.

The fourth criterion by which the credibility of a case study design can be evaluated is reliability, which involves determining whether similar results and conclusions would be found if another sport management researcher conducted the study. Reliability can be established in case study research by documenting (thoroughly operationalizing), using specific procedures (e.g., using a study protocol), and developing a database for the research.

Research Preparation

Before sport management investigators begin their data collection, they need to address several areas of preparation that make up the second phase of the case study research process: skill development, training, creation of case study protocol, screening of potential cases, and the pilot study. The following discussion uses Yin's (2003) explanations to examine these five areas of case study preparation as they apply to sport management research endeavors.

First, the case study researcher needs to develop a number of skills in order to be unbiased and objective, work with a variety of sources, engage in a data collection process characterized by continuous interaction between theory and data, and be prepared for unexpected results (Bickman & Rog, 1998; Yin, 2003). The researcher should be trained in conducting interviews (e.g., what questions to ask and how to ask them; see chapter 8 for more), using a variety of methodologies (e.g., document analysis, observation), and data collection processes. Therefore, the skills required of the case study researcher include being flexible, adaptable, objective, and unbiased, as well as being able to understand and synthesize issues, ask questions, and listen. For instance, regarding flexibility and adaptability, depending on where the data collection takes the researcher, she has to be open to making changes (e.g., following new leads, adding additional cases) throughout the process. Regarding objectivity and being unbiased, the researcher needs to have a grasp of the issues involved but should not bring a preconceived position to the work; rather, he should be open to contradictory findings. One way to reduce bias is by presenting preliminary results and interpretations of the study to scholars and other experts who can provide balance—if the researcher is willing to receive their critiques, alternative explanations, and suggestions for additional data collection.

Researchers can develop the skills required for case study research through reading, cultivating high-quality research strategies, consulting with experienced researchers, and conducting pilot studies. As Stake (1995) explains in *The Art of Case Study Research*, experience is an essential qualification for researchers engaged in case study investigations. Through experience, the case study researcher develops a sense of what activities will result in significant understanding and becomes skilled at "recognizing good sources of data, and consciously and unconsciously testing out the veracity of their eyes and the robustness of their interpretations. It [case study work] requires [both] sensitivity and skepticism" (p. 50). Although novice case study researchers can develop some understanding of case study methodology by reading textbooks, attending research class discussions, and engaging in dialogue about case study research with peers and mentors,

"expertise comes largely through reflective practice" (p. 50). Therefore, to develop skills and expertise in sport management case study research you should engage in case study work and reflect on the process and your involvement. You can do so simply by reflecting on how you built the theoretical foundation of your research, how you designed the case study, how you facilitated the study and collected the data, and how your interpreted the findings.

The second area of preparation for research involves training specific to the selected case study. The lead investigator and any research assistants should have a clear understanding of the study, its purpose and questions, and the possible confirmatory (supportive) or contradictory data that may be collected. Thus, the training should address the study's purpose, questions, case possibilities, and steps, as well as relevant theory and literature, field procedures, types of evidence that will be collected, and reading materials (e.g., other case studies and related articles).

This training should also address the creation of the case study protocol—the third key task in case study preparation—which increases the study's reliability and thus is a vital step in case study work (Bickman & Rog, 1998). The protocol helps throughout the data collection process because it outlines procedures and rules and thus guides the researcher in reporting the results of the study. As Yin (2003) notes, the protocol includes a project overview addressing purpose, objectives, propositions, context, substantive issues, related theory and policy, relevant readings; an operationalization of the field procedures that addresses setting, information sources, schedules, data collection activities, procedures, resources needed (e.g., computer, paper); a listing of the inquiry questions, both general (regarding what will be collected and why) and specific (e.g., asked of interviewees, individual cases); and a report guide (with reference list) addressing how the manuscript will be outlined and formatted, who the intended audience is, and how evidence will be documented. Although this protocol should be followed, the case study researcher in sport management has flexibility throughout the process. Therefore, the case study protocol should be viewed not as a strict guideline but as a process outline and overall agenda.

The fourth key task in the preparation stage involves screening and selecting cases. If only one possible case is available, then this preparation stage is quite simple. For example, a key factor in Sack and Johnson's (1996) single-case study of the Volvo International tennis tournament was the event's location in New Haven, Connecticut. It was easy to select this event and site because Sack and Johnson's study examined theories related to urban politics and because "New Haven has been the site of classic studies of community power over the past 40 years" (p. 2). For many sport management case studies, however, the investigator must choose between many possible cases. For example, for Shaw's (2006) multiple-case study of gender relations, gendered social processes, and sport organizations, she had to select from more than 50 national governing bodies (NGBs) of sport in England. As she notes, "it would have been impossible to collect the required depth of data from them all within the timeframe of this research." Thus, she approached the screening and selection process by first sending a letter of invitation to NGBs "based on a desire to reflect the various ages of these organizations." Eventually, she explains, "after various negotiations regarding the time spent at each organization, and levels of access, three NGBs agreed to participate in the research" (p. 516). Based on the study's objectives and theoretical framework, a primary motivation in selecting the final three NGBs was the fact that they were connected with Sport England (a governmental agency focused on sport development), whose funding criteria included a gender equity requirement.

Researchers can also screen cases for multiple-case study designs by researching the possibilities, talking with knowledgeable people or stakeholders about the potential cases, collecting documentation about the various possibilities, and determining which cases fit the study's purpose and criteria of selection. If many possibilities remain after this process has been completed, the investigator will need to employ random case selection. It should be noted that a case study often requires cooperation and accessibility (Zikmund, 1991) from the organization or via personal relationships or key informants in order to examine the organization's history and inside information. As Shaw and Hoeber (2003) explain in their case study of the influence of gendered discourses in three sport organizations, "the lead author gained access to two of the organizations through personal contacts and to the third organization through a colleague" (p. 355). It is difficult to gain access to company records, reports, and confidential information without assistance from insiders or company and personal contacts. Furthermore, conducting interviews with key stakeholders (e.g., owners, employees) requires cooperation. Take, for instance, Sack and Nadim's (2002) study of a sport licensing company's history

and management decisions. The investigators were able to secure access to "a wide variety of sources" (p. 39), including interviews with company and industry insiders, annual industry publications, financial analyst reports, and the company's internal documents and initial public offering prospectus. Although a sport management case study can still be conducted (e.g., through alternative sources) even without accessibility and cooperation, the data collection process is much more difficult in such instances.

The fifth and final task in case study preparation is to conduct a pilot study, which should help the researcher clarify both substantive (e.g., content, issues) and procedural (e.g., design, questions, logistics) aspects of the study. Similar to the selection of the main case study, often used criteria for selecting the pilot study are convenience, accessibility, and proximity.

Data Collection

Conducting the study—or collecting the data—is the third phase of sport management case study work. This phase involves carrying out the various aspects of the case study research design formulated in the first phase. Although the case study process needs to involve certain steps, the absence of a specific standardized procedure for this research methodology means that investigators must be flexible in their efforts to obtain all the data and information they need (Zikmund, 1991). For instance, the case study researcher will commence her or his investigation with a specific theory in mind but along the way may find data and information that conflict with the theory (Velde et al., 2004). If used effectively, this flexible and in-depth nature of case study work allows the researcher to find valuable information often left unsecured when using other research methodologies (Kirk, 1995). At the same time, because case study investigators deal with unique situations, phenomena, research objectives, and subjects, the case study process is an unstructured research endeavor. Therefore, investigators must be flexible in their research activities and data collection procedures and also cautious about generalizing their findings (Zikmund, 1991).

In the data collection phase, the researcher is securing answers to the questions formulated in the first phase (case study design). The answers come from the literature study, interview data, historical inquiry, document analysis, and other sources of evidence (e.g., physical evidence, cultural artifacts, sport films, and video and audio recordings). Sport management case studies typically involve collecting data from four main **evidence sources**—interviews, observation, historical records and archives, and documents—that we will now explore on the basis of Yin's (2003) work.

Data Sources

Interviews, which are explained in detail in chapter 8, are used in most case study investigations. Case study interviews come in a variety of forms, ranging from open-ended, semi-structured, and unstructured questions to structured and focused questions. For example, in their study of the English Rugby Union, O'Brien and Slack (2004) used 43 semi-structured interviews as their primary data: "As the interviews were semi-structured, questions were not necessarily asked in any firmly prescribed order," the researchers explain. "Questions centered on the constructs outlined in the previous Theoretical Background section, and addressed changes in structure and strategy, interorganizational linkages and resource flows, and particular types of diffusion processes evolving in the field" (p. 22). Shaw's (2006) investigation of national governing bodies in sport used unstructured questions: "Unstructured interviews were also a useful source of data during the participant observation phases and during breaks between interviews," notes Shaw, who considered the unstructured interview "a useful method to use in coffee breaks, before and after interviews, or just when interacting with participants in a more social manner" (p. 519). Case study researchers can also use structured questions in the form of a survey; in fact, Hata and Umezawa (1995) use a questionnaire as their only instrument to examine the use of facilities, programs, and equipment in their case study of a Japanese fitness club. Regardless of the form of interview used in case study research, the strengths of this type of data collection include the fact that interviews can be targeted and tend to yield good insight. Their weaknesses reside in the fact that they can be biased, inaccurate, and reflexive (Yin, 2003). As Long et al. (2004) acknowledged in their study of sponsorship decision making within Canadian university athletic departments, "familiarity with the individuals responsible for the decision can lead to biases in data collection." They added, however, "that after [developing] appropriate qualitative data collection protocols, extant relationships facilitated the collection of richer, valid data." Thus, what was potentially a weakness (the interview technique) was turned into a strength; specifically, since "the

interviewer was knowledgeable of the operations, . . . interviews could focus on the issues at hand, . . . (and) coaches and administrators felt they could trust the interviewer" (p. 140).

Observation is the second frequently used source in case study research in sport management. It involves making field visits and can take the form of direct observation or participant observation. The strengths of observation include reality and contextuality. Its weaknesses involve time consumption, selectivity (e.g., a specific site for observation must be selected), cost, and reflexivity (e.g., researcher must be aware of and evaluate how her involvement has influenced the process being observed) (Yin, 2003). Observation methodology is covered in chapter 9, but the investigation by Sam and Jackson (2006) provides a perfect example of how a sport management case study can integrate observation techniques. In their examination of New Zealand's Ministerial Taskforce on Sport, Fitness, and Leisure, the researchers observed 10 meetings of the task force. Their observations, "produced a mass of field notes, informed and organized according to the project's theoretical frameworks. Ultimately, the aim of observing these meetings was to investigate how both ideas . . . and institutional elements . . . influenced the task force's policy" (pp. 371–372). For this study, the observations both highlighted how the policy process was influenced by organizational structures and documented the political transactions that took place around the task force.

Historical records and archival research constitute the third main source of data in case study work (see chapter 11 for discussion of the methodology associated with these sources). Historical and archival research in sport management case studies can include analyses of sources ranging from personal autobiographies and diaries to organizational charts, minutes, reports, financial spreadsheets, and other business records. For example, the collection of archival materials was one of "two main data-collection steps" in Parent's (2008) case study of organizing committee for the Pan American Games (the Pan American Games Host Society [PAGS]). Parent, who also conducted interviews for her case study, notes that she collected "99 archival documents about PAGS and its stakeholders" from sources such as mass media, organizational Web sites, and documents (e.g., meeting notes, diary entries, summary reports, annual reports). She gathered "data from archival material to better understand the organizing committee structure and to draw a preliminary list of issues, as well as to support, complement, and build on the various aspects raised by the interviews" (p. 143). Overall,

Yin (2003) notes that the advantages of using historical and archival records hinge on the fact that they are stable, unobtrusive, exact, and broad. Their weaknesses involve retrievability, access, selectivity bias (e.g., certain documents may have been discarded for a variety of reasons), and reporting bias.

The fourth case study source—document analysis—is examined in various degrees in other chapters in this textbook. One should consult Yin (2003) for more detailed points regarding the use of documents in case study research because, as Yin notes, "documentary information is likely to be relevant to every case study topic" (p. 85). For example, in Mason and Slack's (2003) study of agents in professional hockey, the researchers note that "data were obtained primarily through the collection of industry documents such as collective bargaining agreements, agent certification programs, salary figures, and state and federal documents" (p. 44). The researchers note that in addition to the industry documentation, they also searched trade publications, legal journals, and various popular press sources. Overall, the documentary sources examined in sport management case study research include materials such as organizational minutes, personal letters, written reports, administrative documents, internal records, newspaper articles, academic literature, and business newsletters. Documents are used in case study work primarily to expand upon and corroborate other sources, and Stevens (2006) uses the phrase "supplemental data" to describe her use of documents in a case study of the merger of the Canadian Amateur Hockey Association and Hockey Canada. The documents addressed in her study include historical materials, "commissioned organizational audits, administrative materials and communiqués, minutes of meetings (such as Board of Directors, Council, and Executive Committee sessions), annual written reports, published program materials, press releases, and newspaper clippings" (p. 80). An often-used methodological approach related to document analysis is content analysis, which is examined in chapter 9.

Collection Requirements

The data collection process for a case study often involves both qualitative sources (e.g., interviews, document analyses) and quantitative sources (e.g., surveys, census records). As Maylor and Blackmon (2005) explain, the data collection process generally involves indirect and unobtrusive methods (e.g., document analysis, historical data) and direct and potentially obtrusive methods (e.g., inter-views, questionnaires, observation). Regardless of the general methodological approach chosen (e.g., qualitative or quantitative) and the specific sources used (e.g., documents, observations, interviews), all gathering of case study evidence in sport management should be guided by three essential requirements based on Yin's (2003) work: the use of multiple sources, the creation of a database, and the establishment of a chain of evidence.

The first requirements that the sport management investigator should use as many sources as possible. Case study analyses necessarily involve collecting evidence from a variety of sources (Bickman & Rog, 1998)—and the more sources used, the better. As Yin (2003) notes, one "major strength of case study data collection is the opportunity to use many different sources of evidence" (p. 97). The use of multiple evidentiary sources involves a process of triangulation, in which data sources complement each other, blend together, and converge on the same findings. Through data triangulation, the researcher asks the multiple data sources (e.g., interviews, documents, observation, historical information) the same research questions in order to corroborate findings. As a result, more than one source of evidence is used to support a particular finding or conclusion. Take, for instance, Sam and Jackson's (2006) study of how the structures of a sport task force influence policy outcomes. The researchers were able to identify and interpret their findings based on several sources. As they note, "no single source of data was taken by itself as evidence of a particular pattern. . . . '[E]vidence' was not drawn from a content analysis of any one source of data but rather from a process of induction from all available texts: observations of consultations (e.g., field notes), interview transcripts, as well as follow-up e-mails and phone calls" (p. 372). In this manner, the convergent use of multiple data sources enables researchers to secure more robust findings and arrive at conclusions that are more accurate, reliable, unbiased, and convincing (Jankowicz, 2005).

A database—the second requirement of data collection in case study research—provides another way to increase a study's reliability. The researcher assembles and organizes the evidence and places the findings in data files. Yin (2003) notes that these files can involve notes (e.g., transcripts of interviews, records of observations, details of document analyses), documents collected throughout the process (e.g., annotated bibliography, copies of reports), tabular materials (e.g., survey results, quantitative observation tabulations), and narratives (e.g., raw answers to protocol questions). In arranging the notes, for example, the researcher can place or classify them in any order (e.g., chronological, sequential, topical) so that they can be retrieved and understood by the researcher or other researchers. As explained by Bickman and Rog (1998), these files—which constitute the case study database—are used as a formal way to document the case study evidence so that it can be reviewed by others. Creating the database also helps the researcher identify themes and insights that can be used in the analysis and discussion sections of the study.

The last requirement in case study data collection is the chain of evidence. Regardless of the data sources used, the researcher should provide a detailed account of the evidentiary process used in the study. This step—which details the process from the creation of the study's questions to the development of the researcher's conclusions based on the evidence—addresses the subject of construct validity and increases a study's reliability, since other researchers can examine the process. This chain of evidence connects the study's purpose, questions, data, and conclusions. It should be revealed through proper and complete citation of sources used, discussion of where and when evidence was collected, illustration of the research design and how procedures were followed and data were correctly collected, and discussion of how the research design and protocol related to the research aims and questions (Bickman & Rog, 1998). This type of chain of evidence is provided in most articles published in peer-reviewed academic journals. One of the best examples is the published case study by Chalip and Leyns (2002). In two lengthy tables spread across three pages, the authors illustrate the research questions, study participants, methodologies, data collection, and key findings associated with each of the four studies in their multiple-case study design. Scholars may also simply illustrate the chain of evidence in paragraph form across several sections of the paper. Regardless of the formatting (e.g., table, paragraph), the presentation of the chain of evidence allows case study researchers to reveal how they moved "from one part of the case study process to another, with clear cross-referencing to methodological procedures and to the resulting evidence" (Yin, 2003, p. 105).

Data Analysis

The fourth phase of case study work in sport management involves analyzing the findings. Here, the researcher examines the data, uses it to address the study's propositions, and assesses how the findings help forward the study's research aims and objectives. According to Yin (2003), case study analysis "depends on an investigator's own style of rigorous thinking, along with the sufficient presentation of evidence and careful consideration of alternative interpretations" (p. 110). Thus, the best case study analyses are accomplished when the researcher exhaustively examines all of the available evidence, explores all possible alternative explanations, focuses on the most significant findings and issues, rigorously separates the findings from the interpretations, and uses and demonstrates expert knowledge of the subject matter.

Researchers can use software to aid in coding and categorizing some data. For example, in Parent and Foreman's (2007) multiple-case study of two major events held in Canada (the 1999 Pan American Games and the 2001 Jeux de la Francophonie) the authors note that "a total of 542,333 words were analyzed with the use of ATLAS.ti 5.0" (p. 23) and "a combination of pattern-matching and inductive content analysis" (p. 25). ATLAS.ti software is designed for use in qualitative research in the social sciences. More information about coding software is provided in chapter 9. Once coding has been completed, the analysis of case study findings typically requires the use of a **general analytic strategy** wherein the researcher examines, categorizes, tabulates, summarizes, condenses, and, if necessary, recombines the data (Bickman & Rog, 1998). Yin (2003) identifies three general analytic strategies that help the researcher treat findings objectively, produce strong conclusions, and rule out alternative explanations. The three strategies are

1. relying on theoretical propositions,
2. creating a rival explanation framework, and
3. developing a case description.

The first general analytic strategy involves relying on theoretical propositions. This strategy ensures that the researcher's collection and analysis of data are guided by the study's propositions, which provide the basis for the study's objectives and research design and which reflect the investigator's research questions, literature review, and hypotheses. For instance, in Stevens' (2006) case study of organizational change in sport (in this case, a merger of amateur hockey organizations), the researcher notes that "data analysis was based on a priori themes drawn from the theoretical perspective for the study, as well as emergent themes that expanded these concepts" (p. 81). Babiak (2007) described a similar approach: "The data [were] analyzed according to the a priori categories of [a theoretical] framework. This process allowed the researcher to categorize answers into areas previously identified but also allowed for the opportunity for alternative themes to emerge" (p. 347).

The second strategy involves creating a rival explanation framework, in which rival explanations are defined and tested by the researcher in the data analysis process. This strategy is illustrated by Mason and Slack (2001), who examined six types of monitoring activities aimed at reducing opportunism among agents in professional hockey. The researchers' analytic strategy relied on a rival explanation framework as they presented "a summary of agent monitoring mechanisms identified in this study, the inherent problems specific to professional hockey that emerged from an analysis of each mechanism, the comments and opinions of stakeholders in the industry, and other industry data" (p. 116). As the researchers note in their conclusion, "using agency theory as a framework, this research has shown that all of the available moni-

toring solutions to agent opportunism in hockey are flawed, although NHLPA [National Hockey League Players' Association] regulation appears the best alternative" (p. 129). Just as Mason and Slack did in this study, sport management researchers should address and reject as many rival explanations as possible. Potential rival explanations may be related to the study's design (e.g., null hypotheses, threats to validity, researcher biases) or to actual situations in the form of direct rivals (where another reason accounts for the outcome), commingled rivals (where other reasons help account for the outcome), rival theories (where another theory explains the results), and societal rivals (where other social trends are involved).

The third general analytic strategy involves developing a case description, in which the researcher frames the analysis (e.g., organizes, describes, identifies causal linkages). For instance, the analysis of a single-case study design often involves writing the details of the case as a descriptive summary

▪ ▪ ▪ ▪ ▪ Beyond General Analytic Strategies ▪ ▪ ▪ ▪ ▪

In addition to these three general analytic strategies, Yin (2003) notes that many types of techniques can be used in conjunction with the general case study analysis strategies. These techniques can help the researcher establish internal and external validity for the case study. One of the most commonly used techniques in both single-case and multiple-case research designs in sport management is pattern matching, in which the researcher compares a predicted pattern with an empirical (actual) pattern. For example, in Smart and Wolfe's (2000) study of intercollegiate athletics, the researchers took a conceptual strategic management perspective—the resource-based view (RBV)—and applied (matched) it to one aspect (a football program) within an intercollegiate athletic department. As they explain, their "purpose was to determine whether the RBV contributes to our understanding of intercollegiate athletic program success" (p. 137). Thus, they compared the predicted pattern—the resource components of RBV (i.e., physical capital, human capital, and organizational capital)—to the empirical or actual pattern (the physical, human, and organizational resources of one university's football program).

Other popular analytic techniques for use in single-case and multiple-case studies include explanation building (using narrative and theory to establish causal linkages through a logical sequence of activities or events), time series analyses (answering how and why questions by analyzing how variables or events are affected over time and comparing these trends with theoretical or rival trends), and logic models (establishing multiple cause-and-effect patterns over time and linking them through a linear or multilinear sequence of events). For example, Amis et al. (2004) used the explanation building technique in their examination of change and transitional processes in sport organizations. They analyzed their findings by applying their theoretical propositions about interests, power, and capacity across a longitudinal dimension. Multiple-case researchers can also use the analytic technique known as cross-case synthesis, in which the researcher analyzes each case in the multiple-case design, searches for patterns across the cases, identifies themes, and looks for similarities and differences (Maylor & Blackmon, 2005).

(Maylor & Blackmon, 2005). For example, in Sack and Nadim's (2002) case study of a sportswear company's slide into bankruptcy, the researchers provided a descriptive summary that included a conceptual framework based on industry competition, an overview of the sport licensing industry, a history of the sport company that addressed its various stages (e.g., pre-public, public, affected by industry forces, strategizing, bankrupt), and an overall discussion and conclusion.

Overall, a complete case study analysis in sport management involves the following components: describing the evidence, analyzing the findings according to the study's propositions and research questions, developing an analytical framework, explaining (and then supporting or rejecting) rival or alternative interpretations, and comparing the results and analysis with other published research. As with data collection, the data analysis process itself should be flexible; in other words, neither data collection nor data analysis should be a rigid or inflexible process in case study work in sport management. For example, as O'Brien and Slack (2003) explain in their case study of professionalization in sport, they generated a coding scheme "a priori to fieldwork," but "further themes emerged while data were being collected" (p. 426). In addition, their data analysis "was an iterative process, constantly moving back and forth between theory and data" (p. 431). Furthermore, as suggested by Bickman and Rog (1998), case study data analysis should include a procedure wherein the conclusions are examined and reviewed by knowledgeable scholars and key informants, such as those interviewed for the study, or the main stakeholders involved. Yin (2003) notes that these reviewers should examine the draft in order to verify that the proper steps were taken and that whatever is being reported as fact and as evidence is indeed accurate; this process increases the accuracy of a study and thus its construct validity as well. In cases where reviewers disagree with the researcher's conclusions and interpretations, the investigator is not obligated to make any changes; however, any disputations of the facts of the study or related findings from the data collection process should be settled.

Case Study Report

The case study is not complete until the researcher has arranged it in a logical structure and written a complete case study report (e.g., journal article, dissertation). Putting together a high-quality final structure and report is vital if the study is to build the body of knowledge in sport management, provide sport management practitioners with useful information, or compare the case study with other case studies (Velde et al., 2004). Therefore, the fifth and final phase of case study research in sport management is to lay out and compose the manuscript. Parts of the case study can even be written up before the completion of data collection and analysis; specifically, the literature review, theoretical framework, and methodology can be written in the early and middle stages of the study.

The layout and composition phase of the sport management case study involves both the general composition and the specific illustrative formatting. The general composition of the case study report is where the researcher describes the case, usually by using a single-narrative format (for a single-case study) or a multiple-narrative approach (for a multiple-case study). The narrative can be organized by chronology, focused on key actors, or focused on processes (Maylor & Blackmon, 2005). Two other approaches (not very common in sport management case studies) are the question-and-answer and the cross-case formats; an excellent example of the question-and-answer format can be found in Slack and Hinings' (1992) study of organizational change in sport. Once the researcher has decided on the general composition approach—that is, narrative, question-and-answer, or cross-case—she or he must then choose a specific illustrative structure to organize the various sections of the study. Let us now use Yin's (2003) work to consider the most commonly used structures in case study research.

One of the most common ways to organize a case study manuscript is through an unsequenced structure, meaning that the researchers do present their case study in a particular order but could just as easily rearrange the sections and present the case study in another sequence. For example, the sections of the case study of the Harlem Globetrotters by Fielding et al. (1999) could have been placed in a variety of orders. Following the historical and brand management sections, the case study included sections addressing the company's mission statement, positioning strategy, corporate partnerships, product, team mascot, fan demographics, brand loyalty, guiding principles of the ownership, promotions, revenue generation, corporate culture, and success measures. Other than the two beginning sections (history and theory), the other sections could have been placed in a variety of other sequences and the case study would still have been just as complete and strong as it is with the structure used by the researchers.

Thus, an unsequenced structure simply means that while the sport management case study needs to be complete, the order in which the sections are presented is not critical. Another example is Berrett and Slack's (1999) multiple-case study of sport sponsorship, which revealed several influences that affected sponsorship activities (yet were out of the control) of the 28 companies studied. In illustrating these influences, Berrett and Slack could have arranged them in various orders. They chose, however, to structure their study by illustrating the competitive environment and then the institutional environment with closer examinations of nearby companies, mimetic (i.e., modeling, imitative) pressures, pressures from personal friendships and relationships, and normative pressures related to the training of the decision makers. The researchers could have placed the sections in a different order and the study would have been just as strong. Similarly, if a researcher uses the unsequenced structure for a case study of a single-sport organization, he or she is not forced to arrange the various sections in a particular order; therefore, the researcher could place the sections regarding the organization's history, development, ownership, stakeholders, consumers, marketing approach, product line, structure, and finances in a variety of orders.

Another common method used to organize sport management case studies is the theory-building structure, in which each section reveals a new aspect of the theory being examined. For example, in an examination of the structural arrangement of minor league baseball franchises, Cousens (1997) used the concept of archetypes as her theoretical framework. With a theory-building structure, she used the sections of her manuscript to explain how the five professional franchises in her multiple-case study design each illustrated one of three conceptual templates: sport-centered archetype, business-centered archetype, or indeterminate archetype. Similarly, the sections in Hill and Kikulis' (1999) study of decision making in university athletics were structured according to the conceptual elements (complexity, politicality, rules of the game) of decision making. Another example is the study of the National Collegiate Athletic Association (NCAA) by Mitchell, Crosset, and Barr (1999). The theory-building structure used in this study follows the model of compliance strategies, which includes punitive, remunerative, preventive, generative, cognitive, and normative strategic actions. Thus, through the use of a theory-building structure, the cases examined in these three studies reveal new and unique aspects of the theory (archetypes, deci-sion making, or compliance strategies) examined in each study.

Two other possible illustrative approaches are the linear-analytic and the chronological structures. In the linear-analytic structure, the study follows a sequence that presents the issue being studied, the theory involved, the literature review, the methodology, the findings, the analyses, the conclusions, the recommendations, and the implications. Kikulis et al. (1995b) examined 36 national sport organizations in their multiple-case study of organizational change in sport; in their report, they included the following sections after their introduction: conceptual framework, methods (including two subsections: sample and data collection; measures and data analysis), results and discussion, and conclusions. Many of the case study reports in sport management academic journals use the linear-analytic structure. In contrast, the chronological approach is used when a researcher wants to look for trends or causes of change in a sport organization or system over a period of time (Velde et al., 2004). For example, in their case study of a tennis tournament, Sack and Johnson (1996) employ the chronological structure to address event origins, strategies to attract the event, stresses, eventual agreement, and organized opposition.

Other possible structures used less commonly in case study reports in sport management include the comparative structure and the suspense structure. In the comparative structure, the researcher compares alternative explanations of the case by repeating or describing the case study from different viewpoints or in terms of different models. This approach can be used when a researcher is repeating a case study but offering alternative perspectives or looking at the study from different angles in order to test theories (Bickman & Rog, 1998). In the suspense structure, the researcher provides the outcomes of the case study first, then analyzes and explains the possible reasons for the study's outcomes; this approach reverses the linear-analytical style.

Yin (2003) explains that a high-quality case study in sport management should have several characteristics. First, it should be unique and should offer some theoretical, policy, or practical significance. For example, Mason, Thibault, and Misener's (2006) case study makes a unique contribution to the academic field and provides practical significance in the management of sport. These researchers use agency theory to examine behavior, management activities, decision-making processes, corruption, and reform attempts by members of the International Olympic Committee (IOC). They illustrate the corruption within the organization, provide explanations of behavior by IOC members and reform attempts within the organization, evaluate how likely the reforms are to reduce similar behavior, and use their theoretical construct "to explain opportunism in this context and contribute to identifying agency problems and understanding how they can be addressed within other nonprofit sport organization environments" (p. 54). Thus, even with its single-case design, the study makes important contributions to both the academic and practical areas of sport management.

The second characteristic of a high-quality sport management case study is completeness, which involves establishing clear study boundaries and an exhaustive and sufficient collection of evidence (i.e., one showing that the researcher studied all possible information). Completeness also means that the study should not have ended because the researcher encountered nonresearch constraints (e.g., inadequate resources, running out of time). The third quality characteristic (already addressed in this chapter) is that the sport management case study should address alternative or rival perspectives (e.g., cultural views, theories, variations among the study's stakeholders). The fourth characteristic of high-quality sport management case studies is that they should present the best and most relevant findings in a neutral manner—that is, present data that support and challenge. The fifth characteristic is that the report is presented in a well-written and engaging manner; in other words, the case study should be written in such a way that those who come into contact with the manuscript will want to continue reading it.

In addition to these five characteristics of high-quality sport management case studies, sport management researchers should ask themselves four key questions upon the completion of their case study research project (Maylor & Blackmon, 2005): (1) Have they conducted the research in a systematic way? (2) Do the narrative, conclusions, and interpretations make sense? (3) Does the evidence they found support the narrative, conclusions, and interpretations they provide? (4) Does their case study reveal or illustrate something interesting and unique? The answers to these questions tell the researchers whether they have conducted a high-quality and thorough sport management case study.

Summary

There are many ways to collect qualitative data, and one of the most common methodological approaches in sport management research is the case study. This social science methodology is conducted in real or practical sport management settings. The studies typically examine in detail a certain phenomenon in sport management. In addition to examining and solving practical issues in the sport industry, case study research in sport management can also involve testing and creating theoretical concepts. The three types of case study research are the explanatory, exploratory, and descriptive approaches. In terms of design, the two major types are the single-case study and the multiple-case study. A case study generally involves an in-depth examination of a single case involving many variables and data collected from multiple sources (e.g., observations of sport managers, surveys of sport event participants, analyses of organizational documents). This chapter covers case study design, processes, and theory development. It also examines how a case study researcher evaluates reliability and validity in a case study and lays out the initial preparatory activities (skill development, training, establishing protocol, selecting cases) necessary for conducting a case study. The data collection stage of case study research in sport management typically involves four main data sources: interviews, observations, historical records, and documents. Case study data analysis techniques typically require the use of a general analytic strategy, in which the researcher examines, categorizes, tabulates, summarizes, condenses, and, if necessary, recombines the data. The chapter concludes with discussion of layout, formatting, and composition of case study reports.

Selected text reprinted from K. Misener
and D.S. Mason, 2009, " Fostering community
development through sporting events strategies:
An examination of urban regime perceptions,"
Journal of Sport Management 23(6), 770-794.

Access the full article online at
www.humankinetics.com/products/all-products/Research-
Methods-and-Design-in-Sport-Management.

ABSTRACT

This article examines the perceptions of members of urban regimes in three cities: Edmonton, Manchester, and Melbourne, regarding the use sporting events for broad-based community outcomes. In Edmonton, members of the urban regime interviewed did not perceive the sporting events strategy to be directly tied to community development objectives. In Manchester and Melbourne, regime members believed that the use of events for development was uniquely tied to communities and community development goals. In addition, regime members in the latter two cities provided examples of symbolic attempts to foster community around the sporting events strategies. While this study could not reveal whether attempts to meet the needs of local communities were being achieved through the sporting events strategies, it is at least encouraging to note that those who control resources and conceive of, oversee, and implement growth strategies within cities view community development as important to these strategies.

TEXT EXCERPTS

A collective case study design was used to explore each of the cities (Stake, 1995). This design employs a joint study of a number of cases to investigate a phenomenon, general population, or general condition which can enhance theory building. Edmonton, Manchester, and Melbourne were chosen for this cross-national research project because they have developed comprehensive event strategies, host-ing a variety of sporting events of different sizes and levels, and have used these events as an integral part of civic development strategies.

....

After establishing the existence of regimes in each city, and classifying them according to the types developed by Stoker and Mossberger (1994), the current study employs in-depth interviews and archival data to examine the perceptions of members of urban regimes in the three cities regarding issues of corporate social responsibility surrounding the events strategy.

■■■■■■■■■■■■■■■■■

Interview questions were developed based on the initial analysis of documentation. In addition, the theoretical framework guided the interview questions, focusing on the sporting event strategy, community participation and partnerships, social inclusion, and city specific community development concerns. These issues are consistent with achieving active and sustainable local communities based on social justice and mutual respect, and finding ways to change the power structures to remove the barriers that prevent people from participating in the issues that affect their lives (McMillan & Chavis, 1986).

■■■■■■■■■■■■■■■■■

Over one hundred documents were collected, representing more than 2300 pages of supporting data. All data were manually coded (Glaser & Strauss, 1967) and managed using N7 qualitative software (Richards, 2005). Themes and key issues that emerged from the data sets were critically analyzed to explore the perceptions of regime members and reflect upon instances where growth coalitions sought to meet the interests of local community. The following results section will present findings from the coded data for each city, as well as representative examples supporting these data.

DISCUSSION QUESTIONS

1. Is the case study research design used here a holistic single-case, an embedded single-case, a holistic multiple-case, or an embedded multiple-case design?

2. What types of data collection sources are used in this study?

3. Can you think of other data (evidence) sources that might have been appropriate to use in this case study research?

4. How were the interviews developed? What guided the interview development process?

5. Referring to the Data Analysis section of the text, how do you think the data in this study were coded? What type of software was used? How do you think the themes and key issues emerged?

6. Did the authors provide enough information? Is there anything else you wish they had addressed in order to help you better understand the case study method and process used in their investigation?

Historical Research

Learning Objectives

After studying this chapter, you should be able to do the following:

- Describe how sport management practitioners can apply the results of historical research
- Discuss the essential tools and materials needed to commence a historical research project
- Understand the importance and considerations of topic selection
- Compare the two major categories of source evidence: primary and secondary sources
- Describe objectivity, reliability, and the factors involved in doing data analysis in historical research
- Compare the two major categories of historical writing

Sport management students have unique needs and interests regarding the use and study of historical aspects and personalities related to the sport industry. As future sport managers, you need to be able to establish and connect historical facts about your sport organization and your organization's industry segment. Doing so enables you to ask the right historical and contextual questions (e.g., What are the past failures and successes of the company and its personnel? How did the company get to its present situation? What is the historical relationship of labor and management? What stages of the business life cycle has the company experienced?), and the answers to these questions give you perspective and guide you in your decision-making processes and strategic planning activities. As Harvard business history professor Richard Tedlow has stated, "studying history helps give you some idea of the domain over which managers actually do have power and influence. It helps you see where you can have an effect. It helps you understand what happened—and what can happen" (Chandler, McCraw, McDonald, Tedlow, & Vietor, 1986, p. 87). With all this in mind, any discussion of qualitative research in sport management research must address historical methodology. Other chapters in this section of the book cover other qualitative research approaches in sport management: surveys (chapter 7), interviews (chapter 8), observation (chapter 9), case studies (chapter 10), and legal research (chapter 12).

 Historical inquiry is an important aspect of research across all disciplines, including the academic fields associated with sport. In fact, numerous scholarly publications (e.g., *International Journal of the History of Sport, Sport History Review, Journal of Sport History*) are devoted entirely to sport history. In a technical sense, historical research often involves searching depositories, digging in archives (i.e., locations that house historical evidence), interviewing people (for contemporary historical topics), examining news sources, exploring museums and libraries, examining business holdings, investigating private collections, and performing other searches and activities. At a basic level, however, the work of a historian is to tell a story, and sport historians are interested, of course, in telling stories related to some aspect of sport. For example, Bob Stewart, Matthew Nicholson, and Geoff Dickson's (2005) analysis of the Australian Football League is a story of "the polices and strategies that were employed by the AFL to achieve its national development aspirations" (p. 96). The sport in which the most historical stories are told is baseball, followed by golf, football,

hockey, basketball, and tennis (McClelland, 2006).

Therefore, at its foundation, any history of sport management events, activities, organizations, or people is simply a story told about an aspect of the sport industry. These stories can range as far back as an ancient historical analysis of crowd control efforts during events at the Roman Colosseum or be as recent as a contemporary historical examination of funding and legislative developments surrounding the support and construction of New Meadowlands Stadium, the newly opened $1.8 billion football stadium for the New York Jets and New York Giants in East Rutherford, New Jersey. Historians who write about sport management tell their stories by researching, describing, and analyzing such topics as past sport industry organizations, events, activities, and personnel. Alexis Smith's (2007) historical story concerns past and present pervasiveness of tobacco products in baseball advertising, as well as the use of tobacco by stakeholders (e.g., players) and the accommodations and silent approval given by the management of professional baseball. Smith believes "that despite the public silence of Major League Baseball against Big Tobacco, the century-old collusion between the baseball industry and tobacco companies continues to thrive at the expense of both players and fans" (p. 122). Therefore, as evidenced here, sport management historians' stories actually help create versions of the past because they must choose a particular focus (e.g., event, person, time frame, topic), select from many options what they consider to be important about the topic, decide what to emphasize in their research, write about certain findings, and then explain their particular analyses and interpretations.

This chapter examines what is involved in the researching, analyzing, interpreting, and writing sport management stories; it focuses on historical research methodology as applied to sport management. "The purpose of historical research," explains McDowell (2002), "is to make sense of a series of events in a specified timeframe, establish their authenticity, understand the connection between them, and interpret their wider significance" (p. 26). Therefore, this chapter helps you (i.e., the academician, student, or practitioner) plan, organize, and complete your sport management history essay, research paper, or project. The chapter addresses issues including the importance and relevance of historical research in sport management, the tools and materials needed to conduct such research, topic selection, and distinguishing and analyzing primary and secondary source material. The chapter concludes with a discussion of the types and process of historical writing in sport management. Numerous sources were used in the research and writing of this chapter; in particular, the chapter is based on three influential historical reference publications: Anthony Brundage's (2002) *Going to the Sources: A Guide to Historical Research and Writing*, W.H. McDowell's (2002) *Historical Research: A Guide*, and Martha Howell and Walter Prevenier's (2001) *From Reliable Sources: An Introduction to Historical Methods*.

Academic Perspective

Because sport management is often an applied discipline in academia, there is a general tendency to push research inquiries in that direction. As Rinehart (2005) explains, "praxis-oriented questions largely have driven research in sport management studies" (p. 498). While historical research can be done (i.e., recognizing historical patterns and trends), history in sport management often involves basic or pure research (i.e., establishing facts). In any case, sport managers and sport management students should know about and be able to interpret historical developments in their field. They should even be able to conduct their own historical research. This is true because sport history research—which for the most part focuses on studying human beings, their actions, connections, and consequences in the sport industry—involves all aspects and subdisciplines of sport management. For example, Marvin Washington and Marc J. Ventresca (2008) used institutional theory to analyze organizational elements in early collegiate basketball in the United States. William Anderson (2006) examined the history of public relations in the former American Football League. Stephen Hardy (2006) examined aspects of sport marketing in his analysis of the early history of ice hockey in America. Laura Cousens and Trevor Slack (2005) examined, among other subjects, governance issues in their historical analysis of North American professional sport firms. John Crompton, Dennis Howard, and Turgut Var (2003) examined the history and trends in public financing of major league sport facilities. Some work, such as the article by Cousens and Slack and another by Miller, Fielding, Gupta, and Pitts (1995), are considered case studies but are discussed in this chapter because of their strong historical documentation and research. As Harvard University business historian Alfred Chandler noted (Chandler et al., 1986), "the case study is precisely what a historian does, what a historian is trained to do" (p. 82). Students in sport management classes and programs are expected to possess knowledge of sport history. They should even consider taking a course in historical methods if doing so fits into their program of study. Even if they do not plan to write the history of their future sport organization, students interested in a career in the sport industry need to have at least some familiarity with historical developments related to the field, as well as an ability to evaluate historical information and research.

History courses are commonplace in institutions of higher education, and most of these courses consist of more traditional forms of history, such as American history, European history, political history, ancient history, constitutional history, social history, and military history. However, many schools—and most sport management programs—offer lecture courses in sport history. For example, the University of New South Wales offers a course titled "Australian Sport: History and Culture," the University of Central Florida offers a two-semester sequence titled "Sport in America," and the University of Windsor teaches a course called "History of Sport in Canada." Even programs that do not offer such courses cover sport history to some degree in various lectures and textbooks used in courses such as sport law, sport sociology, and sport communication. Very few programs offer a sport history methods class, but history term papers, research reports, master's theses, doctoral dissertations, and other projects are frequently written and developed to address topics in sport management. For instance, the book *Build It and They Will Come: The Arrival of the Tampa Bay Devil Rays* (Pedersen, 1997) was developed from a master's thesis on urban sport history and the issues involved with franchise relocation, civic boosterism, facility construction, economics, management, and promotions.

Historical knowledge and research skills are key components of a well-rounded sport management education. In addition to coursework requirements and expectations, most sport management textbooks include chapters devoted to historical subjects. For instance, in the first chapter of *Principles and Practice of Sport Management*, Todd Crosset and Mary Hums (2005) devote 18 pages to historical developments in sport management. As they note, "history suggests that sport managers who are flexible and adaptable to broader changes in society and who have a keen sense of their sport are the most successful" (p. 1). Another book, *Contemporary Sport Management* (Pedersen, Parks, Quarterman, & Thibault, 2011), includes an entire chapter titled "Historical Aspects of the Sport Business Industry."

Even textbooks that do not devote a chapter to sport management history still provide historical foundations throughout the textbook, as is the case with *Sport Marketing*, in which Bernie Mullin, Steve Hardy, and Bill Sutton (2007) interweave historical elements and personalities such as legendary sport marketer Bill Veeck (baseball entrepreneur), Tex Rickard (boxing promoter), and Don Canham (college marketer). The authors note that "historians have [also] recently rediscovered the genius of minority marketers like Rube Foster, who built the first stable professional baseball league for African American players in the 1920s" (p. 15). Sport management students should be familiar with the history of sport management and its various segments, as well as major issues and players (e.g., Billie Jean King, A.G. Spalding) in the historical development of the sport industry.

Practical Applications

As former Harvard Business School faculty member Alonzo McDonald noted (Chandler et al., 1986), "history in business is not useful just as a kind of academic or intellectual exercise"; rather, he states, historical understanding gives practitioners historical context, vision, philosophy, direction, views on issues, reference points, and cultural context. McDonald explains that "if you don't have this kind of idea or historical perspective, there is an enormous temptation to make a managerial mistake" (p. 82). "In a corporate setting," McDonald adds, "if you know your history, you know what to expect" (p. 88). Therefore, in addition to history's educational (i.e., programmatic) and intrinsic (i.e., intellectual) value, it also offers practical value and applicability (i.e., the ability to make high-quality decisions and judgments). For example, Washington and Ventresca (2008) note the possible connection between historical occurrences and amateur basketball's current struggles with issues such as domination by the "NCAA, the debate between the amateurs and the professional nature of college basketball, [and] the role of the media" (p. 31). As a result, they note, their historical study "has implications for sport managers. . . . [Thus] for existing sport managers, we contend that history matters" (p. 31). It is true that the history of sport management has been characterized by discontinuity (i.e., discontinuous changes), but the value of sport management history and research to the practitioner remains whether one views sport management history as linear or cyclical.

The linear or sequential approach to history—studying change over time—is often associated with viewing history as progress. In this view—and similar to what Harvard University historians noted about the importance of historical knowledge to effective managers (Chandler et al., 1986)—improved judgment in sport managers derives from their knowledge and understanding of the past and their ability to learn lessons (i.e., what worked or did not work) found in the experiences of other sport managers who have come before them. In viewing history as progress, sport managers of today build on the knowledge they obtain from the past, and this enlightenment leads to more informed and better decisions and thus a prognosis for a brighter future. Sport managers who know and appreciate their history can make sense of situations and events and choose to engage in informed actions. Therefore, the work of historians also helps by illustrating how elements of the past influence the present, by comparing past and present conditions and issues, and by helping individuals make informed decisions about the present. Historical methodology is a form of research, and thus the study of history is the pursuit of knowledge, which is obtained and disseminated through careful research, collection, evaluation, comparison, and interpretation of source materials. Part of this pursuit involves explaining events of the past and producing a reconstruction of a particular issue in sport history, a personality or individual, an event, or a sport organization. Even the basic work of historians—chronicling the past—offers practical value. One aspect of the work of sport management historians is to provide a record or chronology (timeline) of past sport personalities, organizations, events, and activities. These historians help locate events and personalities in time. Research in sport management topics can add to our field's understanding and to our individual knowledge about people and about social, cultural, and other aspects of past events. But in chronicling the past, historians help distinguish what really happened (i.e., fact) from what might be told (i.e., myth) about what happened. Furthermore, historians' work in chronicling the past provides prospective and future sport managers with an accurate understanding of the past. "The rate of change," according to Vietor (Chandler et al., 1986), is "so fast that simply understanding the context of what has gone on before becomes that much more important if you're going to have any kind of real help in knowing where you're going" (p. 86). Harvard University marketing professor Richard Tedlow adds that one key use of history is "simply getting things, events, and facts into shared memory" (Chandler et al., 1986, p. 82). As students move through sport management programs and into the work force, they are expected to possess some shared knowledge of historical developments in the sport industry. This knowledge gives them context and perspective and helps them interact with others in the field.

The cyclical approach to history involves viewing the past to reveal patterns or cycles (e.g., all sport businesses go through a typical life cycle). For example, Dick Moriarty and Marge Holman-Prpich (1987) examined the topic of patterns, growth, development, and stages when they used a comparative analysis design to explore organizational history in Canadian interuniversity athletics. The work at hand in sport management history is to find connections between events in an attempt to understand or realize a pattern or structure. As Harvard University business professor Thomas McCraw explains, "history is a way of thinking—a way of searching for patterns and trying to see if such patterns recur from one situation to another" (Chandler et al., 1986, p. 82). Researchers are able to impose meaning and pattern on past events through their work of discovery, verification, and description (Brundage, 2002). Therefore, a key purpose of studying and researching sport history is to understand and explain the past and relate it to the present in order to help us understand the sport industry today.

The cyclical approach involves repeated patterns. As Mullin et al. (2007) explain, "as the field continues to progress, sport marketing will move back to a future that was recognized clearly by old-time 'promoters' and 'hustlers' such as Tex Rickard, Bill Veeck, and Don Canham" (p. 15). In this view, it is good to do research and learn about the various phases (e.g., start-up, growth, maturity) of your organization, business, and segment of the sport industry. As noted by former Harvard Business School faculty member Alonzo McDonald (Chandler et al., 1986), "when you don't know any history, however, you are always surprised at what is demanded of you at each of these stages. Managers often do absolutely stupid things that they do not have to do and would not have done if they only understood more about the whole historical sequence" (p. 87). Such understanding provides perspective.

Regardless of whether they use the cyclical or the linear approach, sport historians understand that change occurs, that it occurs for a reason, and that they have to determine—based on their evi-

dence and their interpretation of that evidence—the causal relationship. Change occurs because of a cause, and sport historians must address this problem of cause. As detailed by Howell and Prevenier (2001), the causal factors or principal agents of change can be social, economic, religious, biological, racial, environmental, scientific, technological, or related to inventions, power, public opinion, or mass media (and its components—sources, audience, medium, message). These are causal factors, and sport historians focus their efforts on understanding change and causality. According to McCraw, business historians (and thus sport business historians) "are concerned with identifying change, with identifying the reasons that things happen as they do, and with the balance between inevitability and managerial choice" (Chandler et al., 1986, p. 85).

Whether you view your study of sport history from a linear or sequential perspective or a cyclical perspective, your research and knowledge of the past can help you understand the present, explain contemporary events, and sometimes even predict a sequence of events or an outcome. Therefore, it is the work of sport management historians to discover, verify, describe, contextualize, connect, and interpret past sport history events, activities, organizations, and personalities. Overall, according to McDowell (2002), "the principal task of historians is to provide an informative, accurate and balanced account of individual actions, events and historical trends" (p. 13). Sure, they collect, discover, and report factual information, but they also establish context, identify relationships between facts, and interpret findings. Whether their quests for exploration and explanation are geared toward understanding the past for pure research purposes or to learn from it (build on it or recognize patterns), sport historians are driven and passionate about their projects. They are also professional, which means they are grounded in and follow a prescribed and systematic methodology in their work. Sport historians strive to produce documents that provide both the narrative (i.e., details of events) and the analytical (i.e., details viewed in a broad context or frame).

Research Prerequisites

Those who research, study, and read about historical aspects of sport management generally possess or develop certain qualities. For example, they often have a sense of curiosity, inquiry, and adventure. In their desire to explore the history of the sport industry, they want to find answers to the who, what, when, where, how, and why questions related to their subject. Just as sport management historians tend to possess certain inquisitive qualities, anyone conducting historical research in sport management should have or be able to obtain certain research tools and materials that are necessary in order to complete the task.

Typical materials used in historical research range from the basics (e.g., writing utensils, paper, highlighters, binders, dividers, note cards, organizers) to the more involved (e.g., photocopier, microfilm or microfiche reader, scanner, audio recorder, transcription machine). In our current cyber age, another important research tool is a computer with Internet access; indeed, a personal computer (desk or laptop) is one of the most valuable tools available to sport management historians. They often use a computer to research historical topics by means of online catalogues and library holdings, as well as keyword and database searches. Sport management historians can also use computers, of course, to take and organize research notes; communicate via e-mail with other historians and scholars; categorize files; store and retrieve text and data; run statistical programs (e.g., SPSS) to analyze economic, census, and social data; examine spreadsheets (e.g., Excel); run research software and find information on stored CD-ROM; compile bibliographies; display graphics and present historical data; and locate sources.

Sport management researchers frequently search the conventional and traditional outlets of academic journals, printed books, and hard copies of newspaper and magazine publications. However, the Internet has become more and more widely used in historical investigations in sport as it has developed into a tremendous resource for source material and background information (see the highlight box for a few key resources). For example, Crompton et al. (2003) use the Web site of the *Engineering News-Record* to secure information about cost indexes for their study on sport facility financing. Certain kinds of source material—oral histories, handwritten correspondence, back issues of local newspapers—can be quite difficult or impossible to find online, but online searches and databases do provide an abundance of information and evidence that can help you in your research. Search engines such as Google Scholar are powerful and quite exhaustive. Subject indexes can also be extremely helpful. You can use the Internet to perform searches through archival sources (e.g., the *Sporting News* archives), organizational and governmental Web sites (e.g., for the NCAA), historical journals, electronic databases (of evidence or of bibliographies or histories), library holdings and catalogues (at local, public, and university libraries), historical society records, league and team holdings (e.g., the National Baseball Hall of Fame and Museum), bibliographies and reference lists, abstracts, documents hosted at educational sites, research publications, encyclopedias, newspaper and periodical holdings (e.g., *Street & Smith's SportsBusiness Journal*), annuals, publishers' book listings, special collections, private collections, dissertations and theses, and full-text journal articles.

You should be aware of a few issues when using the Web in your historical research. First, although using the Web for research is often effective and efficient, you will also encounter many Web sites that offer incorrect, unreliable, sensational, incomplete, or biased information and source material. Second, Web pages are frequently moved or deleted, and therefore their availability can be unpredictable. Third, even when using the Web, you cannot locate

Internet Sources for Sport Management Historical Research

A. Bartlett Giamatti Research Center: http://baseballhall.org/museum/experience/library

Engineering News-Record: http://enr.construction.com/Default.asp

Google Scholar: http://scholar.google.com/

NCAA Document Archive: www.ncaa.org/wps/portal (from that page complete a site search for "document archives")

Sporting News: www.sportingnews.com/archives

Street & Smith's SportsBusiness Journal: www.sportsbusinessjournal.com

and retrieve all source material; it is generally just not possible to do a completely exhaustive search.

Topic Selection

In developing a sport management history paper, you should begin by determining an intriguing, feasible, and well-defined topic of investigation. What are your project's objectives? What key questions do you hope the research will answer? Can you locate related and substantial primary and secondary sources? The field of sport management history yields thousands of research possibilities: sport management biographies (e.g., Fred Corcoran, Patty Berg), sport organizational histories (e.g., the tenure of Major League Baseball's Expos [now the Washington Nationals] in Montreal), gender relations and power structures in sport management (e.g., athletic administration in college sport since the Association for Intercollegiate Athletics for Women ceased existence in 1983), international sport and global issues (e.g., the structure of the Paralympics movement since its beginnings in 1948), mass media influences (e.g., the founding of *ABC's Wide World of Sports*), and financial or economic variables (e.g., how the 1932 Summer Olympics turned a profit). Other topics can be found in the myriad issues related to socialization, political influence, symbolism, class issues, sporting traditions, cultural and social movements, or most any other segment of the sport industry.

Pick a topic that is intriguing. Make sure that it can hold your interest, because even the best topics can become mundane over the course of a major research project. Do not hesitate to select a topic that falls outside your specific area of knowledge or your comfort zone. Though it is optimal to select a topic in which you have some background knowledge, researching a unique or new subject area can push you into deeper research that can reveal new areas of discovery and inquiry for you. Regardless, you must find a manageable topic that you can address in a reasonable time frame. To do so, you must consider your interest areas and pick a topic that will sustain your interest.

Pick a topic that contributes to the body of knowledge in the field. For instance, Daniel Mason (1997) contributed something new to the field by taking a different approach to analyzing the National Football League (NFL). Mason used historical research to examine an aspect (agency theory) of organizational behavior within the NFL. For your research, you have to decide whether to research a totally new topic or reexamine an existing topic by looking for new evidence, angles, connections, perspectives, and interpretations. As Marnie Haig-Muir (2004) discovered in doing research for a study on power relations and historical aspects of women's golf, "scant attention is paid to women's achievements. . . . Yet, if the history of golf is approached from another angle and with

a different value perspective, there is a parallel herstory to complement the better-known history of golf" (p. 65). You can generate ideas by asking other scholars and historians and by examining journal articles, books, dissertations, theses, book reviews, conference abstracts, Web resources, and other such materials to see what has been written, what gaps need to be filled, and what new areas of inquiry are emerging. It can take some time to settle on a unique and feasible subject, but you will find that many opportunities, topics, and alternatives are available in the study of sport history. For a topic that has been covered quite a bit (e.g., the Olympics), look at the closely related alternatives (e.g., a unique biographical account) or come at the topic from a new angle (e.g., an original analysis of a certain time frame, management team, or organizational issue). Choosing a good topic is difficult but important if you want to make a significant contribution to the sport management body of knowledge. Even if you are a skillful researcher, a poor topic selection can leave you facing a difficult task in finishing the project and making a meaningful contribution.

Pick a topic that is manageable. For instance, David Shilbury (1993) focused on the topic of corporate structure and culture in his historical and conceptual analysis of the Victorian Football League and its successor, the Australian Football League. Thus he kept his topic manageable by focusing on organizational issues within a particular league's development. The key here is that you should not be *too* ambitious with the scope of your study or the focus of your topic. Selecting a topic can be a difficult process in that many of us are tempted to take on something that is too large (e.g., females in sport management positions in the 20th century) or too narrow (e.g., the commencement of the use of bobblehead dolls in minor league promotions). Because you will need to read, research, synthesize, evaluate, and develop strong knowledge of the sources available on the subject, it is essential to select a manageable topic—that is, one that can be examined thoroughly. Therefore, you should define your topic's scope in a way that is extensive but manageable.

Pick a topic that you can research. If you cannot find primary or secondary sources on the subject in which you are interested, you are going to have a difficult time initiating, researching, writing, and completing the historical analysis. Therefore, at a minimum, you should choose a topic where at least some source material is available for you to draw upon. As noted by McDowell (2002), "your choice of research topic may present you with either the prospect of an abundance of source material or the task of compensating for fragmentary evidence" (p. 75). If you find too much source material, you have probably chosen a topic that is too broad, and you will need to narrow your scope of inquiry in order to have a manageable topic. Your project should, however, be challenging and worth your time, and it should support clear aims and objectives, extend boundaries, be doable in a reasonable amount of time, and enable you to disseminate findings by some means (e.g., publication in a book or article) and build upon it in your future research (McDowell).

The issue of refining a topic generally comes into play when the researcher selects a topic that is too broad. You can refine—or narrow—your topic to something more manageable by looking to limit it to a particular biography, region, focus, time period, aspect, scope, or chronology. Start broad, and then, as you read what other historians have written about the topic or related topics, begin to narrow it. For an example of how these methods work to narrow a topic, consider the study by Washington and Ventresca (2008), who narrowed their topic by selecting a specific sport industry segment (intercollegiate athletics), sport (basketball), country (United States), time frame (1880–1938), and sport management issue (institutional contradiction). Refining your topic is not necessarily something you do at the start of your project; rather, you can refine your topic as you examine the available literature, determine what sources are accessible, limit the scope of your inquiry, or clarify the objectives of your research project.

Source Material

The process of historical research and writing in sport management is both an individualistic and a collaborative endeavor. The work is individualistic because you have to do the research; you go out and examine the evidence (e.g., documents, photographs). The work is collaborative because you rely on the writings of others, including those at the scene (i.e., those involved such as participants and journalists) and those from previous and current generations of historians who have written about the subject. In their quest to uncover, reconstruct, and examine the past, sport historians locate, index, read, and evaluate source materials, and sport management historical inquiry often involves a mixture of source materials: manuscripts, archival findings,

organizational documents (e.g., minutes, reports, memos), government reports, official publications, dissertations, theses, broadcasts, films, sound recordings, interviews, books, book reviews, chapters, periodical and newspaper articles, pamphlets, abstracts, and conference papers, to name a few.

The most common type of source evidence used in sport management history is written communication. Obviously, other tangible remnants of the past can be found (e.g., artifacts, films, weapons, sporting equipment, uniforms, fields, stadiums) and used as source material, but written source material (e.g., business reports, government minutes, personal diaries and letters, newspaper articles) is the type of source most often relied upon by sport management historians. When starting out a sport history project, you should consider the various types of source materials you hope to find and use. If you are still looking for a topic, you may find that knowing the various sources available helps you settle on a subject. Once you pick a topic, use a wide variety of sources in your examination of it. Your various sources of evidence can be grouped into two major categories: primary and secondary.

Primary Sources

The expansion of historical knowledge in the field of sport management—that is, the production of original material and insight—generally results from the discovery, analysis, and interpretation of new or unique primary sources. Thus, advances are most often made when historians construct meaning, create their version of the past, and base their historical arguments (interpretations) on the **primary sources** they find. These sources are raw materials (e.g., relics, remains, eyewitness testimony, speeches) that often contain the answers to questions such as what occurred, how and why it happened, what the context was, what caused it to happen, and who the principal players were.

In sport management research, these raw materials generally take the form of oral and written primary sources. Knowing what is available and being able to obtain primary sources will make or break your research project (unless, of course, you are writing a historiography of your subject, which requires secondary sources). You need to be able to determine the availability (i.e., abundance or scarcity), variety, and accessibility of primary sources for your topic. For instance, you would probably find many and various primary sources readily available if you were writing the history of a sport organization that opened its archives (with, for example, business minutes and other official papers) to you. However, you would probably find a scarcity of primary sources available if you were writing a historical account of a former sport management leader whose files (e.g., diaries, private communication, office memos) were limited or incomplete. Limited availability of primary sources does not necessarily mean that you cannot carry out the project, but it may mean that you have to rely on other types of sources of historical evidence. You can often discover what primary sources are readily available (and have already been consulted by others) by perusing the footnotes and bibliographies of historical books (which are secondary sources) related to your topic. Sources can be found in private collections, hall of fame archives, historical society holdings, published guides, online catalogues, public records offices, museums, institutional and organizational files, newspapers, newsletters, annual reports, census data, and libraries.

You can use several types of primary source material to examine historical events and people in sport management. Oral sources are often valued by sport management historians, but they are used only in contemporary historical research. Other types of primary sources include paintings, photographs, newsreels, documentary and feature films, and sound recording. Again, though, the written primary source material often holds the most value in sport history research and writing. These written accounts may come from active participants (e.g., administrators, legislators, coaches, players), observers (e.g., journalists, fans), or others somehow involved (e.g., bystanders) with the historical event or personality being researched. For this textbook, primary sources used in sport management historical work are categorized into three groups: unpublished manuscripts, published sources, and oral evidence.

Unpublished Manuscripts

Unpublished manuscripts are sources that have been written (i.e., handwritten, keyboarded) but not prepared for mass consumption or public dissemination. These communication materials are generally intended not for the public but for private or limited use. They generally describe the process and rationale by which people acted or made decisions. For example, Anderson (2006) used unpublished manuscripts from the Pro Football Hall of Fame Library (PFHFL) to chronicle how the American Football League (AFL) employed public

relations strategies that led to the league's merger with the NFL. The PFHFL is, according to Anderson, "the largest repository of archival materials related to professional football," and it contains "primary documents such as personal and business correspondence of owners and officials. Reviewing the primary documents helped determine the motives behind industry action" (p. 54).

Unpublished manuscripts often contain both factual and subjective information, but because they were generally not intended for public dissemination sport historians generally assume that they provide a more accurate record of the past than do published materials. They include documents such as minutes of a sport organizational meeting, handwritten notes from a coach preparing for a locker room speech, a starting lineup posted on a dugout wall, or even a personal diary from a sport management leader such as Thomas E. Wilson (founder of Wilson Sporting Goods). For example, when examining historical aspects of a sport organization, it is essential to look at unpublished company records and materials in order to conduct a thorough research project. And yes, some sport organizations do allow scholars to examine their files and go through their archives. For instance, in their study of the Hillerich & Bradsby Company's history and innovative production techniques, sport management researchers Lori Miller, Lawrence Fielding, Mahesh Gupta, and Brenda Pitts (1995) received access to the baseball bat manufacturing company's organizational documents (i.e., annual reports from 1924, 1929, and 1949). When working on such projects, you will need to find a way to access unpublished manuscripts by going through company archives, local depositories, library holdings, or government files.

Some projects provide numerous opportunities to secure unpublished manuscript sources. For example, in Pedersen's (1997) historical research on the building of the domed facility in St. Petersburg, the city government opened its files to the historical work. These files contained hundreds of primary unpublished manuscript sources. This cache is small, however, when compared with the resources available to Stephen Wenn and Scott Martyn (2005) in their analysis of the International Olympic Committee (IOC) and its relationship with the corporate community. As they noted in their study, they had access to sources ranging from organizational records (e.g., IOC marketing reports, IOC meeting and session minutes) to personal correspondence files of one of the key stakeholders (Richard Pound) within the IOC. Because of this privileged access,

Wenn and Martyn's objectivity and critical judgment were challenged (p. 188). After an extensive rebuttal, the authors noted that,

> it has always been our goal as researchers to subject documents and material that have been made available, regardless of their provenance, to scrutiny. Inasmuch as we are fortunate to have been provided access to research material for this paper by Richard Pound, we are very much concerned with our academic responsibilities as historians and have endeavored to provide readers, despite the admitted complexity of events, with a clearly written narrative that can be supported by historical evidence. (p. 189)

As their quote illustrates, just as you would do with any source, you need to approach unpublished manuscripts (and, especially, personal correspondence) with a skeptical mind, a critical analysis, and a desire to triangulate results.

Published Sources

Because you will often lack the time or resources to secure unpublished primary sources, you will find that the materials you encounter most often in your sport management historical research are **published sources** (i.e., any published document). Examples include official records, public documents, letters, memoranda, intimate documents, newspaper articles, legislative debates, company reports, census filings, news accounts, pamphlets, magazine articles, media guides, game day publications, and a host of print media and popular publications. For example, the numerous published sources used in Cousens and Slack's (2005) study include *The New York Times*, *BusinessWeek*, *Brandweek*, *Financial World*, *Advertising Age*, *Fortune*, the *Sporting News*, *Sports Illustrated*, and *USA Today Sports Weekly*. Magazines and newspapers are the most commonly used published source materials in sport management historical research. Newspapers, in particular, provide chronicles of events, advertisements, articles, social and cultural background, columns, opinion pieces, editorials, letters to the editor, photographs, and other information that is helpful in reconstructing, contextualizing, and interpreting past events. You can find newspaper documents by searching the Web, visiting newspaper offices and libraries, viewing CD-ROM versions of the papers, and using microfilm and microfiche machines.

Writings by political figures, opinion leaders, and other major figures in sport management history can often be found in published form (e.g., published personal diaries, personal memoirs). Autobiographies range from the sport marketing genius of Bill Veeck in *Veeck as in Wreck: The Autobiography of Bill Veeck* (Veeck & Linn, 2001) to the steroid controversy illuminated by Jose Canseco in *Juiced: Wild Times, Rampant 'Roids, Smash Hits, and How Baseball Got Big* (2005) to the pioneering efforts by Kathrine Switzer in *Marathon Woman: Running the Race to Revolutionize Women's Sports* (2009). Keep in mind, however, that published primary sources such as autobiographies and other potentially ego-related documents can be unreliable because they often provide partial information, distorted accounts, and only one perspective. They often include inaccuracies in timelines and other information because they are often written years (even decades) after the events in question. Furthermore, as biased accounts, they often suppress controversies, justify past decisions or actions, and, since they are written to impress, contain exaggerations and selectivity. Even with their drawbacks, however, these published primary sources are important in historical research because they provide a perspective that might otherwise be excluded.

Oral Evidence

Evidence gathering in recent historical scholarship has increasingly involved interviews, which can function both as the basis for an independent project (e.g., oral history) and as a complimentary approach when primary and secondary sources have been secured. For example, Cousens and Slack (2005) note that for their study "primary data were gathered from historical documents and from personal interviews conducted with current leaders of professional sport leagues and franchises" (p. 19). Oral sources can include audio recordings of individuals who are deceased or inaccessible, as well as interviews with contemporary persons. As with primary source material, interviews involve people who were active participants, observers, or otherwise associated with the historical event in question. In Patrick Harrigan's (2006) analysis of Canada's national intercollegiate athletic association in the 1960s and 1970s, the relatively contemporary time frame of the topic allowed the researcher to conduct several interviews with executives, athletic administrators, and other stakeholders who were involved in establishing this governing body.

Oral testimony constitutes primary source material that can afford insight into—or provide confirmation, clarification, or supplementation of—written evidence. For example, in Miller and colleagues' (1995) study on the Hillerich & Bradsby Company, the scholars were able to fill gaps in the written record by interviewing a host of organizational employees, including the company president and several vice presidents, coordinators, and managers. This type of oral evidence helps sport management historians reconstruct sport industry events and personalities more vividly, completely, and accurately. The information gained from interviews should add facts, detail, and corroboration and thus should help the historian perform the analysis and interpretation. In addition to the oral testimony that they give, interviewees often provide additional materials (e.g., documents, letters, minutes, memos, artifacts) before, during, and after the interaction.

If you are working on a contemporary historical topic, you may well be able to find individuals who can provide oral testimony. Moreover, many possible participants are eager to talk, so do not hesitate to contact them and ask them to participate. To ensure accuracy of quotations, record the interview if possible. The interview process involves conducting interaction and then recording, transcribing, interpreting, and substantiating the information gathered from the interviewee. Meaningful **oral evidence** depends on the questions you develop and the interviewing techniques you use. The art of interviewing (e.g., question design, selection, type, delivery, sequence, angle, flexibility) is covered in detail in chapter 8.

When considering the use of or evaluating the reliability of oral testimony, you should keep several factors in mind. First, if you are examining a topic where all of the involved parties are deceased or inaccessible, it is of course impossible to conduct an interview and thus oral evidence is not an option (unless archived audio recordings are available). Therefore, oral testimony is generally limited to projects involving events and personalities of the past few decades. Second, because of limitations in oral testimony (e.g., selectivity, partial recollection, sequential difficulties), it is not wise to rely only on oral evidence for any historical project in sport management. Third, interview data need to be critically analyzed. The historian needs to remember that sometimes an interviewee's observations, interpretations, and recollections are biased, distorted, self-serving, or otherwise compromised (e.g., due to limitations on or loss of memory). Thus, it is strongly recommended that you triangulate oral evidence with other primary sources (e.g., published and unpublished written evidence).

Secondary Sources

Source material that is considered secondary generally involves works written by persons who were not involved in or not present at the events about which they are writing. **Secondary sources**— which often provide background knowledge and unique perspectives—are historical works written after the fact by scholars and journalists. Most often, secondary sources are the written documents that historians produce based on their examination of primary sources. These written histories range from scholarly articles and books to textbooks and pamphlets.

Generally, you should read (or at a minimum peruse or scan) the general texts on your topic and then move to more specific and detailed examination of secondary sources by other historians. In addition to examining references and footnotes contained in the secondary source material, you need to determine why the publication was written, the authority of the author, and what information it provides or does not provide. You should triangulate or corroborate the analyses and interpretations of the various authors by testing their writings against the primary sources and other secondary materials. The following paragraphs cover the major secondary sources most often used in sport management research: books, scholarly articles, book reviews, theses and dissertations, and conference papers.

Books

Secondary sources that fit into this category include textbooks, history books, biographies, broad treatises and essays, narrow analyses, monographs, edited compilations, and a host of other publications. These secondary source materials are also quite diverse in terms of scope (e.g., global, biographical), tone (e.g., scholarly, popular), approach (e.g., political, legal, local, labor, diplomatic, social, economic), and style (e.g., narrative, analytical, interpretive). Secondary sources in this category can be based primarily on primary sources, secondary sources, or a combination of the two. Generally, the narrower the topic, the more primary sources are used, since broad topics generally rely more heavily on secondary sources. Take, for example, the historical work surrounding Alvin Ray "Pete" Rozelle. Several secondary sources have been published about this former NFL commissioner, innovator (the Super Bowl, *Monday Night Football*), sport management guru (league merger, "league think"), and overall legendary figure (*Time* magazine's 100 most important people list for the 20th century). In addition to numerous scholarly articles related to Rozelle (e.g., Lomax's 2002 historical study of gambling; Fortunato's 2008 historical study of branding), two Rozelle biographies have recently been published: Jeff Davis' (2007) *Rozelle: Czar of the NFL* and John Fortunato's (2006) *Commissioner: The Legacy of Pete Rozelle*. Although these two secondary sources appeared at about the same time, they each examine, detail, present, and interpret the commissioner's life, work, and legacy in a unique way.

Scholarly Articles

Academic articles published in peer-reviewed journals can serve as extremely useful secondary sources in your historical research. These articles are often the place where you can read about the past in more detail and discover new interpretations of past events. The detailed articles published in scholarly journals are intended for professionals and scholars. The periodicals are generally affiliated with a professional academic organization such as the North American Society for Sport History (NASSH), which offers the *Journal of Sport History*, a quarterly that publishes several research articles in each issue. Plenty of other journals are also devoted to sport history and frequently publish historical articles about sport management (e.g., *Sport History Review*, the *Journal of Olympic History*, *European Sports History Review*, the *International Journal of the History of Sport*). Furthermore, most general sport journals publish occasional articles about sport management history. You can find historical studies related to sport management in journals such as the *Journal of Sport Management* (e.g., Washington & Ventresca, 2008), *Sport Management Review* (e.g., Dabscheck, 2003), the *International Journal of Sport Communication* (e.g., Birot, Pecout, & Cooper, 2008), *Sport Marketing Quarterly* (e.g., Fielding & Miller, 1998), the *International Journal of Sport Management* (e.g., Dobbs, Stahura, & Greenwood, 2005; Inoue, Seifried, & Matsumoto, 2010), the *Journal of Sport and Social Issues* (e.g., Burgos, 2005), and the *International Journal of Sport Management and Marketing* (e.g., Huang, 2006).

Book Reviews

Researching and writing sport management histories can sometimes involve consulting book reviews, which are generally published in academic journals. Take a look at any biannual issue of *Sport History Review* and you will probably find a handful of published book reviews. These articles evaluate and analyze recently published historical books, providing critical analysis and in-depth scrutiny in order to assess the value of the new interpretations provided. For example, in the *Journal of Sport History*, Daniel Simone reviewed Terry Reed's (2005) *Indy: The Race and Ritual of the Indianapolis 500*. Simone (2006) noted the intended audience ("useful to casual auto racing fans and sports scholars" [p. 381]), the book's structure ("wittily organized . . . [with] chapters [arranged] in conjunction with the four turns of the speedway" [p. 381]), and sources used ("a wealth of primary source materials. . . [including] the rich archives at the Indianapolis Motor Speedway Museum" [p. 382]), and the overall analysis ("an important contribution to sport historiography . . . [that] fills a large historiographical gap" [p. 382]).

Theses and Dissertations

Numerous historical works in sport management are published each year as master's theses and doctoral dissertations. These final major projects generally serve as the culmination of an academic program of study (e.g., MA, MS, EdD, PhD); as such, they are in-depth research inquiries based on intensive investigation into specific topics. Dissertations, in particular, are based on primary sources and produce new discoveries and unique areas of investigation, as well as high-quality critiques, summaries, and interpretations. As noted by Brundage (2002), "a dissertation is expected to demonstrate its author's critical acumen, writing abilities, and knowledge of the relevant primary and secondary sources" (p. 25). Theses and dissertations that are sufficiently significant and original are often published as books or divided up into scholarly articles.

Conference Papers

Academic gatherings such as the annual conferences of the NASSH and the North American Society for Sport Management (NASSM) include forums for the reading of scholarly papers, and these papers sometimes address historical sport management topics. They generally present new approaches, analyses, and interpretations of sport management topics. The 2007 NASSM conference provides a good example. The conference organizers received 367 submissions, 226 of which were accepted. Examples of history-related papers presented at the conference include one titled "Introducing and Analyzing Historical Methodology for Sport Management Studies" (Seifried, 2007, p. 300) and another titled "Sport Students' Background Knowledge of the Olympic Games: The Development of a Holistic Sport Event Management Frame of Reference," in which the researchers concluded that "the current knowledge of respondents appears to lack balance between past, present and future, which leads to an unbalanced holistic frame of reference" (van Wyk, Burger, Kluka, & van Schalkwyk, 2007, p. 292).

Data Analysis

Along with possessing or developing the ability to research, investigate, write, take notes, and provide insight and interpretation, those who do historical work in sport management should also be able to perform critical analysis. Historians are rewarded when they exercise, in Brundage's (2002) words, "a blend of diligence, skepticism, imagination, judiciousness, and humor" (p. 7). The pursuit of objectivity should be at the forefront of any sport management historical inquiry.

Although it is impossible to be absolutely objective—you are, after all, examining the past through your own biases (i.e., your values, experiences, time frame, and knowledge)—but you should pursue balance, impartiality, and objectivity in your research endeavors. You should work to keep an open mind, take an impartial approach, and consider all possible alternatives in your selection, analysis, and interpretation of source materials. You will not be able to provide a totally objective or complete reconstruction of the past because you will have to be selective in terms of what you illustrate, ignore, emphasize, and interpret. You should, however, work to provide a history that is as accurate, balanced, and complete as possible. You will make the most accurate and complete conclusions, perspectives, and insights if you can approach your examination of sources with a skeptical and critical eye. It is essential that you have an appreciation of the circumstances and context of the event or personalities involved in your historical inquiry. Try to read and examine your source material through the eyes of those involved. As former Harvard Business School faculty member Alonzo McDonald noted (Chandler et al., 1986), "decisions have consequences, but that does not make it fair for us to judge those who make them

harshly through the benefit of hindsight" (p. 85).

You do not simply describe the historical event, sequence of events, or personalities involved; rather, with skepticism and a questioning approach, you also seek to know (and then explain) why the event occurred or why the individual did or failed to do something. You need to carefully assess the merits of your source materials in terms of both their quality and their reliability. Although reliability is elusive in historical research, still, as noted by Howell and Prevenier (2001), "the historian's basic task is to choose reliable sources, to read them reliably, and to put them together in ways that provide reliable narratives about the past" (p. 2). These authors go on to state that "the central paradox of our profession [is that] historians are prisoners of sources that can never be made fully reliable, but if they are skilled readers of sources and always mindful of their captivity, they can make their sources yield meaningful stories about a past and our relationship to it" (p. 3). They add that sources can be used as evidence only if three basic matters are settled: The source should be comprehensible (understandable), located in a certain time and place, and examined for authenticity.

The process of examining documentary evidence involves numerous considerations. Here are some:

- The publication's credibility, accuracy, and origin
- The source's authorship status and genuineness (established through examination of such factors as handwriting, inaccuracies, language, spelling, and grammar)
- The motives and truthfulness of the author or interviewee
- The personal or public nature of the document
- The amount of time between the event and the writing or recollection of it
- The author's involvement in or proximity to the historical event
- The author's observational skills and perspective (e.g., what is disclosed or not disclosed, what is emphasized or deemphasized)
- The sequence of events (and any factual or sequential errors)
- Whether or not the document makes common sense
- The purpose of the source material (e.g., the audience to whom it was directed, the intention of the document—to influence, to inform, to express oneself)

- Gaps in the record and the consistency of the record with other accounts
- The social and cultural climate of the time

Because historical documents vary greatly in their reliability, researchers in sport management history should assemble, examine, and compare as many sources as possible. For example, many publications are produced with the intention of influencing certain individuals or the public at large; this is often true of newspaper accounts, magazine articles, annuals, media guides, government reports (e.g., stadium construction task forces), and institutional correspondence. Therefore, it is necessary to triangulate and corroborate an organization's ostensibly independent publication or a sport reporter's supposedly objective account with other primary source materials.

Although the study of sport management history may appear mundane because it involves researching the past, the work is in fact dynamic and fresh if you examine the past by means of different and new questions asked from different and new angles and thus arrive at fresh and new perspectives. There is no definitive history of sport management, which means that there is always room for new insight. Complete and exact knowledge of the past can never be achieved, but sport management historians use their background, expertise, and skills to provide knowledge that is as complete and exact as possible and to analyze and interpret it as best they can. New approaches, angles, sources, and questions arise continually and lead to new information and resources, fresh perspectives, unique interpretations, and special contributions that help provide a more complete re-creation of the past. Therefore, after you research your topic, find and authenticate your source material, and read and analyze your various primary and secondary sources, you then work to explain, connect, and interpret your findings. You should make every effort to arrive at your findings and interpretations without prejudice or preconception. By making a conscious effort to limit preconceived thoughts about the subject, you will help reduce the temptation to organize your results, key points, and insights around certain personal thoughts, biases, and expectations.

You should work to provide an insightful and educated opinion on the subject matter. Your interpretations should be as good as possible based on your supporting primary and secondary sources. Interpretation in historical work involves collecting and organizing the factual information and using historical intuition and technique to arrive at logi-

cal and substantiated interpretations. Your opinion is based on primary sources and may differ from what other historians have proposed; it may even cause debate about the subject. New perspectives and insights are not necessarily wrong—just as previous ones are not necessarily wrong. They are simply new approaches, challenges to what others have noted, and unique interpretations.

Unless you are putting together a historiography (made up of secondary sources), your historical research should provide new facts, analyses, and interpretations. For instance, Alan Klein recently wrote a baseball book, *Growing the Game: The Globalization of Major League Baseball* (2006), in which he focused on how teams such as the Los Angeles Dodgers and Kansas City Royals—and the baseball commissioner's office itself, through its Major League Baseball International (MLBI) initiative—have been engaged in global activities for a variety of reasons (e.g., developing baseball talent, marketing the product, growing the game, increasing revenues) and in numerous locations (e.g., Japan, the Dominican Republic, South Africa, South Korea, Italy, Germany, England). Richard Crepeau (2006) reviewed the book:

> As a historian I was troubled by a lack of depth of historical background. There is much about this story that is new, but much, too, that has a deeper history that is glossed over. . . . [However,] these issues can be overlooked given the amount of new information that Klein has been able to assemble on this subject of increasing significance for baseball fans, marketers, and historians. (p. 364)

New interpretation does not mean the same thing as subjective interpretation. Rather, the new interpretations you offer should be objective (as much as possible) interpretations based on the available source material. Even the presence of different interpretations of the same event does not necessarily mean that the interpretations are subjective; it may simply mean that different insights were gained and different interpretations made by looking at the event or personality from different angles. Overall, it is your job to carefully locate, select, read, and evaluate the evidence; attempt to find consensus, connections, and clarifications of discrepancies between the various source materials available to you; and put together the most complete, balanced, and objective re-creation and interpretation that is possible of the organization, event, activity, issue, or personality you are investigating.

Historical Writing

In addition to research skills and investigative acumen, you need to develop strong writing skills in order to publish and present your work effectively. Historical sport management studies and findings are usually disseminated in the form of books, articles, or conference presentations. For the most part, historical writing in sport management can be placed in one of two major categories: the historiographic essay and the research paper.

Historiographic Essay

Conducting historiographic research and writing the historiographic essay involve examining what has already been written and analyzed about a particular historical topic. This historical research into history writing itself involves analyzing the ways (i.e., methods, approaches, interpretations) in which scholars and historians have examined a certain subject or topic. You need to understand the various approaches, angles, dimensions, and interpretations that other historians and scholars have taken in regard to your selected topic. For example, if you wanted to write a historiographic essay on the modern integration of baseball, you would explore how historians have approached this topic, and it would be essential for you to examine primary published sources such as books by Jackie Robinson (*I Never Had It Made*) and Branch Rickey (*Branch Rickey's Little Blue Book*). Your historiographic exploration would also lead you to compare the methodologies and interpretations of secondary source authors, scholars, and historians such as Jules Tygiel (*Baseball's Great Experiment*), Arnold Rampersad (*Jackie Robinson: A Biography*), Scott Simon (*Jackie Robinson and the Integration of Baseball*), Lee Lowenfish (*Branch Rickey: Baseball's Ferocious Gentleman*), and Murray Polner (*Branch Rickey*).

It is also important for students to be knowledgeable about conducting a historiography and writing a historiographic essay because the final requirement for many sport history courses involves putting together such a paper. In the historiographic essay—which is based on secondary sources—you explain how others have analyzed and interpreted the topic in which you are interested. All researchers of sport management historical subjects must know the **historiography** of their research topic in order to establish the foundation of the research paper. It is essential that you know how the topic has been examined and interpreted by other histo-

rians. Thus historiography and the historiographic essay can provide the foundation for a research paper by examining secondary sources (what others have written about the subject) and preparing the historian to examine the primary sources. You can direct historical inquiry and develop research questions effectively only when you know what has already been analyzed and interpreted and what methodology and sources have been used.

You need to develop a manageable historiographic essay. This means that the essay must address a focused and refined topic and total about 20 pages. Generally, these essays include about 20 secondary (not primary) sources, and you need to conduct a complete bibliographic search. Historiographic sources—which can be found by conducting searches as discussed earlier in this chapter—include books and scholarly articles. Remember that recent books and dissertations provide a good starting point in your quest for helpful sources; these publications often provide detailed listings of the secondary sources used. Once you have figured out a topic and secured your secondary sources, it is time to read the sources. You can read or scan each source, but sometimes the most efficient way to figure if the source has information that will help you in your historical research is to focus on the title, table of contents, preface, footnotes, bibliography, introduction, and conclusion. Regardless of how you read and approach the sources, your work here is to examine and take notes about how the various historians approached, analyzed, and interpreted the topic. In addition to determining the similarities, differences, and evolutionary changes in the various historians' analyses, methodologies, and perspectives, you should also evaluate the depth, rigor, and quality of the approaches and interpretations.

After you have taken notes on the various historical approaches, analyses, and interpretations related to your topic, you are ready to write the historiographic essay. This is not a sport management research paper, so keep in mind that you are not writing the history of the topic (although you will provide a little historical information to introduce the topic and some basic facts and illustrations along the way as background and transitional material). You are simply writing about how previous authors have written about the topic. Thus the body of the paper contains analysis and discussion of how scholars and historians have covered your topic. After a paragraph or two introducing the topic, the historiographic essay consists of paragraphs addressing the ways in which various authors have written about the topic.

The essay—as with the research paper discussed next—can move along according to a topical, chronological, or combined approach. This choice is often simply a matter of preference. The topical approach addresses biographical treatments, early works, recent works, agreements and disagreements, and any other topical or thematic breakdown that makes sense for the historical subject being studied. This thematic approach examines one topic or theme at a time, then connects and summarizes the various topics and themes. In the chronological approach, you can also trace a theme or topic, but you generally proceed from the first published source to the most recently published one. Regardless of the approach you choose, your historiographic essay ends with a concluding paragraph or two to summarize the major methodologies and interpretations. The conclusion includes comments about what is still missing in the topic's history and what can be expected in terms of future analysis and interpretation of the topic.

Research Paper

Whereas the historiographic essay is based on secondary sources, the research paper uses both primary and secondary source evidence. The research project involves the application of historical methodology (discovering evidence and examining and interpreting source material). Although the works and interpretations of other scholars and historians (secondary sources) are used, the major emphasis and weight of a research paper is given to the research, discovery, and selection of primary sources. The quality of your research paper will be determined primarily by the type, amount, and reliability of the primary source material you are able to find and examine.

You should analyze and interpret the primary sources according to your knowledge and background, not according to what has already been stated or quoted by other secondary sources. In order to both be certain of the context and establish your own credible interpretation, it is important for you to find and read representative and appropriate primary source material yourself rather than simply citing others' use of and quotes from primary sources. The reason for this is that a history research paper should—through the use and interpretation of primary sources—contribute to the body of knowledge by offering new facts, connections, analyses, and insights. Because of the intensive and self-directed labor, the sometimes considerable expense and time required, and the

specialized digging and analytic skills needed when writing a research paper, this type of history project is generally required only for major research endeavors such as scholarly journal articles, theses, dissertations, conference papers, and books.

The process of putting together a historical methodological research work involves numerous stages. Many of these stages involve preliminary activities or aspects of research already covered earlier in this chapter, such as choosing a general subject area, selecting and refining a topic, defining a title, deciding on a timeline, indexing source material, developing a bibliography, deciding the type of and need for primary and secondary sources, determining accessibility and availability of written and oral source evidence, and evaluating and interpreting findings. The remainder of the chapter focuses on reading source material, developing research questions, recording research notes, arranging a research outline, and preparing (drafting, proofing, and finalizing) the history research paper.

Developing research questions is a necessary step in your sport management history work. There are rigorous procedures and demanding criteria involved in framing sport history questions. You can start by looking for new and novel questions about the sporting past. For example, Washington and Ventresca (2008) were able to examine their evidence through historical (formative time periods) and theoretical (organizational institutionalism) lenses because of their specific and unique research question: "How did U.S. collegiate athletics come to dominate the amateur athletic field of basketball?" (p. 31). The choice of research questions is a selective process because your topic cannot be exhaustive; it must be manageable. You have two options in coming up with your research questions. One is to put the questions together at the start of the project, then refine them as you proceed with the study. The other option is to put the questions together after you have read a good amount of secondary source material in order to determine what other questions have been asked and how your questions are different. Research questions that are too precise or rigid may limit your selection and investigation of source materials. Therefore, it is advisable to generate a broad and flexible list of research questions that allows you to modify your questions as you move along and your research topic becomes clearer and more focused. One example of excellent research questions is Michael Lomax's (2006) analysis of entrepreneurship and revenue maximization in black baseball. Lomax notes that his study involved three research questions: "How did these entrepreneurs employ the business practices developed by black baseball magnates of the late nineteenth century to make the Philadelphia Giants a competitive ball club? How did these entrepreneurs try to expand the Giants' market potential and maximize their revenues? What were the factors that led to the Giants' collapse?" (p. 100).

Once you have settled on a manageable topic, established flexible questions to guide your research, and initiated your search for source material (stages covered earlier in the chapter), you can begin the process of discovery by reading or perusing materials as you collect them. You do not need to wait until all of your primary and secondary sources are in your possession before you start reading, synthesizing, and analyzing the materials. Some sport management historians begin their research by examining (or having an awareness of) the various secondary sources related to their selected research topic. This background knowledge helps provide both a foundation for the study and insight into what other historians have written about and interpreted regarding the chosen topic. Thus, they begin by possessing or putting together a historiographical essay or foundation related to the subject. Developing a historiography (e.g., historiographic essay) can help you as you move into the primary source investigations; it can help you knowing what research questions should be posed, what methods have been used, and what analyses and interpretations have already been made regarding your topic. On the other hand, some sport management historians commence their research by examining primary sources. They believe that this approach provides them with an opportunity to discover—with limited prejudices and preoccupations—new facts, analyses, connections, and interpretations that others may have missed in their examination of primary sources. Still other sport historians combine the two approaches and examine secondary and primary sources at the same time. They are reading primary sources for information and quotes at the same time that they are reading and analyzing secondary sources and understanding what others have extracted from various other primary sources. Regardless of the approach you choose, your initial readings of sources will help you become better informed about your topic and further define and develop it.

When reading and synthesizing source materials, take research notes on note cards or by means of some other vehicle (e.g., notebook, loose-leaf papers in a binder, word processing software).

From the source material you examine, you will record information such as factual details, historical background, summarized and paraphrased material, opinions and quotations, bibliographic information (i.e., citations), and your own comments, notes, and ideas related to the various sources. The amount of information and detail that you record on your note cards depends on your research questions, the objectives of your study, the sources you are investigating, and your overall familiarity with and background knowledge of the history and facts regarding the topic you are researching. For categorization and retrieval purposes, the indexing system you use for your notes should be flexible (e.g., if using note cards, one quote, note, comment, or fact on each card), since you will be arranging and rearranging the notes under a variety of subject headings (e.g., thematic, topical, event-specific, chronological) throughout the development of the sport management research paper.

One often overlooked but helpful developmental stage of writing a research paper is the creation of an outline. Writing an outline focuses your efforts and helps you determine what primary and secondary source materials you may need. For example, in Stacy Lorenz's (2003) history of the development of sport coverage in Canada, the major points of the research paper included the following outline: "The Rise of the Popular Press" (p. 135), "The Expansion of Sports Coverage" (p. 141), "Local Sports Coverage: Civic Boosterism and Community Identity" (p. 148), "National and International Sports Coverage: Creating a World of Sport" (p. 152), and "Conclusion" (p. 155). You should come up with your tentative outline (e.g., introduction, body, major points, conclusion) early on in the process, since doing so will structure your thinking and the project itself. As a result, you will be more efficient in your approach, because you will know where information is and how your thoughts are being arranged. A detailed outline helps you conceptualize the overarching structure, connections, and flow of your historical research paper by providing you with a type of flow chart, mind map, or logical linkage of various components. Such a visual aid can help you develop an overall narrative and specific transitions in the construction of your research paper. Your detailed outline should list the subjects, themes, topics, and issues that you want to explore. It should help you conceptualize the research paper's major structure and specific major points, and it should contain elements such as thematic chapters (if you are working on a book) or topical main headings, sections or subheadings, and even paragraph titles based on various subtopics and subthemes. Your outline will be flexible; you will amend it as you read more source materials and add new subtopics and ideas. Some subtopics and themes will take on greater or lesser significance, and some new areas will reveal themselves as you work through the project.

At some point, of course, you will begin to write your sport management research paper per se. Again, you do not have to wait until you have analyzed all of your sources and assembled all of your research notes before you begin the writing process. Using the outline you created and the research notes you have compiled, you will develop your first draft. Do not worry about proofreading or editing your early drafts; instead, use the early drafts to complete the outline, flesh out the outlined points, create the background, make the connections and transitions between points, develop themes, arrive at new analyses and interpretations, provide description, and structure your argument. You can always bolster your drafts with additional evidence or stylistic and grammatical changes as you go through the rewriting phases.

You can organize your draft according to a chronological (i.e., sequential development) or topical (i.e., thematic) methodological approach. One example of a sequential development is Friedman and Mason's (2001) article examining the influences that led to the relocation of the NFL's Houston Oilers and the public financing of a new stadium in the Oilers' new home of Nashville, Tennessee. Their paper moves from analysis of early negotiations, legislative approvals, and the sale campaign to the stadium referendum, stadium funding, and the eventual relocation of the team. In contrast, an example of a more topical approach can be seen in Fielding and Miller's (1998) historical analysis of the development of, influences on, and responses to the foreign invasion in the American sporting goods market. After introducing the topic and covering the invasion, the researchers then take a topical approach by placing the various strategies according to the components of the marketing mix. Beyond the chronological and topical approaches, many sport management studies use a combination of the two. Mason (1997) took this approach in "examin[ing] the historical development of the National Football League into a single-business entity . . . [and reviewing] some instances of opportunistic agent behavior" (p. 206). You can use the deductive approach by examining a research topic progressively from the general to the specific, or you can use the inductive approach in which particular facts are established and lead to generalizations.

You can also move your paper along a continuum from the less important to the extremely important, from the simple to the complex, or from the widely known to the relatively unknown.

In writing your introduction, make sure that it is intriguing and inviting. You can do so from the first sentence of the paper. For example, John Watterson (2000) opens his examination of a mythical early college football crisis by noting that "in 1944, Frank Menke's *Encyclopedia of Sports* presented one of the most memorable stories in sport history" (p. 291). Such a sentence pulls readers into the narrative. You can even start your paper with a direct quote, as Larry Youngs (2003) did by using a newspaper quote from 1900 in the first sentence of his historical examination of the marketing and establishment of a golf destination site in North Carolina. Regardless of your lead sentence, your introduction should let readers know about the topic, your selection rationale, the method or approach you will be taking, the scope of the paper, the main points, and the overall purpose of the paper. Before you move into the body of the paper, the introduction should also present historiographic information about your topic. Overall, the introduction and background should be well told by means of a narrative that is explanatory and captivating. The rest of the paper should involve telling a good story and providing meaning and context for your story, analyses, and interpretations. Back up your various descriptions and insights with examples, evidence, and appropriate referencing. Your paper should also have strong mechanics: a well-defined structure, natural and strong transitions between points, an engaging writing style, proper syntax, impeccable grammar, and complete footnoting and citing of sources.

You will no doubt write several drafts of your research paper as you go through several rounds of editing and proofreading. Good writing is generally considered rewriting, so you will be writing several drafts of your paper as you go through the process. Your drafts will move from organizing and developing your notes to providing more substantial and detailed information, analyses, and interpretations of the findings. After you write the body of your paper, you are able to go back and rework your introduction and conclusion. In the conclusion, you again cover the main points of the paper and then explain your main conclusions and interpretations based on the evidence that you provided in the body of the paper. Your paper is complete once you add a comprehensive and organized bibliography presented in accordance with the style manual (e.g., APA, MLA, Turabian) used by the intended publication outlet.

Summary

In order to ask the right questions, understand the proper context and perspective, and develop decision-making skills, sport management students can benefit by familiarizing themselves with historical writing and how to conduct historical research. As a future professional in the sport industry, your development of an appreciation for and knowledge of history can help you understand that changes occur in sport management, that these changes occur for various reasons (causes), and that, based on evidence and your own interpretations of that evidence, you can attempt to determine causal relationships involved in those changes.

At its foundation, a sport management historical analysis is simply a story revealed about an aspect, phenomenon, or personality in the sport industry. Therefore, this chapter examines what is involved in researching, analyzing, and interpreting sport management stories. The chapter addresses issues in sport history research methods, prerequisites for conducting such research, and the process of selecting a historical topic to research. The chapter also details the ways in which historians distinguish and analyze primary and secondary source material and the various aspects of historical data analysis. The chapter concludes with an examination of how to format and write historiographic essays and historical research papers.

Selected text reprinted, by permission, from M. Washington and M.J. Ventresca, 2008, "Institutional contradictions and struggles in the formation of U.S. collegiate basketball, 1880-1938," *Journal of Sport Management* 22(1): 30-49.

Access the full article online at
www.humankinetics.com/products/all-products/Research-Methods-and-Design-in-Sport-Management.

ABSTRACT

The prominence of collegiate athletics in amateur athletics is a historically specific outcome. Research in institutional theory is extended by developing an institutional-conflict-based approach to studying institutional changes of U.S. collegiate athletics. Available secondary sources and extensive original data demonstrate how the NCAA came to dominate the governance structure of U.S. amateur basketball. Discourse about the NCAA came to represent the dominant discourse in amateur basketball, and colleges and universities eliminated the noncolleges and nonuniversities from their play schedules. The NCAA developed a set of institutional strategies aimed at increasing its power in U.S. basketball. An institutional-conflict-based approach is useful for analyzing changes in the institutional structure of sports and demonstrates how governance systems and institutional conflicts impact organizational actions. Sport policy makers and managers should consider the historical context and institutional environment of their sport when making decisions.

TEXT EXCERPTS

Historical research requires the systematic collection and analysis of archival data (Ventresca & Mohr, 2002). For this study, we relied on several key primary data sources such as NCAA convention summaries; notes of various meetings between the NCAA, YMCA, and AAU; and individual college athletic histories (see the appendix for a list of sources).

· · · · · · · · · · · · · · · · ·

Our analysis was purposefully driven by process (Kieser, 1994; Van de Ven & Poole, 1995) in an effort to capture the dynamics of actions and reactions of the parties as the struggle over the contested terrain unfolded. This process involved capturing the post hoc interpretations of these events from the vantage point of elapsed time. We used secondary sources to substantial advantage in this phase—the dissertations, existing histories, and other published accounts.

....

Although this is a historical project, we think that this work also has implications for sport managers. A fundamental insight from organizational theory is that organizations and industries are imprinted with the environmental conditions that were in place during the organization or industry's creation (Stinchcombe, 1965). Although the environmental conditions might have changed since the organization or industry's founding, often the structure of the organization or industry does not change. Thus, for existing sport managers, we contend that history matters. Specifically, this project is an example of how existing problems with amateur basketball (dominated by the NCAA, the debate between the amateur and the professional nature of college basketball, the role of the media) might be a consequence of the historical conditions that surrounded basketball during its creation. The implication of this project has implications for other sport-related issues.

....

Historical research requires the systematic collection and analysis of archival data (Ventresca & Mohr, 2002). For this study, we relied on several key primary data sources such as NCAA convention summaries; notes of various meetings between the NCAA, YMCA, and AAU; and individual college athletic histories (see the appendix for a list of sources). Although such primary data sources offer key insights into events as they unfolded and offer the direct point of view of major actors in these organizations (Tuchman, 1994), they fail to provide the interpretive context of retrospective accounts. That is, material documents and texts can be given new meanings as they are separated in time from their original producers and reinterpreted post hoc in the context of "changes in meaning across space and culture" (Hodder, 1994, p. 398).

DISCUSSION QUESTIONS

1 What implications did the authors identify for this historical research, and how did they explain that such historical research matters?

2 Refer to the Topic Selection section of this chapter in your textbook. What aspects of this section are explained by the authors in their article?

3 What primary sources were used in this historical research?

4 Look at this article's appendix. Which sources are secondary sources?

5 How did the authors code their data and conduct their data analysis?

Legal Research

Anita M. Moorman, JD ▪ University of Louisville
John Grady, JD, PhD ▪ University of South Carolina

Learning Objectives

After studying this chapter, you should be able to do the following:

- Identify research topics in sport management that can be studied using legal research methods
- Discuss the characteristics that make legal research similar to or different from other types of traditional research methods
- Understand how legal research methods can complement qualitative and quantitative methods in sport management research
- Design a research project using legal research methods
- Understand the value and benefits of the nonlinear research design and the recursive approach to conducting legal research
- Write a manuscript, thesis, or dissertation using legal research methods

This chapter provides an introduction to legal research, which is a unique process that can be used for understanding and investigating a variety of research topics in sport management. For example, legal research could be used to examine and assess the legality of certain business practices in the industry, or to survey and critique an area of the law or legal principle and provide commentary and recommendations for future action, or to identify legal justifications for particular management practices and management policies. In fact, all of the general research projects listed in the highlight box could involve locating, identifying, and analyzing legal information.

Unlike the research undertaken by law students or lawyers, the work done by researchers in sport management is aimed not at advising a client on a particular point of law but at seeking answers to research questions that can best be answered by using legal sources rather than other types of sources or research methods. For example, a researcher studying the impact of Title IX on Olympic sport might examine Title IX court cases and regulatory guidelines from the U.S. Department of Education and analyze expert commentary from law review articles. Legal research provides an additional and distinct set of tools that sport management researchers can use to find answers to their questions.

Qualities of Legal Research

Legal research can take the form of action research with the goal of problem solving or improving industry practices, or it can be conceptual or empirical; in addition, many legal research papers employ mixed methods. If done properly, legal research can inform our managerial decision making in a positive way and guide us to better management decisions that are both consistent with legal requirements and based on sound reasoning and thought. Although legal research uses a variety of distinctive investigative tools, legal research methods share many common characteristics with other traditional

---

Potential Research Projects Using Legal Research Methods

1. Examining the correctness and impact of a recent court decision

2. Examining the policy and legal intent and impact of a newly enacted statute or newly adopted regulation

3. Examining the threat of litigation arising from certain events in the industry

4. Examining and assessing the legality of certain business practices in the industry

5. Examining the management of risk and/or assessing liability within an organization

6. Surveying and critiquing an area of the law or legal principle, providing commentary, and recommending future action

7. Identifying legal justifications for management practices and management policies

8. Explaining how legal principles contribute to management practices and policies

9. Examining an area of the law from a historical perspective and summarizing both past and recent developments in the field

10. Examining relationships between legal practices and management practices

11. Examining the role of legal counsel and legal representation in the sport industry

12. Examining legal processes such as alternative dispute resolution techniques and trial or appellate procedures

13. Examining the role of legal education in a sport management curriculum

14. Examining rule-making and enforcement processes in amateur and professional sport organizations

15. Examining attitudes and perceptions regarding legal practices and decision making

16. Examining best pedagogical practices in teaching legal issues in sport and sport law

research methods (e.g., quantitative, qualitative, and mixed methods). Similarities include the inductive nature of qualitative research; whereas the qualitative researcher draws conclusions based on observed behavior or events, the legal researcher draws conclusions based on a statement of the law and extrapolates how a particular set of facts fits within the confines of existing law. In other words, the legal researcher determines whether a particular behavior or decision is consistent with current law and a qualitative researcher may evaluate whether a particular behavior or decision is consistent with theorized behavior.

A quantitative researcher, on the other hand, identifies variables and measures relationships that provide predictive or causal explanation for a theory or problem. The purpose of legal research, however, is not to generalize to a whole population; rather, it is problem and issue based. Thus quantitative methods alone rarely produce meaningful understanding of legal issues or outcomes. For example, merely counting the number of sport facility negligence cases (similar to a content analysis) may be of little help in understanding why or how the cases come to fruition. Instead, a researcher may be more interested in identifying case variables, such as whether the defendant was a private or municipally owned facility, the type of sport venue where the injury occurred, the type and severity of injury, and whether the defendant was able to raise any defenses to liability such as comparative negligence, according to which a comparison of the plaintiff's fault in contributing to his or her own injury with the fault of the defendant is claimed to excuse the defendant's liability for negligent conduct. In many cases, legal research methods can (and should) be used to complement quantitative or qualitative methods in to answer the research questions and provide a richer, more in-depth picture of the phenomena being observed (similar to the goals of qualitative research).

Even though traditional quantitative methods are not routinely used in legal research, a number of empirical legal journals are published, and they often use statistical analysis for policy and political analysis. Statistical information can also help researchers develop an understanding of legal issues. For example, several studies are under way to document the increased frequency with which female athletes suffer ACL injuries as compared with their male counterparts (Sokolove, 2008). As managers gain knowledge about health risks, that knowledge shapes their legal duty to operate their athletic programs safely.

Nature of the Law and Legal Research

Fundamental precepts of the law are based on predictability and consistency in the law, yet the law is by nature organic, which means that it is derivative and in some sense is alive. Consider the preceding example regarding an athletic program operator's duty to operate the program safely (Sokolove, 2008). It is a simple matter to state that the operator has a duty to protect participants from known risks, but, as the Sokolove study illuminates, the known risks can be ever-changing. The mere fact that an operator ignores these new risks, fails to properly instruct its female athletes in light of recent discoveries related to ACL injuries, and then later is successfully sued for negligence does not constitute a change in the law. It is merely an application of negligence law to a new and specific set of facts. Furthermore, the standard for imposing negligence liability has not been altered. The operator is still liable only for known risks, and in this example the known risks have changed—but not the underlying legal principle.

This is a good example of the organic nature of the law. Even though the underlying legal principle has not changed, outcomes may differ due to changes in the circumstances or context to which the law is applied. For example, a researcher might apply negligence law in order to understand a facility manager's duty of care to avoid the occurrence of staph infection, but the results of the application may be different in a professional sport context than in the context of campus recreation. Even though the legal obligations may be similar, the context and nature of the sport being played may dictate a different outcome.

Another aspect of the organic nature of the law is the fact that the law can and frequently does change—either slowly, based on changing economic, cultural, political, and societal influences, or suddenly, due to legislative intervention. The sport industry offers several examples of both the slow, plodding kind of change and the more abrupt type. One good example that demonstrates both types of change can be found in spectator liability cases involving observers injured by fly balls at baseball games. Over time, the courts have provided an immunity of sorts for baseball facility operators when spectators are injured by fly balls. In these so called "limited duty" cases, the courts have routinely found no liability so long as the sport facility satisfied certain requirements, including a duty to provide screening in the most dangerous parts of the stadium and the option of reseating patrons to other sections of the stadium if they do not feel safe. However, when one Illinois court decision deviated from this line of cases and found the facility liable for failing to protect the spectator from the harm of fly balls, the Illinois state legislature intervened by passing the Baseball Facility Liability Act (740 ILCS 38 [1993]), which ensures that, at least in the state of Illinois, facilities will not be held liable in spectator injury cases in baseball facilities.

This example also engenders a wealth of public policy debate about the proper role of private business interests (notably the Chicago Cubs and Chicago White Sox) being totally immune from liability at the expense, in some cases, of severely injured fans. A sport management researcher could explore the previous case decisions that served as basis for the "limited duty" rule, focusing specifically on cases in the state of Illinois. The researcher could then analyze the policy reasons the legislature cited in passing the new legislation. Finally, the researcher could determine the impact of the legislation on various stakeholders, including the team, the facility operator, and spectators. Thus, legal research often complements public policy research in identifying issues and problems and recommending responsive solutions and strategies. Another example can be found in sport management research that addresses the growing problem of sexual harassment in the sport industry. This research could result in a policy piece exploring how the context of sport (e.g., non-traditional work hours, athletic trainers working in locker rooms or during team travel) may alter traditional workplace dynamics and may allow incidents of sexually harassing behavior among employees or supervisors to occur. This research would necessarily require an overview and discussion of sexual harassment law as applied to sport organizations in order to further demonstrate the significance of the policy arguments and recommendations.

The law, and consequently legal research, is also fact intensive. Courts are asked to apply the law to a narrowly defined set of facts, such as ruling on the eligibility waiver of a high school athlete who has surpassed the school district's age limit for participating in interscholastic athletics. The court is deliberate in not suggesting how the law might apply in future situations, choosing instead to narrowly tailor its ruling to the set of facts presented in the one case being decided.

Considering both the organic and the fact-intensive nature of the law, it is critical that legal researchers understand the rationale for imposing liability or reaching a particular conclusion. You can develop this type of understanding through systematic analysis of both primary and secondary legal resources. The next section explains legal research techniques and legal sources.

Legal Research Techniques

Legal research tends to be nonlinear. The researcher must employ a combination of techniques and investigate a variety of sources to ensure that the research is comprehensive. In other words, the researcher needs to exhaustively search for and analyze any sources of authority that would be applicable to the research problem. For example, the researcher must find all cases that relate to the legal issue and then, through the process of elimination, narrow the search to sources that are directly on point. As the issue or problem is more clearly understood and defined, additional research is needed.

In a way, legal research can be thought of as solving a puzzle. The pieces of the puzzle are the cases and the laws. Determining how (and whether) they fit together is the researcher's goal in putting the puzzle together. The one main difference with conducting legal research and the puzzle analogy is that extra puzzle pieces are thrown in that may have little or no relevance to the questions you are trying to answer. This is where legal research can become particularly challenging (and fun!), because, as the researcher, you determine what cases are relevant to your research and demonstrate their relevance through your explanation. For example, in studying emergency evacuation in sport facilities for people with disabilities, Grady and Andrew (2007) found that there was not a well-developed body of case law involving evacuation of sport facilities. As a result, they decided to perform in-depth analysis of evacuation cases involving movie theater patrons under the Americans with Disabilities Act (ADA), then analogize how the evacuation of patrons in a movie theater was factually and legally similar to evacuation in sport stadia or arenas.

Making an Analogy

Two techniques are necessary when presenting arguments and interpretation of legal authority. The first technique, mentioned in the preceding example involving evacuation, is the analogy. A researcher must be able to analogize how a given case relates to the current issue or problem. Your research will only rarely reveal a case that contains facts or legal issues identical to those in your current situation. Thus, you will need to locate the cases and authority that are most similar, then argue by analogy that those similarities logically lead to the same conclusion in your case as in the previous ones.

Distinguishing Precedent

The second technique is to distinguish one case from another. For example, when dealing with case law that is not favorable to a particular outcome or is factually dissimilar to the case at hand, the sport management researcher must evaluate the authority in order to determine whether the differences

Distinguishing Precedent: Dusckiewicz v. Carter

In the following case, the parties and the court use both of these two techniques—analogy and distinguishing precedent—to support their arguments and resolve the case. Read the following case, *Dusckiewicz v. Carter,* 52 A.2d 788 (Vt. 1947), then consider the questions that follow the case description.

The complaint is based upon the alleged negligence of the defendant in conducting a wrestling match, resulting in injury to the plaintiff, a spectator at that contest. Carter put on a show at the armory in Rutland on the evening of June 6, 1945. The principal feature of his show was a wrestling match. After the match had been going on for some time, one of the wrestlers threw the other through the ropes in the direction where the plaintiff was seated. When the plaintiff saw the wrestler coming he put up his right hand to protect himself from the oncoming wrestler landing on him and as a result he received a sprained hand and wrist. It is for this injury and resulting alleged damages that the plaintiff seeks to recover.

The defendant asserts that the plaintiff assumed the risk of the danger which resulted in his alleged injury.

As to the question of assumption of risks, an invitee at a place of amusement ordinarily assumes the risk of an obvious danger or of one that is a matter of common knowledge; conversely, such a person does not assume the risk of a hidden or undisclosed danger, not of common knowledge, in the absence of warning or personal knowledge. That the danger

which resulted in the plaintiff's injury was not an obvious danger is self-evident. However, the defendant contends that the plaintiff must be taken to have assumed the risks of the danger which resulted in his injury, because he had personal knowledge of it and also because such danger is a matter of common knowledge.

In support of his argument, defendant cites several baseball cases. These cases hold that an invitee, familiar with the game of baseball, buying a seat in a part of the stands not protected by screens, who is hit by a batted ball during the progress of a ball game proceeding in a normal manner, can not recover, because it is a matter of common knowledge that chance is an important factor in determining the direction a batted ball may take as it leaves the bat.

It is to be noted that while the defendant makes a positive assertion as to the purpose and object of baseball, he is less positive and more cautious in speaking of the purposes and objects of wrestling, "The intent and purpose of a baseball game is to hit the ball as far as possible, and apparently one of the purposes of a wrestling match is to throw a wrestler as far as possible." The number of people who know how a wrestling match is conducted and what may reasonably be expected to happen there is small when compared with the great number who know what may reasonably be expected to happen at a baseball game played in the normal manner.

While the record shows that the plaintiff stated in cross examination that he is a "wres-

(continued)

Distinguishing Precedent   (continued)

tling fan", there is nothing therein showing the rules under which this contest was conducted nor whether such rules permit one wrestler to throw the other from the ring and neither does it appear that the plaintiff had ever seen that done previous to the occasion in question. From what has been hereinbefore stated, it follows that it can not be held as a matter of law that the plaintiff assumed the risks of the danger which resulted in his injury.

Discussion Questions

1. The defendant made an analogy to the baseball cases in order to support his contention that the plaintiff assumed the risk of being injured by a wrestler thrown from the ring. How are the two situations analogous, according to the defendant?

2. The court distinguishes the baseball cases from the defendant's situation as a wrestling spectator. How are the two situations different, such that the baseball cases did not control the outcome of the wrestling case?

A legal researcher who is able to apply the reasoning used in this case can explore its impact on and relevance to current spectator injury cases. The researcher would explore the concept of common knowledge of risks among spectators at sporting events and examine the factors relevant to determining those risks, such as the characteristics and nature of the sport, the prevalence of knowledge about the sport among average consumers, and the actual knowledge of specific injured spectators. In this manner, making comparisons through an analogy or by distinguishing characteristics allows the researcher to advance reasoned arguments in support of conclusions and recommendations.

are sufficient for distinguishing the authority from that of the current situation, thereby rendering it inapplicable or not logically controlling. Making effective use of the techniques of analogy and distinguishing precedent poses the greatest challenge for sport management investigators in doing legal research.

Sources of Legal Information

Legal sources are commonly described either as primary sources or secondary sources. Most sport management research will involve discovery, analysis and analysis of both primary and secondary sources. Primary legal sources are actual statements of the law such as case opinions, statutes, administrative regulations, and constitutions. Secondary legal sources, on the other hand, involve sources that interpret and comment on the law or its application such as law review articles, periodicals, textbooks, and treatises.

Primary Legal Sources

Primary legal sources include constitutions, statutes, rules and regulations, and court decisions.

Such sources represent the actual law, whether it is a decision of the U.S. Supreme Court or a statute enacted by a state. Regardless of the type of legal research you are conducting, you can ultimately rely only on primary legal sources in determining what the law is and what the law requires.

Case Law

One of the most common ways to begin a legal research project is to locate a recent case about the topic at hand. A case or court decision results from a jury verdict or a court order that resolves a case or an issue in a case. For example, suppose that Tiger Woods sued the John Brown Company based on the company's unauthorized use of Woods' name in an advertisement. Woods' lawsuit or case would probably include several different legal claims, such as trademark infringement, violation of the right of publicity, and misappropriation of goodwill. It is possible that John Brown would file a motion for summary judgment, asking the court to dismiss Woods' trademark infringement claim. If the court denied that motion, it would enter an order to that effect, and the order would represent a court decision. Ultimately, when the case went to trial, another court decision would be entered reflecting the outcome of the trial. This final outcome would also be a court decision that might be published depending on the level of court deciding the case. If you wanted to locate and analyze this decision, you would of course need to understand when and where court decisions are published.

Court systems are structured hierarchically—that is, some courts are superior to others. The highest court is usually a supreme or superior court, followed by an intermediate appellate court and then by a district or trial court at the bottom. Most cases originate at the bottom of the hierarchy, at the trial or district court level, and work their way up through the court system. It can take years for a case to move through all levels of the court system. Along the way, any number of court decisions may be entered in a case as it winds its way through the court system toward its ultimate conclusion, and to find court decisions you need to understand how they are reported. We will now explore the federal court system and then the state court system.

In the federal court system, the vast majority of cases originate in the U.S. District Court. The U.S. District Court is the federal trial court and is the first level within the federal court system. Any appeal from a U.S. district court decision would be made to the appropriate U.S. court of appeals. Any party to the district court action may appeal to the U.S. court of appeals. The U.S. courts of appeals represent the second or intermediate appellate level in of the federal court system. After the U.S. court of appeals renders its decision, a party can still request another appellate review by the U.S. Supreme Court. However, the U.S. Supreme Court is not required to hear all appeals; rather, the appellate jurisdiction of the U.S. Supreme Court is considered discretionary, and requests for appeal (known as petitions for certiorari) are rarely granted. The U.S. Supreme Court is the highest court in the land, and its decisions are considered binding on all federal and state courts.

State court systems are organized similarly to the federal courts. Most states have several trial or district courts located in various counties in the state. Most cases originate in the trial or district courts, then follow a similar path as with federal cases; that is, appeals go to an intermediate appellate court or directly to the state supreme court. A decision by a state supreme court is binding on all other courts in that state.

When conducting a **case law analysis**, the researcher must know which level of court is deciding the case, since the level helps determine the **precedential value** of the decision. A decision rendered by the U.S. Supreme Court is binding on all lower federal courts and carries the highest precedential value, whereas a state court decision has limited impact because it applies only to the one state and represents the opinion of just one court. Even a decision by a federal district court establishes binding precedent only on the courts within that district; other federal district courts and the higher court of appeals are not bound by a district court's decision. It is not always easy to recognize the significance of case law, but the ability can be developed by carefully noting the level of the court during your research and relying on secondary sources to put the case decision in the context of case law that existed before the current decision was made. It is relatively simple to determine the level of the court by understanding the information provided in the legal citation for a particular court decision. The accompanying highlight box explains the citation information for the federal courts.

The following sample citations of state reporters follow a format similar to those used in the federal courts: *Maisonave v. Newark Bears Professional Baseball Club*, 881 A.2d 700 (N.J. 2005). This case can be found in volume 881 at page 700 of the Atlantic Reporter, Second Series. This is a 2005 decision of the New Jersey Supreme Court. *Rowe v. Pinellas Sports Auth.*, 461 So. 2d 72 (Fla. 1984). This case can be found in volume 461 at page 72 of the *Southern Reporter, Second Series*, and is a 1984 decision of the Florida Supreme Court. *Kelly v. Marylanders for Sports Sanity, Inc.* 530 A.2d 245 (Md. Ct. App. 1987). This case can be found in volume 530 at page 245 of the *Atlantic Reporter, Second Series*. Notice that this case is a 1987 decision of the Maryland Court of Appeals; thus, it is one of those instances in which an intermediate appellate court decision was published. You can distinguish between decisions of the court of appeals and those of the various state supreme courts by noting the term "App." or "Ct. App." in parentheses with the date. If the citation does not contain "App" or "Ct. App." but gives only the state abbreviation, as in the first two sample citations given here, then the decision was made by the state's highest court (either a supreme court or a superior court).

Constitutions, Statutes, Regulations, and Legislative History

The U.S. Constitution is the supreme law of the land. It both authorizes and restricts conduct of the federal and state governments and defines the protected rights and liberties of private citizens. Similarly, each of the 50 states has its own consti-

Citations in the United States Court System

- **U.S. district courts.** Federal Supplement and Federal Supplement, Second Series (cited F. Supp. or F. Supp. 2d). (Note: These reporters are a continuing series of cases reported by the U.S. district courts from 1932 to the present. It is now in its second series or edition.) Sample citation: *Hoopla Sports and Entertainment, Inc. v. Nike, Inc.,* 947 F. Supp. 347 (N.D. Ill. 1996). The citation tells us that this court decision can be located in volume 947 at page 347 of the Federal Supplement and that the decision was made by the U.S. District Court for the Northern District of Illinois in 1996.

- **U.S. courts of appeals.** Federal Reporter; Federal Reporter, Second Series; and Federal Reporter, Third Series (cited F., F.2d, or F.3d). (Note: These reporters are a continuing series of cases reported by the U.S. courts of appeals from 1880 to the present. It is now in its third series or edition). Sample citation: *National Basketball Association v. Motorola, Inc.,* 105 F.3d 841 (2nd Cir. 1997). The citation tells us that this court decision can be found in volume 105 at page 841 of the Federal Reporter, Third Series and that the decision was made by the U.S. Court of Appeals for the Second Circuit in 1997.

- **U.S. Supreme Court.** U.S. Supreme Court Reports (cited U.S.), Supreme Court Reporter (cited S. Ct.), and Lawyer's Edition (cited L.Ed.2d). (Note: These three reporters all report the same Supreme Court cases. U.S. Supreme Court Reports is the official Supreme Court reporter, but Supreme Court Reporter is user friendly and is the most commonly used.) Sample citation: *PGA Tour, Inc. v. Martin,* 532 U.S. 661, 121 S. Ct. 1879, 149 L. Ed. 2d 904 (2001). As is often the case, this citation refers to all three reporters; this form of citation is called a string cite. The first part of the string is the citation of U.S. Supreme Court Reports (532 U.S. 661). It is followed by the citation of the Supreme Court Reporter (121 S. Ct. 1879) and then by the citation of Lawyer's Edition (149 L. Ed. 2d 904). You may also see a Supreme Court case cited from only one of these three reporters, for example, *PGA Tour, Inc. v. Martin,* 121 S. Ct. 1879 (2001). The citation tells us that this decision can be found in volume 121 of the Supreme Court Reporter on page 1879 and that this decision of the U.S. Supreme Court was rendered in 2001.

tution governing the conduct of state government and citizens of that state. The U.S. Congress and the 50 state legislatures enact laws, known as statutes, that address issues as diverse as ticket scalping, the enforceability of contracts, and the registration of trademarks. Federal statutes are codified (or published) in a series of volumes known as the United States Code (U.S.C.). Each of the 50 states also codifies its state statutes, which are often called civil codes, public laws, session laws, or revised statutes. Both the United States Code and the state statutes are bound and published. Many of the bound volumes contain annotations to categorize court decisions that interpret the statute in question. These annotations are similar to an index and assist the researcher in locating specific court decisions and understanding how the statute has been interpreted and applied by the courts. For example, if you were trying to determine whether a federal district court in your state had ruled in a case involving the Ted Stevens Olympic and Amateur Sports Act, 36 U.S.C.

§ 220501 et seq. (this act created and empowered the United States Olympic Committee), you could use the annotations to locate specific cases decided by courts in your state.

Rather than republish the hardback editions of the U.S. Code each year, the publishers of these volumes instead print supplements to the hardback volume that contain any amendments or modifications that have been made to statutes. This supplement, called a "pocket part," is a softbound pamphlet that can be inserted into a sleeve located inside the back cover of each hardback volume. The publisher uses this process for a number of years before publishing a new series of the hardback volumes. Thus, the most recent amendments to laws will be found in the pocket part, so you must always look there for any changes passed by Congress or the state legislature since the most recent hardback volume was printed. For example, the Sports Agent Responsibility and Trust Act (SPARTA), passed by the U.S. Congress in September 2004 to regulate agents' activities with student athletes, would be cited as the Sports Agent Responsibility and Trust Act, 15 U.S.C. § 7801 et seq. (2004). This citation tells us that the act can be found beginning at Section 7801 in Title 15 of the U.S. Code, which, as explained earlier, is published in several volumes. Because the publisher is not going to reprint all of Title 15 every time Congress passes new laws or amends existing laws, you would have to look in the pocket part to find SPARTA.

Another example is the recent amendment to the Americans with Disabilities Act of 1990. The ADA Amendments Act of 2008 was signed into law on September 24, 2008, and became effective on January 1, 2009. The amendment modifies several significant provisions in the ADA and will naturally be of interest to sport organizations, most of which are subject to the ADA. The official statutory language and legislative history for the Americans with Disabilities Act of 1990, 42 U.S.C. § 12101 et seq. will initially be included in the pocket part until the bound volumes are reprinted. Sport and recreation managers can also gain immediate access to information about such developments from Internet-based sources that are explored later in this chapter.

The U.S. Congress and the state legislatures also create regulatory bodies, such as the Federal Aviation Administration, the Environmental Protection Agency, and the Equal Employment Opportunity Commission. These regulatory bodies are often required to create rules and regulations to fulfill their assigned purposes, and those rules and regulations are codified in the Code of Federal Regulations (C.F.R.), which can be a useful resource for research related to a particular agency's activities. Most state and federal agencies also maintain up-to-date information about rules, regulations, and policies on their Web sites to permit easy access to this information. A partial list of constitutional and statutory resources is contained in the accompanying highlight box.

The sport management researcher must locate and analyze any potentially relevant constitutional provisions, statutes, or regulations to determine their applicability to the research problem. "The body of law represented by statutory law has expanded greatly. Many matters once governed by **common law** (court-made law) are now governed by **statutory law**" (Putman, 2003, p. 49). For example, state dram shop liability statutes in 43 states dictate the requirements for the sale of alcohol to the public. Similarly, administrative agencies such as the Environmental Protection Agency (EPA)

Constitutional and Statutory Resources

- U.S. Constitution
- State constitutions
- Treaties
- Federal statutes (the U.S. Code [U.S.C.])
- State statutes
- Municipal ordinances
- Executive orders and promulgations
- Rules and regulations of federal administrative agencies (CFR)
- Rules and regulations of state administrative agencies
- Attorney general opinions—federal and state

"adopt rules and regulations that have the force of law" (Putman, p. 49). In the context of sport, administrative rules and state statutes increasingly dictate the legal obligations of facility managers regarding the safe operation of their business; for example, administrative rules for environmental protection may dictate procedures for the disposal or recycling of water used to hydrate golf courses or playing fields. Meanwhile, certain state statutes commonly known as recreational user statutes may provide landowners who open their lands for public recreation with immunity from liability when a person is injured while engaged in recreation on the land. As these examples illustrate, statutory law and administrative rules are ripe for further academic research.

Once a researcher has located a relevant state statute, he or she must engage in **statutory analysis** to determine whether "the statute applies, how it applies, and the effect of that application" (Putman, 2003). One particularly challenging part of statutory analysis involves determining whether the required elements of a statute are met by the factual situation at hand. This type of analysis is routinely done by practicing attorneys, but it is also valuable for sport management researchers to consider how the law applies to the various contexts of sport management research. For example, a researcher could analyze whether a statute that provides immunity to state governmental officials could be applied to the athletic director of a state university athletic department or head football coach when a student athlete dies as a result of heat exhaustion during practice. The researcher would likely first need to determine whether employees of the athletic department fall within the definition of government "officials" who are covered by statute and then, if so, determine whether their actions fall within the scope of the immunity statute.

Analyzing **legislative history** also provides a fruitful area of research in sport management because several notable statutory and administrative laws have a long history in the context of sport. The most obvious of these statutory schemes is Title IX, which was passed in 1973 as an amendment to a federal education law ensuring equal opportunity based on gender and was later interpreted to require equal access and opportunity in athletics. Analyzing the legislative history of Title IX is valuable in part because it allows historical comparison of participation in sport by women and girls at the time the law was enacted with the participation opportunities that currently exist in intercollegiate and interscholastic sport. A researcher who investigated this topic could address both legal and sociocultural research questions and could use case law, statutory law, and law review articles to analyze the issue.

Secondary Legal Sources

Secondary legal sources are the backbone of legal research for sport managers because they give the researcher a more in-depth understanding of the legal issues being analyzed. Secondary sources interpret and comment on the law or its application, and they can be found in places such as law review articles, periodicals, textbooks, legal encyclopedias, and treatises. The accompanying highlight box lists some common secondary legal resources. These valuable sources can also help you locate additional or related primary sources. Remember that only primary resources represent the actual law; as a result, secondary resources should never be solely relied on as legal authority.

Treatises are sometimes confused with primary sources due to their breadth and substance. A treatise is typically written by someone considered to be an expert or legal scholar in a particular area of the law, but a treatise such as, for example, *McCarthy on Trademarks* represents Professor Thomas McCarthy's interpretation and analysis of trademark law—it is not in and of itself "the law." Treatises can be particularly useful to legal researchers in developing a greater understanding of a particular area of law (e.g., negligence, anti-trust, trademark, privacy). Another highly persuasive secondary source is the Restatement, which is a comprehensive survey of a specific and major category of law prepared by a group of legal scholars. For example, the Restatement of Contracts summarizes the origin, development, and current application of contract law in the United States, noting differences between individual states, majority positions, and the general rule of

---

Description of Common Secondary Legal Resources

• Legal dictionaries: *Black's Law Dictionary* provides definitions of legal terms and is a must for studying and researching law. Many condensed paperback versions are available.

• Lawyer directories: Martindale-Hubbell is useful for locating attorneys in any state in the United States.

• *Annotated Law Reports* (A.L.R.): This resource provides commentary on and summaries of areas of law. It covers both state and federal courts. The annotation usually includes a case summary along with commentary about the case and how it may or does affect other cases or the current status of the law. A.L.R. is very useful if you wish to study the legal impact of a specific case.

• Legal encyclopedias: Encyclopedias such as *Corpus Juris Secundum* and *American Jurisprudence* (Am. Jur.) function as standard encyclopedias and include topical summaries of numerous legal issues. Each summary includes supporting references to cases, statutes, and other primary and secondary resources. This is a good place to start if you know little or nothing about a topic and want a jumping-off point. These sources do not provide much analysis and may not address the latest developments.

(continued)

■ Treatises, textbooks, casebooks, and hornbooks: Treatises are written by scholars and experts on a particular legal issue or topic. These resources are usually very comprehensive and provide an in-depth examination of an issue or topic. Note, however, that a treatise represents the author's interpretation of the law—it is not the actual law. Treatises can provide the reader with substantial references and resources on a specific topic, and most law libraries hold extensive collections of treatises. Two preeminent publications in the field are the three-volume *Legal Liability and Risk Management for Public and Private Entities* by Betty van der Smissen and *Sports and the Law* by Paul C. Weiler and Gary Roberts. Other sport law treatises are *Sports Law* by Michael J. Bailiff, Tim Kerr, and Marie Dimitri; *Torts and Sports: Legal Liability in Professional and Amateur Athletics* by Raymond L. Yasser; *Sports Law* by George W. Schubert, Rodney K. Smith, and Jesse C. Trended; *Sports and Law: Contemporary Issues* by Herb Appenzeller; *Fundamentals of Sports Law* by Walter T. Champion Jr.; *Sports and the Law: Major Legal Cases* by Charles E. Quirk; *The Law of Sports* by John C. Weistart and Cym H. Lowell; *Essentials of Sports Law* (now in its fourth edition) by Glenn M. Wong; and *Sports Law* by Michael E. Jones.

■ Shepard's Citations: This publication allows the researcher to track a court decision or statute through a citation index listing court decisions that cite previous decisions or interpret specific statutory sections. This resource is useful in locating additional cases once the researcher has located a major or dispositive case. More important, it tracks any treatment of a particular case. Thus, researchers can use it know whether a case they are relying on has been questioned, criticized, followed, reversed, or otherwise interpreted by later court decisions. This knowledge is extremely important so that the researcher can ensure that the court decisions they rely on are indeed still representative of the current legal standard.

■ Legal indexes: The *Index to Legal Periodicals* (ILP) allows the researcher to locate law review articles by topic, author, or both. The ILP is now available both in the traditional book form and electronically. The researcher can use the electronic version to conduct a topical search that yields citation and location information for relevant law review articles.

■ Law review articles: These sources are published primarily by law schools and professional law associations throughout the United States, and numerous law reviews and journals regularly address sport law issues. They include the *Marquette Sports Law Review*; the *Villanova Sports and Entertainment Law Journal*; the *University of Miami Entertainment and Sports Law Review*; the *Seton Hall Journal of Sport and Entertainment Law*; the American Bar Association's *Entertainment and Sports Lawyer*; and *Sports Lawyers Journal*.

■ Academic legal journals: Several academic associations publish journals focused on legal issues. In the field of sport, the Sport and Recreation Law Association publishes the *Journal of Legal Aspects of Sport*, which presents scholarly papers related to legal issues in sport and recreation. Other scholarly publications include *From the Gym to the Jury*; *Sports in the Courts*; the *Sports, Parks and Recreation Law Reporter*; and the *Exercise Standards and Malpractice Reporter*.

■ Business or academic journals: Many current legal issues related to sport are sometimes covered in business and academic journals, many of which include special sections for legal developments. For example, *Sport Marketing Quarterly* features a regular column titled Marketing and the Law, and the *Journal of Public Policy & Marketing* offers a similar feature.

■ Business magazines and newspapers: Current developments in the sport industry often have a legal impact, and the sport industry is often covered in business magazines and daily newspapers. For example, the filing of a case is often reported in the print and online versions of major newspapers, and *Street and Smith's SportsBusiness Journal* also reports often on recent legal developments and issues. Such articles can help sport managers identify key issues and stay current regarding legal developments in the sport industry.

law for all issues related to contracts. Restatements can help researchers develop a better understanding of the principle and theory of law, if the reader has some familiarity with the law already.

The process of locating and reviewing secondary sources is similar to the process for conducting a traditional literature review in other research methods. The goal of the process in this case is to gain an understanding of the current state of the law whereas the goal of the literature review is to gain an understanding of the current state of knowledge in the field. The wide availability of electronic resources provides an almost endless supply of secondary sources that can be used by the researcher to gain an understanding of the issues being investigated. For example, a Google search for "trademark protection of school colors" produced more than 29,000 results with contemporary commentary by legal scholars, practicing attorneys, law students, and industry experts, as well as related legal documents. This type of search can serve as a good starting point in your effort to gain a preliminary understanding of relevant issues. However, the initial search must be complemented by a search for secondary sources using a traditional legal search engine, such as LexisNexis Academic, to ensure the credibility of the research.

Use of secondary sources is a required part of the legal research process, since primary sources alone are unlikely to give the researcher a comprehensive understanding of the topic (secondary sources are also insufficient in and of themselves—both are needed). By expanding the legal research process to include secondary sources, particularly law reviews in the trademark example just mentioned, the researcher can more fully understand the complexity of the legal issues. In fact, after locating the relevant case decision, the researcher would be wise to rely on secondary sources early on in the research process to get a better idea of the available case law on this issue and to determine which case law is still good law. After the researcher reads a few law review articles on point and develops an understanding of the key legal issues, he or she can then return to locating additional case law related to the research question of whether color schemes can be protected as trademarks in the context of collegiate sport merchandise. This **iterative approach** or **recursive approach**, in which the legal researcher goes back and forth between primary and secondary sources, shares a goal with qualitative research—gaining a rich understanding of the complex legal

issues being studied. The researcher must rely on both types of legal resources in order to answer the research question and develop an awareness of the industry implications of such cases.

The researcher may then be able to expand his or her search to include industry publications in order to determine how the industry has responded to the current legal decision. Findings from this part of the research process may be more valuable to sport management research since they can provide insight about how management practice is influenced by the evolving nature of the law—in the example of the trademark case, understanding the impetus for specific changes in collegiate licensing practices that this case creates.

Electronic Search Engines and Databases

The availability and efficiency of electronic and Web-based research continues to expand and improve. Researchers can now perform a great deal of their research by means of computer. Both primary and secondary sources are often readily available through a variety of electronic databases or on the Web. Although electronic and Web-based sources may never replace a trip to the law library, growth in this area has been tremendous. Many law schools now provide students with access to electronic databases known as Westlaw and Lexis, which allow the researcher to search topically or for a specific case or statute. Some law libraries provide access to these databases only to law students; in that instance, LexisNexis Academic, available through most college and university libraries, is also a valuable research tool. It allows you search top news; general news; company, industry, and market news; legal news; company financial information; law reviews; federal case law; the U.S. Code; and state legal resources. In the event that your library does not have access to any of these resources, you can use several additional Web-based research sites.

In addition to electronic databases, many electronic subscription services are available to keep abreast of current legal developments specific to the sport industry. Many of these services are free, such as FindLaw, which offers a free subscription to a weekly e-mail that lists current developments in sport law. An excellent paid subscription (with discount rates for students) is available from *Sports Litigation Alert*, which provides a detailed biweekly summary of recent sport law developments. Several other excellent electronic resources are described a bit later in the chapter.

Legal Blogs and Internet Searches

Thanks to Google, Yahoo, and other Internet search engines, legal information can often be accessed with just a click of the mouse. For example, if you enter the search term "sport law" into Google, Google's search engine will return more than 190,000 results if you happened to enclose the term within quotations marks to limit the number of hits (using quotation marks limits the search to the phrase per se, rather than bringing up results that include the two words in any order). If you didn't enclose "sport law" within parentheses, the Google search will instantly return more than 36 million hits. This capability can be both a benefit and a detriment. The speed and ease of such a search is a great benefit, but of course it could take weeks to sort through 190,000 results, and tackling more than 36 million would be nearly impossible. So, for maximum effectiveness, our searches need to be as specific and detailed as possible.

Google and other search engines can also be used very effectively to locate current developments in sport law that are relevant to a chosen topic. For example, assume that you are a sport or recreation manager and have been following a pending lawsuit. In the past, it might have taken days or even weeks after a final decision was made for you to learn of the decision and access a copy of the court's order or opinion. Today, however, notification of the final decision is often made almost simultaneously with the decision itself, and the written decision or order is often made available within hours or even minutes. Almost every major news outlet delivers the news via the Internet, thus enabling you to receive instant notification of breaking news stories. A good example of just how useful these services are to a sport or recreation manager can be found by considering a case in which a collegiate baseball player, Andrew Oliver, sued the NCAA. The case was watched with great interest by most college athletic administrators since it challenged the authority of the NCAA to enforce its eligibility rules and regulations. If you had subscribed to one of the many available daily e-mail news updates, you would have been notified immediately when the Ohio state court invalidated the NCAA rule restricting the manner in which athletes considering a professional offer may use legal representation.

In addition, within just a few hours, you could have accessed a great deal of legal commentary interpreting, analyzing, and criticizing the court's decision. This kind of immediate response to legal developments can be very useful to a sport manager.

In addition to search engines and news alerts, researchers can benefit from a number of legal blogs. Blogs (short for Web logs) originated as Web sites where individuals posted commentary or personal diaries. In the past, most blogs were not very useful research sources, particularly for legal research, because they primarily represented the personal opinion of the blogger and contained anonymous and random comments by the blog's readers. It was very difficult to discern whether the blogger possessed any particular expertise or knowledge to use in evaluating the credibility of his or her posts. Thus, the Web made it possible for every person with an opinion or a little knowledge about anything to share it via the Internet. Legal research, however, must lead to verifiable and credible conclusions. For example, a blog post casting Andrew Oliver as "the Curt Flood of college athletics" may make for interesting conversation, but it is not useful or reliable when trying to understand the Andrew Oliver decision, the court's reasoning, or the legal impact of the decision. Today, however, although blogs may still be viewed with some skepticism when conducting legal research, a number of credible legal authorities provide opinions, commentary, and legal analysis via blogs. These legal blogs, such as the Sports Law Blog, constitute a useful legal resource for tracking current legal developments, reviewing credible commentary about legal issues, and linking to additional resources related to legal developments. Researchers still should exercise caution when citing these sources unless they are able to satisfy themselves that the information is credible enough to support their conclusions. And even if a researcher is going to rely upon these sources, he or she needs to take care to cite them properly in order to assure that the reader understands that a particular statement or conclusion is based on a secondary source (not a primary source) and thus represents opinion or analysis of a blogger—not necessarily the opinion or analysis of a court or legal expert or authority. If used cautiously and properly, legal blogs are quite effective as research tools. The accompanying highlight box lists a number of Web sites, search engines, electronic resources, and sport law blogs that can help you rapidly identify current developments in sport law and conduct more in-depth research.

General Legal Research

Searchable databases that cover a broad range of topics, including general federal and state law information and federal and state court decisions:

FindLaw: www.findlaw.com

Refdesk.com: www.refdesk.com

LLRX.com (law and technology resources for legal professionals): www.llrx.com

National Center for State Courts: www.ncsc.org/default.aspx

Law Crawler—Legal Web & Databases Search: www.lawcrawler.com

The 'Lectric Law Library: www.lectlaw.com/ref.html

American Law Sources On-Line: www.lawsource.com/also

Government Research Sources

Web sites, some searchable, that provide information about government agencies, governmental functions, Congress, and general information:

United States Patent and Trademark Office: www.uspto.gov

United States Geological Survey: www.usgs.gov

United States Federal Trade Commission: www.ftc.gov

United States Department of Labor: www.dol.gov

United States House of Representatives: www.house.gov

United States Senate: www.senate.gov

THOMAS (legislative information from the United States Library of Congress): http://thomas.loc.gov

United States Supreme Court: www.supremecourtus.gov

University-Sponsored Research Sites

Searchable databases and links that include general research regarding state and federal court decisions, the Constitution, and state and federal statutes, as well as Web sites focused on a single topic (e.g., Title IX, hazing):

The Legal Information Institute at Cornell University Law School: www.law.cornell.edu

University of Iowa Gender Equity in Sports Project: http://bailiwick.lib.uiowa.edu/ge/

Alfred University study of high school hazing: www.alfred.edu/news/html/hazing_study.html

Jurist Legal News & Research at the University of Pittsburgh: http://jurist.law.pitt.edu/

Sports Law: Internet and Library Resources (Indiana State University): http://library.indstate.edu/about/units/instruction/sportslaw.htm

Law Journal and Association Sites

Web sites with sport law links and general information about sport law studies and research:

Emory Law School: www.law.emory.edu/

National Sport Law Institute: http://law.marquette.edu/jw/nsli

Sport and Recreation Law Association: www.srlaweb.org

Sport Law Blogs

Sports Law Blog: http://sports-law.blogspot.com

The Sports Law Professor: http://thesportslawprofessor.blogspot.com

College of Sports Law News—Willamette University: http://blog.willamette.edu/wucl/journals/sportslaw

ABA Journal Law News Now: www.abajournal.com/topic/entertainment+sports+law

Connecticut Sports Law: http://ctsportslaw.com

Golka's Athlete Agent Regulation Blog: www.gaarb.com

Sports Agent Blog: www.sportsagentblog.com

Recreation Law: http://rec-law.blogspot.com

Title IX Blog: http://title-ix.blogspot.com

Design and Implementation

As with other research designs, designing legal research in the field of sport management requires a clearly defined research plan. The researcher needs to conduct adequate preliminary research to correctly identify the research problem or legal issue to be examined and generate research questions. Otherwise, the researcher could spend countless hours reviewing court decisions, electronic databases, and journal articles with little to show the effort. The following three phases represent a good approach to designing and conducting legal research in sport management: (1) identifying the research question, (2) organizing the research plan, and (3) writing the paper. These phases involve several nonlinear steps.

Identifying the Research Question

Identifying and defining the research question is by far the most important step in the research process. To define a research question, take the following steps: (a) identify the topic, issue, or current development that gives rise to the research question, (b) narrow the general topic or issue to identify the legal issue, and (c) write the research question.

Identifying Current Issues or Developments

To identify current issues or developments with legal implications, it is helpful to search current business and professional literature to stay on top of industry developments. For example, when the University of Kentucky (UK) terminated head men's basketball coach Billy Gillispie at the end of the 2008-2009 season, several questions were raised about what, if any, buyout would be paid to Gillispie, who had never executed a formal extensive contract with UK but instead had been employed for the previous 2 years pursuant to a simple 3-page memorandum of understanding (MOU) (Tipton, 2009). Gillispie and UK eventually filed separate lawsuits against each other, and the legal issues raised in the case may have implications that extend beyond the University of Kentucky and affect all future college coaches' contract negotiations.

If the issue or problem is not clearly identified and narrowly defined, you will find it difficult to focus your research sufficiently to produce meaningful results. Clearly defining the issue helps you discover key words, phrases, and terms that may facilitate your research. Several good sources of recent developments in the sport industry are available. The *Chronicle of Higher Education* includes sections on college athletics that report recent educational, administrative, business, and legal developments. Several industry publications, such as *Sports Business Daily* and *Street and Smith's Sports-Business Journal*, also report on emerging business and legal issues. Findlaw.com offers free online weekly updates pertaining specifically to legal issues in sport, and several sport law blogs are now available that regularly track and update emerging legal issues in sport. In addition, news outlets often report on developing trends and issues in the sport industry. Thus, from a single current development in the business of sport, numerous legal issues may emerge. Once the general issue has been clearly identified, it becomes easier to identify legal issues.

Identifying the Legal Issues

To identify the legal issues, sport management researchers review secondary source materials. Legal encyclopedias, treatises, digests, law review articles, and textbooks can all help the researcher gain a preliminary understanding of the legal issues and principles associated with his or her research question. For example, imagine that you want to research whether coaches can be fired for violent behavior. Determine what areas of law are implicated: labor relations, assault and battery, teacher rights, employment law, or contract law. You could use encyclopedias and treatises to help you sift information and narrow your search to what ultimately may be a simple question of either contract law (Does the coach have a contract, and if so, what does it say about termination?) or employer–employee relations (Is the coach an employee at will, or must the school demonstrate just cause to terminate?). Digests will provide references to court decisions related to your issue or subject. If you have discovered that your issue relates to a specific state or federal statute, check the statute for annotations that address related statutes, legislative history, law review articles, and court decisions. You might also consult a textbook chapter on contract law or sport law for an overview of issues related to coaches' contracts. Finally, law review articles may have already examined a variety of issues regarding termination of coaches' contracts or wrongful termination of public employees, and you must do a thorough search for all relevant secondary sources in order to avoid duplicating someone else's research efforts and to purposely select an area of research that is either understudied or subject to confusion regarding the current state of the law due to inconsistent judicial decisions.

For another example, imagine that you are a researcher interested in studying the broad topic of gender equity in athletics. You must narrow your focus to a specific legal issue connected to the broader topic and demonstrate why it is important to examine this legal issue in greater detail. If you review a few secondary sources and even some primary sources (e.g., case decisions), you will discover that in order to impose liability on an educational institution under Title IX, a plaintiff must prove that the educational institution had notice of discrimination based upon sex and acted with deliberate indifference in remedying the alleged discrimination. This standard contains at least three elements: first, that the educational institution had notice of something alleged to be sex discrimination; second, that the alleged discriminatory conduct must be on the basis of sex; and third, that the educational institution acted with deliberate indifference toward the discrimination. Any one of these three elements could be a sufficient area for further legal analysis and study; for instance, it would be appropriate to narrow a research question down to defining and understanding the concept of deliberate indifference since that standard is applied in Title IX cases. This step can be the most difficult one because we may want instinctively to address larger, more global issues, but if we narrow our topic and research question at the outset, it is more likely that we will make a meaningful contribution to the body of knowledge in the chosen area of the law.

Writing the Research Question

Your final research question should integrate specific facts and issues associated with the problem. For example, if you wanted to study the issue of "slip and fall liability" in arenas, you would need to limit your search to negligence cases involving sport facilities in order to avoid bringing up hundreds of cases involving hotels or restaurants that might not be applicable. Conversely, if you wanted to understand the types of warning provided to prevent slips and falls from occurring, you might purposely seek out cases involving facilities where warning signs are often used, such as restaurants, grocery stores, and casinos. Therefore, narrowing the scope of your research question is critically important in your initial efforts to locate a relevant body of case law.

Consider the following example of how to define a research question. In *Board of Supervisors of Louisiana State University et al. v. Smack Apparel* (2008), the United States Court of Appeals for the Fifth Circuit held that a university's school colors can be protected as stand-alone trademarks. The appellate decision represented a major shift in broadening the scope of trademark protection for collegiate institutions and has serious implications for the licensing programs at universities with high-profile athletic programs where licensing royalties represent a significant source of revenue. In starting the research process by locating relevant case law, the researcher is able to narrowly focus the legal issues being studied without getting bogged down in peripheral legal issues that are irrelevant to the research question. The danger of getting bogged down by unrelated issues is particularly acute for student researchers, who may be performing the legal research process for the first time.

In this example, the initial research question could be stated as follows: What is the scope of protection for college trademarks and logos? By locating case law using a keyword search for "trademark" and "color scheme," reading the Smack Apparel decision, and reviewing additional secondary sources, the researcher can further refine the research question to something like this: "Are color schemes used by collegiate athletic programs subject to trademark protection under federal trademark laws?" Once a research question has been identified, narrowed, and written down, the researcher enters phase 2 and begins to organize a research plan.

Organizing the Research Plan

Once you have defined your legal research question, you must then conduct your research and locate all relevant authorities that address your question. This phase involves repeating a number of tasks, including locating secondary and primary sources related to your research question and reviewing and analyzing the sources to determine whether they are relevant to your research question.

It can be a daunting task to organize all the general information, cases, statutes, legal commentary, and legal or academic journal articles, but it is necessary to do so if you are going to effectively answer your research question. You will be able to integrate the information more efficiently if you summarize every case, define and redefine your issue as you gain a better understanding of the issue, and search other jurisdictions for cases which have both similar or dissimilar facts related to the same legal issue. The benefit in using cases with dissimilar facts is for the researcher to be able to show how a court decided a case with the same legal issue but under a different set of facts. Next, you will want to locate any relevant statutory laws. For example, if your issue deals with gender equity in sport, you will soon learn that you need to consider not only the specific federal statute and federal regulations (Title IX of the Education Amendments of 1972) but also numerous court decisions that can help you interpret and understand the statute and the regulations. In addition, the U.S. Department of Education has issued policy statements, guidelines, and rules or regulations dealing with enforcement issues under Title IX specifically applicable to athletics. Finally, scholars frequently write treatises, law review articles, and other commentary on this subject, and you could literally find more than 100 articles about Title IX and athletics.

In summarizing case law, the format described in the accompanying highlight box is helpful and gives the student researcher as well as the reader an easier way to organize and digest the cases and to make sense of them as a whole. Often referred to as the IRAC format (for issue, rule, analysis, and conclusion), this method is frequently used by law students in briefing a case as a quick and easy way to summarize cases and distinguish the legal principles from cases involving similar fact patterns. A brief statement of the facts is also customarily included.

Summarizing Cases: The IRAC Approach

- Statement of facts: Identify the relevant facts involved in the case.
- Issue: State the legal issue or question that will be answered.
- Rule: Identify the rule of law used to decide this issue. This element should include a brief summary of relevant cases, relevant statutory language, and other information needed to understand the law.
- Analysis: This section should include a detailed analysis of the law from the rule of law section and how it applies to the statement of facts section in order to answer the question identified in the issue section.
- Conclusion: A short restatement of the case based on how the rule of law was applied to the facts.

The best advice for organizing the voluminous amount of information is to repeatedly look back to the original problem and research question. You can continually revise your research question as you review and analyze additional information. Limit or narrow the inquiry to only those bits of information that provide an answer to the original problem or research question. Your information and analysis can then be organized and presented in a number of ways, which are discussed in greater detail in the following section on the legal writing process.

During this phase of the research, the process is nonlinear. The researcher moves back and forth between primary and secondary sources, integrating the information rather than providing a linear summary of each source. For example, a researcher exploring the impact of the Americans with Disabilities Act on student athletes might begin by examining law review articles about students with learning disabilities. By beginning the search with secondary sources, the student is better able to grasp the big picture and understand the major legal issues at stake, such as the rights of students under the ADA. The secondary sources often lead the student to locate important cases that deal directly with the topic (student athletes with disabilities) and may also require searching for any new cases that have been decided since the law review articles were published. This iterative process of going back and forth from secondary sources to primary sources in order to focus the research question is very similar to the qualitative research process, where one may go back into the field after initial data analysis to collect more data in order to better understand the phenomenon being investigated. This iterative process is most effective when it is applied in a conceptual approach known as an inverted pyramid analytical approach (Dernbach, Singleton, Wharton, & Ruhtenberg, 2007). Figure 12.1 illustrates the fact that as the researcher reviews and analyzes primary and secondary sources simultaneously, the research question continues to become more clearly defined and focused, and the researcher can hone in on only those sources that logically relate to the conclusions and implications.

Writing the Paper

Legal writing differs from other styles of writing. The purpose of legal research is problem or issue based, and individual research papers or products of legal research can serve a variety of objectives. Writing an undergraduate paper allows students to develop the skills of critical thinking and problem

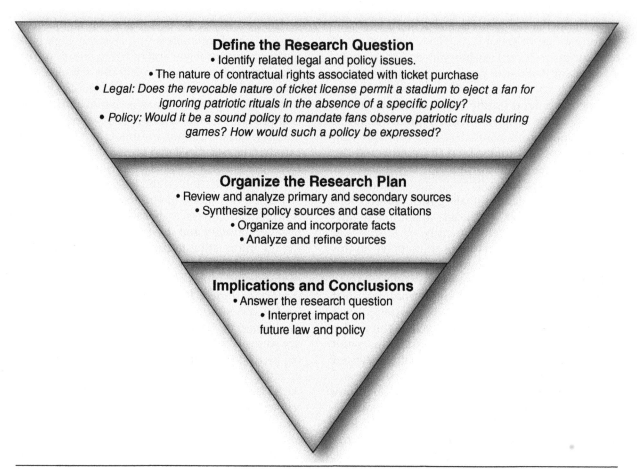

Figure 12.1 The inverted pyramid analysis. The goal of the recursive approach is to continually narrow the focus of the research.

solving that are needed in order to narrowly define their topic. A graduate research paper may be focused on permitting that student to gain a certain level of expertise in a specific legal area or topic. A master's thesis or dissertation integrates the element of gaining expertise on a broader legal topic with additional components related to in-depth discussion, analysis, and recommendations.

A typical master's thesis or doctoral dissertation follows a linear research process: identify a research topic or question, conduct and organize a literature review, design a methodology, collect and analyze data, report the results of the data analysis, and discuss how the results compare with the previous literature or knowledge in the field. A linear approach suggests that each step must be performed in order, that later steps cannot be taken until earlier steps are completed, and that there is no need to go back and repeat any of the earlier steps based upon outcomes in the later stages of the process. The linear approach is simple and effective for a number of research projects, but not for legal research projects.

As discussed in regard to phase 2, legal writing requires a recursive approach (Dernbach et al., 2007). With the recursive approach, you are working on later steps even as you are completing earlier steps, and you must revisit the earlier steps as your knowledge grows during the later steps. In a recursive approach, then, you are not just locating and summarizing sources; instead, as you locate a source, you must initially analyze it in order to help refine your issue and determine whether it is relevant and applicable to your topic. Thus the first step in writing is to conduct a tentative analysis of each source and try to locate gaps in your research or analysis. The recursive approach involves much back and forth between research, analysis, writing, and rewriting.

Legal writing does not involve data collection or analysis, nor are there results to report from any data collection or analysis. Instead legal writing goes back and forth, just as our research design is nonlinear. Identify issues, plan and begin your research, and then analyze your initial research, narrow the issue, and begin writing. Begin to organize the paper, then conduct more research, analyze it, and continue writing the paper. Further analysis will lead to additional research, which in turn leads to more revision. Each step of your progress involves fewer tasks, since you are narrowing the problem and eliminating or reorganizing sources.

According to Dernbach and colleagues (2007), three steps are critical to good legal writing. First, begin writing early—just as soon as you have a grasp of what the law is and how it applies to your issue or problem. By writing early, it is easier to keep focused on the problem. Second, allow plenty of time for editing. The editing process is time consuming and essential if you are to tie all the research together in a logical way and concentrate your analysis and discussion on the problem. Last, step away from the paper, take a break from it, then return to carefully read the entire paper from beginning to end. This step will reveal organizational flaws, unclear discussion points, or even gaps in the research. If you don't see these problems, you are not reading carefully. Organizational flaws and logical gaps result naturally from a recursive research approach, and you need to be willing to completely reorganize entire sections or move entire pages or paragraphs to address organizational flaws or disconnected discussion.

Common Legal Manuscripts and Papers

A legal manuscript can take many forms for students, faculty, and practitioners. The most common legal manuscripts for student researchers are the thesis, dissertation, and expert research project. Typical scholarly output for faculty and practitioners includes law review articles, academic journal articles, practitioner journal articles, and public policy pieces. Researchers who work for private foundations or public organizations often write "white papers" and position papers to express the organization's position on a matter of public policy. For example, the Disability Sport Initiative of the Sport in Society center at Northeastern University frequently creates white papers and position papers addressing issues that affect athletes with disabilities. When President Obama signed the United Nations' 2006 Convention on the Rights of Persons with Disabilities on behalf of the United States, the center was asked to prepare commentary and a position paper about the impact that the U.S. adoption of the convention would have on current treatment of athletes with disabilities under the Americans with Disabilities Act. In this way, managers and administrators working in a variety of areas in the sport industry may be asked to opine or contribute viewpoints regarding matters of social, public, or economic policy that would require legal research and writing. Thus, even if a sport manager is not preparing traditional legal manuscripts, it is useful to have a solid foundation in legal research and writing. The following sections discuss theses, dissertations, scholarly articles, and law reviews in greater depth.

Writing the Thesis

A sport management thesis using legal research methods is appropriate and encouraged for master's degree students and possibly for honors undergraduate students. The amount of information used in a legal thesis may be greater than that used in a quantitative or qualitative study, but legal research skills may be easier for students to learn and apply quickly to their projects. Thesis topics with a legal focus are quite popular given that sport law is constantly evolving, which prompts academic and practitioners to produce much literature and scholarly debate about sport law topics that can serve as the basis for a thesis project. Even a cursory review of the Sports Law Blog (http://sports-law.blogspot.com/) reveals many sport law topics involving college and professional sport issues that could be sufficiently developed into a thesis.

Once the student researcher has identified a topic area, perhaps the biggest remaining challenge is that of narrowing the purpose of the study to analyze a particular legal issue in sufficient depth to make a meaningful contribution to the sport law scholarship. While the student researcher may want to analyze a legal topic area comprehensively, it may be more manageable—and thus more successful—to analyze a narrower legal issue in greater depth. Thus it is critical to draft manageable research questions. Consider the following example of a topic that is sufficiently narrow to serve as a doable thesis project. A master's student with a background in coaching wants to focus his thesis generally on Title IX. He wants to explore cases where women's athletic programs received inferior treatment as compared their male counterparts' programs. Rather than looking at all relevant cases, the student could narrow his focus to cases where the coach filed a Title IX complaint arguing that the program was being treated unfairly. The student could narrow the topic even further to look at claims of retaliation by the athletic program against the coach after the coach filed a Title IX complaint. By narrowing the focus of the thesis, the student makes the project feasible by honing in on a more manageable amount of information and resources to digest. The student is more likely to succeed in completing the thesis project if he can envision the end result through the lens of a sufficiently narrow purpose statement and related research questions—and how his analysis is leading him toward his goal.

Even if the focus of a thesis project is not entirely on legal issues, the student may still be able to use legal research methods. For example, a student working on a sport finance thesis regarding revenues and expenditures of college athletic departments might move her study forward by analyzing Equity in Athletics Disclosure Act (EADA) reports to determine the financial picture of all schools in a certain athletic conference. Her project could also involve a sport law component if she examines Title IX compliance, since the EADA reports also contain participation numbers comparing male and female enrollments. Projects that involve more than one discipline of sport management research have the potential to make a valuable contribution to the sport management literature, and the researcher may be able to increase the project's rigor and strengthen his or her findings by using multiple research methods.

As mentioned earlier, the methods section of a thesis project that uses legal research methods looks quite different from that of a quantitative or qualitative research project. This is true because the legal researcher is not justifying the appropriateness of the methods used; rather, a professor with expertise in legal research methods will help the student design the research in such a way as to capture all of the relevant information from the various primary and secondary sources and to analyze this information in order to develop a deeper understanding of the legal issues and their implications. In other words, it is unlikely that the student will need to defend an accepted method for locating legal resources; instead, the researcher will explain the steps used to ensure that all of the relevant legal materials and resources were identified, reviewed, and sufficiently analyzed. For example, a U.S. Supreme Court decision frequently contains the majority opinion as well as one or more concurring or dissenting opinions. It would be expected that the researcher would analyze all parts of such an opinion in order to understand all sides of the legal issue. It would be superfluous to include a notation stating that the majority, concurring, and dissenting opinions were analyzed and describing how the analysis was conducted. Instead, the researcher

could simply state that relevant cases were located and analyzed. The actual analysis and discussion of the majority, concurring, and dissenting opinions in the manuscript conveys to the reader that the researcher followed an appropriate and rigorous research process.

One common methodological mistake in legal research is to rely on a secondary legal source for principal legal analysis. For example, assume that a court decides a case and issues its findings and opinion. Frequently, a secondary source (e.g., newspaper or law journal) will publish an article summarizing or discussing the decision. If a researcher wishes to use the findings and rationale from that case to support an argument or position, he or she must review, analyze, and cite the actual case—not the secondary source summarizing the case. Thus, if the researcher included a statement such as "the court held that the Patriots could enforce the acceleration clause contained in its Personal Seat License Agreement," the correct resource for this statement is the court decision itself. The court's opinion is the only appropriate source for findings, reasoning, or holding (i.e., decision) of the court. If, instead of citing the court decision to support this statement, the researcher followed the statement with a citation of the secondary news source, the researcher's methodology would be flawed. If, on the other hand, the researcher included the statement, "The Patriots have been sharply criticized for suing their own ticketholders during the economic crisis," this statement could appropriately be supported by a citation of the secondary news source discussing the criticism, since it does not describe any legal aspect of the decision but merely the existence of public criticism surrounding the case.

Writing a Legal Dissertation

A legally focused dissertation in sport management is, admittedly, quite rare, because a dissertation focused mainly on case law or statutory analysis would be unlikely to follow the traditional five-chapter dissertation format used for most sport management dissertations. In addition, the student might face resistance from dissertation committee members who are unfamiliar with the nature of legal research. If you do contemplate undertaking a legal dissertation, you would be strongly encouraged to seek out a dissertation committee chair or active committee member with expertise in legal research. It is much more common, however, for a student to undertake a sport management dissertation that considers a legal issue alongside a sport management or marketing practice. For example, a dissertation focused on the practice of ambush marketing at the Olympics would necessarily include a legal component analyzing domestic or international laws intended to combat ambush marketing. Thus, although the research questions might be mainly focused on issues such as sponsorship protection, activation, or proper leveraging of sport sponsorships, the student could also include a legal component analyzing special legislation enacted to protect the event and its sponsors from ambush marketing.

The format of a legal dissertation might deviate from the traditional chapter format depending on the research questions posed. While the introduction would likely contain all required parts of a traditional dissertation introduction (e.g., purpose statement, significance), subsequent chapters might deviate from the norm. Depending on the purpose of the study, the literature review could include a significant amount of case law or statutory analysis to lay the groundwork for the study. For example, a study by Carroll (2007) examined the problem of

Legal Manuscripts Commonly Created by Student Researchers and Sport Managers

■ **Predictive memo.** The purpose of writing a predictive memo is to predict how a future court might rule on a particular legal issue. This type of research project likely involves reviewing the relevant case law and consulting law review articles or other secondary sources. The student researcher must be able to synthesize the primary and secondary sources and distinguish the facts and law of the given hypothetical fact pattern in order to effectively predict how a court would rule. The necessary legal research skills would be similar to, yet less advanced than, the skills required for a legal thesis or dissertation.

■ **Position statement.** In writing a position statement, the researcher takes one side of a legal argument (i.e., takes a position) and argues that a court or policy-making body should rule or make a decision in favor of that position. For example, a researcher could take a position in favor of nonsmoking policies in stadiums and arenas on college campuses. The position could be supported by case law, other academic research such as policy articles, and analysis and critique of any pending legislation. A position statement could be expanded into a larger research project examining other states or municipalities that have enacted similar legislation and how these new laws affected the sport industry in terms of attendance or other factors.

■ **White paper.** A white paper is often produced by researchers on behalf of a public or nonprofit organization's efforts in order to explain their group's opinions regarding a certain legal topic, particularly where there is vigorous debate about the topic. For example, public funding of sport stadia and the economic and noneconomic benefits of such investment would be a proper subject for a white paper authored by sport economists or researchers in urban planning with an interest in downtown revitalization. Although the goal of a white paper is not to take sides as is the purpose of a position statement, the white paper likely presents a more balanced analysis of the arguments on all sides of the issue and cites other authorities to support its propositions.

■ **Case summary.** Writing a case summary is one of the most basic tasks of legal research—and one of the most important. A good case summary is beneficial to the sport management researcher if it precisely identifies the legal issue that the court was asked to consider, then puts the court's holding into context related to the existing case law in the legal topic area. Thus, the student must develop, over time, the ability to synthesize cases and make sense of them in the larger body of existing case law. A first-year law professor often asks his or her students the question, "What does this case stand for?" The professor is trying to get the students to understand the legal principles delineated in the case and how they either conform to or disagree with existing case law. Writing effective case summaries requires the ability to spot issues, understand the law, and appreciate how the particular facts of a case dictated the court's decision.

hazing in athletics with the goal of reviewing existing case law but also providing management recommendations to athletic departments for preventing this practice from occurring. The literature review, therefore, necessarily included a component summarizing the hazing cases involving athletic teams.

While the literature review might resemble a traditional one, the results and discussion chapters for a legal dissertation may be structured quite differently from those in a traditional dissertation manuscript. The focus of the results chapter will likely involve analysis of the case law or statutory analysis, examining similarities and differences between cases with similar fact patterns or making a determination regarding variations in state laws covering a specific legal topic area. The last chapter, the discussion, continues the analysis presented in the results chapter and thus will likely include analysis and reconciliation of conflicting case law or analysis of scholarly debate about a particular legal issue or topic area. The discussion chapter of a legal dissertation is also likely to include treatment of the industry implications of the legal issues presented. For example, the ambush marketing dissertation topic could include discussion about how various stakeholders (event organizers, national governing bodies, host country, and local businesses) can come together to address the problem of ambush marketing in a comprehensive manner.

Writing Scholarly Publications for Faculty and Practitioners

Sport management faculty and practitioners produce a variety of legal manuscripts. The most common legal papers are law review articles, academic journal articles, commentaries, and practitioner memos. Law students also write what are known as case notes and comments. A case note is a detailed analysis of a single recently decided case that is likely to have significant impact in an area of the law. For example, when the Supreme Court decided the *PGA Tour, Inc. v. Martin* case holding that the PGA discriminated against Casey Martin for not permitting him to use a golf cart as a reasonable accommodation for his disability, it was a landmark decision. As a result, many case notes were written by law students analyzing and critiquing the decision and discussing its potential impact on future cases involving athletes with disabilities. On the other hand, a comment is a more in-depth examination of an area of the law. For example, rather than limit the analysis only to a discussion of the Casey Martin decision, a comment

might examine how the reasonable accommodation required under the Americans with Disabilities Act has been applied to sport organizations. This is a much broader topic and will involve much more analysis than one would find in a case note. While these types of articles are commonly written by law students, advanced sport management students and sport management faculty could certainly write similar types of manuscripts.

For sport management faculty members, it is critical to determine the publication outlet for a legal manuscript before writing it. If the outlet is a law review or law journal, a specific citation style is required, and the primary focus of the article must be a rigorous legal analysis of a legal principle or development. If the outlet is an academic journal, such as the *Journal of Sport Management* or *Sport Marketing Quarterly*, a different citation and writing style is expected. In this latter example, an academic journal article must not only provide a rigorous discussion of the legal issues but also explain the relevance of the legal issue to the management of sport. Reviewers for the academic journal may or may not have law degrees or other expertise in legal research. They may be expecting to see the traditional linear paper with an introduction, literature review, methods, discussion, and conclusion. As discussed earlier, however, legal writing is not linear, and the sport management researcher will need to take this into consideration. Thus, the introduction of a legal manuscript needs to be more detailed and descriptive of the research question and relevance to the industry; it must clearly identify the purpose of the paper (at the end of the introduction) and specify exactly how the discussion is organized.

The following paragraph from a legal manuscript published in an academic journal provides a good example of how to tell reviewers and readers how a paper is organized and where it will take the reader.

> However, the collision between political uses of sport and private business interests has created some new legal challenges for sport managers. This article provides an analysis of the legal labyrinth surrounding the Bush-Cheney re-election campaign's use of "Olympics" in campaign advertising. First, this article examines the law establishing protections for the USOC and Olympic marks and symbols to determine if, in fact, the USOC had a viable legal claim against the Bush-Cheney re-election campaign's unauthorized use of "Olympics." Next, the possible application of other federal and state law, including the Lanham Act, is examined to determine if the USOC and other U.S. sport properties have

alternative legal claims that could provide viable remedies against the unauthorized use of trademarks in political advertising campaigns. This article also explores laws and case law regarding false and deceptive campaign advertising to determine if this provides a viable legal challenge to political advertising campaigns utilizing sport organization trademarks without authorization. Finally, this article suggests Congress may need to revisit the latitudes afforded political speech to prevent what may become a dangerous trend of political candidates misleading or misrepresenting their association with, or implying an endorsement by, sport organizations. (McKelvey & Moorman, 2007)

Fortunately, for sport management scholars and practitioners who are interested in legal research, at least one academic legal journal is available. The *Journal of Legal Aspects of Sport* combines the best of both worlds, which means that the researcher does not need to convince an editorial board that legal issues are a good fit for the journal or worry that reviewers may not understand the nature of legal research and writing. The *Journal of Legal Aspects of Sport* also adheres to the same citation style as other academic journals and is peer reviewed—an important professional consideration for sport management faculty seeking tenure and promotion.

Summary

This chapter introduces you to legal research and legal writing. It is not necessary to be a lawyer in order to effectively use legal research for inquiry and investigation. Legal research can complement existing research methods, and many research studies have incorporated a variety of research methods, including legal research. Many research questions are best answered by using legal research in whole or in part. Thus, the researcher should embrace these skills. The nonlinear nature of legal research can initially pose a challenge for sport management researchers. In order to help you meet this challenge, this chapter explains how to identify research topics in sport management that are best studied using legal research methods, how to develop a focused legal research question, and how to approach writing papers addressing law and policy issues in sport management using a recursive approach.

Selected text reprinted, by permission, from S. McKelvey and J. Grady, 2008, "Sponsorship program protection strategies for special sport events: Are event organizers outmaneuvering ambush marketers?" *Journal of Sport Management* 22(5): 550-586.

Access the full article online at www.humankinetics.com/products/all-products/Research-Methods-and-Design-in-Sport-Management.

ABSTRACT

Companies invest millions of dollars to become "official sponsors" of major global sporting events. The tremendous publicity and consumer audiences generated by such events provide an attractive marketing opportunity for companies other than the event's official sponsors who seek to associate themselves in the minds of the public with the goodwill and popularity of these events. This activity, known as ambush marketing, poses significant legal and business challenges for sport event organizers seeking to protect both the financial investment of official sponsors and the integrity of their sponsorship programs. With rising sponsorship stakes, event organizers have become increasingly proactive in their efforts to combat ambush marketing. This article examines the implementation and effectiveness of a variety of evolving sponsorship program protection strategies including: pre-event education and public relations initiatives; on-site policing tactics; contractual language in athlete participation and spectator ticket agreements; and the enactment and enforcement of special trademark protection legislation.

TEXT EXCERPTS

Given the significant financial investments of official sponsors, as well as the tremendous publicity and consumer audiences generated by major sporting events, it has become increasingly important for event organizers to adopt proactive sponsorship program protection strategies for the following reasons: "(1) to protect the integrity and financial viability of the event; (2) to build the event 'brand' and goodwill in it for the future; and (3) to fulfill contractual obligations to sponsors" (Ambush marketing, 2003).

....

Following an overview of the practice of ambush marketing and its legal parameters, this article examines four over-arching sponsorship program protection strategies increasingly used by event organizers: (1) pre-event education and public relations initiatives; (2) on-site policing, which ranges from confiscation of nonsponsor product and signage to the creation of "clean zones"; (3) the use of contractual language in athlete participation agreements and on spectators' tickets; and (4) the enactment and enforcement of special trademark protection legislation (the term "event organizers" is used throughout this article to refer generally to the governing bodies and leagues that, in essence, own and manage the special sport event discussed herein). The current article builds upon prior research examining the effectiveness of ambush marketing prevention measures (Curthoys & Kendall, 2001; Hartland & Skinner, 2005; McAuley & Sutton, 1999; McKelvey

& Grady, 2004). Additional research, review of internal documents provided by event organizers, and findings from the 2006 FIFA World Cup, are used to illuminate these sponsorship program protection strategies and provide "best practices" guidance for event organizers of future special sport events.

....

Hence, in the U.S., there remain no adjudicated cases applying federal or state laws directly to the practice of ambush marketing, resulting in a historical reluctance of event organizers to challenge the practice using the courts.

....

Another reason that event organizers have been reluctant to bring suit against ambush marketers is the fear of an adverse court ruling.

DISCUSSION QUESTIONS

1. How do the authors use current events to explain the purpose of their study?

2. How do the authors explain the need to present both legal and nonlegal (i.e., policy or business practice) issues?

3. Do the authors use primary and secondary sources correctly in this section? How so?

4. What is the basis of the authors' critique of NCAA policy and practice?

5. Legal research articles typically use very few tables or graphs, but occasionally a visual representation of

legal information can aid readers' understanding of the legal applications under discussion. How do the authors use a graphic to help readers better understand the statutory requirements of LOAR?

6. It is important for scholarly articles to identify a study's implications for future research. How do the authors of this article accomplish this?

7. What types of resources did the researchers rely on?

part IV

Statistical Methods in Sport Management

Part IV covers quantitative techniques that address analyses of structure, relationships between variables, significance of group differences, and prediction of group membership. Unlike the outline of a typical quantitative statistics textbook, these analyses are ordered not by the specific number of dependent variables incorporated in the analysis. Instead, since sport managers tend to use research to investigate an existing situation or provide solutions to an existing problem (see chapter 1), the quantitative analyses discussed here are ordered according to their general purpose. For example, a sport manager wishing to develop or refine a survey should consult chapter 13 to learn about analyses of structure. Similarly, those seeking to uncover positive or negative relationships between variables of interest should consult chapter 14, those desiring to uncover differences between groups (e.g., males and females) should explore chapter 15, and those who want to predict group membership (e.g., season ticket holders) should examine chapter 16. In grouping the analyses by purpose, our goal is to create a user-friendly text.

Throughout part IV, we provide procedural steps for conducting each analysis by means of SPSS, which is a popular statistical software package originally released in 1968 and since updated many times. SPSS has developed a reputation for being user friendly, and, as such, is widely at prominent universities and colleges. The procedural steps presented in part IV correspond to SPSS 17.0, but it is important to note that the company was recently acquired by IBM, and is now known as SPSS: An IBM Company. Therefore, it is possible that the procedural steps outlined in Part IV may not be applicable to future versions of the software package. Fortunately, user guides for each iteration of SPSS are commonly available and should outline any updates to the procedural steps discussed in this text.

Chapter 13 discusses Cronbach's alpha, exploratory factor analysis, principal component analysis, and confirmatory factor analysis. Though Cronbach's alpha is only a method of assessing internal consistency reliability, and is, therefore, less powerful than the other statistics mentioned in this chapter, it is included to correspond with other procedures that can be performed in SPSS. Chapter 14 addresses bivariate correlation, simple linear regression, multiple regression, and path analysis. Chapter 15 covers the t-test, one-way analysis of variance (ANOVA), one-way analysis of covariance (ANCOVA), factorial ANOVA, factorial ANCOVA, one-way multivariate analysis of variance (MANOVA), one-way multivariate analysis of covariance (MANCOVA), factorial MANOVA, and factorial MANCOVA. Finally, chapter 16 addresses discriminant analysis, logistic regression, and cluster analysis.

chapter 13

Analyses of Structure

Learning Objectives

After studying this chapter, you should be able to do the following:

- Discuss the importance of reliability and validity
- Describe and categorize the statistical techniques used to analyze structure according to their appropriate usage
- Understand the similarities and differences between an exploratory factor analysis and a principal component analysis
- Describe the general purpose of a confirmatory factor analysis
- List the common types of fit indices with their corresponding values that indicate good fit of the data to the model

The purpose of this chapter is to introduce and explain a number of statistical techniques used to analyze structure. Analyses of structure are relevant when the researcher questions the underlying structure of an instrument or is interested in reducing the total number of independent variables. As such, analyses of structure can be performed to examine or enhance the reliability or validity of a study, which can increase the researcher's confidence in the results.

Importance of Reliability and Validity

As mentioned in chapter 4, reliability and validity are important components in research design. **Reliability**, the consistency of the results obtained, concerns the extent to which the instrument yields the same results in repeated trials. The types of reliability are interobserver reliability, test–retest reliability, and internal consistency reliability. **Validity**, the extent to which an instrument accurately measures the target it was designed to measure, helps a researcher determine whether or not an instrument addresses its designed purpose. The types of validity are content validity, criterion validity, and construct validity.

Questionnaires must be both reliable and valid in order for researchers to have confidence in the data collected with the instrument. In other words, items measuring the same construct should generate consistent responses and be pertinent to the construct that the items are intended to measure. As reliability and validity increase, measurement error decreases. However, it is possible for a test to be reliable but not valid. For instance, if a research methods instructor included items on an exam that were not covered in class lectures or reading materials, the items could demonstrate reliability through consistency of response even as they fail to constitute a valid assessment of learning material covered in the course—assuming that the purpose of giving the exam is to measure the extent to which students learned about the topics covered in the course.

The procedures discussed in this chapter are often used by sport management researchers to support the reliability or validity of a survey. For example, Cronbach's alpha is a specific measure of internal consistency reliability, whereas exploratory factor analysis, principal component analysis, and confirmatory factor analysis address construct

validity. Given that the quality of a study's results are related directly to the quality of the instrument used to collect data, it is easy to see the importance of collecting data by means of reliable and valid instruments.

Cronbach's Alpha

A popular method for measuring the internal consistency reliability of a group of items is the Cronbach's alpha coefficient, often referred to as simply *Cronbach's alpha* or *Cronbach's* α. In short, **Cronbach's alpha** measures how well a set of variables or items measures a single, unidimensional latent construct. It is essentially a correlation between the item responses in a questionnaire; assuming the statistic is directed toward a group of items intended to measure the same construct, Cronbach's alpha values will be high when the correlations between the respective questionnaire items are high. Cronbach's alpha values range from 0 to 1, and, in the social sciences, values at or above 0.7 are desirable, but values well above 0.9 may not be desirable as the scale is likely to be too narrow in focus (Nunnally & Bernstein, 1994). In addition to providing the Cronbach's alpha result for the entire construct, SPSS also provides item-specific information, such as "Cronbach's Alpha if Item Deleted" (i.e., the estimated value of Cronbach's alpha for the overall construct if the given item is removed from the analysis), "Corrected Item-Total Correlation" (i.e., the Pearson correlation of the item with the total scores on all items, where low values indicate weaker correlations with the overall scale), and "Squared Multiple Correlation" (i.e., the R^2 for an item when it is predicted from all other items in the scale, where lower values indicate that the item is

SPSS Cronbach's Alpha Procedure

1. Statistics → Scale → Reliability Analysis
2. Move each studied variable to the Variable box.
3. Statistics: Check Means and Scale If Item Deleted.
4. Continue.
5. OK

not contributing well to internal consistency). The accompanying highlight box provides the SPSS procedure for calculating Cronbach's alpha.

▪ ▪

Cronbach's Alpha Example

Verner, Hecht, and Fansler (1998) set out to develop a valid survey for assessing athletics donor motivation. Drawing on an extensive literature review and qualitative interviews with donors, the researchers identified 14 dimensions of donor motivation, then reduced that number to 12 after expert review and field testing of potential survey items. A pilot test of the survey was distributed to 500 randomly selected athletics donors, 50 from each of the 10 Missouri Valley Conference member institutions. The final number of responses was 296 (for a 59 percent response rate), and 255 of those surveys were deemed to be usable. The survey items were subjected to a battery of statistical tests, and Cronbach's alpha was used to measure the internal consistency of the identified athletics donor motivations. These motives included participating in secondary events ($\alpha = .84$), public recognition ($\alpha = .77$), giving of time and energy ($\alpha = .91$), inside information ($\alpha = .86$), priority treatment ($\alpha = .72$), philanthropy ($\alpha = .83$), collaboration ($\alpha = .83$), create ($\alpha = .83$), change ($\alpha = .86$), curiosity ($\alpha = .85$), power ($\alpha = .84$), and loyalty ($\alpha = .53$). Thus the Cronbach's alpha of the loyalty motive fell below the recommended threshold of 0.7 prescribed by Nunnally and Bernstein (1994). In light of the substandard Cronbach's alpha value (as well as substandard fit indices in a confirmatory factor analysis, as discussed later), the researchers decided to drop the loyalty motive from the survey. Thus, the final version of the survey contained 11 factors that addressed motives for athletics donor giving. At the same time, however, the researchers recommended additional research to examine the loyalty factor due to the potential effect of environmental and behavioral factors presumed to be present in their selected sample.

▪ ▪

Exploratory Factor Analysis and Principal Component Analysis

When researchers question an instrument's underlying structure or want to reduce the number of independent variables, they may find it appropriate to perform an analysis of structure such as an **exploratory factor analysis** (EFA) or a **principal component analysis** (PCA). These analyses share a common goal: combining several related, independent variables into fewer, more basic, underlying factors, thus revealing a less-complicated "internal structure" that conforms to the data. Essentially, EFA and PCA are variable reduction techniques, and they reduce the number of variables by determining which variables cluster together, which results in groupings of variables that, it is hoped, measure a common construct. The process is atheoretical, meaning that it is not driven by a pre-selected theory and uses statistical cutoffs to reduce a set of variables to a more concise set, which supports its exploratory nature. As a result, researchers must always ensure that the results of these variable reduction techniques correspond to real-world entities (i.e., the researcher should examine the results for content or face validity). If successful, the EFA and PCA procedures identify a new set of variables that explains all or nearly all of the variance that was formerly explained by the larger set of variables.

Statisticians generally agree that larger sample sizes are preferable to smaller sample sizes because they tend to minimize the probability of error, maximize the accuracy of population estimates, and increase the generalizability of results, but statisticians are somewhat divided when it comes to recommending a sample size for EFA and PCA. Some statisticians recommend an absolute minimum sample size, and Guadagnoli and Velicer's (1988) review of studies that offered such recommendations found that the recommendations ranged from 50 (Barrett & Kline, 1981) to 400 (Aleamoni, 1976). In addition, Comfrey and Lee (1992) suggest that "the adequacy of sample size might be evaluated very roughly on the following scale: 50 (very poor), 100 (poor), 200 (fair), 300 (good), 500 (very good), $\geq$ 1000 (excellent)" (p. 217). However, other statisticians contend that it is simplistic to set an absolute minimum for sample size. These statisticians insist that sample size should be calculated based on the number of items in the questionnaire, and their recommendations range from using at least a 5:1 subject-to-item ratio (Gorsuch, 1983; Hatcher, 1994) to using at least a 10:1 subject-to-item ratio (Nunnally, 1978). The lack of consensus among statisticians about using an absolute minimum or subject-to-item ratio in calculating EFA and PCA sample size is unfortunate, because the consequences of an insufficient sample size are quite significant: unstable loadings (Cliff,

1970); random, nonreplicable factors (Aleamoni, 1976; Humphreys, Ilgen, McGrath, & Montanelli, 1969); and lack of generalizability to the population (MacCallum, Widaman, Zhang, & Hong, 1999). Until a consensus is reached, it is best for researchers to use metrics from both camps when considering the adequacy of their sample size and to interpret sample size as conservatively as possible.

Before discussing the procedures used in analyses of structure, we will address some of the unique terminology associated with such analyses. **Variables** are often referred to as *factors* or, in a PCA, as *components*. A variable is typically made up of individual questionnaire items that load together on a particular dimension or factor. A key output of any EFA or CFA is a **factor loading,** which is interpreted as the Pearson correlation coefficient of an original variable with a factor. Similar to a correlation coefficient, factor loadings range from −1.00 (perfect negative correlation) to +1.00 (perfect positive correlation), and though variables may have some loadings on all factors, they usually have high loadings on only one factor. **Extraction** is the process by which factors are determined from a larger set of variables. Upon evaluating the factor loading data, the researcher can identify a particular factor as a variable and name it accordingly to reflect what the items collectively measure.

Specific terms are also used to correspond to the measurement of variance in variable reduction techniques. An **eigenvalue** indicates the amount of variance explained by each factor or component. Eigenvalues are commonly represented within scree plots, which graph the magnitude of each eigenvalue (vertical axis) against their ordinal numbers (horizontal axis). Scree plots are useful in determining the maximum number of factors for retention. The term *communality* refers to the variance in observed variables accounted for by common factors. Communalities allow the researcher to examine how individual variables reflect the sources of variability, and they are most commonly used in EFAs.

The primary distinction between EFA and PCA resides in the fact that in a PCA all sources of variability (unique, shared, and error variability) are analyzed for each observed variable, whereas in an EFA only shared variability is analyzed. As a result, PCA analyzes variance, and EFA analyzes covariance. Essentially, PCA is used to find optimal ways of combining variables into a small number of subsets, and EFA is used to identify the structure of underlying variables and to estimate measurements of latent factors (i.e., constructs that cannot

be measured directly). PCA is most often the preferred method of factor extraction when the goal is to extract the maximum variance from a data set, resulting in a few uncorrelated components. If a researcher initially intends to run a regression analysis (see chapter 14) but is unable to do so because the observed variables are highly correlated, a PCA allows the researcher to create uncorrelated linear combinations of weighted observed variables (i.e., principal component scores) that explain a maximal amount of variance in the data. Simply stated, the goal of a PCA is to explain the same amount of variance with fewer variables. For instance, PCA would be very useful for a researcher who desired to shorten a 150-item scale into a smaller, more concise, instrument.

However, if the goal of the analysis is to identify the number of latent factors and the underlying factor structure of a set of variables, EFA may be the preferred variable reduction technique. In this sense, EFA allows a researcher to explore a possible underlying factor structure for a set of measured variables without imposing a preconceived structure on the model.

PCA groups independent variables that share common variance, and then subjects these factors to a process called rotation for further adjustments. *Orthogonal rotation* is most commonly used, since its goal is to determine a final set of factors that are uncorrelated with each other, which is often a researcher's goal when developing a survey with unique factors. The types of orthogonal rotation include varimax, quartimax, and equimax and they are generally used when a researcher wants to maximize the generalizability of the results. Oblique rotation, on the other hand, allows factors to be correlated with each other; consequently, oblique rotation maximizes the fit of the data and structure.

When conducting a PCA, the researcher, of course, ultimately decides whether to retain a factor. Fortunately, several guidelines are available to help researchers make such decisions. First, researchers can consult **Kaiser's rule** (Kaiser, 1960), which dictates retaining only components whose eigenvalues are greater than 1. Second, researchers can examine the scree plot for a sharp bend in the line. Stevens (1992) recommends retaining all components with eigenvalues in the sharp descent of the line before the first bend where the leveling effect occurs. Third, the researcher can set a predetermined threshold for variance explained and can retain and interpret any factors that account for a certain amount of total variance. If this option is employed, Stevens (1992) recommends using 70 percent as the minimum threshold for variance explained. Finally, the researcher can make retention decisions based on an assessment of model fit. If the number of correlations that are reasonably close is small (typically <.05), it can be assumed that the model is consistent with the empirical data. Of course, the possibility remains that a researcher might encounter different retention recommendations when using more than one set of retention guidelines. In this case, more specific information from the output may lead the researcher to make an informed decision. For instance, Stevens (1992) states that Kaiser's rule has been shown to be quite accurate when the number of original variables is <30 and the communalities are >.70, or when $N >$ 250 and the mean communality is $\geq$.60. Additionally, Mertler and Vannatta (2005) note that use of the scree test with $N > 250$ provides fairly accurate results, provided that most of the communalities are somewhat large (i.e., >.30). The accompanying highlight box provides the SPSS procedure for calculating a principal component analysis.

SPSS Factor Analysis Procedure

1. Analyze → Data Reduction → Factor
2. Move each studied variable to the Variable box.
3. Descriptives: Check Initial Solution and Reproduced.
4. Continue.
5. Extraction: Check Correlation Matrix, Unrotated Factor Solution, Scree Plot, and Eigenvalue.
6. Continue.
7. Rotation: Check Varimax and Rotated Solution.
8. Continue.
9. Scores: Check Save as Variables and Regression.
10. Continue.
11. Options: Check Sorted by Size.
12. Continue.
13. OK

Principal Component Analysis Example

Chen (2004) studied the factors affecting individuals' participation decisions regarding athletics-related professional associations. Since these associations are nonprofit and are formed voluntarily by athletic administrators or coaches, membership enrollment and retention are crucial to the organization's survival.

Based on prior research, Chen proposed a four-factor model to illustrate decisions about participation by members of athletics-related associations: utilitarian, solidary, purposive, and informative incentives. Utilitarian incentives (UI) are material rewards or tangible benefits given only to members of the association. Solidary incentives (SI) reflect members' emotional attachment to the association and are beneficial to their occupational affinity, sense of belonging, professional identification, and friendship through social interaction with other members. Purposive incentives (PI) provide satisfaction for those who are intrinsically motivated to appeal to social norms, occupational standards, and political ideologies underlining the organization's goals and values system. Finally, informative incentives (II) involve information provided by the associational network that could benefit members either tangibly with timing or transferable value (e.g., discount programs, new jobs) or intangibly for their professional growth (e.g., research data, new knowledge).

A total of 415 individuals voluntarily participated in the study out of a sample of 820 who were asked to participate (for a 50.61 percent response rate). The entire sample was randomly split into two halves (samples A and B), and sample A was treated as a calibration group that was subjected to a principal component analysis. The eigenvalues for UI, SI, PI, and II ranged from 1.113 to 4.069, indicating a four-factor model. UI, SI, PI, and II independently contributed 8.10 percent to 29.06 percent variance to the solution and cumulatively contributed 62.3 percent of the total variance. Communalities for UI, SI, PI, and II ranged from .55 to .75, thus meeting the standards prescribed by Hair, Anderson, Tatham, and Black (1998), and each of the extracted factors contained 3 or 4 items that were highly correlated with the expected constructs of the conceptual framework. Ultimately, after considering the aforementioned guidelines for factor retention, Chen elected to retain all four factors, resulting in a model that featured utilitarian, solidary, purposive, and informative incentives as predictors of participation decisions in athletics-related professional associations (see table 13.1).

Table 13.1 **Remaining 14 Items With Means (M), Standard Deviation (SD), Coefficients of h2, and Factor Loadings (FL) Using Direct Oblimin Rotation of EFA for Calibration Sample (n = 208)**

Factors	Items	M	SD	h2	FL
UI	U1. Have more opportunities of leisure and recreation	2.33	.91	.66	.645
	U2. Obtain benefits of membership (discounts and programs)	2.11	1.07	.75	.869
	U3. Receive free journals, magazines, or membership gifts	2.32	.92	.66	.740
SI	S4. Gain affinitive feelings from organizational activities	3.48	1.21	.60	.709
	S5. Have a sense of belonging to my prestigious profession	3.10	1.26	.55	.618
	S6. Meet with my friends, colleagues, or celebrities	3.04	1.32	.70	.842
PI	P7. Engage in collective decisions (voting, making policy)	2.58	1.12	.60	.679
	P8. Express my political ideology and professional freedom	2.31	1.13	.62	.804
	P9. Exercise my leadership or fellowship in the profession	2.75	1.06	.62	.567
	P10. Appeal to social values and occupational standards	2.77	1.15	.61	.727
II	I11. Gather information regarding new jobs and programs	4.00	.76	.55	.704
	I12. Enhance understanding of updated knowledge and regulations	4.04	.86	.58	.599
	I13. Exchange new ideas and methods of administration and coaching	4.11	.91	.60	.658
	I14. Learn about future trends through networking	4.31	.84	.64	.765

UI = utilitarian incentives; SI = solidary incentives; PI = purposive incentives; II = informative incentives

Reprinted, by permission, from L. Chen, 2004, "Membership incentives: Factors affecting individuals' decisions about participation in athletics-related professional associations," *Journal of Sport Management* 18(2): 111-131.

Exploratory Factor Analysis Example

Given that brand association is one of four elements that are proposed to determine brand equity (the others being brand awareness, brand loyalty, and perceived quality), Ross, James, and Vargas (2006) set out to develop a scale for measuring team brand associations in professional sport. The authors followed Churchill's (1979) procedure for scale development (discussed in chapter 5) and, as part of this procedure, employed an exploratory factor analysis. The researchers first used a free-thought technique to discover the specific sport team associations that individuals hold regarding their favorite sport team. Thought-listing forms were distributed to undergraduate students, and, of the 40 forms distributed, 37 were completed and considered useable for analysis. The researchers and two coders conducted a content analysis of the

218 individuals in order to form the 70 initial items of the team brand association scale (TBAS).

These 70 items were administered to a convenience sample of 395 students, and 367 responses were completed and deemed useable for further analysis. These data were submitted to an exploratory factor analysis, and retention decisions were based on the Kaiser criterion (Kaiser, 1960), the scree test (Zwick & Velicer, 1982), examination of a fit statistic named the root mean square error of approximation (RMSEA) (Browne & Cudeck, 1993), parallel analysis (Zwick & Velicer), and extent of interpretability (Fabrigar, Wegener, McCallum, & Strahan, 1999). Each of the factor retention tests suggested a different number of factors to be retained; specifically, the Kaiser criterion suggested 13 factors, the scree test 3 factors, the RMSEA 4 factors, the parallel analysis 7 factors, and interpretability 10 factors. After thoroughly examining the factor loadings for each potential model structure in light of the potential hazards of overfactoring and underfactoring, in addition to the extent to which the solutions were interpretable, the researchers decided to retain 10 factors.

The resulting 10-factor solution accounted for 64.7 percent of the total variance explained by the model. The retained factors and their interpretations are as follows:

- Nonplayer personnel: concerns such as individual coaches of the team, team management, and the owners of the team

- Team success: concerns such as a team's success in competition, perceived quality of players, and perceived quality of the team itself

- Team history: historical thoughts regarding the team, its history of success, and the history of the team's personnel

- Stadium community: thoughts regarding favorite professional team's home stadium or arena and the community and area surrounding the home venue

- Team play characteristics: thoughts regarding specific characteristics that a team displays on the field of play, how the team goes about scoring, and specific characteristics ascribed to the team's play

- Brand mark: thoughts regarding identifying marks such as the logo, symbol, and colors

- Consumption experience: thoughts regarding concessionary aspects and social interaction related to a particular team (e.g., eating specific foods, consuming beverages, going to games with friends)

- Characteristics of sport: thoughts regarding characteristics of the sport being played and competition with rivals

- Commitment: thoughts regarding an individual's enduring affiliation with a particular professional sport team (length, continued regularity, and general notion of affiliation)

- Organizational attributes: thoughts regarding specific attributes of the sport organization as a whole, the organization's loyalty to fans, management's actions, and brand personality

Confirmatory Factor Analysis

As the term suggests, the major difference between **confirmatory factor analysis** (CFA) and the pre-viously discussed exploratory factor analysis (EFA) and principal component analysis (PCA) is that the latter two procedures determine an underlying model that best fits the data, whereas CFA allows the researcher to confirm the fit of the data with a predetermined model that is typically based on prior research. Therefore, EFA and PCA are tools for theory building, whereas CFA is a tool for theory testing. As a result, a CFA is often performed after an EFA or PCA.

In order to perform a confirmatory factor analysis, the researcher first must ensure that the proposed model is identified. An identified model allows the researcher to determine the unique values of the structural parameters from the observed interrelationships. Models can be identified by either the three-indicator rule or the two-indicator rule. The three-indicator rule allows for model identification if every factor has at least three indicators (e.g., survey items), no manifest variable is an indicator for more than one factor, and the error terms are not correlated. The two-indicator rule allows for model identification if every factor has at least two indicators, no manifest variable is an indicator for more than one factor, the error terms are not correlated, and the covariance matrix for the latent variables does not contain zeroes.

After the model identification is confirmed, CFA uses the user-specified model to generate a predicted set of item interrelationships (i.e., correlations or covariances). The difference between the predicted interrelationships and the observed interrelationships is referred to as a *fitted residual*, which is then divided by its estimated standard error to create a standardized residual. Since standardized residuals are independent of units of measurement, they are more clearly interpretable by the researcher.

A CFA analyzes the goodness of fit of the model proposed by the researcher by examining the overall size of the fitted residuals that it produces. These fit indices can be generally grouped into three categories: absolute fit, comparative fit, and parsimonious fit (Kelloway, 1998). Tests of absolute fit address the ability to reproduce the correlation or covariance matrix, and these fit indices include the root mean squared residual (RMR; values of <.05 indicate good fit), root mean square error of approximation (RMSEA; values of <.05 indicate good fit), goodness-of-fit index (GFI; values of >.9 indicate good fit), and the adjusted goodness-of-fit index (AGFI; values of >.9 indicate good fit). Tests of comparative fit make comparisons between the model of interest and a model that is known in advance to provide a poor fit to the data. These indices include the normed fit index (NFI; values >.9 indicate good fit), non-normed fit index (NNFI; values of >.9 indicate good fit), and the comparative fit index (CFI; values of >.9 indicate good fit). Finally, parsimonious fit indices are concerned primarily with the cost-benefit trade-off of fit and degrees of freedom (Kelloway). These indices include the parsimonious normed fit index (PNFI; no commonly accepted standard but higher values are better) and the parsimonious goodness-of-fit index (PGFI; no commonly accepted standard but higher values are better).

A typical confirmatory factor analysis requires a fairly large sample size. Jackson (2003) recommended that researchers adopt a sample size strategy for CFA that is similar to a common method used for path analysis. That is, minimum sample size should be calculated in terms of a ratio of cases to free parameters. A ratio of 20 cases per parameter is preferable, but a ratio of 10 cases per parameter may also be sufficient. In situations when CFA models are analyzed when the sample is not large, Marsh and Hau (1999) provide the following recommendations:

1. Use indicators with good psychometric characteristics that will each also have relatively high standardized factor loadings (e.g., >.60).

2. It may be possible to generate more trustworthy solutions by estimating the model with equality constraints imposed on the unstandardized loadings of the indicators of the same factor.

3. When the indicators are categorical items instead of continuous scales, it may be better to analyze them in groups known as parcels rather than individually.

A CFA cannot be calculated via SPSS software and requires specialized software for expedient calculation (e.g., AMOS, LISREL, EQS).

▪ ▪

Confirmatory Factor Analysis Examples

Both of the aforementioned examples for PCA (Chen, 2004) and EFA (Ross et al., 2006) incorporated a CFA after their variable reduction analysis to confirm the proposed models generated upon completion of the PCA and EFA, respectively. Recall that Chen was interested in the factors affecting individuals' participation decisions in athletics-related professional associations, and he divided his sample into sample A and sample B. Sample A was subjected to a PCA, and sample B was subjected to a CFA. For the CFA, Chen linked each questionnaire item with one of the four hypothesized determinants of participation decisions: utilitarian, solidary, purposive, and informative incentives. The resulting fit indices (GFI = .96, RMR = .048, AGFI = .94, CFI = .94) indicated acceptable fit of the data to the model and supported the factorial validity of the scale.

Similarly, recall that Ross et al. (2006) were interested in developing a scale for measuring team brand associations in professional sport. An EFA performed on the initial 70-item version of the questionnaire resulted in a 10-factor model: nonplayer personnel, team success, team history, stadium community, team play characteristics, brand mark, consumption experience, characteristics of sport, commitment, and organizational attributes. Ultimately, the EFA reduced a 70-item instrument to a 50-item instrument, and a subsequent expert panel review of these 50 items further reduced the instrument to 41 items assessing 11 factors (the factor addressing characteristics of the sport was renamed rivalry, and the factor addressing consumption experience was dichotomized into social interaction and concessions factors). A CFA was performed on the remaining items, resulting in acceptable or better fit indices (RMSEA = .074, CFI = .95).

▨ ▪ ▨ ▪ ▨ ▪ ▨

Summary

This chapter reviews statistical tools used to analyze structure. Cronbach's alpha is a popular method for measuring the internal consistency reliability of a group of items. Exploratory factor analysis (EFA) and principal component analysis (PCA) are variable reduction techniques used in an attempt to combine several related independent variables into fewer, more basic underlying factors. The primary distinction between EFA and PCA is that in a PCA all sources of variability (unique, shared, and error variability) are analyzed for each observed variable, whereas in an EFA only shared variability is analyzed (i.e., PCA analyzes variance, and EFA analyzes covariance). PCA is used to find optimal ways of combining variables into a small number of subsets, whereas EFA is used to identify the structure of underlying variables and to estimate measurements of latent factors. Finally, confirmatory factor analysis (CFA) allows the researcher to confirm the fit of the data in respect to a predetermined model that is typically based on prior research.

ADVANCED READING

Cronbach's Alpha

Gauthier, R., & Hansen, H. (1993). Female spectators: Marketing implications for professional golf events. *Sport Marketing Quarterly, 2*(4), 21–28.

Hansen, H., & Gauthier, R. (1993). Spectators' views of LPGA golf events. *Sport Marketing Quarterly, 2*(1), 17–25.

Hansen, H., & Gauthier, R. (1994). The professional golf product: Spectators' views. *Sport Marketing Quarterly, 3*(4), 9–16.

Ross, S., James, J., & Vargas, P. (2006). Development of a scale to measure team brand associations in professional sport. *Journal of Sport Management, 20*(2), 260–279.

Principal Component Analysis

Inglis, S., Danylchuk, K., & Pastore, D. (1996). Understanding retention factors in coaching and athletic management positions. *Journal of Sport Management, 10*(3), 237–249.

Pastore, D., Goldfine, B., & Riemer, H. (1996). NCAA college coaches and athletic administrative support. *Journal of Sport Management, 10*(4), 373–387.

Pastore, D., & Meacci, W. (1994). Employment process for NCAA female coaches. *Journal of Sport Management, 8*(2), 115–128.

Staurowsky, E., Parkhouse, B., & Sachs, M. (1996). Developing an instrument to measure athletic donor behavior and motivation. *Journal of Sport Management, 10*(3), 262–277.

Exploratory Factor Analysis

Alexandris, K., Kouthouris, C., Funk, D., & Chatzigianni, E. (2008). Examining the relationships between leisure constraints, involvement and attitudinal loyalty among Greek recreational skiers. *European Sport Management Quarterly, 8*(3), 247–264.

Hardin, R., Andrew, D., Koo, G., & Bemiller, J. (2009). Motivational factors for participating in basic instruction programs. *Physical Educator, 66*(2), 71–84.

Konter, E. (2009). Towards adaptation of self and other versions of the Revised Power in Soccer Questionnaire for Turkey. *European Sport Management Quarterly, 9*(3), 311–332.

Seo, W., & Green, B. (2008). Development of the Motivation Scale for Sport Online Consumption. *Journal of Sport Management, 22*(1), 82–109.

Vlachopoulos, S., Theodorakis, N., & Kyle, G. (2008). Assessing exercise involvement among participants in health and fitness centres. *European Sport Management Quarterly, 8*(3), 289–304.

Confirmatory Factor Analysis

Chang, K., & Chelladurai, P. (2003). Comparison of part-time workers and full-time workers: Commitment and citizenship behaviors in Korean sport organizations. *Journal of Sport Management, 17*(4), 394–416.

Gladden, J., & Funk, D. (2002). Developing an understanding of brand associations in team sport: Empirical evidence from consumers of professional sport. *Journal of Sport Management, 16*(1), 54–81.

MacLean, J., & Chelladurai, P. (1995). Dimensions of coaching performance: Development of a scale. *Journal of Sport Management, 9*(2), 194–207.

Selected text reprinted, by permission, from A. Rudd, S. Mullane, and S. Stoll, 2010, "Development of an instrument to measure the moral judgments of sport managers," *Journal of Sport Management* 24(1): 59-82.

Access the full article online at www.humankinetics.com/products/all-products/Research-Methods-and-Design-in-Sport-Management.

ABSTRACT

The purpose of this study was to develop an instrument to measure the moral judgments of sport managers called the Moral Judgments of Sport Managers Instrument (MJSMI). More specifically, our intention was to measure moral judgment on a unidimensional level given past research suggesting moral judgment is a unidimensional construct (Hahm, Beller, & Stoll, 1989; Kohlberg, 1984; Piaget, 1932; Rest, 1979, 1986). The MJSMI contains 8 moral dilemmas/stories in the context of sport management. Sport managers respond to the dilemmas on a four-point Likert scale. Three pilot studies were undertaken to develop the MJSMI. Exploratory factor analysis and internal consistency analysis were the primary methods for assaying reliability and validity. Results consistently showed that sport managers' responses vary depending on the nature of the moral scenario and thus do not indicate a unidimensional construct. The reasons for inconsistent responses are thoroughly discussed.

TEXT EXCERPTS

It is important to note that item development was an iterative process. Items were removed and new ones developed based on reliability and validity analyses from the pilot studies.

. . . .

Before administering the instrument, the MJSMI was assessed for content validity. This was ascertained through expert review (Johnson & Christensen, 2004).

. . . .

All 78 students completed the instrument. Given the larger sample size, an exploratory factor analysis was conducted to assess the unidimensionality of the instrument with the caveat that the sample was still somewhat small. Principal axis factoring was chosen as the extraction method along with an orthogonal factor rotation (Varimax).

. . . .

Principal axis factoring with an orthogonal rotation (Varimax) extracted two factors based on the Kaiser Criterion (i.e., selecting factors with eigenvalues greater than 1.00; Henson & Roberts, 2006).

. . . .

Although internal consistency does not automatically imply reliability and validity, an instrument should demonstrate a strong degree of internal consistency if one intends to measure any given construct on a unidimensional level (or at least the subscales should be internally consistent). It is not possible to use summative scaling if the items do not yield consistent responses. Good item discrimination is needed to clearly interpret scores. Furthermore, internal consistency can provide some evidence of construct validity if the theoretical construct (in this case moral judgment) is believed to yield consistent responses across scenarios (Cronbach & Meehl, 1955). However, the results from this study suggest that there are certain elements of the various scenarios within the MJSMI that caused one's decision, or moral reasoning, to fluctuate. One possibility may be that moral judgment cannot be measured on a unidimensional level. Or, it may be that additional work is needed to improve the wording contained in the MJSMI scenarios to evoke more consistent responses across scenarios.

DISCUSSION QUESTIONS

1 What is the purpose of the Moral Judgments of Sport Managers Instrument (MJSMI)?

2 Provide a general description of the final version of the MJSMI.

3 What potential limitations do researchers face when adopting a scenario-based approach to survey development?

4 What reasoning do the authors provide to support their conclusion that it would be unwise to aggregate the MJSMI items into a total score?

5 What three reasons do the authors provide in respect to the question of why responses may change depending on the type of moral scenario?

6 Compare the authors' arguments for and against using the MJSMI (in its current state) for research purposes.

Relationships Between Variables

Learning Objectives

After studying this chapter, you should be able to do the following:

- Provide a general description of the statistical techniques used to determine the degree of relationship between variables
- Compare the meaning of positive and negative correlations
- Categorize standard multiple regression, sequential multiple regression, and stepwise multiple regression according to their appropriate usage
- Discuss the differences between the forward-selection, stepwise-selection, and backward-deletion regression techniques
- Differentiate between exogenous and endogenous variables
- Compare the various statistical techniques used to determine the degree of relationship between variables on the basis of their limitations and appropriate usage

One function of statistical tests is to determine the degree of relationship between variables. Specifically, statistical tests can be used to address research questions proposing that one or more (independent) variables have a positive or negative effect on one or more (dependent) variables. Table 14.1 lists the various assumptions for procedures that test the degree of relationship between variables. The purpose of this chapter is to describe statistical tests that can be used to determine the degree of relationship between variables: bivariate correlation, simple linear regression, multiple regression, and path analysis.

Bivariate Correlation

Bivariate correlation evaluates the degree of relationship between two quantitative variables without distinction between the independent and dependent variables. Correlation may also be used

Table 14.1 **Assumptions for Procedures That Test the Degree of Relationship Between Variables**

Assumptions	Bivariate correlation	Simple linear regression	Multiple regression	Path analysis
The independent variables are fixed.			X	X
The independent variables are measured without error.			X	X
The relationship between the independent variables and the dependent variable is linear.			X	X
The mean of the residuals for each observation on the dependent variable over many replications is zero.			X	X
Errors associated with any single observation of the dependent variable are independent of (i.e., not correlated with) errors associated with any other observation on the dependent variable.			X	X
The errors are not correlated with the independent variables.			X	X
The variance of the residuals across all values of the independent variables is constant (i.e., there is homoscedasticity of the variance of the residuals).			X	X
The errors are normally distributed.			X	X
The model accurately reflects the actual causal sequence.				X
The structure equation for each endogenous variable includes all variables that are direct causes of that particular endogenous variable.				X
There is a one-way causal flow in the model.				X
The relationships between variables are assumed to be linear, additive, and causal in nature.				X
All exogenous variables are measured without error.				X

to determine the relationship between three or more variables, and in these cases the technique is referred to as multiple correlation. In **bivariate** correlation-based analyses, a correlation coefficient is used to measure the association between two quantitative variables. When both variables are collected at the interval or ratio levels of measurement, a parametric test is incorporated that features a **Pearson correlation coefficient** (r), named after its developer, Karl Pearson. The SPSS procedures used to calculate a Pearson correlation are presented in the accompanying highlight box. If both collected variables are at the ordinal level of measurement, a nonparametric test with a **Spearman correlation coefficient** (rs or ρ) is used; this test is named after Charles Spearman, who devised it. The SPSS procedures used to calculate a Spearman correlation are found in the accompanying highlight box.

SPSS Pearson Correlation Procedure

1. Analyze → Correlate → Bivariate
2. Select appropriate variables.
3. Check Pearson.
4. OK

SPSS Spearman Correlation Procedure

1. Analyze → Correlate → Bivariate
2. Select appropriate variables.
3. Check Spearman.
4. OK

Regardless of whether the test used is parametric or nonparametric, the correlation coefficient represents a quantitative value that describes the relationship between two variables. Correlations can be positive or negative in nature. In a positive correlation, as the value of one of the variables increases, the value of the second variable increases. Likewise, as the value of one of the variables decreases, the value of the other variable decreases. In a negative correlation, as the value of one of the variables increases, the value of the second variable

decreases, and vice versa. Negative correlations are sometimes described as inverse correlations.

A **correlation coefficient** (i.e., a Pearson r or a Spearman r or ρ) can range from −1.00 to +1.00. Values closer to −1.00 or +1.00 indicate stronger relationships, and values closer to 0 indicate weaker relationships. A correlation coefficient of −1.00 or +1.00 describes a perfect negative relationship or a perfect positive relationship, respectively. It is rare to encounter either a perfect negative or perfect positive correlation, but it is possible. For example, if one were to compare the number of tickets sold for the Super Bowl with the number of spectators who in fact attended the event, a perfect positive correlation would be possible. That is, if every spectator who purchased a ticket attended the game, the relationship between the number of tickets sold and the number of attending spectators would result in a perfect positive correlation. On the other hand, a correlation coefficient of 0 indicates no relationship between the two variables. Returning to the Super Bowl example, a researcher might not expect a relationship between the amount paid by each spectator for his or her ticket and the spectator's quantitative score on a European history exam. Of course, correlation coefficients are also accompanied by p-values in a statistical output, so a correlation should be significant (typically, where $p < .05$) before it is interpreted.

One issue that researchers must consider when calculating a correlation is whether or not they have a sufficient sample size. The sample size for a bivariate Pearson correlation is determined by three factors: significance level, power level, and effect size. The significance level is the researcher-defined acceptability of a Type I error (typically, this value is 0.05). Recall from chapter 5 that a Type I error occurs when the null hypothesis is true but the researcher concludes that it is false (i.e., the researcher rejects the null hypothesis). Therefore, a significance level of .05 means that the researcher is accepting a 5 percent chance that the results obtained in the study are purely due to chance. On the other hand, the power level is inversely related to the significance level, since the power level is the researcher-defined acceptability of a Type II error. A Type II error occurs when the null hypothesis is false but the researcher concludes that it is true (i.e., the researcher fails to reject the null hypothesis). Power levels are typically set at 0.80, which makes the probability of committing a Type II error approximately four times that of the probability of committing a Type I error in the typical analysis. Effect size is an objective and standardized measure of the magnitude of the observed effect (Field, 2005). Effect sizes are measured on a scale of 0 to 1, where 0 indicates no effect size and 1 represents a very high effect size. Cohen's (1988, 1992) widely referenced recommendations for Pearson correlations are 0.10 for a small effect size, 0.30 for a medium effect size, and 0.50 for a large effect size (the medium effect size value is most commonly used). By plugging the significance level, power level, and effect size into Cohen's (1992) calculation formula, the researcher can calculate a minimum sample size of 85 for Pearson correlation at a 0.05 level of significance, a power of 0.80, and a medium effect size (i.e., $r = .30$). A number of free and convenient sample size calculators are available online and can be found by using a standard Internet search engine.

In summary, a bivariate correlation can indicate (1) whether there is a relationship between two variables, (2) the direction of the relationship (i.e., positive or negative), and (3) the strength or magnitude of the relationship. Remember, however, that correlation does not necessarily indicate causality. For example, if a researcher investigates employees in a sport organization and uncovers a positive correlation between job satisfaction and organizational commitment, it can be concluded that higher job satisfaction scores are generally associated with higher organizational commitment scores. It cannot, however, be inferred that job satisfaction causes organizational commitment, or that organizational commitment causes job satisfaction, on the basis of a correlation analysis alone. Correlation is a necessary—but not a sufficient—condition for causation. The only way causation can be shown is via an experimental study in which an independent variable is manipulated in order to bring about an effect.

▬▬▬▬▬▬▬▬▬▬▬▬▬▬▬▬▬▬▬▬▬▬▬▬▬

Correlation Example

Lyberger and Pastore (1998) surveyed a group of 370 health club facility operators in order to examine the relationship between an operator's awareness of, knowledge about, and perceptions of compliance with the Americans with Disabilities Act (ADA). The questionnaire included measures of (a) awareness of the ADA, (b) knowledge about the ADA, (c) perceptions of ADA regulations, (d) self-perceived level of compliance with the ADA, and (e) demographic information. A lower-than-expected response rate of 13.5 percent prompted the use of a correlation matrix to explore the potential relationships between the independent variables (i.e., health club facility operators' awareness, knowledge, and perceptions) and the dependent variable (self-perceived level of compliance). Note that a correlation matrix allows for calculation of several bivariate correlations simultaneously.

The results indicated significant positive relationships between (a) awareness and self-perceived level of compliance ($r = .49$, $p < .05$), (b) awareness and perceptions ($r = .39$, $p < .01$), and (c) knowledge and perceptions ($r = .53$, $p < .01$). When all results of the study were taken into account, the findings suggested that low levels of awareness are associated with low to moderate levels of self-perceived compliance, that facility operators are only moderately knowledgeable and generally perceptive about the ADA, and that they are not fully complying with ADA regulations.

▬▬▬▬▬▬▬▬▬▬▬▬▬▬▬▬▬▬▬▬▬▬▬▬▬

Simple Linear Regression

Simple linear regression is similar to bivariate correlation in that it analyzes the relationship between two variables. However, an added benefit of simple linear regression analysis is that it produces a regression equation that can be used for prediction purposes. A regression equation is essentially a formula that produces a best-fit line that describes the relationship of the independent and dependent variables. Such information allows the researcher to predict a value for the dependent variable based on a value of the independent variable. For example, simple linear regression analysis could be applied to the Lyberger and Pastore (1998) study of health club facility operators in order to predict a health club facility operator's self-perceived level of compliance given a known level of awareness for that particular operator (see Correlation Example).

Another advantage of a simple linear regression over bivariate correlation is that simple linear regression results provide an R^2 value (also referred to as the **coefficient of determination**), which allows the researcher to determine the extent to which the independent variable successfully predicts the dependent variable. R^2 values range from 0 (no linear relationship) to 1.0 (perfect linear relationship). Lower values of R^2 indicate that additional independent variables need to be added to the model in order to improve prediction of the dependent variable (see the accompanying highlight box for the simple linear regression calculation procedure for SPSS).

SPSS Simple Linear Regression Procedure

1. Analyze → Regression → Linear
2. Move DV to Dependent Variable box.
3. Move IV to Independent(s) box.
4. Select appropriate method.
5. Statistics: Check Estimates, Model Fit, R Squared Change, Descriptives, Part and Partial Correlations, and Collinearity Diagnostics.
6. Continue.
7. Options: Select appropriate criteria.
8. Continue.
9. OK

Researchers are still somewhat divided concerning the minimum sample size for regression analyses. Stevens (1992) offers a simple subject-to-predictor ratio (n/k, where n = sample size and k = number of predictors) of 15:1 to provide a reliable regression equation. Since simple linear regression by definition has only one predictor (i.e., one independent variable), a minimally defined model according to Stevens would only require 15 subjects. Of course, this ratio is also used for multiple regression (discussed later in this chapter), where more than one independent variable is possible. Alternatively, Tabachnick and Fidell (1996) recommend calculating regression sample size by using one of the following two formulas: $n \geq 50 + 8(k)$ for multiple correlations, or $n \geq 104 + k$ for individual predictors (where n = sample size and k = number of predictors). They suggest calculating sample size with both formulas and using the larger value in order to be most conservative. In cases where statisticians fail to reach consensus regarding sample size, it is often more prudent to select the most conservative estimate (i.e., the estimate that requires the largest sample size).

▪ ▪

Simple Linear Regression Example

Park, Andrew, and Mahony (2008) surveyed a convenience sample of 128 respondents to explore the role that trait curiosity plays in initial sport interest. The researchers hypothesized that trait curiosity, or an individual's typical pattern of curiosity across situations, would be positively related to an individual's initial interest levels across 10 novel sports (i.e., sports that were relatively new and did not have a long history of fan interest). In other words, the researchers predicted that individuals who had high levels of trait curiosity would be naturally predisposed to being interested in new and emerging sports. The researchers used 20 items from the Melbourne Curiosity Inventory to measure trait curiosity and created a novel sport index to measure one's interest in watching 10 novel sports.

In order to examine whether trait curiosity was useful in predicting an individuals' initial interest in new sports, a simple linear regression was performed. The overall model revealed a significant result [$F(1, 126) = 27.5$; $p < .001$] and indicated that about 18 percent of the variance in novel sport spectatorship was explained by the model ($R^2 = 0.18$). The *beta value* (β) for trait curiosity in the equation was .42. In a regression equation, the β is analogous to the Pearson r in correlation; that is, it represents the relationship between the independent variable (in this case, trait curiosity) and the dependent variable (initial interest in novel sports). As trait curiosity increased, the intention to watch novel sports also increased significantly. However, given that trait curiosity scores explained only 18 percent of the variance in novel sport spectatorship, the researchers suggested future research to determine other predictors of initial interest levels of novel sports.

▪ ▪

Multiple Regression

Multiple regression is an extension of simple linear regression that allows the researcher to expand the number of independent variables in the regression equation. Consequently, the purpose of a multiple regression analysis is to create a regression equation for predicting the dependent variable from a group of independent variables. For example, a sport marketing researcher might want to determine which combination of spectator motives (e.g., drama, escape, aesthetic qualities, vicarious achievement, social interaction, national pride, economics or gambling, adoration, violence, sport interest) best predicts media consumption behavior of mixed martial arts fans (see Kim, Greenwell, Andrew, Lee, & Mahony, 2008). In this case, multiple regression results would allow the researcher to determine the best combination of predictors (independent variables, in this case spectator motives) that significantly predict the desired outcome (dependent variable, in this case media consumption).

The default method for multiple regression in SPSS allows for simultaneous input of all predictor variables (independent variables) into the equation; this method is often referred to as **standard multiple regression** in textbooks and as Enter in SPSS. These variables are then analyzed individually on the basis of their ability to significantly predict the dependent variable. More specifically, the effect of each independent variable on a dependent variable is assessed as if it had been entered into the equation after all other independent variables had been entered. At that point, each independent variable is then evaluated in terms of what it adds to the prediction of the dependent variable (Tabachnick & Fidell, 1996). Independent variables that do not significantly account for variance in the dependent variable should be dropped from the equation, leaving a final regression equation that includes a group of significant independent variables that predict the dependent variable (see the accompanying highlight box for the multiple regression calculation procedure for SPSS).

SPSS Multiple Regression Procedure

1. Analyze → Regression → Linear
2. Move DV to Dependent Variable box.
3. Move IV to Independent(s) box.
4. Select appropriate method.
5. Statistics: Check Estimates, Model Fit, R Squared Change, Descriptives, Part and Partial Correlations, and Collinearity Diagnostics.
6. Continue.
7. Options: Select appropriate criteria.
8. Continue.
9. OK

When a researcher wants to examine the influence of several predictor independent variables in a specific order, he or she should employ **sequential multiple regression** (also referred to as **hierarchical multiple regression**). In this approach, the researcher specifies a particular order in which

variables are entered into the analysis. A rationale for using this technique would be that past research has led the researcher to believe that one variable may be more influential than others in the set of predictors. As a result, the researcher may want to enter the more established predictor into the model first, followed by other predictor variables in order to determine the value that each subsequent variable adds to the predictive model, above and beyond the value added by the more established predictor variable.

Finally, when studies are exploratory in nature, **stepwise multiple regression** (also referred to as **statistical multiple regression**) may be employed. Stepwise multiple regression is typically used in cases where a researcher has a large set of independent variables and needs to determine which specific independent variables make meaningful contributions to the overall prediction. Here are descriptions of three variations of stepwise multiple regression:

- **Forward-selection multiple regression**: The independent variable that has the highest correlation with the dependent variable (on the basis of a correlation matrix) is entered into the model first and assessed in terms of its contribution to the prediction of the dependent variable (in terms of R^2). Then, the remaining independent variables are subjected to a correlation matrix to determine which has the highest correlation with the dependent variable. This particular variable is then added into the equation and assessed in terms of the improvement of prediction of the dependent variable in the existing model in terms of a significant change to R^2 (ΔR^2). This process continues until the point at which new predictor variables stop making significant contributions to the prediction of the dependent variable. In a simplistic sense, forward selection operates in much the same way that professional players are selected by sport teams. Each team manager selects a player based on the anticipated contributions of that player to the team, followed by the second-best player, the third-best player, and so on.

- **Stepwise-selection multiple regression**: This variation is similar to forward selection except that, at each step, tests are performed to determine the significance of each independent variable already in the equation as if it were to enter last. In forward selection, once a variable has been entered into the analysis, it remains there. However, in stepwise selection, if a variable entered into the analysis measures much of the same construct as another, the reassessment that occurs at each step may determine that the initial variable no longer contributes anything to the overall analysis. Subsequently, the initial variable would then be dropped in the analysis because it no longer serves as a substantial contributor.

■ **Backward-deletion multiple regression**: This variation computes an equation with all predictors included, followed by a significance test (a partial F-test) for every predictor as if each were entered last in order to determine the level of contribution to overall prediction. At this point in the analysis, the variable with the smallest partial F is compared to a preselected "F to remove" value that typically coincides with the significance level preselected by the researcher. If the predictor variable is not significant (i.e., the partial F value of the independent variable is less than the "F to remove" value), it is removed from the analysis and a new equation with the remaining predictors is computed and subjected to another test of the resulting smallest partial F. This procedure continues until only significant predictors remain in the equation. The backward-deletion variation is often preferable to the forward-selection variation because of its ability to deal with suppressor effects, which occur when a predictor has a significant effect but only when another variable is held constant. In a general sense, backward deletion operates much like the television show *Survivor*, at least in theory; if, at each stage of the competition, the true weakest link was voted off the island until a cohort of true survivors remained, then *Survivor* would be analogous to backward deletion.

Stepwise multiple regression analysis is not often employed in sport management research, but given the need for more exploratory research in the field, it could be very popular in the future. For example, the study of mixed martial arts spectators mentioned earlier (Kim et al., 2008) was exploratory in nature and appropriately used the backward-deletion variation of stepwise multiple progression to pare down its original group of 10 spectator motives. Ultimately, the researchers calculated two backward-deletion stepwise multiple regressions to determine that sport interest, vicarious achievement, and national pride motives were significant predictors of media consumption for males, whereas sport interest and drama motives were significant predictors of media consumption for females. Sport marketers can use these results to develop specific marketing strategies for each group or to use any common motives among the two

groups (in this case, sport interest) to design a more general marketing campaign that would positively influence media consumption among both groups.

While standard multiple regression is employed in the majority of sport management studies, both sequential and stepwise multiple regression hold a distinct advantage over standard multiple regression in that one variable is added at a time and thus each is continually checked for significant improvement in the prediction of the dependent variable. Sequential multiple regression calls for the researcher to add variables based on a theory or plan, whereas stepwise multiple regression uses statistical analyses for inclusion or deletion decisions.

Multiple Regression Example

DeSchriver's (2007) study concerning Freddy Adu and attendance in Major League Soccer provides an excellent example of standard multiple regression in the sport management context. The purpose of this study was to analyze the relationship between game-specific attendance in Major League Soccer (MLS) and the presence of Freddy Adu in matches during the 2004 season. Individual game attendance, as reported by MLS, served as the dependent variable for this study, and the researcher included the following eight independent (predictor) variables:

- AduRoad: categorical variable representing games in which DC United and Freddy Adu played as the visiting team
- Team fixed-effects variables: categorical variables that account for all market-specific characteristics (population, racial composition, income, ticket price) that are constant for a single team in an individual season but can vary across teams
- Promotional activity variables: group of three categorical variables representing the presence of promotional activities (i.e., complementary giveaway item, fireworks promotional day, doubleheader with U.S. national team)
- Weekday/weekend: variable denoting games played on Friday, Saturday, or Sunday since a positive relationship was expected between weekend contests and attendance
- Visitor All-Stars: variable measuring the attractiveness, or star quality, of the opposing team after controlling for on-field success
- Weather: variable denoting games played during favorable weather conditions since a positive relationship was expected between

favorable weather conditions and attendance

- Home team performance: variable measured by the average points per game earned by the home team before the game in question (3 points for a win, 1 point for a tie, 0 points for a loss)

- Previous season visiting team performance: variable measuring the visiting team's on-field performance in the 2003 season (calculated in similar fashion to the home team performance variable)

In all, the regression equation explained 67 percent of the variation in game-specific attendance, and 9 of the 22 independent variables were statistically significant at the .05 level. Using the generated regression equation, and holding all other variables constant, the researcher concluded that an additional 10,958 spectators per game attended games in which Freddy Adu was playing. Furthermore, the researcher estimated that these additional spectators generated about $3.25 million in revenue from ticket, concession, and merchandise sales during the 2004 season, making Freddy Adu's $500,000 annual salary appear to be a sound investment.

▬ ▬

Path Analysis

Path analysis is an extension of regression that analyzes correlations within a set of variables in order to examine the pattern of causal relationships. The process typically involves generating a **path diagram** with arrows depicting the direction of causation between variables. This path diagram is developed a priori (i.e., the model is hypothesized prior to the analysis phase). In short, path analysis incorporates multiple applications of multiple regression to estimate causal relationships, both direct and indirect, between several variables and to test the acceptability of the path diagram hypothesized by the researcher. Often, two or more path diagrams are analyzed according to the best-fitting model for the collected data, and the best-fitting model is typically recommended by the researcher as the best model for advancement of theory.

Path analysis offers many distinct benefits. First, it provides an overall indication of the fit between the model and the theory. Second, the analysis can incorporate latent variables, which are variables that cannot be measured directly but can be approximated with other measures (e.g., human intelligence is not directly measurable but is often approximated by performance on intelligence tests). Note that when a path analysis incorporates unobservable latent variables in the model, the analysis is often referred to as structural equation modeling. Third, multiple dependent variables and intervening (i.e., mediating) variables can be analyzed simultaneously. One disadvantage of path analysis is that more complicated models (e.g., structural equation modeling) require specialized statistical software, such as LISREL, AMOS, or EQS.

Path diagrams typically feature a series of variables with arrows connecting each variable to another variable that it is hypothesized to influence in some manner. As a result, some variables have arrows pointing to them, some have arrows pointing away from them, and some have both. Researchers typically use the term **endogenous variable** to describe a variable that is being explained by the model (i.e., a variable that has an arrow pointing toward it) and the term **exogenous variable** to describe a variable that is not explained by the model (i.e., a variable that does not have an arrow pointing toward it). Whereas endogenous variables are assumed to have their variance explained by the exogenous variables included in the model, the variability of exogenous variables is assumed to be explained by other variables outside the causal model.

Path coefficients are calculated to estimate the strength of the relationships in the hypothesized causal model. In essence, path coefficients are analogous to the r value in correlation and the beta (β) value in regression. Therefore, path coefficient values can range from −1.00 to +1.00, and higher values indicate stronger relationship between the two variables of interest, whereas lower values indicate weaker relationship. Again, as with the r value in correlation and the beta (β) value in regression, path coefficients should be significant before researchers draw conclusions pertaining to these results.

A **fit index** gives the researcher an indication of how well the data fits the proposed model (see chapter 13 for a more detailed review). Fit indices can be generally grouped into three categories: absolute fit (χ^2: chi-square; RMR: root mean square residual; RMSEA: root mean square error of approximation; GFI: goodness-of-fit index; and AGFI: adjusted goodness-of-fit index), comparative (or relative) fit (NFI: normed fit index; NNFI: nonnormed fit index; CFI: comparative fit index; and IFI: incremental fit index), and parsimonious fit (PNFI: parsimonious normed fit index; PGFI: parsimonious goodness-of-fit index; and PCFI: parsimonious comparative fit index). Tests of absolute fit are concerned with the ability to reproduce the correlation or covariance matrix. Tests of comparative fit make comparisons between the model of interest and a model that is known in advance to provide a poor fit to the data. Parsimonious fit indices are concerned primarily with the cost-benefit trade-off of fit and degrees of freedom (Kelloway, 1998). Table 14.2 lists the fit indices by category, along with their recommended values for acceptable fit.

Researchers must ensure that they meet the minimum sample size requirements for a path analysis before interpreting any results. Kline (1998) recommends a minimum of 10 times as many cases as parameters under examination in the model. A parameter is a presumed relation between observed and latent variables (i.e., an arrow in the model). The number of parameters in a model often exceeds the number of variables, because a variable may have multiple paths associated with it. Kline further notes that 20 times as many cases as parameters is ideal and that fewer than 5 times as many cases as parameters is insufficient for significance testing of model effects. Hoyle (1995) recommends an absolute minimum sample size of 100 to 200 for confidence in the goodness-of-fit tests associated with path analysis. The SPSS procedure for calculating a path analysis is presented in the accompanying highlight box (models with latent variables require more sophisticated software packages, such as AMOS, LISREL, and EQS).

SPSS Path Analysis Procedure

1. Analyze → Regression → Linear
2. Move endogenous variables to Dependent Variable box.
3. Move exogenous variables to Independent(s) box.
4. Select Enter.
5. Statistics: Check Model Fit and Collinearity Diagnostics.
6. Continue.
7. OK

Path Analysis Example

Cunningham, Sagas, Dixon, Kent, and Turner (2008) gathered data from 138 upper-level undergraduate sport management students (71 interns, 67 non-interns) to examine the effect of internships on students' career-related affect and intentions. For undergraduate sport management students, the internship is typically the last field experience in an academic program, and it often serves as the final professional preparation for students before they decide whether or not to enter the sport management profession. The

---

Table 14.2 **Recommended Values of Absolute, Comparative, and Parsimonious Fit Measures**

ABSOLUTE		COMPARATIVE		PARSIMONIOUS	
Test	Value	Test	Value	Test	Value
χ^2	p >.05	NFI	>.90	PNFI	>.50
RMR	<.05	NNFI	>.90	PGFI	>.50
RMSEA	<.10	CFI	>.90	PCFI	>.50
GFI	>.90	IFI	>.90		
AGFI	>.90				

Note: χ^2 = chi-square; RMR = root mean square residual; RMSEA = root mean square error of approximation; GFI = goodness-of-fit index; AGFI = adjusted goodness-of-fit index; NFI = normed fit index; NNFI = non-normed fit index; CFI = comparative fit index; IFI = incremental fit index; PNFI = parsimonious normed fit index; PGFI = parsimonious goodness-of-fit index; and PCFI = parsimonious comparative fit index

researchers hypothesized that, given the proximity of the internship to the decision to enter the sport management profession, the internship experience can potentially influence subsequent career-related affect and behaviors, namely anticipated career satisfaction, occupational commitment, and intention to enter the sport management profession.

One hypothesis of this study specifically addressed the expected interrelationships between anticipated career satisfaction, occupational commitment, and intention to enter the profession. The authors asserted that "if a person strongly identifies with and has an emotional attachment to a profession, it is likely that he or she will make efforts to and will actually join that profession" (p. 47). They expected that anticipated career satisfaction would lead to occupational commitment, which, in turn, would result in intention to enter the profession: "Occupational commitment will mediate the positive relationship between anticipated career satisfaction and intention to enter the profession" (p. 47).

To test the aforementioned hypothesis, the authors incorporated structural equation modeling—a special case of path analysis that includes latent variables. Specifically, the researchers compared two competing models: (1) a fully mediated model in which the effects of anticipated career satisfaction on intention to enter the sport management profession are seen only through occupational commitment, and (2) a partially mediated model in which the effects of anticipated career satisfaction on intention to enter the sport management profession are seen both independently and through occupational commitment. The results indicated that occupational commitment did indeed mediate the relationship between anticipated career satisfaction and intention to enter the profession,

and the variances explained in both occupational commitment (81 percent) and intention to enter the sport management profession (43 percent) were quite large. These results underline the important roles that anticipated career satisfaction and occupational commitment play in predicting an undergraduate student's intentions to enter the sport management profession.

▪ ▪

Summary

This chapter introduces statistical tests that can be used to determine the degree of relationship between variables. The specific statistical test needed depends upon the number of independent (predictor) and dependent (criterion or outcome) variables under investigation. Bivariate correlation evaluates the degree of relationship between two quantitative variables without distinction between the independent and dependent variables. Simple linear regression analyzes the relationship between two variables and produces a regression equation that can be used for prediction purposes. Multiple regression allows the researcher to predict a dependent variable from a group of independent variables. Path analysis incorporates multiple applications of multiple regression to estimate causal relationships, both direct and indirect, between several variables and to test the acceptability of the path diagram hypothesized by the researcher. Structural equation modeling is a specific type of path analysis that allows inclusion of latent variables and requires specialized statistical software for calculation. Table 14.3 summarizes the statistical tests presented in this chapter, as well as the variable conditions required for each test.

Table 14.3 **Summary of Procedures That Test the Degree of Relationship Between Variables**

Test	Quantitative IV	Quantitative DV	Purpose
Bivariate correlation	1 IV	1 DV	Relationship
Simple linear regression	1 IV	1DV	Relationship and prediction
Multiple regression	2+ IVs	1 DV	Relationship and prediction
Path analysis	2+ IVs	1+ DV(s)	Relationship and causality

IV = independent variable; DV = dependent variable

ADVANCED READING

Correlation

Armstrong-Doherty, A. (1996). Resource dependence-based perceived control: An examination of Canadian interuniversity athletics. *Journal of Sport Management, 10*(1), 49–64.

Park, S., & Kim, Y. (2000). Conceptualizing and measuring the attitudinal loyalty construct in recreational sport contexts. *Journal of Sport Management, 14*(3), 197–207.

Multiple Regression

Danylchuk, K. (1993). The presence of occupational burnout and its correlates in university physical education personnel. *Journal of Sport Management, 7*(2), 107–121.

Hardin, R., Andrew, D.P.S., Koo, G., & Bemiller, J. (2009). Motivational factors for participating in basic instruction programs. *Physical Educator, 66*(2), 71–84.

Kim, S., Andrew, D.P.S., & Greenwell, T.C. (2009). An analysis of spectator motives and media consumption behaviour in an individual combat sport: Cross-national differences between American and South Korean mixed martial arts fans. *International Journal of Sports Marketing & Sponsorship, 10*(2), 157–170.

Kim, S., Greenwell, T.C., Andrew, D.P.S., Lee, J., & Mahony, D.F. (2008). An analysis of spectator motives in an individual combat sport: A study of mixed martial arts fans. *Sport Marketing Quarterly, 17*(2), 109–119

Libkuman, T., Love, K., & Donn, P. (1998). An empirically based selection and evaluation system for collegiate football. *Journal of Sport Management, 12*(3), 220–241.

Path Analysis (Structural Equation Modeling)

Bauer, H., Stokburger-Sauer, N., & Exler, S. (2008). Brand image and fan loyalty in professional team sport: A refined model and empirical assessment. *Journal of Sport Management, 22*(2), 205–226.

Cunningham, G., & Mahoney, K. (2004). Self-efficacy of part-time employees in university athletics: The influence of organizational commitment, valence of training, and training motivation. *Journal of Sport Management, 18*(1), 59–73.

Cunningham, G., Sagas, M., Dixon, M., Kent, A., & Turner, B. (2005). Anticipated career satisfaction, affective occupational commitment, and intentions to enter the sport management profession. *Journal of Sport Management, 19*(1), 43–57.

Kim, M., Chelladurai, P., & Trail, G. (2007). A model of volunteer retention in youth sport. *Journal of Sport Management, 21*(2), 151–171.

Kwon, H., & Armstrong, K. (2006). Impulse purchases of sport team licensed merchandise: What matters? *Journal of Sport Management, 20*(1), 101–120.

Trail, G., & Chelladurai, P. (2002). Perceptions of intercollegiate athletic goals and processes: The influence of personal values. *Journal of Sport Management, 16*(4), 289–310.

Research Methods and Design in Action
Journal of Sport Management

Selected text reprinted, by permission, from Y.K. Kim and G. Trail, 2010, "Constraints and motivators: A new model to explain sport consumer behavior," *Journal of Sport Management* 24(2): 190-210.

Access the full article online at www.humankinetics.com/products/all-products/Research-Methods-and-Design-in-Sport-Management.

ABSTRACT

This study focused on developing a model to explain relationships among constraints, motivators, and attendance, and empirically test the proposed model within the spectator sport context. The proposed model explained 34% of variance in Attendance. Results showed that Attachment to the Team, an internal motivator, entered first and explained approximately 21% of the variance in attendance. Lack of Success, an internal constraint, entered next and explained almost 10% additional variance. Leisure Alternatives, an external constraint entered next and explained an additional 3%. The ability to properly evaluate constraints and motivators gives sport marketers the opportunity to more effectively serve existing fans, as well as attract new fans.

TEXT EXCERPTS

The relationship between the key independent variables (i.e., constraints and motivators) and attendance was examined by using a stepwise regression analysis in SPSS 15.0. We allowed all variables (both motivators and constraints) to be examined simultaneously and the variable that explained the most variance on attendance entered first. The variable that entered next explained the most remaining variance in attendance, and so on. Latent variable scores of theorized constructs were computed following Jöreskog's (2000) technique and used in the regression analysis. Latent variable scores are considered to provide means of overcoming measurement error common in all measured variables to some degree, and have the ability to represent multiple aspects of a theorized construct when they are well constructed, valid, and reliable (Hair et al., 1998).

. . . .

Analysis was performed using SPSS Regression and SPSS Explore for evaluation of assumptions. Univariate outliers in the DV and in the IVs are sought using extreme values output from the Explore analysis. Following Hair et al.'s (1998) protocol, normality, linearity, and homoscedasticity assumptions were simultaneously assessed by analyzing residuals scatter plots. To examine the degree of multicollinearity and its effects on the results, we employed a two-part process (condition indices and the decomposition of the coefficient variance) developed by Belsley, Kuh, and Welschi (1980) and made comparisons with the conclusions drawn from the variance inflation factor (VIF) and tolerance values.

••••••••••••••••

Errors of prediction (residuals) were normally distributed around predicted DV scores and the residuals had almost no correlation with predicted scores, indicating that normality and linearity assumptions were met.

••••••••••••••••

In the current study, internal motivators and internal constraints explained a major portion of variance (31%) in attendance and a much greater amount of the variance than external motivators (not significant) and external constraints

(3%). This result supports Crompton et al.'s (2005) notion that internal factors are more influential predictors of leisure participation than external factors. However, the role of external factors should not be disregarded solely based on the findings from this research. This small amount of variance explained by external factors might be true only for the particular team or the sample used in this study, if the above explanation for insignificant external motivators is also applied to external constraints. Thus, the proposed model needs to be retested with different samples and different teams.

••••••••••••••••

The direction of the beta coefficient indicated that fans were internally constrained from attending the team's games when the team was unsuccessful. This supports Snyder, Lassegard, and Ford's (1986) supposition that people dissociate themselves from unsuccessful others to protect their self-esteem.

DISCUSSION QUESTIONS

1 How did the authors define constraints in their study?

2 What constraints had been previously identified by sport management researchers?

3 What four purposes did the authors state for the study?

4 Based on the authors' description of their stepwise regression analysis procedure, which of the three variations of stepwise regression analysis did they use? Does the selected variation of stepwise regression analysis control for suppressor effects? Given the exploratory nature of the study, could

the authors have used another variation of stepwise regression analysis?

5 How did the authors test their data set to ensure that it met the assumptions for multiple regression? Were any modifications required in order to meet those assumptions? Why or why not?

6 What rationale do the authors provide for testing the proposed model with different samples and different teams?

7 What study limitations are conceded by the authors, and what future research suggestions do they offer?

Significance of Group Differences

Learning Objectives

After studying this chapter, you should be able to do the following:

- Provide a general description of the statistical techniques used to determine the significance of group differences

- Compare the purpose of one-sample, independent-samples, and paired-samples t-tests

- Discuss the advantage of conducting a single ANOVA rather than multiple t-tests

- Describe the difference between one-way and factorial tests

- Provide a general description of interaction effects between levels of independent variables and how they are typically interpreted

- Compare the various statistical techniques used to determine the significance of group differences on the basis of their limitations and appropriate usage

On occasion, sport management researchers incorporate statistical tests to determine whether groups of subjects or study participants differ from each other according to one or more variables. A primary purpose of testing for group differences is to determine a causal relationship between the independent and dependent variables. The various assumptions for procedures that test the significance of group differences can be found in table 15.1. This chapter describes nine statistical tests that can be used to explore potential group differences: t-test, one-way

Table 15.1 Assumptions for Procedures That Test the Significance of Group Differences

Assumptions	T-test	ANOVA	ANCOVA	MANOVA	MANCOVA
The observations within each sample must be independent of one another.	X	X	X		
The populations from which the samples were selected must be normal.	X	X	X		
The populations from which the samples were selected must have equal variances (homogeneity of variance).	X	X	X		
A linear relationship exists between the dependent variable and the covariate.			X		
The regression slopes for a covariate are homogenous (i.e., the slope for the regression line is the same for each group).			X		
The covariate is reliable and is measured without error.			X		
The observations within each sample must be randomly sampled and must be independent of each other.				X	X
The observations of all dependent variables must follow a multivariate normal distribution in each group.				X	
The population covariance matrices for the dependent variables in each group must be equal.				X	
The relationships between all pairs of DVs for each cell in the data matrix must be linear.				X	
The distributions of scores on the dependent variables must be normal in the populations from which the data were sampled.					X
The distributions of scores on the dependent variables must have equal variances.					X
Linear relationships must exist between all pairs of DVs, all pairs of covariates, and all DV–covariate pairs in each cell.					X

analysis of variance (ANOVA), one-way analysis of covariance (ANCOVA), factorial ANOVA, factorial ANCOVA, one-way multivariate analysis of variance (MANOVA), one-way multivariate analysis of covariance (ANCOVA), factorial MANOVA, and factorial MANCOVA. The appropriate test is determined on the basis of the number of categories in the independent variable, the total number of independent variables, and the total number of dependent variables. Many of the aforementioned parametric procedures have nonparametric equivalents that can be used in situations where the data do not meet the stringent assumptions indicated in table 15.1. For example, the Mann-Whitney U test is the nonparametric alternative to the independent-samples t-test, and the Kruskal-Wallis test is the nonparametric alternative to ANOVA.

T-Test

The most basic statistical test that measures group differences is the **t-test**, which is appropriately used when the researcher wishes to determine whether two groups, as defined by the independent variable, differ on the basis of a selected dependent variable. More specifically, the t-test allows a researcher to compare a categorical independent variable with two groups on the basis of an interval- or ratio-scaled dependent variable. For example, if a researcher wants to determine whether male and female spectators at a professional tennis tournament differ on the basis of merchandise consumption (i.e., total amount spent on event-related purchases) on a particular day during the tournament, he or she could address that research question by performing a t-test with gender as the dichotomous categorical independent variable and total amount spent as the ratio-scaled dependent variable.

A t-test is used to calculate group differences by examining the means and variation of both groups. The difference between the means of the groups is divided by the standard error of the difference (i.e., the variance for each group is divided by the number of subjects in each group). The variance is simply the square of the standard deviation (see chapter 5). This calculation results in a t-value, which can be referenced in a table of significance to test for a significant difference between the groups. Fortunately, SPPS automates this process, and the procedure for calculating a t-test within SPSS is found below. Relevant SPSS output for a t-test includes t-value, degrees of freedom, and p-value.

SPSS T-Test Procedure

1. Analyze → Compare Means → Paired-Samples T-Test
2. Move both variables to Paired Variables box.
3. Move IV to Fixed Factor box.
4. OK

The three basic types of t-tests featured in SPSS are the **one-sample t-test**, the **independent-samples t-test**, and the **paired-samples t-test**. The one-sample t-test examines whether the mean of one variable differs from a value specified by the researcher. The independent-samples t-test compares the means of two independently sampled groups (e.g., differences between males and females on a test score); therefore, the independent-samples t-test examines whether the mean scores of two groups can be considered significantly different. The paired-samples t-test compares the mean scores of two identical tests from the same group; essentially, the paired-samples t-test measures whether the mean of a single group is different when measured at different times. For example, if an instructor in a research methods class wanted to test whether her presentation of research methods materials had a positive effect on the students' demonstrated research methods knowledge, she could give the final exam on the first and last days of class and compare the mean scores of the two identical tests. The instructor would be hoping, of course, to be able to use the results from a paired-samples t-test to show improvement in student achievement as measured by the exam.

T-Test Example

Job satisfaction is one of the most widely studied concepts in the field of management in general, and Whisenant, Pedersen, and Smucker (2004) set out to determine how female sport journalists establish satisfaction levels. To justify their study, these researchers employed Adams' (1963) theory of inequity, which asserts that subordinates and supervisors are most satisfied when the ratio between their received benefits (e.g., pay, seniority, job status) and organizational contributions (e.g., effort, education, organizational tenure) is similar to the ratio they perceive to be the case for their co-workers. In other words, employees base their job satisfaction on their evaluation of their working conditions in respect to referent others (e.g., friends, family, co-workers, other employees in the industry, and even self-comparisons in the context of past jobs or experiences).

Whisenant and colleagues (2004) compared the referent-selection process used by female sport journalists in determining their level of satisfaction in five areas of job satisfaction. The researchers addressed the following six research questions:

1. To what extent do the participants make referent comparisons and multiple referent comparisons when considering their own level of satisfaction with five facets of job satisfaction?
2. Which referent choices are selected for each facet?
3. Which referent choices are selected as the most important for each facet?
4. To what extent do the referent selections deemed to be the most important for each facet of job satisfaction differ based on the demographic characteristics of the participant?
5. To what extent was there a satisfaction difference in the administrators making referent comparisons and multiple referent comparisons as opposed to those not making comparisons?
6. To what extent do the most important referent choices influence the satisfaction levels of each facet?

Various analyses were undertaken to address each of these research questions, including a series of t-tests used to determine satisfaction differences between administrators who made referent comparisons and multiple referent comparisons and those who did not make comparisons (i.e., research question 5). A total of 78 members of the Association for Women in Sports Media (AWSM) participated in the study (26 percent response rate). Job satisfaction was measured via the Job Descriptive Index (JDI) in conjunction with a referent-comparison scale. Scores on the JDI range from 0 to 54, and higher scores represent higher levels of job satisfaction. The t-test results indicated a significant ($p < .05$) pay difference between journalists making pay-referent comparisons (34.17 ± 16.56) and those not making pay-referent comparisons (43.50 ± 9.48), but there were no significant satisfaction differences between those making multiple referent comparisons and those making single comparisons. Therefore, female sport journalists who did not compare their pay with others were more satisfied with

their pay than those who did make such comparisons. This study provided useful information to sport management practitioners who might confront employee issues associated with job satisfaction.

▪ ▪

One-Way ANOVA

A **one-way analysis of variance** (ANOVA) tests the significance of group differences between two or more groups. A one-way ANOVA offers a distinct advantage over the t-test if the researcher is exploring differences between more than two groups (i.e., if the independent variable has more than two levels). It is appropriate to use the one-way ANOVA when the independent variable is defined as having two or more categories and the dependent variable is quantitative (i.e., interval- or ratio-scaled). The "one-way" descriptor is used by the researcher to denote the presence of one independent variable. (A one-way ANOVA is an alternative to an independent-samples t-test much in the same way that a repeated-measures ANOVA is an alternative to a paired-samples t-test.) Returning to the example used earlier in the t-tests explanation, if for some reason a researcher hypothesized that merchandise consumption at a professional tennis tournament might vary according to the tennis skill level of the spectator (defined as beginner, intermediate, or advanced), he could address the question by means of an ANOVA that used skill level as the categorical independent variable and total amount spent as the ratio-scaled dependent variable.

Given that the one-way ANOVA and the t-test share a common purpose, one might wonder why researchers use a one-way ANOVA rather than multiple t-tests to test for the significance of group differences. For instance, if a researcher wanted to compare the test scores of groups A, B, and C, he or she could either use a one-way ANOVA or three independent-samples t-tests to test for significant group differences. Three independent-samples t-tests could test for significant differences between (1) groups A and B, (2) groups B and C, and (3) groups A and C. However, as mentioned in chapter 5, researchers should avoid a Type I error rate at all costs (recall that a Type I error occurs when the null hypothesis is true but the researcher concludes that it is false), and each multiple comparison inflates the Type I error chance. In other words, in this scenario, the Type I error chances for a one-way ANOVA at the .05 level would be 5 percent ($1 - .95 = .05$), but the Type I error chances for three independent-samples t-tests, each conducted at the .05 level of significance, would be 14 percent (.95 × .95 ×.95 = .86; 1 − .86 = .14). Simply stated, the ANOVA controls for Type I error better than the t-test does in cases where multiple comparisons are needed.

The ANOVA simultaneously evaluates significance of mean differences on a selected dependent variable by analyzing variance as opposed to mean differences. ANOVA partitions the total amount of variance in the data into two separate components: (1) variance between subjects (sometimes referred to as between-groups variability) and (2) variance expected due to chance (sometimes referred to as the error variance or within-groups variability). The test statistic for the ANOVA is called the F ratio, and it consists of the variance between subjects (i.e., between-groups variability) divided by the variance expected due to chance (i.e., within-groups variability). Larger values of the F ratio typically correspond to significant differences between the groups. According to Gravetter and Wallnau (1999), plausible explanations for a significant F ratio include a treatment effect (i.e., the various treatments, or group characteristics, actually cause the difference) or random chance (i.e., the differences occur simply due to chance). Higher F ratios make the latter explanation less plausible.

The F ratio of the ANOVA tells you that some sort of statistically significant differences exist somewhere between the groups, but in cases where three or more groups are being evaluated by the ANOVA, further testing is needed to determine which specific groups are significantly different from each other. As a result, post hoc tests are required in conjunction with ANOVAs featuring three or more categories in the independent variable. A **post hoc test** is a comparison of the statistical difference between group means calculated after (i.e., "post") having conducted an ANOVA. Also known as **multiple comparisons**, post hoc tests vary in terms of their conservatism. Some of the more popular post hoc tests are Newman-Keuls, Duncan, Fisher's LSD (least significant difference), Tukey, and Scheffé. The general purpose of post hoc analyses is to determine specific differences between the levels of the independent variable while controlling the Type I error rate. With this purpose in mind, the Tukey and Scheffé post hoc tests are recommended over the Newman-Keuls, Duncan, and Fischer's LSD for their superior ability to control the Type I error rate while making comparisons. The Tukey post hoc analysis is considered an excellent option for pairwise group comparisons, and the Scheffé post hoc analysis is most appropriate for explor-

atory research since it examines all pairwise and complex contrasts simultaneously. The accompanying highlight box features the SPSS procedure for calculating a one-way ANOVA with a Tukey and a Scheffé post hoc analysis.

SPSS One-Way ANOVA Procedure

1. Analyze → Compare Means → One-Way ANOVA
2. Move DVs to Dependent List box.
3. Move IV to Factor box.
4. Post Hoc: Check Scheffé and Tukey.
5. Continue.
6. Options: Check Descriptive, Homogeneity of Variance, and Means Plot.
7. Continue.
8. OK

One-Way ANOVA Example

Given the increasing occupational demands placed on National Collegiate Athletic Association (NCAA) athletic directors over the past several decades (Bradley, 1993; Lea & Loughman, 1993), it is natural to assume that these heightened occupational stressors might lead to higher perceived occupational stress levels. According to Greenberg's (1993) framework, occupational stress is a complex construct consisting of sources of work stress (e.g., intrinsic job demands), individual personality characteristics, and extra-organizational stressors (e.g., family or financial crisis). Extending from Greenberg's sources of stress, Copeland and Kirsch (1995) devised a study to determine whether perceived stress levels of intrinsic administrative tasks differed among NCAA Division I, II, and III athletic directors. Given that Division I programs are generally associated with a larger, higher-profile structure (Landry, 1983) than are the smaller financially based Division II programs (Cuneen, 1992) or the more academically oriented Division III programs (McFarlane, 1986), the researchers anticipated that perceived occupational stress levels among NCAA athletic directors would vary based on the division level in which the respective athletic director served.

Copeland and Kirsch (1995) searched the literature to uncover the administrative responsibilities most salient to athletic directors and subsequently developed a specific measure of perceived occupational stress that included the following facets:

- Personal relations with personnel
- Policy decision making
- Budget demands
- Program organization and development
- Gender equity guidelines
- Maintenance of a competitive program
- Completion of task demands on time
- Affirmative action (EOE) guidelines
- Firing
- Public relations
- Event management
- Fundraising
- Compilation of NCAA data
- Role ambiguity

In addition, a general measure of perceived occupational stress was adapted from a previously published study (Hartman, 1981).

In order to test for differences of perceived occupational stress, both as a general construct and in terms of more specific performance tasks, the researchers calculated a one-way analysis of variance (ANOVA) followed by a Scheffé post hoc multiple pairwise comparison. In the analysis, divisional status served as the independent variable, and each ANOVA featured a specific measure of perceived occupational stress, either from the list of stress facets or from the average of the items used as a general measure, as the dependent variable.

The results indicated significantly higher perceived occupational stress levels in relation to policy decision making for Division I athletic directors (3.32 ± .75) when compared with their Division II counterparts (2.81 ± .92). The researchers speculated that the more complex and higher-profile nature of Division I athletics might be more demanding in the task of defining policy. In addition, Division II athletic directors (3.48 ± 1.12) reported significantly higher perceived occupational stress in relation to fundraising than did Division III athletic directors (2.68 ± 1.00). The researchers concluded that smaller, academically oriented Division III athletic programs may not rely as heavily on external funding as do their Division II counterparts. Overall, the results of this study indicated that occupational stress (a) exists among college athletic directors, (b) is represented in budgeting and firing functions in relation to intrinsic tasks, and (c)

is perceived, despite some task-related differences, similarly across NCAA divisions.

One-Way ANCOVA

A **one-way analysis of covariance** (ANCOVA) is similar to a one-way ANOVA in that it tests the significance of group differences between two or more groups on the basis of one independent variable, but it does so by controlling for the potential influence of one or more covariates. A **covariate** is an independent variable not manipulated by the researcher that has an effect on the dependent variable. The effect of a covariate can be statistically controlled, which allows for development of a clearer picture of the independent variable's direct impact on the dependent variable by increasing the statistical power of the analysis. Returning to our earlier example involving merchandise consumption, if a researcher hypothesized that merchandise consumption at a professional tennis tournament might vary according to the tennis skill level of the spectator (defined as beginner, intermediate, or advanced) and wished to control for the potential influence of expendable monthly income, he or she could address that research question by means of an ANCOVA that used skill level as the categorical independent variable, total amount spent as the ratio-scaled dependent variable, and expendable monthly income as the covariate.

In general, two rationales are plausible for the inclusion of one or more covariates in a model. First, any variables that should theoretically correlate with the dependent variable or that have been shown to correlate with the dependent variable in similar types of subjects (as supported by prior research) should be considered as possible covariates. Second, upon examination of a correlation matrix of the variables in a study, if a researcher uncovers variables that are significantly correlated with the dependent variable and that have low correlations among themselves (in cases where more than one covariate is being used), such variables may be chosen as covariates. In cases where multiple covariates are selected, it is important to ensure that these covariates do not correlate highly with each other (roughly $r < .40$ is recommended), since highly correlated covariates essentially remove the same error variance from the dependent variable (Mertler & Vannatta, 2005). In other words, if a researcher identifies two possible covariates but the second covariate is highly correlated with the first covariate, then the second covariate would contribute very little to improving the design and resultant analysis. In such cases, only one of the highly correlated covariates should be entered into the analysis. The accompanying highlight box features the SPSS procedure for calculating a one-way ANCOVA.

SPSS One-Way ANCOVA Procedure

1. Analyze → General Linear Model → Univariate
2. Move DV to Dependent Variable box.
3. Move IV to Fixed Factor box.
4. Move covariate(s) to Covariate box.
5. Model: Check Full Factorial.
6. Continue.
7. Options: Move IV and covariates to Display Means box. Check Descriptive Statistics, Estimates of Effect Size, and Homogeneity Tests.
8. Continue.
9. OK

One-Way ANCOVA Example

Given its potential to affect organizational outcomes, the construct of organizational culture has received increased interest over the past few years (Slack & Parent, 2006). As noted by Steensma, Jansen, and Vonk (2003), organizational culture is a set of core values, behavioral norms, and behavioral patterns that influence the ways in which people in organizations behave. Organizational culture has been shown to impact many organizational outcomes, including job satisfaction (Bateman & Strasser, 1984). Sosa and Sagas (2006) specifically explored the effects of organizational culture on job satisfaction among academic athletic directors employed within athletic departments that sponsored NCAA Division I basketball programs. The researchers sent an abbreviated organizational culture profile (OCP; Cable & Judge, 1997) instrument, a job satisfaction scale (Cammann, Fichman, Jenkins, & Klesh, 1983), and a demographic assessment to academic athletic directors at 327 Division I basketball schools, and 152 usable responses were collected after two rounds of data collection (46 percent response rate). The OCP is a 28-item survey

assessing the following seven facets of organizational culture:

- Competitiveness (having an achievement orientation, emphasizing quality, being different from others, and being competitive)
- Social responsibility (being reflective, having a good reputation, being socially responsible, and having a clear guiding philosophy)
- Supportiveness (being team oriented, sharing information freely, being people oriented, and collaborating)
- Innovation (being quick to take advantage of opportunities, taking risks, and taking individual responsibility)
- Emphasis on rewards (emphasizing fairness, opportunities for professional growth, high pay for good performance, and praise for good performance)
- Performance orientation (having high expectations for performance and enthusiasm for the job, being results oriented, and being highly organized)
- Stability (being calm, emphasizing security of employment and low conflict)

After collecting the organizational culture data, the researchers conducted a cluster analysis (see chapter 16) to determine whether any naturally occurring clusters could be determined based on the participants' responses. This analysis revealed that two distinct cultures were present in the sample: one cluster with higher responses on the seven facets of organizational culture and another cluster with lower, yet still moderate, responses on the seven facets.

After completing the cluster analysis, the researchers calculated a one-way ANCOVA in which the administrators' job satisfaction was the dependent variable and organizational culture was the independent variable. The organizational culture variable grouped participants into one of two categories: high organizational culture and moderate organizational culture. Two covariates were included in the analysis: institutional budget size and occupational tenure. Budget was regarded as a covariate since budget size varies in Division I athletic departments. The researchers also controlled for years in position because prior research had noted that change in academic directors can result in a change in culture due to new leadership (Hallett, 2003). After controlling for the effects of institutional budget size and occupational tenure, ANCOVA results showed that administrators in departments with strong organizational cultures had higher job satisfaction (6.16 ± .89) than did administrators with moderate organizational cultures (5.5 ± .89). Therefore, the results of this study provided support for the idea that organizational culture is related to individual job satisfaction in a collegiate athletic department setting.

■ ■

Factorial ANOVA

A **factorial analysis of variance** (ANOVA) is similar to a one-way ANOVA, with the exception that it allows for the simultaneous analysis of two or more independent variables with a single dependent variable. The term "factorial" implies more than one independent variable, but sometimes researchers will describe a factorial statistic more concisely by inserting the specific number of independent variables before the word "way" when describing the statistic (e.g., two-way ANOVA, three-way ANOVA). Returning again to our example about merchandise consumption, if a researcher hypothesized that merchandise consumption at a professional tennis tournament might vary according to gender and the tennis skill level of the spectator (defined as beginner, intermediate, or advanced), she or he could address that research question by performing a factorial ANOVA with gender and skill level as the categorical independent variables and total amount spent as the ratio-scaled dependent variable.

In addition to testing for the individual effects of each independent variable on the dependent variable, a factorial ANOVA also tests for any **interaction effects** between levels of the independent variables. In other words, a factorial ANOVA with two independent variables (a two-way ANOVA) tests for significance of the first independent variable and the second independent variable and for interaction effects between the two independent variables. In this scenario, the effect of the first or second independent variable in isolation on the dependent variable is called a main effect. The interaction of the two independent variables is called the interaction effect. An interaction effect occurs when the effect of one independent variable depends on different levels of another independent variable. When interpreting the results of a factorial ANOVA, any potential interaction effects supersede any potential main effects. In other words, if the interaction effect is significant, it does not make much sense to interpret any potentially significant main effects; that is, knowledge of an interaction effect is more informative than the presence of main effects. However, if the interaction effect is not

significant, the researcher may proceed to interpret any significant main effects.

Significant interaction effects are typically interpreted through the use of a **cell-means plot**, which, for two independent variables, features two straight lines. If these lines are parallel, an interaction effect is not present. If the lines are not parallel and do not cross within the values of the graph, an **ordinal interaction effect** is present (e.g., see figure 15.1 on page 237). If the lines are not parallel and do cross within the values of the graph, a **disordinal interaction effect** is present (e.g., see figure 15.2 on page 237). When an ordinal interaction effect is present, the researcher may choose to examine and interpret main effects since the interaction is not as pronounced as in a disordinal interaction (Newman & Newman, 1994). However, as with the one-way ANOVA, post hoc analysis will be required to determine group differences when significant independent variables have three or more levels.

Once the researcher has determined significance of an independent variable via the F ratio, he or she can use effect size values to determine the strength of the relationship. Effect size is calculated for each independent variable and the interaction effect, and it is represented by the eta-squared value (η^2). The eta-squared value indicates the proportion of variance in the dependent variable that is explained by the independent variables, and values greater than .50 denote significant importance. The accompanying highlight box features the SPSS procedure for calculating a factorial ANOVA.

SPSS Factorial ANOVA Procedure

1. Analyze → General Linear Model → Univariate
2. Move DV to Dependent Variable box.
3. Move IVs to Fixed Factor box.
4. Model: Check Full Factorial.
5. Continue.
6. Options: Check Descriptive Statistics, Estimates of Effect Size, and Homogeneity Tests.
7. Continue.
8. Post Hoc: Select post hoc method.
9. Continue.
10. OK

Factorial ANOVA Example

Generation Y (Gen Y), a segment of the population born between 1977 and 1994, has generated a great deal of interest from marketing researchers because of its large size (78 million), which is three times the size of its Generation X predecessor (Lim & Turco, 1999) and makes up nearly 25 percent of the United States population (Gardyn & Fetto, 2000). Even the sport industry has devoted attention to Gen Y consumers through expanded media coverage of events such as the X Games and the Gravity Games, which specifically target Gen Y consumers. In 2001, McCarthy noted that action sports, also known as extreme sports, boasted more than 58 million consumers between the ages of 10 and 24 "who wield $250 billion in buying power" (p. 2).

Citing the rise in consumer and corporate interest in action sports, Bennett, Henson, and Zhang (2003) developed a study to examine Gen Y's perceptions of action sports, with a specific focus on the expressed popularity of action sports and the relationship between action sports interest and use of the media. A number of research questions were developed to guide the study:

1. What are Gen Y perceptions of action sports?
2. Are action sports as preferred as traditional sport events among members of Gen Y?
3. What are the action sport viewing preferences of members of Gen Y?
4. What is the relationship between Internet usage and perceived computer competency and interest in action sports?
5. What is the relationship between television viewing and interest in action sports?

A total of 367 middle school and high school students responded to the questionnaire developed by Bennett et al. (2003). The questionnaire was based on Bennett and Henson's (2003) earlier study of action sport perceptions among college students, but its content was modified to be readable by a younger sample. The survey included items assessing demographics, participants' sport-related viewing preferences, and viewing habits and support for action and traditional sports.

Citing prior findings of Bennett and Henson (2003), the researchers wanted to examine the relationships of gender and grade level to action sport interest. As a result, they used two factorial ANOVAs with gender (2 levels: male and female) and grade level (5 levels: grades 8, 9, 10, 11, and 12) as independent variables for both analyses. The dependent variable

in the first analysis was action sport popularity; in the second analysis, the dependent variable was action sport familiarity. For action sport popularity, neither the grade main effect nor the interaction of grade and gender was statistically significant, but the gender main effect was statistically significant [$F(1, 329) = 17.58$, $p < .001$]. Examination of the mean scores for each gender revealed that males tended to think action sports would become more popular in the future than females did, but the effect size was rather small ($\eta^2 = .049$). Similarly, the results for the second analysis investigating action sport familiarity featured nonsignificant findings for the grade main effect and the interaction of grade and gender but significant findings for the gender main effect [$F(1, 329) = 39.17$, $p < .001$]. Males reported a higher familiarity with action sports than did females, and the effect size for this result ($\eta^2 = .103$) was slightly larger than for the first analysis. Although the researchers anticipated greater action sport interest in lower grades, that expectation was not supported. The authors speculated that any age-related differences may be more generationally based than dependent on simple increases in age.

Factorial ANCOVA

A **factorial analysis of covariance** (ANCOVA) is similar to a factorial ANOVA in that it allows for simultaneous analysis of two or more independent variables with a single dependent variable, but it does so by controlling for the potential influence of one or more covariates. In our merchandise consumption example, if for some reason a researcher hypothesized that merchandise consumption at a professional tennis tournament might vary according to gender and the tennis skill level of the spectator (defined as beginner, intermediate, or advanced) and wished to control for the potential influence of expendable monthly income, he or she could address that question by means of a factorial ANCOVA with gender and skill level as the categorical independent variables, total amount spent as the ratio-scaled dependent variable, and expendable monthly income as the covariate.

Like the factorial ANOVA, the factorial ANCOVA examines the independent variables for both main and interaction effects, and significant interaction effects supersede main effects. However, the factorial ANCOVA controls for one or more covariates, and these covariates should be selected on the basis of theoretical or statistical reasoning. Key outputs of the factorial ANCOVA include the F ratio and accompanying p-value, the effect size (as measured by eta squared: η^2), and the cell-means plot if an interaction effect is present. The accompanying highlight box features the SPSS procedure for calculating a factorial ANCOVA.

SPSS Factorial ANCOVA Procedure

1. Analyze → General Linear Model → Univariate
2. Move DV to Dependent Variable box.
3. Move IVs to Fixed Factor box.
4. Move covariate(s) to Covariate box.
5. Model: Check Full Factorial.
6. Continue.
7. Options: Move IVs and covariates to Display Means box. Check Descriptive Statistics, Estimates of Effect Size, and Homogeneity Tests.
8. Continue.
9. OK

Factorial ANCOVA Example

When communicating a message to a target audience, the characteristics of a spokesperson can be as important as the message itself. As a result, spokespersons for persuasive communications (i.e., advertisements, promotional messages, development campaigns, and announcements) are strategically selected based on their characteristics in order to appeal to and influence the attitudes and behaviors of their intended audience. Since individuals cannot process every aspect of a message they encounter, researchers analyze cues, or factors that trigger information processing or influence an individual's motivation to process persuasive communication. Cues that refer to characteristics of the presenter of a message are called source cues (e.g., the source's attractiveness, race, celebrity status, similarity to the recipient of the message), and they have been shown to influence how recipients respond to a particular communication (Berschied, 1966; Dembroski, Lasater, & Ramirez, 1978; Petty, Cacioppo, & Schumann, 1983; White & Harkins, 1994; Whittler, 1989).

Armstrong (2000) designed a study to examine African American students' responses to race as a source cue of the spokesperson featured in a persuasive sport communication. More specifically, the study moderated two independent variables, race of the source and message of the source, in a hypothetical scenario concerning the increase of student fees to finance a university's sport facility. The following four experimental conditions were developed:

1. A photograph of an African American male student and a listing of his race, gender, major, age, college attended, and year in college, along with an editorial containing strong arguments prepared by him in support of the increase in student fees to finance a sport facility

2. A photograph of an African American male student and a listing of his race, gender, major, age, college attended, and year in college, along with an editorial containing weak arguments prepared by him in support of the increase in student fees to finance a sport facility

3. A photograph of a Caucasian male student and a listing of his race, gender, major, age, college attended, and year in college, along with an editorial containing strong arguments prepared by him in support of the increase in student fees to finance a sport facility

4. A photograph of a Caucasian male student and a listing of his race, gender, major, age, college attended, and year in college, along with an editorial containing weak arguments prepared by him in support of the increase in student fees to finance a sport facility

Therefore, the four scenarios allowed the researcher to moderate race (African American or Caucasian) and strength of message (strong or weak) within the experimental design.

The sample for the study included 110 college-aged students who were randomly assigned to an experimental group (n = 72) or a control group (n = 38). Those assigned to the experimental group were randomly assigned to one of the four experimental scenarios detailed previously. Participants responded to a number of measures that were later used as dependent variables, including (1) attitude toward the issue of increasing student fees to finance a sport facility, (2) evaluation of the message, (3) total number of thoughts generated by the respondent, (4) thought positivity, (5) target of the thoughts, (6) argument recall, (7) source credibility, and (8) influence of communication. Data were also collected concerning the extent to which the respondent identified with his or her ethnicity, and that information was included as a covariate in the model. Therefore, a total of eight factorial ANCOVAs were calculated; for each analysis, race of source and quality of argument were independent variables, ethnic identification was a covariate, and one of the eight mentioned variables was the dependent variable.

The results of the analyses, listed by dependent variable, were as follows:

1. Attitude measures: nonsignificant interaction effect but significant main effects for race of source [$F(1, 70) = 4.08$; $p = .048$] and quality of argument [$F(1, 70) = 5.54$; $p = .02$]. Respondents who were exposed to the African American source responded more favorably to the attitude measures ($M = 4.67$) than respondents who were exposed to the Caucasian source ($M = 3.96$). Respondents who were exposed to the strong argument responded more favorably to the attitude measures ($M = 4.79$) than respondents who were exposed to the weak argument ($M = 3.84$).

2. Message evaluation: nonsignificant interaction effect and main effect for race of the source but significant main effect for quality of argument [$F(1, 70) = 22.43$; $p < .001$]. Respondents rated the strong argument as being of higher quality ($M = 5.94$) than the weak argument ($M = 4.03$).

3. Total number of thoughts: nonsignificant interaction effect, main effect for race of source, and main effect for quality of argument.

4. Thought positivity: significant disordinal interaction (see figure 15.1) between race of source and quality of argument on recipients' thought positivity [$F(1, 71) = 8.70$; $p = .004$]. The interaction indicated that the quality of the arguments made a significant difference in the positivity index score that resulted from the participants' exposure to the editorials containing weak arguments delivered by the African American or the Caucasian source.

5. Target of the thoughts: nonsignificant interaction effect, main effect for race of source, and main effect for quality of argument.

6. Argument recall: nonsignificant interaction effect, main effect for race of source, and main effect for quality of argument.

7. Source credibility: significant ordinal interaction (see figure 15.2) between race of source and quality of argument on the recipients' source credibility ratings [$F(1, 70) = 3.97$; $p = .05$]. The

interaction indicated that the African American source received a higher credibility rating than the Caucasian source when presenting the same message.

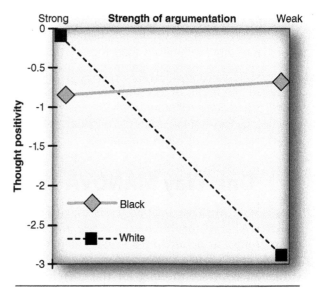

Figure 15.1 Interaction between the race of the source presenting the message and the quality of the argument in the message on the respondents' thought positivity.

Reprinted, by permission, from K. Armstrong, 2000, "African-American students' responses to race as a source cue in persuasive sport communications," *Journal of Sport Management* 14(3): 208-226.

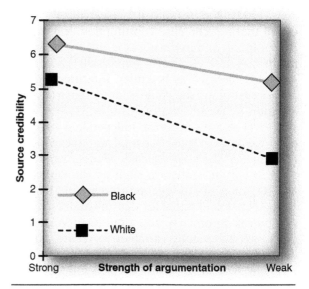

Figure 15.2 Interaction between the race of the source presenting the message and the quality of the argument in the message on the respondents' rating of the credibility of the source as a spokesperson on the topic.

Reprinted, by permission, from K. Armstrong, 2000, "African-American students' responses to race as a source cue in persuasive sport communications," *Journal of Sport Management* 14(3): 208-226.

8. Influence of communication: nonsignificant interaction effect but significant main effects for race of source [$F(1, 70) = 4.91; p = .03$] and quality of argument [$F(1, 70) = 10.68; p = .002$]. Respondents were more influenced by the African American source ($M = 3.86$) than by the Caucasian source ($M = 3.03$). Respondents who received the strong argument ($M = 4.20$) were more influenced than those who were exposed to the weak argument ($M = 2.72$).

Overall, the results of this study showed that race of source and quality of argument had some effect on selected outcomes of the recipients, although perhaps not as much of an effect as anticipated.

▬ ▬

One-Way MANOVA

A **one-way multivariate analysis of variance** (MANOVA) tests for differences between two or more groups, as defined by a single independent variable and in respect to two or more dependent variables, while controlling for the correlations between the dependent variables. The term *one-way* denotes the presence of one independent variable, and the term *multivariate* signifies the presence of two or more dependent variables. The dependent variables selected for inclusion in the multivariate analysis should be correlated to some degree and should share a common conceptual meaning (Stevens, 1992). For example, if a researcher hypothesized that merchandise consumption and media consumption at a professional tennis tournament might vary according to the tennis skill level of the spectator (defined as beginner, intermediate, or advanced), he or she could address that research question by means of a one-way MANOVA with skill level as the categorical independent variable and total amount spent and total amount of media consumed as the ratio-scaled dependent variables.

Multivariate statistics, such as the one-way MANOVA, operate by creating a linear combination of the dependent variables that maximizes group differences. In other words, a one-way MANOVA combines dependent variables to create a new dependent variable that is analyzed for group differences according to the selected independent variable.

According to Tabachnick and Fidell (1996), MANOVA offers several advantages over its univariate counterpart, ANOVA. First, since several dependent variables are measured simultaneously, the chance of discovering the actual changes that result based on the selected independent variables increases significantly. Second, MANOVA may reveal differences not shown in separate ANOVAs through the testing of multiple dependent variables simultaneously. Third, the alternative to MANOVA (i.e., the use of several univariate ANOVAs) leads to an inflated Type I error rate. Finally, compared to ANOVA, MANOVA incorporates the intercorrelations of the dependent variables into the analysis via the linear combination of the dependent variable. The disadvantages of MANOVA include the fact that it is substantially more complicated than ANOVA, requires several important assumptions to be met, and can sometimes produce ambiguous results with respect to the effects of independent variables on individual dependent variables (Tabachnick & Fidell). Therefore, researchers should be prudent when making the decision to include additional dependent variables in their studies.

The most common overall test statistic for a MANOVA is **Wilks' lambda** (λ), and other test statistics for MANOVA include Pillai's Trace, Hotelling's Trace, and Roy's Largest Root. Values for Wilks' lambda range from 0 to 1, and the statistic is an inverse criterion, meaning that lower values are indicative of significant results (opposite of the case with F ratio). Wilks' lambda tests the overall hypothesis that all groups are equal on the combination of dependent variables. If this null hypothesis is accepted (i.e., the result is not significant), the analysis ends at that point. However, a significant Wilks' lambda prompts the calculation of several univariate analyses (ANOVAs) to determine which of the dependent variables is being affected by the independent variable.

When multiple ANOVAs are required to interpret significant differences noted by a MANOVA, a Bonferroni adjustment is typically used to ensure that the overall Type I error rate remains constant. A **Bonferroni correction** is calculated by dividing the overall alpha level (α-level) of the analysis (typically .05) by the number of dependent variables (e.g., the Bonferroni correction for a MANOVA with three independent variables would be $.05 \div 3 = .0167$). The Bonferroni-adjusted alpha level is then used as a criterion for determining the presence of significant results within the ANOVAs. Of course, just as mentioned in the discussion of the one-way ANOVA, post hoc analyses are then required for all significant independent variables with three or more levels. The accompanying highlight box features the SPSS procedure for calculating a one-way MANOVA.

SPSS One-Way MANOVA Procedure

1. Analyze → General Linear Model → Multivariate
2. Move DV to Dependent Variable box.
3. Move IV to Fixed Factor box.
4. Model: Check Full Factorial.
5. Continue.
6. Options: Move IV to the Display Means box. Check Descriptive Statistics, Estimates of Effect Size, and Homogeneity Tests.
7. Continue.
8. Post Hoc: Move IV to the Post Hoc Test box. Select post hoc method.
9. Continue.
10. OK

▪ ▪

One-Way MANOVA Example

Organizational justice, or the study of individuals' perceptions of fairness within the workplace, has been a popular topic among business and psychology scholars for a number of years due to its demonstrated effect on numerous important organizational outcomes (Greenberg, 1990). Organizational justice is generally thought to be composed of three facets: distributive justice (perceived fairness of the decision outcome), procedural justice (perceived fairness of the process used to make the decision), and interactional justice (perceived fairness of the interpersonal treatment experienced during the delivery of the decision). Of course, the construct is also applicable in the context of sport. For example, imagine a scenario where an athletic director at a small college needed to replace worn lockers for his or her athletes but had only enough financial resources to purchase new lockers for a few teams. In this case, the student athletes' perceptions of fairness could be determined by one or more of the following factors: (a) whether or not their teams' lockers were replaced (distributive justice: Deutsch, 1975; Homans, 1961; Leventhal, 1976), (b) the procedures that the athletic director followed to reach the final conclusion (procedural justice: Folger

& Konovsky, 1989; Sweeney & McFarlin, 1993), and (c) the manner in which the athletic director informed the athletes of the decision (interactional justice: Bies & Moag, 1986).

Building on prior research that sampled coaches and administrators at NCAA institutions (Mahony, Hums, & Riemer, 2002, 2005), Mahony, Riemer, Breeding, and Hums (2006) conducted a study to explore the effect of one aspect of organizational justice—distributive justice—on college athletes and other college students. Given that distributive justice is most often exemplified in resource distribution situations, Tornblom and Jonsson (1985, 1987) classified the various distribution methods under three primary principles: (1) equity (those who contribute more to the organization deserve more of the resources), (2) equality (everyone should receive an equal share of the resources), and (c) need (those with less of the resources deserve more). In regards to the equity principle, Tornblom and Jonsson argued that allocations could be based on productivity, effort, or ability. Similarly, distributions based on equality include equality of opportunity (each has an equal chance to receive the distribution), equality of results (distributions are equal over the long term), and equality of treatment (all distributions are equal in a given situation).

Mahony et al. (2006) recruited 300 participants from an NCAA Division I institution who were equally distributed between a college athletics scenario and a sport business scenario. Each group of 150 participants consisted of an equal distribution ($n = 30$) within each of five groups: male nonathletes, male revenue sport athletes (i.e., football and basketball at this particular institution), male nonrevenue sport athletes, female nonathletes, and female athletes (all female sports at this institution were classified as nonrevenue sports). Participants were asked to provide their fairness perceptions associated with six scenarios (distribution and reduction of money, facilities, and support services) according to the following nine principles: equality of treatment, equality of results, equality of opportunity, productivity, effort, ability, revenue production, spectator appeal, and need. Two of these principles—revenue production and spectator appeal—represent new equity principles that were specific to the sport setting.

A series of nine one-way MANOVAs (consisting of three sets of three one-way MANOVAs each) was used to determine the effect that group membership (in one of the five previously mentioned groups) might have on responses regarding the perceived fairness of the nine principles in the collegiate sport scenario. The results indicated significant differences in only two instances: (1) the set of equality variables in the money scenario [Wilks' λ = .82; F(24, 489.7) = 2.53, p < .001, partial η^2 = .05] and (2) the set of equity variables for the facility scenario [Wilks' λ = .61; F(40, 517.6) = 2.53, p = .002, partial η^2 = .12]. Post hoc analyses revealed significant differences between female athletes and male revenue-sport athletes in the money scenario, as well as significant differences between (a) male nonathletes and female nonathletes and (b) male nonathletes and male nonrevenue-sport athletes in the facility scenario. Similar one-way MANOVA analyses were conducted for the sport business scenario, but no significant findings were observed. The results of the study furthered our understanding of perceptions of distributive justice in the sport setting.

One-Way MANCOVA

A **one-way multivariate analysis of covariance** (MANCOVA) tests for differences between two or more groups, as defined by a single independent variable and in respect to two or more dependent variables, while controlling for the correlations between the dependent variables and the potential influence of one or more covariates. For example, if a researcher hypothesized that merchandise consumption and media consumption at a professional tennis tournament might vary according to the tennis skill level of the spectator (defined as beginner, intermediate, or advanced) and wished to control for the potential influence of expendable monthly income, he or she could address that research question by means of a one-way MANCOVA with skill level as the categorical independent variable, total amount spent as the ratio-scaled dependent variable, and expendable monthly income as the covariate.

Like the one-way MANOVA, the one-way MANCOVA relies on linear combinations of the dependent variable for data analysis. Therefore, the researcher needs to evaluate the overall multivariate hypothesis via Wilks' lambda (lower values of Wilks' lambda correspond to significant results). Since the one-way MANCOVA controls for the influence of one or more covariates, the researcher must follow up a significant Wilks' lambda result by conducting a series of ANCOVAs (with an appropriate Bonferroni correction) to control for the potential influence of the covariate(s). Finally, the researcher must calculate the appropriate post hoc analyses in order to complete the analysis. The accompanying highlight box features the SPSS procedure for calculating a one-way MANCOVA.

SPSS One-Way MANCOVA Procedure

1. Analyze → General Linear Model → Multivariate
2. Move DV to Dependent Variable box.
3. Move IV to Fixed Factor box.
4. Move covariate(s) to Covariate box.
5. Model: Check Full Factorial.
6. Continue.
7. Options: Move IV to the Display Means box. Check Descriptive Statistics, Estimates of Effect Size, and Homogeneity Tests.
8. Continue.
9. Post Hoc: Move IV to the Post Hoc Test box. Select post hoc method.
10. Continue.
11. OK

One-Way MANCOVA Example

Advertisers have recently ventured into the medium of sport video games in order to reach their target audiences, but are in-game advertisements really effective? Cianfrone, Zhang, Trail, and Lutz (2008) set out to answer this question by designing an experimental study to assess the effectiveness of in-game advertisements within three consumption domains: cognitive, affective, and conative. The cognitive domain is the thinking stage of consumption, and it includes awareness and knowledge components (typically measured via brand recall and brand awareness surveys). The affective domain involves attitudes and feelings, and it usually measured by consumers' preferences for brands. The conative domain is related to the level of desire for consumption action—the motivational state that specifically examines intent to purchase. All of these domains are hypothesized to occur prior to the behavioral stage, which is usually measured by the volume, frequency, and longevity of consumption (Lavidge & Steiner, 1961).

In-game advertising in sport video games is typically positioned as sport sponsorship. For example, EA Sports' NCAA Football games have featured the Old Spice Red Zone, an on-screen logo displayed when the player advances inside the opponent's 20-yard line, and the Pontiac Drive Summary, an on-screen logo that features the Pontiac logo next to information about a scoring drive. One advantage of placing such advertisements in sport video games is that, unlike television commercials, these advertisements cannot be avoided or skipped. However, as noted by Cianfrone and colleagues (2008, p. 196), "to date, there is no evidence that sport video game in-game advertising enhances consumers' awareness of the sponsoring brand, which is often seen as a basic goal of any sponsorship or advertisement." To remedy this void, these researchers set out to determine the effect of advertising in sport video games on the cognitive, affective, and conative consumption domains.

For their study, Cianfrone et al. (2008) recruited a total of 89 college undergraduate students at a large university with a strong football tradition in the southeastern United States. These students specifically reported regular use of EA Sports' NCAA Football games for a minimum of 30 minutes each week. The participants were randomly assigned to either an experimental (n = 45) or control (n = 44) group. Both groups played one game consisting of four 3-minute quarters, but the control group played the 2003 version of EA Sports' NCAA Football game, which featured no in-game advertisements, while the experimental group played the 2005 version, which featured three forms of in-game advertisement (Old Spice Red Zone, Pontiac Drive Summary, and Pontiac Player of the Game). Both groups were instructed to score as many points as possible in an attempt to get a high score, which would increase the number of times that members of the experimental group were exposed to the Old Spice Red Zone and the Pontiac Drive Summary.

Before game play, participants completed a questionnaire assessing demographics, behavioral involvement, and identification level; after game play, they completed a questionnaire assessing cognitive, affective, and consumption domains (i.e., unaided recall, aided recall, recognition, brand attitude, and purchase intention). A one-way MANCOVA was conducted for the consumption variables in the cognitive, affective, and consumption domains to compare mean scores between the experimental and control conditions after adjusting for the effects of behavioral consumption and identification level variables. In other words, the cognitive, affective, and consumption domains served as the dependent variable, the assignment to either the experimental or control group served as the independent variable, and the covariates included the behavioral consumption and identification level variables. Since the cognitive domain consisted of three

dependent variables, the affective domain consisted of two dependent variables, and the conative domain consisted of two dependent variables, three one-way MANCOVAs were conducted, one for each domain.

For the first MANCOVA, the mean scores of the cognitive variables for the experimental group were significantly (p < .017) higher than for the control group after adjusting for the effects of behavioral involvement and identification level. The experimental group reported much greater brand awareness in terms of unaided recall, aided recall, and recognition than did the control group, thus indicating an awareness of in-game advertising and the ability to distinguish the advertised brands from nonadvertised brands (see figure 15.3). No significant findings were uncovered for the remaining two MANCOVAs assessing the affective and conative domains. Overall, these results showed that in-game advertising within sport video games can serve as an effective method for enhancing brand awareness.

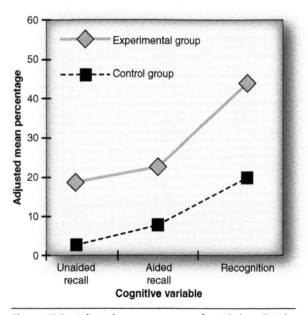

Figure 15.3 Adjusted mean percentage of unaided recall, aided recall, and recognition for experimental and control groups.

Reprinted, by permission, from B. Cianfrone et al.,2008, "Effectiveness of in-game advertisements in sport video games: An experimental inquiry on current gamers," *International Journal of Sport Communication* 1(2): 195-218.

Factorial MANOVA

A **factorial multivariate analysis of variance** (MANOVA) allows for simultaneous analysis of the effect of two or more independent variables on two or more related dependent variables while controlling for the correlations between the dependent variables. For instance, if a researcher hypothesized that merchandise consumption and media consumption at a professional tennis tournament might vary according to the gender and tennis skill level of the spectator (defined as beginner, intermediate, or advanced), he or she could address that research question by means of a factorial MANOVA with gender and skill level as the categorical independent variables and total amount spent and total amount of media consumed as the ratio-scaled dependent variables.

As mentioned earlier, multivariate statistics function by creating a linear combination of the dependent variables entered into the analysis. In the case of a factorial design with multiple independent variables, a different linear combination of dependent variables is formed for each main effect and each interaction (Tabachnick & Fidell, 1996). Thus, using the tennis example, three new dependent variables would be created: (1) a linear combination that would maximize the separation between males and females, (2) a linear combination that would maximize the separation between skill levels, and (3) a linear combination that would maximize the separation between the various cells of the interaction between gender and skill level.

Pertinent outputs of a factorial MANOVA include (1) the MANOVA results (Wilks' lambda, F ratio, degrees of freedom, p-value, and effect size), including the main effects of each independent variable on the combined dependent variable and the main effect for the interaction between independent variables; (2) the univariate ANOVA results (F ratio, degrees of freedom, p-value, and effect size), including the main effect for each independent variable and dependent variable and a comparison of means to indicate which groups differ on each independent variable; and (3) post hoc results (mean differences and levels of significance). The accompanying highlight box features the SPSS procedure for calculating a factorial MANOVA.

SPSS Factorial MANOVA Procedure

1. Analyze → General Linear Model → Multivariate
2. Move DVs to Dependent Variable box.
3. Move IVs to Fixed Factor box.
4. Move covariate(s) to Covariate box.
5. Model: Check Full Factorial.
6. Continue.
7. Options: Move each IV to the Display Means box. Check Descriptive Statistics and Estimates of Effect Size.
8. Continue.
9. OK

Factorial MANOVA Example

Although collegiate athletic departments in the United States sponsor both men's and women' sports, little is known about the specific attendance motives for spectators of many of these sports. To further complicate the situation, college sport marketers are often charged with the task of marketing a variety of both men's and women's sports. While many collegiate sport marketers devote the majority of their attention to revenue-producing sports (e.g., football, men's basketball, and, in some cases, women's basketball), marketers would benefit from knowing whether the motives for attending games are similar or different across sports. Robinson and Trail (2005) conducted a study to determine whether gender or type-of-sport differences exist in motives for attendance and in attachment to various aspects associated with a team.

Sport fans and spectators watch or attend sporting events for different reasons, and identifying their motivations is critical to understanding and satisfying these consumers. Researchers have identified key motivation factors and developed scales to measure sport consumers' motives (Funk, Mahony, & Ridinger, 2002; Kahle, Kambara, & Rose, 1996; Milne & McDonald, 1999; Sloan, 1989; Trail & James, 2001; Wann, 1995). Trail and James evaluated previous scales (Wann, 1995; Milne & McDonald, 1999) and proposed the motivation scale for sport consumption (MSSC), which uses nine factors to explain the motives of the fans watching or attending sport events: vicarious achievement, acquisition of knowledge, aesthetics, social interaction, drama, physical attractiveness of the participants, escape, family, and physical skill of the participants. Trail, Fink, and Anderson's (2003) model of sport spectator consumption suggested that sport fans attend sporting events due to one or a combination of these motives.

Another key predictor of sport consumption behavior can be found in points of attachment, which are various sport-related entities with which a spectator can identify. Trail, Robinson, Dick, and Gillentine (2003) posited that sport consumers could be attached to various sport-related entities and that the levels of attachment could differ across types of sport consumers (e.g., fans, spectators). Points of attachment examined in Robinson and Trail's (2005) study included team, players, coach, community, sport, university, and level of sport.

The participants (N = 669) in Robinson and Trail's (2005) study included spectators at three intercollegiate contests at a university that participates in the NCAA Atlantic 10 Conference for football (n = 222) and the Colonial Athletic Association for men's basketball (n = 234) and women's basketball (n = 213). The participants completed questionnaires consisting of two scales: the motivation scale for sport consumption (Trail & James, 2001) and the point of attachment index (Trail, Robinson, et al., 2003).

As part of the study, a factorial (two-way) MANOVA was calculated with gender (male and female) and sport (football, men's basketball, and women's basketball) as the independent variables and with motives and points of attachment as dependent variables. The results regarding motives indicated significant main effects for gender [F(7, 620) = 2.16, p = .036] and type of sport [F(14, 1240) = 3.00, p < .001], but the interaction effect was not significant. Scheffé post hoc analyses revealed that (a) women were more motivated by knowledge than men, (b) women's basketball spectators were more motivated by aesthetics and knowledge than were football spectators, and (c) men's basketball spectators were more motivated by knowledge and physical skill than were football spectators.

The results regarding points of attachment indicated significant main effects for gender [F(7, 620) = 3.30, p = .002] and type of sport [F(14, 1240) = 6.37, p < .001], but the interaction effect was not significant. Scheffé post hoc analyses revealed that (a) women were more attached to players and to the sport than men were, (b) women's basketball spectators were more attached to the player and the university than football spectators were, (c) men's basketball spectators were more attached to players and the university than football spectators were, (d) football spectators were more attached to the coach and the sport than men's basketball spectators were, and (e) women's basketball spectators were more attached to the players and the coach than men's basketball spectators were. Collectively, the results of this study provided pertinent information to collegiate sport marketers that could be used to develop marketing plans for each of the analyzed sports.

Factorial MANCOVA

A **factorial multivariate analysis of covariance** (MANCOVA) allows for simultaneous analysis of the effect of two or more independent variables on two or more related dependent variables while controlling for the correlations between the dependent variables and the potential influence of one or more covariates. For instance, if a researcher hypothesized that merchandise consumption and media consumption at a professional tennis tournament might vary according to the gender and tennis skill level of the spectator (defined as beginner, intermediate, or advanced) and wished to control for the potential influence of expendable monthly income, he or she could address that research question by means of a factorial MANCOVA with gender and skill level as the categorical independent variables, total amount spent and total amount of media consumed as the ratio-scaled dependent variables, and expendable monthly income as the covariate.

Relevant outputs of a factorial MANCOVA include (1) the MANCOVA results (Wilks' lambda, F ratio, degrees of freedom, p-value, and effect size), including the main effects of each independent variable on the combined dependent variable and the main effect for the interaction between independent variables; (2) the univariate ANCOVA results (F ratio, degrees of freedom, p-value, and effect size), including the main effect for each independent variable and dependent variable and a comparison of means to indicate which groups differ on each

SPSS Factorial MANCOVA Procedure

1. Analyze → General Linear Model → Multivariate
2. Move DV to Dependent Variable box.
3. Move IVs to Fixed Factor box.
4. Move covariate(s) to Covariate box.
5. Model: Check Full Factorial.
6. Continue.
7. Options: Move each IV to the Display Means box. Check Descriptive Statistics, Estimates of Effect Size, and Homogeneity Tests.
8. Continue.
9. OK

independent variable; and (3) post hoc results (mean differences and levels of significance). The accompanying highlight box features the SPSS procedure for calculating a factorial MANCOVA.

■ ■

Factorial MANCOVA Example

As mentioned earlier (Bennett et al., 2003), action sports are an increasingly popular sport industry segment, particularly for Generation Y (Gen Y) consumers. Indeed, Gen Y consumers generally account for approximately 60 percent of the action sport market segment (Bennett et al.). Given that Gen Y consumers constitute a very sought after market segment, it is not surprising that businesses have used action sports as a platform to access this typically elusive market segment. These corporations have used numerous strategies to reach Gen Y consumers, including commercials, athlete endorsement, venue signage, and even a combination of these strategies, as is often offered in promotional packages by action sport event producers (Brockinton, 2001).

Cianfrone and Zhang (2006) devised a study to explore the differential effects of these four strategies on brand recall and recognition among Gen Y consumers. They recruited 253 students enrolled at a large university in the southeastern United States. These students were targeted for participation in the study because they occupied the upper half of the Gen Y age bracket and identified as part of the target market. The study's participants were randomly assigned to one of the following eight groups:

- Experimental TV commercial group
- Control TV commercial group
- Experimental athlete endorsement group
- Control athlete endorsement group
- Experimental venue signage group
- Control venue signage group
- Experimental combined promotion group
- Control combined promotion group

Based on the group to which they were assigned, members of the experimental groups watched various motocross video programs as the intervention. After watching these programs, each group responded to a questionnaire that measured unaided recall, aided recall, and brand recognition. A factorial MANCOVA was then conducted to examine the differential effectiveness, as measured by the recall and recognition rates, between treatments and among promotional types, while controlling for the influence of previous

action sport consumption. More specifically, the factorial MANCOVA featured two independent variables (experimental condition and promotional format), three dependent variables (unaided recall, aided recall, and brand recognition), and five covariates that controlled for previous action sport consumption (*general consumption*: visiting action sports websites, purchasing action sports apparel, etc.; *board activity*: participation in surfing, wakeboarding, or skateboarding; *Gravity Games*: days of the 2002 Gravity games attended or number of episodes watched; *common activity*: participation in inline skating or motocross motorcycling; and *street activity*: participation in BMX biking or street luging).

A significant ordinal interaction effect [Wilks' λ = .696, $p < .001$, $\eta^2 = .166$] of experimental condition and promotional format was observed (see figure 15.4). The television commercial was the most effective in promoting unaided recall, aided recall, and recognition of brand, followed by the combined promotion, athlete endorsement, and venue signage. The experimental group in this study was required to watch footage that included commercial breaks in a controlled environment to ensure that the treatment effect was administered; however, since such conditions are not placed upon television viewers in real life settings, this approach may have inflated the effect of television commercials in this study. Regardless, the results of this study provide a first glance at the effect

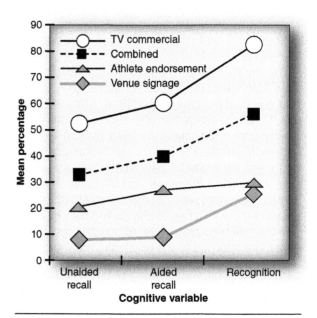

Figure 15.4 Mean percentage of unaided recall, aided recall, and recognition for promotional types.

Reprinted, by permission, from B. Cianfrone and J. Zhang, 2006, "Differential effects of television commercials, athlete endorsements, and venue signage during a televised action sports event," *Journal of Sport Management* 20(3): 322-344.

of promotional formats on Gen Y consumers of action sport events. The results may be applied by organizations seeking to advertise by means of action sport events to help them select an effective way to convey their messages and by action sport event producers, who must convey the value of each available promotional format and set prices for advertising packages.

Summary

This chapter reviews a number of statistical tests used to explore the significance of group differ- ences. These procedures include the t-test, one-way analysis of variance (ANOVA), one-way analysis of covariance (ANCOVA), factorial ANOVA, factorial ANCOVA, one-way multivariate analysis of vari- ance (MANOVA), one-way multivariate analysis of covariance (MANCOVA), factorial MANOVA, and factorial MANCOVA. The appropriate test is determined by the number of categories in the independent variable, the total number of indepen- dent variables, and the total number of dependent variables. Table 15.2 provides a summary of the distinguishing factors of procedures that test the significance of group differences.

Table 15.2 **Summary of Procedures that Test the Significance of Group Differences**

Test	Categorical IV	Quantitative DV	Covariate
T-test	1 IV (2 levels)	1 DV	
One-way ANOVA	1 IV (2+ levels)	1 DV	
One-way ANCOVA	1 IV (2+ levels)	1 DV	1+ covariate(s)
Factorial ANOVA	2+ IVs (2+ levels)	1 DV	
Factorial ANCOVA	2+ IVs (2+ levels)	1 DV	1+ covariate(s)
One-way MANOVA	1 IV (2+ levels)	2+ DVs	
One-way MANCOVA	1 IV (2+ levels)	2+ DVs	1+ covariate(s)
Factorial MANOVA	2+ IVs (2+ levels)	2+ DVs	
Factorial MANCOVA	2+ IVs (2+ levels)	2+ DVs	1+ covariate(s)

ADVANCED READING

T-Test

Fink, J., Cunningham, G., & Kensicki, L. (2004). Using athletes as endorsers to sell women's sport: Attractiveness vs. expertise. *Journal of Sport Management, 18*(4), 350–367.

Kyle, G., Kerstetter, D., & Guadagnolo, F. (2003). Manipulating consumer price expectations for a 10K road race. *Journal of Sport Management, 17*(2), 142–155.

McDaniel, S. (2003). Reconsidering the relation- ship between sensation seeking and audience preferences for viewing televised sports. *Jour- nal of Sport Management, 17*(1), 13–36.

One-Way ANOVA

Auld, C., & Godbey, G. (1998). Influence in Canadian national sport organizations: Per- ceptions of professionals and volunteers. *Journal of Sport Management, 12*(1), 20–38.

Doherty, A., & Danylchuk, K. (1996). Trans- formational and transactional leadership in interuniversity athletics management. *Journal of Sport Management, 10*(3), 292–309.

Kim, C., & Kim, S. (1998). Segmentation of sport center members in Seoul based on attitudes toward service quality. *Journal of Sport Manage- ment, 12*(4), 273–287.

One-Way ANCOVA

Kavussanu, M., Seal, A.R., Phillips, D.R. (2006). Observed prosocial and antisocial behaviors in male soccer teams: Age differences across adolescence and the role of motivational variables. *Journal of Applied Sport Psychology, 18*, 326–344.

Sosa, J., & Sagas, M. (2006). Assessment of organizational culture and job satisfaction on NCAA academic administrators. *Applied Research in Coaching and Athletics Annual, 21*, 130–154.

Factorial ANOVA

Cuneen, J. (1992). Graduate-level professional preparation for athletic directors. *Journal of Sport Management, 6*(1), 15–26.

Fink, J., Parker, H., Brett, M., & Higgins, J. (2009). Off-field behavior of athletes and team identification: Using social identity theory and balance theory to explain fan reactions. *Journal of Sport Management, 23*(2), 142–155.

One-Way MANOVA

Cunningham, G., Bruening, J., & Straub, T. (2006). The underrepresentation of African Americans in NCAA Division I-A head coaching positions. *Journal of Sport Management, 20*(3), 387–413.

Pritchard, M., & Funk, D. (2006). Symbiosis and substitution in spectator sport. *Journal of Sport Management, 20*(3), 299–321.

Turner, B., & Chelladurai, P. (2005). Organizational and occupational commitment, intention to leave, and perceived performance of intercollegiate coaches. *Journal of Sport Management, 19*(2), 193–211.

One-Way MANCOVA

Hausenblaus, H.A., & Mack, D.E. (1999). Social physique anxiety and eating disorder correlates among female athletic and nonathletic populations. *Journal of Sport Behavior, 22*(4), 502–514.

Vescovi, J., Murray, T., Fiala, K., & VanHeest, J. (2006). Off-ice performance and draft status of elite ice hockey players. *International Journal of Sports Physiology & Performance, 1*(3), 207–221.

Factorial MANCOVA

Doherty, A., & Carron, A. (2003). Cohesion in volunteer sport executive committees. *Journal of Sport Management, 17*(2), 116–141.

Molinero, O., Salguero, A., Tuero, C., Alvarez, E., & Márquez, S. (2006). Dropout reasons in young Spanish athletes: Relationship to gender, type of sport and level of competition. *Journal of Sport Behavior, 29*(3), 255–269.

Robinson, M., Trail, G., & Kwon, H. (2004). Motives and points of attachment of professional golf spectators. *Sport Management Review, 7*(2), 167–192.

Selected text reprinted, by permission, from M. Yoshida and J. James, 2010, "Customer satisfaction with game and service experiences: Antecedents and consequences," *Journal of Sport Management* 24(19): 338-361.

Access the full article online at www.humankinetics.com/products/all-products/Research-Methods-and-Design-in-Sport-Management.

ABSTRACT

Sport marketing researchers have generally studied two types of satisfaction at sporting events: game satisfaction and service satisfaction. One gap in the literature is studying the two types together. A model of the relationships between service quality, core product quality, game and service satisfaction, and behavioral intentions is proposed and tested. Data were collected from spectators at a professional baseball game in Japan ($n = 283$) and at two college football games in the United States ($n = 343$). The results in both Japan and the United States indicate that game atmosphere was a strong predictor of game satisfaction whereas stadium employees and facility access were the major antecedents of service satisfaction. Game satisfaction had a significant impact on behavioral intentions across the two settings, although the service satisfaction-behavioral intentions relationship was significant only in Japan. The research findings, managerial implications, limitations, and directions for future research are discussed.

TEXT EXCERPTS

Services marketing researchers suggest that a customer's perceptions of a core product and ancillary services may coexist as antecedents of customer satisfaction and behavioral intentions (Mittal, Kumar, & Tsiros, 1999; Parasuraman, Zeithaml, & Berry, 1994). Surprisingly, there is a lack of research in sport marketing examining both the core product (e.g., player performance and team characteristics) and ancillary services (e.g., concessions, facility amenities, and security) together.

Using SPSS 15.0, descriptive statistics (means, standard deviations, and correlations) were calculated and are reported in Table 1. The mean factors scores pertaining to core product quality are slightly higher than those of the factors pertaining to service quality. To assess group differences between the Japanese and United States samples, a multivariate analysis of variance (MANOVA) was conducted with the proposed nine constructs (see Table 1). The results indicated the MANOVA null hypothesis of equality of the mean scores for the nine constructs between the two groups was rejected at the .01 significance level (Wilk's Lambda = .685, F[9, 616]= 31.45, $p < .01$; see Table 1). A univariate analysis of variance (ANOVA) was employed for each of the nine constructs to identify more specific differences across the two samples (see Table 1). The computed F values for facility access, facility space, player performance, game satisfaction, and behavioral intentions were statistically significant and were 36.31, 12.50, 63.30, 20.95, and 20.67, respectively (see Table 1).

. . . .

The results indicated that facility functionality and behavioral intentions were more highly evaluated by the United States spectators than by the Japanese spectators, whereas player performance and game satisfaction were more highly assessed by the Japanese spectators than by the United States spectators. Partial eta-squared (ηp^2) was also computed as an index of effect size (Cohen, 1973; see Table 1). Partial eta-squared is similar to $R2$ in a regression analysis and can be deemed as the amount of variance in a dependent variable that is explained by a categorical independent variable. The partial eta-squared values for the nine constructs ranged from .01 to .09, indicating that the contributions of the two groups to the dependent variables were small.

. . . .

Since little effort has been made to identify the antecedents and consequences of satisfaction in the context of sporting events, we believe the study makes a significant contribution to the literature in four different ways.

DISCUSSION QUESTIONS

1 How do the authors define customer satisfaction, service satisfaction, and game satisfaction?

2 What samples were collected for the study, and what justification was provided for collecting samples from different settings?

3 Given the study's multiple purposes, the authors conducted a number of statistical analyses (e.g., descriptive statistics, MANOVA, ANOVA, exploratory factor analysis, confirmatory factor analysis, structural equation modeling). Which of the procedures incorporated by the authors specifically assesses group differences?

4 How did the authors interpret the results of the MANOVA and ANOVA procedures?

5 What contributions do the authors claim their study makes to the literature?

6 What study limitations are conceded by the authors, and what future research suggestions do they offer?

chapter 16

Prediction of Group Membership

Learning Objectives

After studying this chapter, you should be able to do the following:

- Provide a general description of the statistical techniques that allow prediction of group membership

- Describe how discriminant analysis can be viewed as the reverse of MANOVA

- Discuss the purpose and appropriateness of hierarchical, K-means, and two-step clustering

- Compare the various statistical techniques that allow for prediction of group membership on the basis of their limitations and appropriate usage

At times, sport managers may be interested in determining which factors serve as the best predictors of membership in a particular group. For example, what factors best predict whether an individual will purchase season tickets for a professional sport team rather than multiple individual game tickets? Which personality traits best predict whether a sport management intern is best placed in sales or in marketing? What combination of variables best predicts whether an individual will vote for or against a referendum to provide public funding for the construction of a new sport arena that may attract new business developments to the local area? Researchers addressing such questions will get the most help from statistical tests that allow researchers to determine which combination of independent variables is the best predictor of membership in a particular group. Assumptions for procedures that predict group membership are found in table 16.1.

Discriminant Analysis

Discriminant analysis seeks to identify a combination of independent variables, measured at the interval level, that best predicts membership in a particular group, as measured by a categorical independent variable. According to Stevens (1992), the two basic purposes of discriminant analysis are to describe major differences between groups following a MANOVA analysis (see chapter 15 for a review of MANOVA) and to classify individuals into groups based on a combination of measures. When discriminant analysis is used for the former purpose, it is often referred to as descriptive discriminant analysis, and, much like exploratory factor analysis (see chapter 13), the researcher must ultimately provide a meaningful name for the various significant groups. However, if the discriminant analysis is being used for purposes of prediction or classification, the researcher's goal is to determine dimensions that serve as the basis for reliably and accurately classifying subjects into groups. In either case, the linear combination of independent variables used to discriminate among groups is referred to as a discriminant function.

In many ways, discriminant analysis can be viewed as the reverse of MANOVA. Recall that MANOVA allows a researcher to compare the scores of two or more groups on a combination

Table 16.1 Assumptions for Procedures That Predict Group Membership

Assumptions	Discriminant analysis	Logistic regression	Cluster analysis
The observations of the predictor variables must be randomly sampled and must be independent of one another.	X		
The sampling distribution of any linear combination of predictors is normal.	X		
The population covariance matrices for the predictor variables in each group must be equal.	X		
The relationships between all pairs of predictors within each group must be linear.	X		
Several problems may occur if too few cases relative to the number of predictor variables exist in the data.		X	X
Relies on a goodness-of-fit test as a means of assessing the fit of the model to the data.		X*	
Sensitive to high correlations between predictor variables.		X	X
Extreme values of predictor variables should be examined carefully (sensitivity to outliers).		X	X
Sample needs to be representative of the population.			X

*Small cell sizes may inhibit power.

of dependent variables in an attempt to discover potentially significant group differences. In such an analysis, the independent variables are the grouping variables, and the dependent variables are the predictors. This process is reversed in discriminant analysis, in which the dependent variables serve as the grouping variables and the independent variables serve as the predictors. For descriptive discriminant analysis, the researcher determines the discriminant functions (i.e., linear combinations of independent variables) that maximize the differences between the groups in question. However, in cases where group prediction is the goal of the analysis, the researcher typically uses discriminant function scores to predict the group from which the participants came.

A discriminant analysis provides several important results for a researcher. First, the summary of the discriminant functions, similar to factors in an exploratory factor analysis (see chapter 13), includes coefficients for each discriminant function (these are analogous to regression coefficients or beta weights), eigenvalues for each discriminant function, and Wilks' lambda (λ) information (analogous to an F-test). The discriminant function with the largest eigenvalue provides for maximum discrimination among the groups examined, and the Wilks' lambda serves as a significance test for each of the discriminant functions, thus providing the researcher with information about the degree to which significant group differences exist in the independent variables after the effects of any previous functions have been removed. (Note that Wilks' lambda is an inverse criterion, which means that higher values of Wilks' lambda are indicative of significant results.) Once the significant discriminant functions have been identified, the researcher can then name these functions by examining the variables most related to them.

Similar to multiple regression (see chapter 14), discriminant analysis allows for several variations concerning the entry of independent variables into the analysis. The SPSS default is standard, or direct, discriminant analysis, in which each independent variable is entered simultaneously. Sequential, or hierarchical, discriminant analysis allows the researcher to specify a particular order of entry for the independent variables. Stepwise, or statistical, discriminant analysis dictates that predetermined statistical criteria will determine the order in which independent variables are entered into the analysis.

Discriminant analysis is quite sensitive to sample size, so researchers should ensure that their sample is large enough to generate confidence in results. Stevens (1992) recommends a 20:1 ratio of total sample size to number of variables, meaning that a discriminant analysis with 5 variables would require a minimum of 100 subjects. The accompanying highlight box reviews the SPSS procedure for conducting a discriminant analysis.

SPSS Discriminant Analysis Procedure

1. Analyze → Classify → Discriminant
2. Move the DV to the Grouping Variable box.
3. Define Range: Indicate the lowest and highest group value.
4. Continue.
5. Move IVs to the Independents box.
6. Statistics: Check Means, Univariate ANOVAs, and Box's M.
7. Continue.
8. Select either Enter or Stepwise*.
9. Classify: Check Compute From Group Sizes, Summary Table, Leave-One-Out Classification, Within-Groups Matrix, and Combined-Groups Plot.
10. Continue.
11. Save: Check Discriminant Scores.
12. Continue.
13. OK

*Note: If Stepwise is selected, select Method and check Wilks' Lambda, Use F-Value, and Summary of Steps, then click Continue.

Discriminant Analysis Example

In one of the first sport management studies to employ discriminant analysis, Brown (1990) sought to identify significant predictors of student success in a graduate program of sport management at a major research institution in the United States. The study was also designed to identify significant predictors of success in securing initial employment. To address this latter purpose, a discriminant analysis was calculated in which job acquisition was the dependent variable. Job acquisition was split into three groups: group 1 included all respondents who found a job within 1 year of graduation; group 2 included all respondents who found employment more than 1 year after graduation; and group 3 included respondents who had not accepted or had not found employment in the sport management field at the time of data collection.

A number of independent variables were included in the discriminant analysis:

- UGPA: overall undergraduate grade point average from all institutions attended
- PE: undergraduate major in physical education, recreation, or similar field
- BUS: undergraduate business major (or related field)
- JOURN: undergraduate major in journalism, English, communications, or similar field
- GRE-A%: analytical percentile score on the Graduate Record Exam
- FTSM: total years of full-time employment in a sport management or related position upon application
- EXC: total years of active undergraduate involvement in extracurricular activities
- OFF: total number of years of offices held in undergraduate extracurricular activities
- FTNSM: total years of full-time employment in a non–sport management (or related) position upon application
- AGE: age upon application to the program
- GRE-V%: verbal percentile score on the Graduate Record Exam
- GRE-Q%: quantitative percentile score on the Graduate Record Exam
- GGPA: final graduate grade point average

The results of the discriminant analysis included a nonsignificant Wilks' lambda for each discriminant function. Therefore, the results indicated that, in the population observed, the set of independent variables did not discriminate between the three job groups identified by the researcher. In her discussion of the results, Brown (1990) noted that future studies might employ other variables or recategorize the outcome variable. Indeed, potential independent variables that could affect a graduate's success in securing employment might include psychological factors such as interpersonal skills, creativity, leadership, and perseverance, which are often listed in job descriptions as desirable attributes in a candidate. Inclusion of such psychological variables might help explain why particular individuals are successful in securing employment in the field soon after matriculation.

Logistic Regression

Logistic regression is an extension of multiple regression that can be used in cases where the dependent variable is categorical in nature. The simplest and most common type of logistic regression is binary logistic regression, which is used in situations where the dependent variable is dichotomous, meaning that only two response options are available (e.g., yes or no, pass or fail, member or nonmember, guilty or not guilty). When the dependent variable in a logistic regression has more than two categories, the procedure is commonly referred to as multinomial logistic regression. Contrary to multiple regression, however, logistic regression reports a probability, ranging from 0 to 1, that specifies the precise probability of a particular outcome. More specifically, logistic regression specifies the odds probability of the dependent variable occurring as the values of the independent variables change. Essentially, the regression equation in a binary logistic regression predicts the probability of whether an individual (defined by the independent variables) will fall into one of two categories.

Though logistic regression shares the same purpose as discriminant analysis and is based on multiple regression, logistic regression is considerably more flexible than both discriminant analysis and multiple regression. Here are three reasons: First, logistic regression requires no assumptions about the distribution of the independent variables (e.g., independent variables do not have to be normally distributed or linearly related or have equal variances within each group). Second, logistic regression can analyze independent variables of all types, including continuous, discrete, and dichotomous variables (recall that discriminant analysis requires independent variables to be at least at the interval level of measurement). Finally, logistic regression is able to produce nonlinear models, thus allowing the researcher to explore potential relationships that are nonlinear in nature.

The pertinent output from a logistic regression includes goodness-of-fit tests, a classification table for the dependent variable, and a table of coefficients for independent variables included in the model. The goodness-of-fit tests allow the researcher to examine the contributions of each independent variable to the model, as well as overall model fit. The classification table for the dependent variable compares the predicted values for the dependent variable with the observed values from the data, thus providing an indication of the overall accuracy of the model in classifying individuals. The coefficients for independent variables included in the model are similar to multiple regression coefficients (see chapter 14). This table also provides the odds ratio (often depicted as Exp(β), the exponentiation of the β coefficient, or ψ), which is the ratio of the odds of being classified in one category of the dependent variable based on the values of the independent variables. According to Mertler and Vannatta (2005), the odds ratio represents the increase (or potentially the decrease, if the value is less than 1) in odds of being classified in a dependent variable category when the independent variable increases by 1. In other words, the odds ratio denotes the percent odds that an individual will be classified into a particular dependent variable group given a 1-unit increase in the respective independent variable.

Researchers are still somewhat divided concerning the minimum sample size for logistic regression analyses. For example, Hosmer and Lemeshow (1989) recommend a minimum of 10 cases per independent variable, whereas Pedhazur (1997) recommends that the sample size be at least 30 times the number of parameters being estimated. As mentioned earlier, in cases where statisticians fail to reach consensus regarding sample size, it is often prudent to select the most conservative estimate (i.e., the estimate that requires the largest sample size). The accompanying highlight box reviews the SPSS procedure for conducting a logistic regression.

SPSS Logistic Regression Procedure

1. Analyze → Regression → Binary Logistic
2. Move the DV to the Dependent box.
3. Move IVs to the Covariates box.
4. Select Methods.
5a. Select Categorical (if any IVs are categorical).
5b. Move any categorical IVs to the Categorical Covariates box.
6. Select Contrast Method and Reference Category.
7. Continue.
8. Options: Check Appropriate Options.
9. Continue.
10. OK

Logistic Regression Example

Yokum, Gonzalez, and Badgett (2006) were interested in predicting the long-term viability of a minor league baseball team. Specifically, they explored whether a particular minor league team, the San Angelo Colts of the independent Central Baseball League, would be successful in attracting attendance over an extended period of time. The San Angelo Colts represented a resurrected franchise that had previously existed from 1948 to 1957 and was reborn in 2000 with a new stadium that could accommodate approximately 4,000 spectators.

The long-term viability of the San Angelo Colts was of particular interest to these researchers due to several demographic and sociodemographic factors that seemed threatening to the future financial success of the franchise. First, San Angelo, a small city in west Texas, experienced a population decline from 94,000 to 88,000 between the 1990 and 2000 censuses, even as other Texas population areas averaged a 28.2 percent increase. The economic development of the region was hampered by the loss of manufacturing jobs, declining school enrollment, and the migration of youth to urban areas. Second, San Angelo was ranked 195th out of 210 demographic metropolitan areas in disposable income by Nielsen Media Research. Clearly, team investors were counting on the potential popularity of minor league baseball to counteract these negative economic factors.

While the study incorporated a number of analyses, and a logistic regression on cross-sectional data was used to supplement other forecasts made by the researchers. The logistic regression used data from a cross-sectional 9-year history of the Central Baseball League. Data were collected from the teams for the period from 1994 to 2002, during which 10 league teams failed for various reasons and 8 teams did not fail. In this logistic regression model, the factors analyzed from each of these 18 teams included the following:

- Previous year's attendance
- Age of stadium
- Economic and entertainment competition for a market's entertainment dollars
- Population size of county in which the team was located

The dichotomous dependent variable in this analysis was whether or not the team survived financially during the time period, and teams were coded either with a 1 (team still existed) or a 0 (team failed during the time period).

The results of the logistic regression revealed that none of the four independent variables were significant predictors of team existence at the .05 level of significance. A subsequent analysis of the data convinced the researchers that the presence of severe multicollinearity issues prevented the estimation of reliable coefficients for the cross-sectional logistic model. Multicollinearity occurs when two or more predictor variables in a regression are highly correlated, which negatively affects the calculations of individual predictors in a specified model. Using these insignificant coefficients as variables, the researchers concluded that the average predicted probability of success for the San Angelo Colts was 38.2 percent.

Cluster Analysis

Cluster analysis, sometimes referred to as **segmentation analysis** or **taxonomy analysis**, is often used in market research to partition a general population of consumers into market segments in order to better understand the similarities and differences between various groups of consumers. Cluster analysis is used to classify objects or individuals into mutually exclusive and collectively exhaustive groups. Simply stated, cluster analysis helps researchers identify objects or individuals similar to one another based on some specified criterion. Essentially, cluster analysis accomplishes its task by identifying a set of groups that both minimize within-group variation and maximize between-group variation (i.e., objects or individuals within groups are similar to each other yet distinctly different from objects or individuals in other statistically defined groups). Whereas discriminant analysis analyzes group membership for a number of known, researcher-specified groups, cluster analysis is used when the researcher does not know the number of groups in advance but wishes to establish groups and then analyze group membership.

Cluster analysis works by measuring the "distance" between data points, and it uses these distance measurements to form similar and dissimilar clusters or groups. Although several mathematical calculations for distance are available, the most common measure of distance employed in cluster analysis is Euclidean distance, which calculates distance as if calculating the length of the third side of a right triangle (i.e., the hypotenuse).

SPSS allows for three general approaches to cluster analysis: hierarchical clustering, K-means clustering, and two-step clustering. **Hierarchical**

clustering is most appropriate for smaller samples (n < 250) and requires the user to select a definition of distance, select a linking method for forming clusters, and determine how many clusters best suit the data. Similar to multiple regression (see chapter 14), hierarchical clustering allows the user to set a statistical threshold for inclusion in or exclusion from the formed clusters. In forward clustering, also referred to as agglomerative clustering, small clusters are formed by using a high similarity index threshold, and the threshold is gradually relaxed to establish broader and broader clusters. Backward clustering, also called divisive clustering, starts with a low threshold that is gradually increased, thus increasing the total number of clusters as the procedure progresses. Hierarchical clustering is often followed by K-means clustering to verify the composition of clusters according to the number of groups determined via the hierarchical clustering technique.

K-means clustering requires the researcher to specify the number of clusters in advance, after which an algorithm calculates how to assign cases to the K clusters. More specifically, K-means clustering uses Euclidean distance to minimize within-cluster variance and maximize variability between clusters. As such, K-means clustering can be used to verify the composition of clusters according to

SPSS Cluster Analysis Procedure

1. Analyze → Classify → Hierarchical Cluster or K-Means Cluster or TwoStep Cluster
2. Move variables to the Variables list.
3. In the Cluster group, select Cases or Variables, as appropriate.
4. In the Display group, select Statistics and Plots.
5. Click Statistics and select the appropriate options.
6. If applicable, in the Cluster Membership group, select Range of Solutions and specify number of clusters.
7. In the Plots subdialog box, select Dendogram, All Clusters, and Vertical.
8. Continue.
9. OK

the number of groups determined via the hierarchical clustering technique. K-means clustering is a preferred technique for large data sets ($n > 1,000$), which contrasts with the relatively smaller sample size that the hierarchical clustering technique can accommodate.

Two-step clustering is most appropriate for very large samples and is typically the method chosen when data are categorical (though the procedure can also accommodate continuous data). Two-step clustering operates by creating preclusters and subsequently clustering those preclusters via hierarchical methods in order to reach a solution. In essence, two-step clustering features two algorithms so that the researcher can first pass through the data to identify preclusters, then use hierarchical methods to treat those preclusters as individual cases for subsequent analysis.

■ ■

Cluster Analysis Example

McGehee, Yoon, and Cárdenas (2003) analyzed the involvement and travel of recreational runners in North Carolina. Specifically, they set out to test Havitz and Dimanche's (1990) Proposition XI, which states that "an individual's involvement profile with a recreational activity, tourist destination, or related equipment is positively related to frequency of participation, travel, or purchase (p. 189)." In order to test Proposition XI within the context of recreational runners, McGehee et al. formulated the following four hypotheses:

- H1: Recreational runners with high levels of involvement in overnight road race travel will participate in significantly more races than will recreational runners with medium levels of involvement in overnight road race travel.

- H2: Recreational runners with high levels of involvement in overnight road race travel will prepare for races significantly more than will recreational runners with medium levels of involvement in overnight road race travel.

- H3: Recreational runners with high levels of involvement in overnight road race travel will report significantly more overnight trips than will recreational runners with medium levels of involvement in overnight road race travel.

- H4: Recreational runners with high levels of involvement in overnight road race travel will spend significantly more in running-related expenditures than recreational runners with medium levels of involvement in overnight road race travel.

Before McGehee and colleagues could address these hypotheses, they needed a way to measure the construct of involvement. They developed 9 Likert-scale items featuring a semantic differential format to measure involvement, and they included those items in a comprehensive survey that also featured demographic measures and behavioral characteristics. The survey was distributed to 222 runners who volunteered to participate in the study. Once the survey results had been compiled into a spreadsheet, the researchers needed a way to distinguish the respondents based on their level of involvement.

Having no knowledge of how many distinct groups might be present in their data set, the researchers split their sample into two halves and employed a hierarchical cluster analysis on the first split sample. The results from this procedure indicated a two-cluster solution, meaning that the sample's responses to the involvement items could allow for two distinct groups. In order to confirm the two-cluster solution, a K-means cluster procedure was performed with the entire sample to ensure that two meaningful and distinguishable segmented groups were present. Recall that the K-means cluster procedure requires the researcher to specify the number of clusters in advance, so the researchers used the results from the hierarchical cluster analysis to support the predetermination of a two-cluster solution for the K-means cluster analysis. The results indicated two clusters—a medium involvement cluster and a high involvement cluster—and all involvement items significantly differed between the two groups ($p < .001$). A subsequent stepwise discriminant analysis confirmed that 97.6 percent of the entire sample was correctly classified under a two-factor solution.

Once these two groups were formed, the researchers used a series of independent sample t-tests to test their four proposed hypotheses (see chapter 15). The results indicated partial support for H1, no support for H2, partial support for H3, and full support for H4. Overall, the findings provided mixed support for Proposition XI; however, the delineation of two distinct participation groups on the basis of involvement should be of interest to marketers who may develop specific marketing strategies to attract one or both groups.

■ ■

Summary

This chapter reviews a number of statistical tests that aid in predicting group membership. Discriminant analysis seeks to identify a combination of independent variables, measured at the interval level, that best predicts membership in a particular group, as measured by a categorical independent variable. Logistic regression is an extension of multiple regression that can be used in cases where the dependent variable is categorical in nature. As compared with discriminant analysis, logistic regression is a more flexible technique that specifies the odds probability of the dependent variable occurring as the values of the independent variables change. Finally, cluster analysis is used to classify objects or individuals into mutually exclusive and collectively exhaustive groups based on some specified criterion. Table 16.2 summarizes the procedures that predict group membership.

Table 16.2 Summary of Procedures that Predict Group Membership

Test	IV	Categorical DV
Discriminant analysis	2+ IVs (quantitative)	1 DV (2+ categories)
Logistic regression	2+ IVs (categorical or quantitative)	1 DV (2 categories)
Cluster analysis	N/A*	N/A*

IV = independent variable; DV = independent variable

*Cluster analysis is an interdependence analysis.

ADVANCED READING

Discriminant Analysis

Ambrozic, F., Bednarik, J., Petrovic, K., & Sueman, R. (1999). Model characteristic of voluntary sport organisations in Slovenia. *European Journal for Sport Management, 6,* 28–38.

Li, M., & Burden, W. (2004). Institutional control, availability of internal resources and other related variables in affecting athletic administrator's outsourcing decisions. *International Journal of Sport Management, 5*(4), 295–305.

Logistic Regression

Bennett, G., & Cyree, K. (2002). Team payroll and performance in Major League Baseball: Are championships purchased? *International Journal of Sport Management, 3*(1), 74–86.

Reese, J., & Nagel, M. (2001). The relationship between revenue and winning in the National Football League. *International Journal of Sport Management, 2*(2), 125–133.

Sack, A., Singh, P., & Thiel, R. (2005). Occupational segregation on the playing field: The case of Major League Baseball. *Journal of Sport Management, 19*(3), 300–318.

Cluster Analysis

Kim, C., & Kim, S. (1998). Segmentation of sport center members in Seoul based on attitudes toward service quality. *Journal of Sport Management, 12*(4), 273–287.

Luna-Arocas, R., & Tang, T. (2005). The use of cluster analysis to segment clients of a sport center in Spain. *European Sport Management Quarterly, 5*(4), 381–413.

Ross, S.D. (2007). Segmenting sports fans using brand associations: A cluster analysis. *Sport Marketing Quarterly, 16,* 15–24.

Wang, C., Koh, K., & Chatzisarantis, N. (2009). An intra-individual analysis of players' perceived coaching behaviours, psychological needs, and achievement goals. *International Journal of Sports Science & Coaching, 4*(2), 177–192.

Woolf, J. (2008). Competitive advantage in the health and fitness industry: Developing service bundles. *Sport Management Review, 11*(1), 51–75.

Selected text reprinted, by permission, from A.L. Sack P. Singh, and R. Thiel, 2005, "Occupational segregation on the playing field: The case of Major League Baseball," *Journal of Sport Management* 19(3): 300-318.

Access the full article online at www.humankinetics.com/products/all-products/Research-Methods-and-Design-in-Sport-Management.

ABSTRACT

Occupational segregation by race and gender, though less common now than in the past, continues to be the norm rather than the exception in the sport industry. The purpose of this study was twofold. First, occupational segregation on the baseball playing field, often referred to as stacking, was discussed in light of human capital and social closure theories. Second, an attempt was made to replicate and extend a multivariate analysis of stacking by Margolis and Piliavin (1999) that challenges the dominant social science paradigm for explaining stacking. The present study uses more recent data than the Margolis and Piliavin study, as well as multinomial logistic regression analysis. The results reveal that stacking persists in Major League Baseball. They also reveal that the effect of race/ethnicity on assignments to playing positions is reduced when one controls for skills and physical characteristics such as speed and power hitting. The implications of this finding for sport management are examined.

TEXT EXCERPTS

The (population) of players included in this study included all hitters, including designated hitters, comprising the opening day rosters of the 30 professional baseball teams in the 1999 major-league season. Pitchers were omitted from the population because their performance data are significantly different from nonpitchers. Players who saw very little playing time, such as pinch hitters and runners or players brought up from the minor leagues on a part-time basis, were also omitted by restricting the sample to players with 50 or more at bats. The final sample size once pitchers and partial players were omitted was 299. Player position, performance, and personal-attributes data were obtained from the 1998 and 1999 Major League Handbook (James, 1999). All data were double-checked for accuracy against those posted by other sources, such as (Sports Illustrated) and (Associated)

Press. Data on race/ethnicity were obtained primarily from the complete set of Topps Baseball cards for the 1999 season and the web sites of the various teams.

. . . .

The dependent variable was player position. Four positions were categorized and the coding followed largely from previous research (Margolis & Piliavin, 1999). The catcher position was coded as 1. Second base and shortstop were coded as 2; first and third base as 3; and outfield as 4. For players playing more than one position and the designated hitter, the coding was determined by the position they played most frequently. This four-category variable was adequate for the preliminary analysis, which consisted of a contingency table and bivariate analysis. The categorical nature of this coding scheme, however, made it less appropriate in the regression analysis.

. . . .

This analysis also used multinomial logistic regression, which is better suited for categorical dependent variables.

. . . .

Table 3 presents the odds of being in one playing position or another by race. The relevant statistic for interpreting this table is the odds ratio. For instance, the odds of being in the outfield rather than catching if a player is African American are 46.9 times higher than the odds of being in the outfield rather than catching if the player is White. The difference in odds for African Americans being in the infield rather than catching compared with Whites is also significant. Being Latino is a significant predictor of being in the outfield versus catching, but it is not significant in the infield/catcher comparison. The Wald statistic and its associated *p* value indicate level of significance.

DISCUSSION QUESTIONS

1 Explain the concept of stacking.

2 What main conceptual flaw in the previous literature led to the development of this study? What were the purposes of this study?

3 What was the dependent variable for the multinomial logistic regression, and how was it categorized?

4 What were the independent variables for the multinomial logistic regression, and how were they categorized?

5 How did the regression model change when the speed and slugging average variables were added to the model and controlled?

6 What study limitations are conceded by the authors, and what future research suggestions are forwarded?

7 What do the authors conclude is the real challenge for future segregation research?

Glossary

advocacy/participatory paradigm—Research paradigm insisting that research inquiry is intertwined with politics and a political agenda and that it contains an action agenda for reform that may change the lives of participants and researchers and the institutions in which individuals work or live.

applied research—Type of research, classified according to application, that is carried out to solve a specific problem or provide a solution to a practical question.

backward-deletion multiple regression—Type of stepwise multiple regression used to compute an equation with all predictors included, followed by a significance test (a partial F-test) for every predictor as if it were entered last in order to determine the level of contribution to overall prediction; at each stage of the analysis, the weakest nonsignificant variable is removed from the equation until only significant predictors remain.

basic research—See *pure research*.

bivariate correlation—Statistic used to evaluate the degree of relationship between two quantitative variables without distinction between the independent and dependent variables.

Bonferroni correction—Statistical adjustment typically used to ensure that the overall Type I error rate remains constant across a series of analyses.

case—Primary unit of analysis in case study research that can involve a sport management issue, event, organization, decision, or policy or any sport industry phenomenon.

case law analysis—Process of identifying, reviewing, analyzing, and briefing court decisions as they relate to a research topic and to each other.

case study—Oft-used sport management research strategy in which an investigator uses a variety of data collection sources (e.g., interviews, surveys, observations, document analyses) in order to understand a phenomenon in the sport industry.

cell-means plot—Common graphing method used to interpret an interaction effect (two parallel lines indicate no interaction effect; nonparallel lines indicate an interaction effect).

census—The sampling of an entire population.

closed question—Type of question, often associated with quantitative research, that requires the respondent to choose from a list of predetermined responses.

cluster analysis—Statistical test used to classify objects or individuals into mutually exclusive and collectively exhaustive groups. Also referred to as *segmentation analysis* or *taxonomy analysis*.

coding—Process of reducing raw data into smaller, more manageable collections of similar data.

coefficient of determination (R^2)—Outcome of regression analysis allowing the researcher to determine the extent to which the independent variable successfully predicts the dependent variable; R^2 values range from 0 (no linear relationship) to 1.0 (perfect linear relationship).

common law—Legal precedent established through judicial decisions made by a court.

conceptual framework—A novel collection of related ideas developed by a researcher that link concepts from the literature.

confirmatory factor analysis (CFA)—Theory testing tool that allows a researcher to confirm the fit of the data in respect to a predetermined model typically based on prior research.

constructivism—Research paradigm rooted in the assumption that individuals seek understanding of the world in which they live and work and that they develop subjective meanings of their experiences.

construct validity—An examination of how accurately an instrument measures its target by how it measures or correlates with a theorized psychological construct.

content analysis—Use of an analytic method (e.g., thematic analysis, textual analysis, document analysis, discourse analysis) to unobtrusively examine some form of sport communication (e.g., team Web sites, sport magazines, organizational reports).

content validity—An assessment of how well a measure or instrument represents a construct.

correlation coefficient—Primary outcome of interest in a correlation analysis (values can range from -1.00 to +1.00, where values closer to -1.00 or +1.00 indicate stronger relationships and values closer to 0 indicate weaker relationships).

covariate—Independent variable not manipulated by the researcher that has an effect on the dependent variable and can be statistically controlled for by the researcher.

criterion validity—An examination of how accurately an instrument measures its target by comparing the instrument with some future or current criteria.

Cronbach's alpha (α)—Statistic that measures how well a set of variables or items measures a single, unidimensional latent construct

data anomalies—Unusual or unexpected data points that vary from what might be expected.

Delphi questionnaire—Series of increasingly probing questionnaires on an identified topic.

demand characteristics—An experimental artifact where research study participants form an interpretation of the experiment's purpose and unconsciously change their behavior as a result.

descriptive research—Type of research, classified according to objective, that uses surveys, interviews, or observations to focus on what is happening rather than why it happens.

descriptive statistics—Data analysis techniques used to describe or summarize data collected on a set of subjects that constitute the sample of interest.

discriminant analysis—Statistical test used to identify a combination of independent variables, measured at the interval level, that best predicts membership in a particular group as measured by a categorical independent variable.

disordinal interaction effect—Type of interaction effect that can be detected when the lines on a cell-means plot are not parallel and cross within the values of the graph.

double-barreled question—Type of closed question that requests respondent views on two separate issues within the same item.

effect size—An objective and standardized measure of the magnitude of the result of statistical analysis.

eigenvalue—Amount of total variance explained by each factor in a factor analysis.

empirical research—Type of research, classified according to the presence of data, that uses data to support the development of new ideas, theories, and explanations.

endogenous variable—Variable in a path diagram that is assumed to have its variance explained by other variables in the model (i.e., a variable that has an arrow pointing toward it).

epistemology—Philosophical study of how knowledge is acquired that assumes knowledge about the presence of a construct because of existing related knowledge.

ethnography—Naturalistic methodological process by which social scientists enter a real setting (in the field) to conduct research through processes such as observing, listening, and interviewing.

evidence source—Data collection source for a case study (e.g., historical record, participant observation, subject interview, document analysis).

exogenous variable—Variable in a path diagram that is not explained by the model (i.e., a variable that does not have an arrow pointing toward it).

experimenter effects—Any of a number of subtle cues or signals from an experimenter that affect the response of participants in an experiment.

explanatory research—Type of research, classified according to objective, that attempts to clarify why and how there is a relationship between two or more variables.

exploratory factor analysis (EFA)—Variable reduction technique used to assess share variance (i.e., covariance) and allow the researcher to identify the number of latent factors and the underlying factor structure of a set of variables.

exploratory research—Type of research, classified according to objective, that is often used when the research question or problem is not particularly well defined, is flexible in nature, and focuses on hypothesis development rather than hypothesis testing.

extraction—Process by which factors are determined from a larger set of variables.

fact—Notion so firmly supported by evidence that there is no longer a compelling reason to continue testing the notion.

factorial analysis of covariance (ANCOVA)—Parametric statistical test used to explore group differences and allow for simultaneous analysis of two or more independent variables with a single dependent variable while controlling for the potential influence of one or more covariates.

factorial analysis of variance (ANOVA)—Parametric statistical test used to explore group differences and allow for simultaneous analysis of two or more independent variables with a single dependent variable.

factorial multivariate analysis of covariance (MANCOVA)—Parametric statistical test used to explore group differences and allow for simultaneous analysis of two or more independent variables with two or more dependent variables while controlling for the correlations between the dependent variables and the potential influence of one or more covariates.

factorial multivariate analysis of variance (MANOVA)—Parametric statistical test that explores group differences and allows for simultaneous analysis of two or more independent variables with two or more dependent variables while controlling for the correlations between the dependent variables.

factor loading—Key output of an exploratory factor analysis or a principal component analysis that is interpreted as the Pearson correlation coefficient of an original variable with a factor; values can range from –1.00 (perfect negative correlation) to +1.00 (perfect positive correlation).

field notes—Primary source of data in sport management observation research, consisting of recorded and written comments by investigators regarding their observations while they were in the research setting.

filter question—Type of closed question that allows respondents to skip a series of questions that may not apply to them.

fit index—Collection of values that gives the researcher an indication of how well the data fit the proposed model.

focus group—Collection of 8 to 12 participants in a group interview setting; commonly used in marketing research.

follow-up reminder—Method used to increase survey response rates that involves reminding individuals within a sample who have not yet participated in the study that they have the chance to participate.

forward-selection multiple regression—Type of stepwise multiple regression in which the independent variable that has the highest correlation with the dependent variable (on the basis of a correlation matrix) is entered into the model first and assessed in terms of its contribution to the prediction of the dependent variable (in terms of R^2), after which the remaining independent variables are added to the model one at a time in descending order (after being subjected in each new round to a correlation matrix to determine the remaining one that has the highest correlation with the dependent variable) until the pool of remaining independent variables contains only nonsignificant predictors of the dependent variable.

frame error—Type of error in which the list from which the sample is drawn does not contain all members of the population.

general analytic strategy—Type of strategy, based on Yin's (2003) work, in which the case study researcher relies on theoretical propositions, creates a rival explanation framework, and develops a case description.

hierarchical clustering—Type of cluster analysis most appropriate for use with smaller samples (n < 250) and requiring the user to select a definition of distance, select a linking method for forming clusters, and determine how many clusters best suit the data.

hierarchical multiple regression—See *sequential multiple regression*.

historiography—Study of the methods used and interpretations made by researchers in their examination of a certain historical subject, event, or phenomenon.

human subjects—Human participants in a research study.

hypothesis—Educated prediction of a research outcome.

independent-samples t-test—Type of t-test used to compare the means of two independently sampled groups and examine whether the mean scores can be considered significantly different from each other.

inducement—Method used to increase survey response rates that involves giving some type of reward to the participant in return for completing the questionnaire.

inferential statistics—The collecting and analyzing of information from samples in order to draw conclusions about the larger population.

informant—Interview participant who helps guide the identification of additional participants.

informed consent—Formal acknowledgment by research subjects that they are voluntarily participating in a specific research study.

institutional review board (IRB)—A committee responsible for approving, monitoring, and reviewing research at organizations and agencies, such as universities, with the primary purpose of protecting the welfare of human participants.

interaction effect—Interaction between two independent variables that occurs when the effect of one independent variable depends on varying levels of another independent variable.

interview—Two-way exchange between researcher and subject, usually conducted face-to-face or via telephone, that allows the researcher to incorporate a human element into the data collection process.

introductory letter—Method used to increase survey response rates by notifying potential respondents of the purpose and importance of the study.

iterative or recursive approach—Nonsequential research strategy that involves undertaking research and writing activities simultaneously and working on later steps as the researcher is completing earlier steps; requires the researcher to engage actively and simultaneously in research, analysis, writing, and rewriting.

K-means clustering—Type of cluster analysis that requires the researcher to specify the number of clusters in advance and then use an algorithm to calculate how to assign cases to the K clusters.

Kaiser's rule—Rule often consulted in a principal component analysis which dictates that only components whose eigenvalues are greater than 1 should be retained.

leading question—Closed question that influences responses by pressuring the respondent to respond in a certain manner.

legislative history—Any materials such as committee reports, analysis by legislative counsel, committee hearings, floor debates, and records of actions taken on proposed legislation. Legislative history can be useful in understanding the congressional intent of legislation such if the legislation is intended to address a specific kind of problem or provide a specific kind of remedy. The legislative history provides a context in which the law is being enacted.

Likert scale—Closed question that allows the respondent to indicate the extent to which she or he agrees with a particular statement (usually on a five-, seven-, or nine-point scale).

list question—Closed question that allows the respondent to select more than one option to a particular item.

literature review—A stage of the research process in which the investigator identifies, summarizes, and analyzes previously published research related to his or her research problem.

logistic regression—Statistics test allowing for prediction of group membership in cases where the dependent variable is categorical in nature.

member checking—Method of validity assessment for interview transcription whereby participants are asked to confirm report accuracy.

mixed-methods research—A research project involving both qualitative and quantitative techniques.

motivational confounding—Related to factors that affect one's agreeableness to participate in experiments; a differential dropout rate in experimental between-subject conditions would be indicative of motivational confounding.

multiple-case study—Examination or comparison of two or more individual cases.

multiple comparison—See *post hoc test*.

multiple regression—Extension of simple linear regression that allows the researcher to expand the number of independent variables in the regression equation.

netnography—Online observation methodology in which research is conducted in a virtual setting (e.g., message boards, chat rooms, blogs, microblogs); also referred to as webnography, digital ethnography, and cyberethnography.

nonprobability sampling—Techniques used in selecting subjects for inclusion in a research study in which the probability, or odds, of getting a particular group of subjects cannot be calculated.

nonresponse bias—A systematic difference between respondents and nonrespondents in the data collection phase of a research study.

nonresponse error—Type of error involving the extent to which subjects included in the sample fail to provide usable responses and are systematically different from those who respond to the survey.

observation research site—Environment or field where a sport management researcher can collect data by observing people's behavior and interactions in their natural setting.

one-sample t-test—T-test that tests whether the mean of one variable differs from a value specified by the researcher.

one-way analysis of covariance (ANCOVA)—Parametric statistical test used to analyze the significance of group differences between two or more groups on a specified dependent variable while controlling for at least one covariate.

one-way analysis of variance (ANOVA)—Parametric statistical test used to analyze the significance of group differences between two or more groups on a specified dependent variable.

one-way multivariate analysis of covariance (MANCOVA)—Parametric statistical test used to analyze the significance of group differences between two or more groups as defined by a single independent variable in respect to two or more dependent variables while controlling for correlations between dependent variables and the potential influence of one or more covariates.

one-way multivariate analysis of variance (MANOVA)—Parametric statistical test used to analyze the significance of group differences between two or more groups as defined by a single independent variable in respect to two or more dependent variables while controlling for correlations between the dependent variables.

ontology—Study of the philosophy of knowledge that deals with questions concerning what entities exist or can be said to exist and how such entities can be grouped, related within a hierarchy, and subdivided according to similarities and differences.

open question—Type of question often associated with qualitative research that allows the respondent to address the queried information with an unrestricted response.

operationalize—To measure a concept on the basis of its definition.

oral evidence—Primary source materials such as oral testimony, interviews, and tape recordings of individuals, participants, observers, or stakeholders associated with a historical event, personality, or phenomenon.

ordinal interaction effect—Type of interaction effect that can be detected when the lines on a cell-means plot are not parallel yet do not cross within the values of the graph.

paired-samples t-test—Type of t-test used to compare the mean scores of two identical tests from the same group and determine whether the mean of a single group varies when measured at different times.

paradigm—Mind-set or way of thinking.

participant observation—Procedure similar to ethnography wherein a researcher joins or spends time in a sport management setting (e.g., an athletic department) and uses various methodologies (e.g., observing, interviewing) in order to understand a human social phenomenon.

path analysis—Extension of regression that analyzes correlations in a set of variables in order to examine the pattern of causal relationships.

path coefficient—Value in a path analysis used to estimate the strength of relationships between two variables in the hypothesized model; analogous to correlation coefficient in a regression analysis.

path diagram—A priori pictorial representation of a path analysis that depicts all variables and their hypothesized relationships with other variables.

Pearson correlation coefficient (r)—Parametric test used to evaluate the degree of relationship between two variables measured at the interval or ratio levels of measurement.

peer review—The process of evaluating an author's research through critical examination by experts in the field in order to determine if the research is worthy of being published in a journal or presented at a conference.

pilot study—Small-scale administration of a survey prior to the main administration; often uses a similar sample.

plagiarism—Using the ideas, writings, or drawings of others as one's own.

population—The group of cases, meeting particular criteria, that the researcher intends to generalize his or her results to.

post hoc test—One of a group of specific analyses conducted after a general test of significant group differences to determine specific differences between the levels of the independent variable while controlling the Type I error rate (typically required when the independent variable of interest has three or more levels). Also referred to as *multiple comparison.*

postpositivism—Research paradigm that stresses the need to identify and assess causes that influence outcomes.

pragmatism—Research paradigm concerned primarily with applications and solutions to research problems.

precedential value—Importance or significance of a court decision based on the level of court issuing the ruling; depending on the level of the court issuing the decision, may be a binding precedent (which must be applied or followed) or a persuasive precedent (which is merely used as guidance by a subsequent court).

predictive research—Type of research, classified according to objective, that forecasts the likelihood that particular phenomena will occur in given circumstances.

prenotification—Practice of notifying potential respondents of a forthcoming survey prior to administering the survey.

primary legal source—Actual statement of the law, such as a case opinion, statute, administrative regulation, or constitution (only primary legal sources can be relied on in determining the law and what it requires).

primary research—Type of research, classified according to the source of data, that involves the collection of original data specific to a research project.

primary source—Raw source material, most often in the form of an unpublished manuscript, published source, or oral evidence.

principal component analysis (PCA)—Variable reduction technique that assesses all sources of variability (unique, shared, error) and allows the researcher to find optimal ways of combining variables to explain the same amount of variance with fewer variables.

principle—Collection of one or more thoroughly tested theories combined in a way that guides behavior.

probability sampling—Techniques used in selecting subjects for inclusion in a research study in which the probability, or odds, of getting a particular group of subjects can be calculated.

published source—Documentary evidence involving a primary source published for public dissemination (e.g., autobiography of a sport manager, news article about a sporting event, media guide for a college basketball team).

pure research—Type of research, classified according to application, that is undertaken to gain a better understanding of a theoretical concept without regard for a specific problem or issue. Also referred to as *basic research*.

qualitative research—Research involving non-quantitative or nonstatistical techniques used to gain an in-depth understanding of a research problem, typically involving smaller numbers of subjects.

quantitative research—Research using statistical techniques to explain phenomena.

questionnaire—Method of collecting data that involves posing a set of questions to a study participant; typically delivered in person or via the mail or Internet.

ranking question—Closed question that asks the respondent to place responses in order of importance.

reliability—Extent to which a data collection instrument yields the same results on repeated trials.

research—"Systematic process of discovery and advancement of human knowledge" (Gratton & Jones, 2010, p. 4).

research design—The structure of the research project being implemented in order to answer the research questions.

research dissemination—The process of sharing the findings from a research study, commonly including but not limited to publishing in research journals and presenting at scholarly conferences.

research proposition—Guideline developed during the research design process based on the case study's theoretical foundation; supplies the sport management researcher with direction and sets boundaries regarding what should be examined in the research study.

response error—Error resulting from the communication process in which the respondent is unable or unwilling to respond to all items in a survey.

research problem—The topic of inquiry in a research study.

research questions—A formal statement defining what the research study is intended to investigate or answer.

sample—The subset of the population used as subjects in a research study.

sampling error—Error that occurs when the sample drawn from a population is not representative of the entire population.

scientific dishonesty—The fabrication, falsification, or plagiarism in proposing or conducting research or in reporting research results.

secondary legal source—Source that interprets and comments on the law or its application (e.g., law review article, periodical, textbook, legal encyclopedia, treatise).

secondary research—Type of research, classified according to the source of data, that relies on existing sources of data rather than collecting original data specific to a research project.

secondary source—Source material that involves historical work written after the fact by individuals (e.g., historians, journalists) not involved or not present at the events about which they are writing.

segmentation analysis—See *cluster analysis*.

semantic differential—Slight variation of the Likert-scale closed question that measures the respondent's reaction along a scale with contrasting adjectives at each end.

sequential multiple regression—Method of multiple regression analysis that allows the researcher to specify the particular order in which variables are entered into the analysis in order to analyze their individual ability to significantly predict the dependent variable. Also referred to as *hierarchical multiple regression*.

simple linear regression—Statistical test used to determine the degree of relationship between an independent variable and a dependent variable that produces a regression equation useful for prediction purposes.

significance level—The degree of evidence required in order to accept that an occurrence is unlikely to have happened by chance.

single-case study—In-depth examination of one case (e.g., analysis of a unique sport management example, organization, or phenomenon).

social desirability—Phenomenon involving the tendency of individuals to respond in a manner that makes them appear better than they are.

Spearman correlation coefficient (rs or ρ)—Nonparametric test that evaluates the degree of relationship between two variables measured at the ordinal level of measurement.

sponsorship—Method for increasing survey response rates that involves having an esteemed individual endorse or directly encourage the potential respondent to participate in the study.

sport management—"Any combination of skills related to planning, organizing, directing, controlling, budgeting, leading, and evaluating within the context of an organization or department whose primary product or service is related to sport and/or physical activity" (DeSensi, Kelley, Blanton, & Beitel, 1990).

standard multiple regression—Method of multiple regression analysis that allows for simultaneous input of all predictor variables (independent variables) into the equation in order to analyze their individual ability to significantly predict the dependent variable.

statistical error—Incorrect conclusions being drawn from statistical hypothesis testing; includes Type I and Type II forms of error.

statistical multiple regression—See *stepwise multiple regression*.

statistical power—The probability of rejecting the null hypothesis when the null hypothesis is false; the ability in statistical testing to detect a difference when it truly exists.

statistical significance—The likelihood that a result is caused by something other than chance.

statutory analysis—Process of applying and analyzing legislation to determine whether and how a statute applies to a given situation or problem.

statutory law—Law enacted by a legislative body (e.g., state legislature, U.S. Congress).

stepwise multiple regression—Method of multiple regression analysis, most appropriate for exploratory studies, that allows input of independent variables into the model based upon predetermined quantitative criteria. Also referred to as *statistical multiple regression*.

stepwise-selection multiple regression—Type of stepwise multiple regression that is similar to forward-selection multiple regression except that tests are performed at each step to determine the significance of each independent variable already in the equation as if it were to enter last, which may determine that one of the initial variables no longer significantly contributes to the overall analysis.

structured interview—Interview conducted on the basis of a prescribed list of questions asked of each participant.

survey—The act of collecting information.

taxonomy analysis—See *cluster analysis*.

technical variance—A type of error variance that emanates from the use of technical instruments.

theoretical framework—A collection of related ideas or concepts that have been previously established in the literature.

theme—Topic used to organize groups of repeating ideas that emerge from coding.

theoretical research—Type of research, classified according to the presence of data, that incorporates findings from past research to develop new ideas, theories, and explanations in the absence of data analysis.

theory—Explanation of a phenomenon that can be used to make testable predictions supported by prior research.

threatening question—Closed question in which a respondent may have a vested interest in concealing the information requested.

treatise—Summary and interpretation of the current state of the law, typically written by someone considered an expert or legal scholar in a particular area of the law.

t-test—The most basic statistical test used to determine group differences; appropriately used when the researcher wishes to determine if two groups, as defined by the independent variable, differ on the basis of a selected dependent variable .

two-step clustering—Type of cluster analysis most appropriate for very large samples and typically chosen when data are categorical (although the procedure can also accommodate continuous data).

unpublished manuscript—Primary source material consisting of a written record not copied for mass consumption or public dissemination (e.g., sport organization's meeting minutes, sport management leader's personal diary).

unstructured interview—Interview containing open-ended questions and allowing the researcher greater flexibility in obtaining data.

validity—Extent to which an instrument accurately measures the target that it was designed to measure.

variability—Measure of how scores are dispersed or spread in relationship to the mean value.

variable—Term typically used to refer to a number of individual questionnaire items that load together on a particular dimension or factor.

Wilks' lambda (λ)—The most common overall test statistic for a multivariate analysis of variance (MANOVA).

References

Adams, J.S. (1963). Toward an understanding of inequity. *Journal of Abnormal and Social Psychology, 67*(5), 422–436.

Aitchison, C.C. (2005). Feminist and gender research in sport and leisure management: Understanding the social-cultural nexus of gender-power relations. *Journal of Sport Management, 19,* 422-441.

Aitchison, C.C., Brackenridge, C., & Jordan, F. (1999). *Gender equity in leisure management.* Reading, UK: Institute of Leisure and Amenity Management.

Aleamoni, L.M. (1976). The relation of sample size to the number of variables in using factor analysis techniques. *Educational and Psychological Measurement, 36,* 879–883.

Altheide, D.L. (1996). *Qualitative media analysis.* Thousand Oaks, CA: Sage.

American Psychological Association. (2002). Ethical Principles of Psychologists and Code of Conduct. www.apa.org/ethics/code/index.aspx.

Amis, J. (2005). Interviewing for case study research. In D.L. Andrews, D.S. Mason, & M.L. Silk (Eds.), *Qualitative methods in sports studies* (pp. 104–138). Oxford: Berg.

Amis, J., Pant, N., & Slack, T. (1997). Achieving a sustainable competitive advantage: A resource-based view of sport sponsorship. *Journal of Sport Management, 11*(1), 80–96.

Amis, J., Slack, T., & Hinings, C.R. (2004). Strategic change and the role of interests, power, and organizational capacity. *Journal of Sport Management, 18*(2), 158–198.

Anderson, W.B. (2006). American v. National Football League: Using public relations to "win" a war against a monopoly. *Public Relations Review, 32*(1), 53–57.

Andrew, D.P.S., & Grady, J. (2005). Access Now v. Southwest Airlines: A net loss for Web users with disabilities? *Sport Marketing Quarterly, 14*(1), 54–56.

Andrew, D.P.S., & Kent, A. (2007). The impact of perceived leadership behaviors on satisfaction, commitment, and motivation: An expansion of the Multidimensional Model of Leadership. *International Journal of Coaching Science, 1*(1), 37–58.

Angrosino, M.V. (2002). *Doing cultural anthropology: Projects for ethnographical data collection.* Prospect Heights, IL: Waveland.

Angrosino, M.V. (2007). *Naturalistic observation.* Walnut Creek, CA: Left Coast.

Apostolopoulou, A. (2005). Vertical extension of sport organizations: The case of the National Basketball Development League (NBDL). *Sport Marketing Quarterly, 14*(1), 57–61.

Armstrong, K. (2000). African-American students' responses to race as a source cue in persuasive sport communications. *Journal of Sport Management, 14*(3), 208–226.

Auerbach, C.F., & Silverstein, L.B. (2003). *Qualitative data: An introduction to coding and analysis.* New York: New York University Press.

Babbie, E. (1986). *The practice of social research.* Belmont, CA: Wadsworth.

Babiak, K. (2007). Determinants of interorganizational relationships: The case of a Canadian nonprofit sport organization. *Journal of Sport Management, 21*(3), 338–376.

Barber, E.H., Parkhouse, B.L., & Tedrick, T. (2001). A critical review of the methodology of published research in the *Journal of Sport Management* from 1991 through 1995 as measure by selected criteria. *International Journal of Sport Management, 2*(3), 216–236.

Barrett, P.T., & Kline, P. (1981). The observation to variable ratio in factor analysis. *Personality Study and Group Behavior, 1,* 23–33.

Baseball Facility Liability Act, 745 ILCS 38 (1993).

Bateman, T., & Strasser, S. (1984). A longitudinal analysis of the antecedents of organizational commitment. *Academy of Management Journal, 27,* 95–112.

Battenfield, F.L., & Kent, A. (2007). The culture of communication among intercollegiate sport information professionals. *International Journal of Sport Management and Marketing, 2*(3), 236–251.

Beaulieu, N.D., & Zimmerman, A.M.G. (2005). The New England Patriots: Making the team. Harvard Business School Coursework No. 9-905-011, 1–29.

Bechtol, D.L. (2002). Structured observation description of the managerial roles and activities of selected NCAA Division I athletic directors. *International Journal of Sport Management, 3*(1), 11–33.

Bennett, G., & Hardin, B. (2002). Management behaviors of an elite intercollegiate baseball coach. *International Journal of Sport Management, 3*(3), 199–214.

Bennett, G., & Henson, R. (2003). Perceived status of the action sports segment among college students. *International Sports Journal, 7*(1), 124–138.

Bennett, G., Henson, R., & Zhang, J. (2003). Generation Y's perceptions of the action sports industry segment. *Journal of Sport Management, 17*(2), 95–115.

Berg, B.L. (2004). *Qualitative research methods for the social sciences* (5th ed.). Boston: Pearson.

Berg, B.L. (2007). *Qualitative research methods for the social sciences* (6th ed.). Boston: Pearson.

Bernard, H.R. (2006). *Research methods in anthropology: Qualitative and quantitative approaches.* Oxford, UK: AltaMira.

Berrett, T., & Slack, T. (1999). An analysis of the influence of competitive and institutional pressures on corporate sponsorship decisions. *Journal of Sport Management, 13*(2), 114–138.

Berschied, E. (1966). Opinion change and communicator–communicatee similarity and dissimilarity. *Journal of Personality and Social Psychology, 4,* 670–680.

Bickman, L., & Rog, D.J. (1998). *Handbook of applied social research methods.* Thousand Oaks, CA: Sage.

Bies, R.J., & Moag, J.F. (1986). Interactional justice: Communication criteria of fairness. In R.J. Lewicki, B.H. Sheppard, & M.H. Bazerman (Eds.), *Research on negotiations in organizations* (Vol. 1, pp. 43–55). Greenwich, CT: JAI Press.

Birot, L., Pecout, C., & Cooper, C. (2008). Cinema Sports News (1940–1944): Between factual information and propaganda. *International Journal of Sport Communication, 1*(2), 219-240.

Bishop, R. (2003). Missing in action: Feature coverage of women's sports in *Sports Illustrated. Journal of Sport and Social Issues, 27*(2), 184–194.

Boshoff, G.B.E. (1997). Barefoot sports administrators: Laying the foundation for sports development in South Africa. *Journal of Sport Management, 11*(1), 69–79.

Boucher, R.L. (1998). Toward achieving a focal point for sport management: A binocular perspective. *Journal of Sport Management, 12,* 76-85.

Bowen, H.K. (2006). The Salt Lake Organizing Committee: 2002 Olympics. Harvard Business School Coursework No. 9-604-092, 1–21.

Bradley, M. (1993, September). In the thick of it. *Athletic Management, 5,* 16–22.

Branch, D. (2000). SMQ Profile/Interview. *Sport Marketing Quarterly, 9*(2), 61–64.

Branch, D. (2008). The Charlotte Bobcats: (Re)launching a new (old) NBA franchise. *Sport Marketing Quarterly, 17*(1), 57–62.

Brandt, A.M. (1978). Racism and research. The case of the Tuskegee syphilis study. *Hastings Center Report, 8*(6), 21–29.

Bricknell, L. (2001). Doing ethnography: A reflexive comment. In C. Hallinan & J. Hughson (Eds.), *Sporting tales: Ethnographic fieldwork experiences* (pp. 7–20). New South Wales: Australian Society for Sports History.

Brief, A.P., & Dukerich, J.M. (1991). Theory in organizational behavior: Can it be useful? In B.M. Staw & L.L. Cummings (Eds.), *Research in Organizational Behavior* (pp. 327-352). Greenwich, CT: JAI Press.

Brockinton, L. (2001, August 20). Sponsors still loyal despite sinking TV ratings. *Street & Smith's SportsBusiness Journal,* p. 22.

Brown, R.S., & O'Rourke, D.J., III. (2003). *Case studies in sport communication.* Westport, CT: Praeger.

Brown, S. (1990). Selecting students for graduate academic success and employability: A new research direction for sport management. *Journal of Sport Management, 4*(2), 133–146.

Browne, M., & Cudeck, R. (1993). Alternative ways of assessing model fit. In K. Bollen & J. Long (Eds.), *Testing structural equation models* (pp. 136–162). Beverly Hills: Sage.

Bruening, J.E., & Lee, M.Y. (2007). The University of Notre Dame: An examination of the impact and evaluation of brand equity in NCAA Division I-A football. *Sport Marketing Quarterly, 16*(1), 38–48.

Brundage, A. (2002). *Going to the sources: A guide to historical research and writing* (3rd ed.). Wheeling, IL: Harlan Davidson.

Bryman, A., & Bell, E. (2007). *Business research methods* (2nd ed.). Oxford: Oxford University Press.

Buchanan, D., Boddy, D., & McCalman, J. (1988). Getting in, getting on, getting out, and getting back. In A. Bryman (Ed.), *Doing research in organizations* (pp. 53–67). London: Routledge.

Burgos, A. (2005). Entering Cuba's other playing field: Cuban baseball and the choice between race and nation, 1887–1912. *Journal of Sport and Social Issues, 29*(1), 9–40.

Byrd, J., & Utsler, M. (2007). Is stereotypical coverage of African-American athletes as "dead as disco"? An analysis of NFL quarterbacks in the pages of *Sports Illustrated. Journal of Sports Media, 2*(1), 1–28.

Cable, D., & Judge, T. (1997). Interviewers' perceptions of person–organization fit and organizational selection decisions. *Journal of Applied Psychology, 82,* 562–577.

Cammann, C., Fichman, M., Jenkins, D., & Klesh, J. (1983). Assessing the attitudes and perceptions of organizational members. In S. Seashore, E. Lawler, P. Mirvis, & C. Cammann (Eds.), *Assessing organizational change: A guide to methods, measures and practices* (pp. 71-138). New York: Wiley.

Campion, M.A. (1993). Article review checklist: A criterion checklist for reviewing research articles in applied psychology. *Personnel Psychology, 46*(3), 705–718.

Canseco, J. (2005). *Juiced: Wild times, rampant 'roids, smash hits, and how baseball got big.* New York: HarperCollins.

Carroll, D.M. (2009). Commercial programming at a single-sport cable channel: Strategies and practices at Golf Channel. *International Journal of Sport Communication, 2*(4), 484–499.

Carroll, M.S. (2007). *An analysis of case law regarding the liability of interscholastic and intercollegiate institutions for sport-related hazing.* Unpublished manuscript.

Caza, A. (2000). Context receptivity: Innovation in an amateur sport organization. *Journal of Sport Management, 14*(3), 227–242.

Chadwick, S., & Arthur, D. (2007). *International cases in the business of sport.* Burlington, MA: Elsevier/Butterworth-Heinemann.

Chalip, L. (1992). The construction and use of polysemic structures: Olympic lessons for sport marketing. *Journal of Sport Management, 6*(2), 87–98.

Chalip, L. (1997). Action research and social change in sport: An introduction to the special issue. *Journal of Sport Management, 11*(1), 1–7.

Chalip, L., & Leyns, A. (2002). Local business leveraging in a sport event: Managing an event for economic benefit. *Journal of Sport Management, 16*(2), 132–158.

Chalip, L., & Scott, E.P. (2005). Centrifugal social forces in a youth sport league. *Sport Management Review, 8*(1), 43–67.

Chambliss, D., & Schutt, R. (2006). *Making sense of the social world* (2nd ed.). Thousand Oaks, CA: Pine Forge.

Chandler, A.D., McCraw, T.K., McDonald, A.L., Tedlow, R.S., & Vietor, R.H.K. (1986, January/February). In A.M. Kantrow (Ed.), Why history matters to managers. *Harvard Business Review, 64*(1), 81–88.

Charmaz, K. (1983). The grounded theory method: An explication and interpretation. In R.M. Emerson (Ed.), *Contemporary field research: A collection of readings* (pp. 109–126). Boston: Little and Brown.

Charmaz, K. (2002). Qualitative interviewing and grounded theory analysis. In J.F. Gubrium & J.A. Holstein (Eds.), *Handbook of interview research: Context & method* (pp. 675–694). Thousand Oaks, CA: Sage.

Charmaz, K. (2005). Grounded theory in the 21st century: Applications for advancing social justice studies. In N.K. Denzin & Y.S. Lincoln (Eds.), *The Sage handbook of qualitative research* (pp. 507–535). Thousand Oaks, CA: Sage.

Chelladurai, P. (1978). *A contingency model of leadership in athletics.* Unpublished doctoral dissertation, Department of Management Sciences, University of Waterloo, Canada.

Chelladurai, P. (1990). Leadership in sports: A review. *International Journal of Sport Psychology, 21,* 328–354.

Chelladurai, P., & Riemer, H.A. (1997). A classification of the facets of athlete satisfaction. *Journal of Sport Management, 11,* 133–159.

Chelladurai, P., Imamura, H., Yamaguchi, Y., Oinuma, Y., & Miyauchi, T. (1988). Sport leadership in a cross-national setting: The case of Japanese and Canadian university athletes. *Journal of Sport and Exercise Psychology, 10,* 374–389.

Chen, L. (2004). Membership incentives: Factors affecting individuals' decisions about participation in athletics-related professional associations. *Journal of Sport Management, 18*(2), 111-131.

Cherryholms, C.H. (1992). Notes on pragmatism and scientific realism. *Educational Researcher, 2*(6), 13–17.

Choi, J., & Park, S. (2007). The comparison of research trends between *Journal of Sport Management* and *Korean Journal of Sport Management. International Journal of Asian Society for Physical Education, Sport, and Dance, 5*(2), 10–15.

Choi, J.A., Stotlar, D.K., & Park, S.R. (2006). Visual ethnography of on-site sport sponsorship activation: LG Action Sports Championships. *Sport Marketing Quarterly, 15*(2), 71–79.

Churchill, G.A., Jr. (1979). A paradigm for developing better measures of marketing constructs. *Journal of Marketing Research, 16*(1), 64–73.

Cianfrone, B., & Zhang, J. (2006). Differential effects of television commercials, athlete endorsements, and venue signage during a televised action sports event. *Journal of Sport Management, 20*(3), 322–344.

Cianfrone, B., Zhang, J., Trail, G., & Lutz, R. (2008). Effectiveness of in-game advertisements in sport video games: An experimental inquiry on current gamers. *International Journal of Sport Communication, 1*(2), 195–218.

Clavio, G., & Pedersen, P.M. (2007). Print and broadcast connections of ESPN: An investigation of the alignment of editorial coverage in *ESPN The Magazine* with ESPN's broadcasting rights. *International Journal of Sport Management, 8*(1), 95–114.

Cleland, J. (2009). The changing organizational structure of football clubs and their relationship with the external media. *International Journal of Sport Communication, 2*(4), 417–431.

Cliff, N. (1970). The relation between sample and population characteristic vectors. *Psychometrika, 35,* 163–178.

Cochran, W.G. (1963). *Sampling techniques* (2nd ed.). New York: Wiley.

Cohen, J. (1988). *Statistical power analysis for the behavioral sciences* (2nd ed.). New York: Academic Press.

Cohen, J. (1992). A power primer. *Psychological Bulletin, 112*(1), 155–159.

Comfrey, A.L., & Lee, H.B. (1992). *A first course in factor analysis.* Hillsdale, NJ: Erlbaum.

Conn, J.H. (1991). Content analysis of athletic policies from selected interscholastic athletic handbooks. *Journal of Sport Management, 5*(2), 144–152.

Copeland, B., & Kirsch, S. (1995). Perceived occupational stress among NCAA Division I, II, and III athletic directors. *Journal of Sport Management, 9*(1), 70–77.

Costa, C.A. (2005). The status and future of sport management: A Delphi study. *Journal of Sport Management, 19*(2), 117–142.

Cousens, L. (1997). From diamonds to dollars: The dynamics of change in AAA baseball franchises. *Journal of Sport Management, 11*(4), 316–334.

Cousens, L., & Barnes, M.L. (2009). Sport delivery in a highly socialized environment: A case study of embeddedness. *Journal of Sport Management, 23*(5), 574–590.

Cousens, L., & Slack, T. (2005). Field-level change: The case of North American major league professional sport. *Journal of Sport Management, 19*(1), 13–42.

Crepeau, R.C. (2006). [Review of the book *Growing the game: The globalization of Major League Baseball*]. *Journal of Sport History, 33*(3), 363–364.

Creswell, J., & Clark, V. (2007). *Designing and conducting mixed methods research.* Thousand Oaks, CA: Sage.

Creswell, J.W. (2007). *Qualitative inquiry and research design: Choosing among five approaches* (3rd ed.). Thousand Oaks, CA: Sage.

Creswell, J.W. (2009). *Research design: Qualitative, quantitative and mixed methods approaches* (3rd ed.). Thousand Oaks, CA: Sage.

Crompton, J.L., Howard, D.R., & Var, T. (2003). Financing major league facilities: Status, evolution, and conflicting forces. *Journal of Sport Management, 17*(2), 156–184.

Crosset, T.W., & Hums, M.A. (2005). History of sport management. In L.P. Masteralexis, C.A. Barr, & M.A. Hums (Eds.), *Principles and practice of sport management* (2nd ed.) (pp. 1–18). Sudbury, MA: Jones and Bartlett.

Crotty, M. (1998). *The foundations of social research: Meaning and perspective in the research process.* London: Sage.

Crow, R.B., & Bradish, C.L. (2002). Bridging the gap: How *Sport Marketing Quarterly* is working to fulfill its mission. *Sport Marketing Quarterly, 11*(2), 76–79.

Cuneen, J. (1992). Graduate-level professional preparation for athletic directors. *Journal of Sport Management, 6*(1), 15–26.

Cuneen, J., & Parks, J.B. (1997). Should we serve sport management practice or sport management education? A response to Weese's perspective. *Journal of Sport Management, 11*, 125–132.

Cuneen, J., & Sidwell, M.J. (1998). Gender portrayals in *Sports Illustrated for Kids* advertisements: A content analysis of prominent and supporting models. *Journal of Sport Management, 12*(1), 39–50.

Cunningham, G.B. (2007). Opening the black box: The influence of perceived diversity and a common in-group identity in diverse groups. *Journal of Sport Management, 21*, 58–78.

Cunningham, G.B., & Sagas, M. (2007). Gender differences in the impact of treatment discrimination. *Journal of Applied Social Psychology, 37*, 3010–3024.

Cunningham, G.B., Sagas, M., Dixon, M., Kent, A., & Turner, B.A. (2008). Anticipated career satisfaction, affective occupational commitment, and intentions to enter the sport management profession. *Journal of Sport Management, 19*, 43–57.

Dabscheck, B. (2003). Paying for professionalism: Industrial relations in Australian Rugby Union. *Sport Management Review, 6*(2), 105–125.

Daddario, G., & Wigley, B.J. (2006). Prejudice, patriarchy, and the PGA: Defensive discourse surrounding the Shoal Creek and the Augusta National controversies. *Journal of Sport Management, 20*(4), 466–482.

Daft, R. (1995). Why I recommended that your manuscript be rejected and what you can do about it. In L.L. Cummings and P.J. Frost (Eds.), *Publishing in the organizational sciences* (2nd ed., pp. 164–182). London: Sage.

Daprano, C.M., Costa, C.A., & Titlebaum, P.J. (2007). Building on success: Volunteer management at the Midwest Tennis Classic. *Sport Management Review, 10*(1), 97–123.

Davis, J. (2007). *Rozelle: Czar of the NFL.* New York: McGraw-Hill.

Deci, E.L., & Ryan, R.M. (1985). *Intrinsic motivation and self-determination in human behavior.* New York: Plenum Press.

Delong, T.J., Cheek-Clayton, T., & Reed, D. (2005). Changing times at the NBA. Harvard Business School Coursework No. 9-405-004, 1–26.

Dembroski, T.H., Lasater, T.M., & Ramirez, A. (1978). Communicator similarity, fear arousing communications, and compliance with health care recommendations. *Journal of Applied Social Psychology, 8*, 254–269.

Denzin, N.K., & Lincoln, Y.S. (1998b). *Strategies of qualitative inquiry.* Thousand Oaks, CA: Sage.

Denzin, N.K., & Lincoln, Y.S. (Eds.). (1998a). *Collecting and interpreting qualitative materials.* Thousand Oaks, CA: Sage.

Denzin, N.K., & Lincoln, Y.S. (Eds.). (2005). *The Sage handbook of qualitative research* (3rd ed.). Thousand Oaks, CA: Sage.

Derian, D. (2008, January). Career corner: Behind the scenes at Major League Baseball. *Profiles of the Game.* www.profilesofthegame-digital.com/profilesofthegame/200801/?u1=texterity.

Dernbach, J.C., Singleton, R.V., Wharton, C.S., & Ruhtenberg, J.M. (2007). A practical guide to legal writing and legal method (3rd ed.). New York: Aspen.

DeSchriver, T. D. (2007). Much adieu about Freddy: The relationship between MLS spectator attendance and the arrival of Freddy Adu. *Journal of Sport Management, 21*(3), 438-451.

DeSensi, J.T., Kelley, D.R., Blanton, M.D., & Beitel, P.A. (1990). Sport management curricular evaluation and needs assessment: A multifaceted approach. *Journal of Sport Management, 4*, 31–58.

Deutsch, M. (1975). Equity, equality, and need: What determines which value will be used as the basis of distributive justice? *Journal of Social Issues, 31*, 137–150.

DeWalt, K.M., & DeWalt, B.R. (2002). *Participant observation: A guide for fieldworkers.* Walnut Creek, CA: AltaMira.

Dillman, D.A. (2000). *Mail and Internet surveys* (2nd ed.). New York: Wiley.

Dittmore, S.W., Mahony, D.F., Andrew, D.P.S., & Hums, M.A. (2009). Examining fairness perceptions of financial resource allocations in U.S. Olympic sport. *Journal of Sport Management, 23*(4), 429-456.

Dittmore, S.W., Mahony, D.F., Andrew, D.P.S., & Phelps, S. (2007). Is sport management research diverse? A five-year analysis of dissertations. *International Journal of Sport Management, 8*(1), 21–31.

Dixon, M.A., & Bruening, J.E. (2006). Retaining quality workers: A case study of work-family conflict. *Sport Management Review, 9*(1), 79–103.

Dixon, M.A., & Bruening, J.E. (2007). Work-family conflict in coaching I: A top-down perspective. *Journal of Sport Management, 21*, 377–406.

Dixon, M.A., & Warner, S. (2010). Employee satisfaction in sport: Development of a multi-dimensional model in coaching. *Journal of Sport Management, 24*(2), 139-168.

Dobbs, M.E., Stahura, K.A., & Greenwood, M. (2005). Founding professional sports leagues: A statistical analysis, 1871–1997. *International Journal of Sport Management, 6*(1), 15–29.

Doherty, A., & Murray, M. (2007). The strategic sponsorship process in a non-profit sport organization. *Sport Marketing Quarterly, 16*(1), 49–59.

Donnelly, M. (2006). Studying extreme sports: Beyond the core participants. *Journal of Sport & Social Issues, 30*(2), 219–224.

Dooley, L.M., & Linder, J.R. (2003). The handling of nonresponse error. *Human Resource Development Quarterly, 14*(1), 99–110.

Drayer, J., & Rascher, D.A. (2007). The use of simulation technology in sport finance courses: The case of the Oakland A's Baseball Business Simulator. *Sport Management Education Journal, 1*(1), 53–65.

Duquette, G.H., & Mason, D.S. (2004). Finding a home market: Franchise ownership in the Canadian Hockey League. *Sport Management Review, 7*(1), 79–102.

Dusckiewicz v. Carter, 52 A.2d 788 (Vt. 1947).

Dwyer, B., Kim, Y., & Gray, D. (2008). For love or money: Exploring and developing a motivational scale for fantasy football participation. *Proceedings of the 2008 North American Society for Sport Management Conference*, 196.

Eckstein, R., & Delaney, K. (2002). New sports stadiums, community self-esteem, and community collective conscience. *Journal of Sport & Social Issues, 26*(3), 235–247.

Edmunds, H. (1999). *The focus group research handbook*. Lincolnwood, IL: American Marketing Association.

Edwards, A., & Skinner, J. (2009). *Qualitative research in sport management*. Oxford, UK: Elsevier.

Edwards, A., Skinner, J., & Gilbert, K. (2005). Towards a critical theory of sport management. *International Journal of Sport Management, 6*(3), 233–251.

Edwards, D.J. (1998). Types of case study work: A conceptual framework for case-based research. *Journal of Humanistic Psychology, 38*(3), 36–70.

Evans, S.B. (2008). Whose stats are they anyway? Analyzing the battle between Major League Baseball and fantasy game sites. *Texas Review of Entertainment & Sports Law, 9*(2), 335–351.

Fabrigar, L., Wegener, D., McCallum, R., & Strahan, E. (1999). Evaluating the use of exploratory factor analysis in psychological research. *Psychological Methods, 4*, 272–299.

Fairley, S. (2003). In search of relived social experience: Group-based nostalgia sport tourism. *Journal of Sport Management, 17*(3), 284–304.

Fairley, S., Kellett, P., & Green, B.C. (2007). Volunteering abroad: Motives for travel to volunteer at the Athens Olympic Games. *Journal of Sport Management, 21*, 41–57.

Fantasy Sports Trade Association. (2008). Fantasy sports industry grows to a $800 million industry with 29.9 million players. www.prweb.com/releases/2008/7/prweb1084994.htm.

Fetterman, D.M. (1989). *Ethnography: Step by step*. Newbury Park, CA: Sage.

Field, A. (2005). *Discovering statistics using SPSS*. Thousand Oaks, CA: Sage.

Field, A.P. (2001). Meta-analysis of correlation coefficients: A Monte Carlo comparison of fixed- and random-effects models. *Psychological Methods, 6*, 161–180.

Fielding, L.W., & Miller, L.K. (1998). The foreign invasion of the American sporting goods market. *Sport Marketing Quarterly, 7*(3), 19–29.

Fielding, L.W., Miller, L.K., & Brown, J.R. (1999). Harlem Globetrotters International, Inc. *Journal of Sport Management, 13*(1), 45–77.

Fink, J.S., & Cunningham, G.B. (2005). The effects of racial and gender dyad diversity on work experiences of university athletics personnel. *International Journal of Sport Management, 6*, 199–213.

Fischman, M.W. (2000). Informed consent. In B.D. Sales & S. Folkman (Eds.), *Ethics in research with human participants* (pp. 49–58). Washington, DC: American Psychological Association.

Folger, J.P., Hewes, D.E., & Poole, M.S. (1984). Coding social interaction. In B. Dervin & M.J. Voigt (Eds.), *Progress in communication sciences* (Vol. 4, pp. 115–161). Norwood, NJ: Ablex.

Folger, R., & Konovsky, M.A. (1989). Effects of procedural and distributive justice on reactions to pay raise decisions. *Academy of Management Journal, 32*, 115–130.

Fontana, A., & Frey, J.H. (2005). The interview: From neutral stance to political involvement. In N.K. Denzin

& Y.S. Lincoln (Eds.), *The Sage handbook of qualitative research* (pp. 695–727). Thousand Oaks, CA: Sage.

Forsyth, C.J., & Thompson, C.Y. (2007). Helpmates of the rodeo: Fans, wives, and groupies. *Journal of Sport & Social Issues, 31*(4), 394–416.

Fortunato, J. (2006). *Commissioner: The legacy of Pete Rozelle.* Lanham, MD: Taylor.

Fortunato, J.A. (2008). Pete Rozelle: Developing and communicating the sports brand. *International Journal of Sport Communication, 1*(3), 361–377.

Fox, J.R. (1961). Pueblo baseball: A new use for old witchcraft. *Journal of American Folklore, 74*(291), 9–16.

Frankfort-Nachimas, C., & Nachimas, D. (1996). *Research methods in the social sciences* (5th ed.). London: Arnold.

Frei, F.X., & Campbell, D. (2006). Moneyball (A): What are you paying for? Harvard Business School Coursework No. 9-606-025, 1–7.

Friedman, M.T., & Mason, D.S. (2001). "Horse trading" and consensus building: Nashville, Tennessee and the relocation of the Houston Oilers. *Journal of Sport History, 28*(2), 271–291.

Friedman, M.T., & Mason, D.S. (2007). (Re)building a brand in the minor leagues: The Nashville Ice Flyers, 1997–98. *Sport Marketing Quarterly, 16*(3), 174–182.

Frisby, W., Crawford, S., & Dorer, T. (1997). Reflections on participatory action research: The case of low-income women accessing local physical activity services. *Journal of Sport Management, 11*(1), 8–28.

Frisby, W., Reid, C., Millar, S., & Hoeber, L. (2005). Putting "participatory" into participatory forms of action research. *Journal of Sport Management, 19*(4), 367–386.

Frosdick, S., & Marsh, P. (2005). *Football hooliganism.* Devon, UK: Willan.

Funk, D., Mahony, D., & Ridinger, L. (2002). Characterizing consumer motivation as individual difference factors: Augmenting the Sport Interest Inventory (SII) to explain level of spectator support. *Sport Marketing Quarterly, 11*(1), 33–44.

Gallmeier, C.P. (1989). Traded, waived, or gassed: Failure in the occupational world of ice hockey. *Journal of Sport and Social Issues, 13*(1), 25–45.

Gardyn, R., & Fetto, J. (2000, June). Demographics: It's all the rage. *American Demographics 22*(6), 72.

George, A.L., & Bennett, A. (2005). *Case studies and theory development in the social sciences.* Cambridge, MA: MIT Press.

Ghauri, P., & Gronhaug, K. (2005). *Research methods in business studies* (3rd ed.). Harlow, Essex, England: Pearson.

Girginov, V. (2001). Strategic relations and sport policy making: The case of Aerobic Union and School Sports Federation Bulgaria. *Journal of Sport Management, 15*(3), 173–194.

Gorsuch, R.L. (1983). *Factor analysis* (2nd ed.). Hillsdale, NJ: Erlbaum.

Grady, J. (2007). Fantasy stats case tests limits of intellectual property protection in the digital age. *Sport Marketing Quarterly, 16*(4), 230–231.

Grady, J., & Andrew, D.P.S. (2003). Legal implications of the Americans with Disabilities Act: Changing guidelines, structures, and attitudes in accommodating guests with disabilities. *Journal of Legal Aspects of Sport, 13*(3), 231–252.

Grady, J., & Andrew, D.P.S. (2006). Emergency preparedness for individuals with disabilities. *Journal of Physical Education, Recreation and Dance, 77*(2), 10–11.

Grady, J., & Andrew, D.P.S. (2007). Equality of access to emergency services for people with disabilities under the Americans with Disabilities Act. *Journal of Legal Aspects of Sport, 17*(1), 1–25.

Gratton, C., & Jones, I. (2004). *Research methods for sport studies.* London: Routledge.

Gratton, C., & Jones, I. (2010). *Research methods for sports studies* (2nd ed.). New York: Routledge.

Gravetter, F.J., & Wallnau, L.B. (1999). *Essentials of statistics for the behavioral sciences* (3rd ed.). Pacific Grove, CA: Brooks/Cole.

Green, B.C. (2001). Leveraging subculture and identity to promote sport events. *Sport Management Review, 4*(1), 1–19.

Green, B.C. (2005). Building sport programs to optimize athlete recruitment, retention, and transition: Toward a normative theory of sport development. *Journal of Sport Management, 19*(3), 233–253.

Green, P.E., & Tull, D. (1978). *Research for marketing decisions* (4th ed.). Englewood Cliffs, NJ: Prentice-Hall.

Greenberg, J. (1990). Organizational justice: Yesterday, today, and tomorrow. *Journal of Management, 16,* 399–432.

Greenberg, J. (1993). *Comprehensive stress management.* Dubuque, IA: Brown & Benchmark.

Guadagnoli, E., & Velicer, W.F. (1988). Relation of sample size to the stability of component patterns. *Psychological Bulletin, 103,* 265–275.

Gubrium, J.F., & Holstein, J.A. (2002). From the individual interview to the interview society. In J.F. Gubrium & J.A. Holstein (Eds.), *Handbook of interview research: Context & method* (pp. 3–32). Thousand Oaks, CA: Sage.

Gummessen, E. (1991). *Qualitative methods in management research.* Newbury Park, CA: Sage.

Haig-Muir, M. (2004). Handicapped from birth? Why women golfers are traditionally a fairway behind. *Sport History Review, 35*(1), 64–82.

Hair, J.F., Anderson, R.E., Tatham, R.L., & Black, W.C. (1998). *Multivariate data analysis* (5th ed.). Upper Saddle River, NJ: Prentice Hall.

Hallett, T. (2003). Symbolic power and organizational culture. *Sociological Theory, 21*(2), 128–149.

Hanis-Martin, J.L. (2006). Embodying contradictions: The case of professional women's basketball. *Journal of Sport and Social Issues, 30*(3), 265–288.

Hardy, S. (2006). "Polo at the Rinks": Shaping markets for ice hockey in America, 1880–1900. *Journal of Sport History, 33*(2), 157–174.

Harrigan, P.J. (2006). Asserting authority: The Canadian Intercollegiate Athletic Union, 1961–1975. *Sport History Review, 37*(2), 150–175.

Harrolle, M.G., & Trail, G.T. (2007). Ethnic identification, acculturation, and sport identification of Latinos in the United States. *International Journal of Sport Marketing and Sponsorship, 8*, 234-253.

Hartman, P. (1981). What directors of athletics do about stress. *Athletic Administration, 15*, 15–17.

Hata, O., & Umezawa, N. (1995). Use of fitness facilities, equipment, and programs. A case study of a Japanese fitness club. *Journal of Sport Management, 9*(1), 78–84.

Hatch, A. (2002). *Doing qualitative research in educational settings*. Albany: State University of New York Press.

Hatcher, L. (1994). *A step-by-step approach to using the SAS system for factor analysis and structural equation modeling*. Cary, NC: SAS Institute.

Havitz, M., & Dimanche, F. (1990). Proposition for testing the involvement construct in recreation. *Leisure Sciences, 12*, 179–195.

Heinonen, H. (2002). Finnish soccer supporters away from home: A case study of Finnish national team fans at a World Cup qualifying match in Liverpool, England. *Soccer & Society, 3*(3), 26–50.

Henderson, K.A., & Bialeschki, D. (1993). Professional women and equity issues in the 1990s. *Parks and Recreation, 28*(3), 54-59.

Henderson, K.A., & Bialeschki, D. (1995). Career development and women in the leisure services profession. *Journal of Park and Recreation Administration, 13*(1), 26-42.

Hesse-Biber, S.N., & Leavy, P. (2006). *The practice of qualitative research*. Thousand Oaks, CA: Sage.

Hill, B., & Green, B.C. (2008). Give the bench the boot! Using manning theory to design youth sport programs. *Journal of Sport Management, 22*(2), 184–204.

Hill, L., & Kikulis, L.M. (1999). Contemplating restructuring: A case study of strategic decision making in interuniversity athletic conferences. *Journal of Sport Management, 13*(1), 18–44.

Hoeber, L. (2007). "It's somewhere on the list but maybe it's one of the bottom ones": Examining gender equity as an organizational value in a sport organization. *International Journal of Sport Management and Marketing, 2*(4), 362–378.

Homans, G.C. (1961). *Social behavior: Its elementary forms*. New York: Harcourt, Brace & World.

Hopwood, M.K. (2005). Applying the public relations function to the business of sport. *International Journal of Sports Marketing and Sponsorship, 6*(3), 174–188.

Hosmer, D., & Lemeshow, S. (1989). *Applied logistic regression*. New York: Wiley.

Howell, M., & Prevenier, W. (2001). *From reliable sources: An introduction to historical methods*. Ithaca, NY: Cornell University Press.

Hoyle, R.H. (1995). *Structural equation modeling*. Thousand Oaks, CA: Sage.

Huang, Q., & Brewer, R.M. (2008). Improving communication effects and value in professional soccer: An analysis of the Chinese Super League. *International Journal of Sport Communication, 1*(1), 108–121.

Huang, Y. (2006). An analysis of sport business in the Great China region from a strategic perspective. *International Journal of Sport Management and Marketing, 1*(4), 349–358.

Hughson, J., & Hallinan, C. (2001). The ethnographic turn in sport studies. In C. Hallinan & J. Hughson (Eds.), *Sporting tales: Ethnographic fieldwork experiences* (pp. 3–6). New South Wales: Australian Society for Sports History.

Huisman, M., & van der Zouwen, J. (1999). Item nonresponse in scale data from surveys: Types, determinants, and measures. In J.M.E. Huisman (Ed), *Item nonresponse: Occurrence, causes, and imputation of missing answers to test items* (pp. 63-90). Leiden: DSWO-press.

Humphreys, L.G., Ilgen, D., McGrath, D., & Montanelli, R. (1969). Capitalization on chance in rotation of factors. *Educational and Psychological Measurement, 29*(2), 259–271.

Hums, M.A., Moorman, A.M., & Wolff, E. (2003). The inclusion of the Paralympics in the Olympic and Amateur Sports Act: Legal and policy implications for integration of athletes with disabilities into the United States Olympic Committee. *Journal of Sport and Social Issues, 27*, 261–275.

Hussey, J., & Hussey, R. (1997). *Business research*. Basingstoke: Macmillan.

Jackson, D.L. (2003). Revisiting sample size and number of parameter estimates: Some support for the *N:q* hypothesis. *Structural Equation Modeling, 10*, 128–141.

Jankowicz, A.D. (2005). *Business research projects* (4th ed.). London: Thomson.

Johnson, J.M. (2002). In-depth interviewing. In J.F. Gubrium & J.A. Holstein (Eds.), *Handbook of interview research: Context & method* (pp.103–119). Thousand Oaks, CA: Sage.

Jones, M.J., & Schumann, D.W. (2000). The strategic use of celebrity athlete endorsers in *Sports Illustrated:*

An historic perspective. *Sport Marketing Quarterly, 9*(2), 65–76.

Kahle, L.R., Boush, D.M., & Phelps, M. (2000). Good morning, Vietnam: An ethical analysis of Nike activities in Southeast Asia. *Sport Marketing Quarterly, 9*(1), 43–52.

Kahle, L.R., Kambara, K.M., & Rose, G.M. (1996). A functional model of fan attendance motivations for college football. *Sports Marketing Quarterly, 5*(4), 51–60.

Kaiser, H.F. (1960). The application of electronic computers to factor analysis. *Educational and Psychological Measurement, 20*, 141–151.

Kane, M.J. (1988). Media coverage of the female athlete before, during, and after Title IX: *Sports Illustrated* revisited. *Journal of Sport Management, 2*(2), 87–99.

Kassing, J.W., & Sanderson, J. (2010). Fan–athlete interaction and Twitter tweeting through the Giro: A case study. *International Journal of Sport Communication, 3*(1), 113–128.

Kawulich, B.B. (2005). Participant observation as a data collection method. *Forum: Qualitative Social Research, 6*(2), Art. 43. www.qualitative-research.net/fqs-texte/2-05/05-2-43-e.htm.

Kay, J., & Laberge, S. (2002). The "new" corporate habitus in adventure racing. *International Review for the Sociology of Sport, 37*(1), 17–36.

Kellett, P., & Fielding, L. (2001). Marketing for participation, managing for success: The Louisville Racquet Club. *Sport Management Review, 4*(21), 221–239.

Kelley, S.W., & Turley, L.W. (2004). The effect of content on perceived affect of Super Bowl commercials. *Journal of Sport Management, 18*(4), 398–420.

Kelloway, E.K. (1998). *Using LISREL for structural equation modeling: A researcher's guide.* Thousand Oaks, CA: Sage.

Kemmis, S., & Wilkinson, M. (1998). Participatory action research and the study of practice. In B. Atweh, S. Kemmis, & P. Weeks (Eds.), *Action research in practice: Partnerships for social justice in education* (pp. 21–36). New York: Routledge.

Kent, A., & Campbell, R.M. (2007). An introduction to freeloading: Campus-area ambush marketing. *Sport Marketing Quarterly, 16*(2), 118–122.

Kent, A., & Turner, B. (2002). Increasing response rates among coaches: The role of prenotification methods. *Journal of Sport Management, 16*, 230–238.

Kihl, L. (2007). Moral codes, moral tensions and hiding behind the rules: A snapshot of athletic administrators' practical morality. *Sport Management Review, 10*, 279–305.

Kihl, L., & Richardson, T. (2009). "Fixing the Mess": A grounded theory of a men's basketball coaching staff's suffering as a result of academic corruption. *Journal of Sport Management, 23*(3), 278–304.

Kihl, L.A., Richardson, T., & Campisi, C. (2008). Toward a grounded theory of student-athlete suffering and dealing with academic corruption. *Journal of Sport Management, 22*(3), 273–302.

Kikulis, L.M., Slack, T., & Hinings, B. (1995a). Does decision making make a difference? Patterns of change within Canadian national sport organizations. *Journal of Sport Management, 9*(3), 273–299.

Kikulis, L.M., Slack, T., & Hinings, B. (1995b). Toward an understanding of the role of agency and choice in the changing structure of Canada's national sport organizations. *Journal of Sport Management, 9*(2), 135–152.

Kim, S., Andrew, D.P.S., & Greenwell, T.C. (2009). An analysis of spectator motives and media consumption behavior in an individual combat sport: Cross-national differences between American and South Korean mixed martial arts fans. *International Journal of Sports Marketing and Sponsorship, 10*(2), 157–170.

Kim, S., Greenwell, T.C., Andrew, D.P.S., Lee, J., & Mahony, D.F. (2008). An analysis of spectator motives in individual combat sport: A study of mixed martial arts fans. *Sport Marketing Quarterly, 17*(2), 109–119

Kirk, R.E. (1995). *Experimental design: Procedures for the behavioral sciences* (3rd ed.). Pacific Grove, CA: Brooks/Cole.

Klein, A.M. (2006). *Growing the game: The globalization of Major League Baseball.* New Haven, CT: Yale University Press.

Kline, R.B. (1998). *Principles and practice of structural equation modeling.* New York: Guilford Press.

Kozinets, R.V. (1997). "I want to believe:" A netnography of the X-Philes' subculture of consumption. *Advances in Consumer Research, 24*, 470–475.

Kraft, P., & Lee, J.W. (2009). Protecting the house of Under Armour. *Sport Marketing Quarterly, 18*(2), 112–116.

Krippendorff, K. (2004). *Content analysis: An introduction to its methodology.* Thousand Oaks, CA: Sage.

Krueger, R.A., & Casey, M.A. (2000). *Focus groups: A practical guide for applied research* (3rd ed.). Thousand Oaks, CA: Sage.

Lachowetz, T., Dees, W., Todd, S., & Ryan, E. (2009). Savannah Sand Gnats: Macro strategies for using identity to increase attendance in minor league baseball. *Sport Marketing Quarterly, 18*(4), 222–227.

Lai, F. (1999). Floorball's penetration of Australia: Rethinking the nexus of globalisation and marketing. *Sport Management Review, 2*(2), 133–149.

Landry, D. (1983). What makes a top college athletic director? *Athletic Administration, 18*(2), 20.

Lavidge, R.J., & Steiner, G.A. (1961). A model for predictive measurements of advertising effectiveness. *Journal of Marketing, 25*(6), 59–62.

Lea, M., & Loughman, E. (1993, October). Crew, compliance, touchdowns and torts: The growth of the modern athletics department, its legal needs and models for satisfying them. *Athletics Administration*, 48–51.

Lee, S., Seo, W.J., & Green, C. (2008, May). Why do people play fantasy sports? *Proceedings of the North American Society for Sport Management Conference* 167.

Leventhal, G.S. (1976). The distribution of rewards and resources in groups and organizations. In L. Berkowitz & E. Walster (Eds.), *Advances in experimental social psychology* (Vol. 9, pp. 91–131). New York: Academic Press.

Li, M., & Cotton, D. (1996). Content analysis of the introductory course in sport management. *Journal of Sport Management, 10*(1), 87–96.

Li, M., Pitts, B., & Quarterman, J. (2008). *Research methods in sport management.* Morgantown, WV: Fitness Information Technology.

Lim, C., & Turco, D. (1999). The next generation in sport: Y. *Cyber-Journal of Sport Marketing, 3*(4). http://pandora. nla.gov.au/nph-arch/1999/Z1999-Nov-1/http://www. cjsm.com/vol3/lim34.htmwww.ausport.gov.au/full-text/1999/cjsm/v3n4/lim34.htm.

Lincoln, Y. S., & Guba, E. G. (1985). *Naturalistic inquiry.* Beverly Hills, CA: Sage.

Lindlof, T.R., & Taylor, B.C. (2002). *Qualitative communication research methods* (2nd ed.). Thousand Oaks, CA: Sage.

Lofland, J., Snow, D., Anderson, L., & Lofland, L.H. (2006). *Analyzing social settings: A guide to qualitative observation and analysis* (4th ed.). Belmont, CA: Wadsworth.

Lomax, M.E. (2002). "Detrimental to the league": Gambling and the governance of professional football, 1946–1963. *Journal of Sport History, 29*(2), 289–311.

Lomax, M.E. (2006). Black baseball entrepreneurs in the Quaker City: The Philadelphia Giants and the rise and fall of the NACBC. *Sport History Review, 37*(2), 100–129.

Long, J., Thibault, L., & Wolfe, R.A. (2004). A case study of influence over a sponsorship decision in a Canadian university athletic department. *Journal of Sport Management, 18*(2), 132–157.

Lorenz, S.L. (2003). "In the field of sport at home and abroad": Sports coverage in Canadian daily newspapers, 1850–1914. *Sport History Review, 34*(2), 133–167.

Lovett, D.J., & Lowry, C.D. (1995). Is liberal feminism working in the NCAA? *Journal of Sport Management, 9*(3), 263–272.

Lyberger, M.R., & Pastore, D. (1998). Health club facility operators perceived level of compliance with the Americans with Disabilities Act. *Journal of Sport Management, 12*, 138–145.

Lynn, S., Hardin, M., & Walsdorf, K. (2004). Selling (out) the sporting woman: Advertising images in four athletic magazines. *Journal of Sport Management, 18*(4), 335–349.

MacCallum, R.C., Widaman, K.F., Zhang, S., & Hong, S. (1999). Sample size in factor analysis. *Psychological Methods, 4*, 84–99.

Mack, N., Woodsong, C., MacQueen, K.M., Guest, G., & Namey, E. (2005). *Qualitative research methods: A data collector's field guide.* Research Triangle Park, NC: Family Health International.

Mahony, D.F., Riemer, H., Breeding, J., & Hums, M. (2006). Organizational justice in sport organizations: Perceptions of college athletes and other college students. *Journal of Sport Management, 20*(2), 159–188.

Mahony, D.F., Hums, M.A., & Riemer, H.A. (2002). Distributive justice in intercollegiate athletics: Perceptions of athletic directors and athletic board chairs. *Journal of Sport Management, 16*, 331–357.

Mahony, D.F., Hums, M.A., & Riemer, H.A. (2005). Bases for determining need: Perspectives of intercollegiate athletic directors and athletic board chairs. *Journal of Sport Management, 19*, 170–192.

Mahony, D.F., Hums, M.A., Andrew, D.P.S., & Dittmore, S.W. (2010). Organizational justice in sport. *Sport Management Review, 13*(2), 91-105.

Malhotra, D., & Hout, M. (2006). Negotiating on thin ice: The 2004–2005 NHL dispute (A). Harvard Business School Coursework No. 9-606-038, 1–20.

Marsh, H.W., & Hau, K.T. (1999). Confirmatory factor analysis: Strategies for small sample sizes. In R.H. Hoyle (Ed.), *Statistical strategies for small sample research* (pp. 252–284). Thousand Oaks, CA: Sage.

Martin, C.L. (1990). The employee/customer interface: An empirical investigation of employee behaviors and customer perceptions. *Journal of Sport Management, 4*(1), 1–20.

Martino, J.P. (1993). *Technological forecasting for decision making* (3rd ed.). New York: McGraw-Hill.

Mason, D.S. (1997). Revenue sharing and agency problems in professional team sport: The case of the National Football League. *Journal of Sport Management, 11*(3), 203–222.

Mason, D.S., & Slack, T. (2001). Evaluating monitoring mechanisms as a solution to opportunism by professional hockey agents. *Journal of Sport Management, 15*(2), 107–134.

Mason, D.S., & Slack, T. (2003). Understanding principal-agent relationships: Evidence from professional hockey. *Journal of Sport Management, 17*(1), 37–61.

Mason, D.S., Thibault, L., & Misener, L. (2006). An agency theory perspective on corruption in sport: The case of the International Olympic Committee. *Journal of Sport Management, 20*(1), 52–73.

Mason, J.G., Higgins, C.R., & Wilkinson, O.J. (1981). Sports administration education 15 years later. *Athletic Purchasing and Facilities, 5*(1), 44–45.

May, R.A.B. (2001). The sticky situation of sportsmanship: Contexts and contradictions in sportsmanship among high school boys basketball players. *Journal of Sport and Social Issues, 25*(4), 372–389.

Maylor, H., & Blackmon, K. (2005). *Researching business and management: A roadmap for success.* Basingstoke: Palgrave Macmillan.

McCarthy, M. (2001, August 14). ESPN's promotion of X Games goes to extremes. *USA Today.*

McClelland, J. (2006). The history of golf: Reading pictures, viewing texts. *Journal of Sport History, 33*(3), 345–357.

McCormick, B.P. (1996). N = 1: What can be learned from the single case? *Leisure Sciences, 18*(4), 365–369.

McDaniel, C., & Gates, R. (1991). *Contemporary marketing research.* St. Paul, MN: Harcourt.

McDonald, M.A., & Milne, G.R. (1999). *Cases in sport marketing.* Sudbury, MA: Jones & Bartlett.

McDowell, W.H. (2002). *Historical research: A guide.* Harlow, England: Pearson.

McEvoy, C.D., & Morse, A.L. (2007). An investigation of the relationship between television broadcasting and game attendance. *International Journal of Sport Management and Marketing, 2*(3), 222-235.

McFarlane, E. (1986). *Tenure considerations for individuals in full time teaching faculty positions with dual responsibilities in intercollegiate athletics.* Unpublished doctoral dissertation, West Virginia University, Morgantown.

McGehee, N.G., Yoon, Y., & Cárdenas, D. (2003). Involvement and travel for recreational runners in North Carolina. *Journal of Sport Management, 17,* 305–324.

McGlone, C., & Martin, N. (2006). Nike's corporate interest lives strong: A case of cause-related marketing and leveraging. *Sport Marketing Quarterly, 15*(3), 184–188.

McKay, J. (1996). *Managing gender: Affirmative action and organizational power in Australian, Canadian and New Zealand sport.* New York: State University of New York Press.

McKelvey S., & Moorman, A. (2007). Bush-whacked: Has political speech crossed the line and infringed on sport organizations' intellectual property rights? *Journal of Sport Management, 21,* 79-102.

McNary, E., & Pedersen, P.M. (2008). The written and photographic coverage of sports in a youth magazine: A content analysis of *Sports Illustrated for Kids (SIK). The Journal of Youth Sports, 3*(3), 9–13.

Mehta, R., & Sivadas, E. (1995). Comparing response rates and response content in mail versus electronic mail surveys. *Journal of the Market Research Society, 37,* 429–493.

Mercado, H.U. (2008). *Market segmentation based on subcultural socialization: A case study.* Unpublished doctoral dissertation, Florida State University.

Merriam, S.B. (1998). *Qualitative research and case study applications in education.* San Francisco: Jossey-Bass.

Mertens, D.M. (1998). *Research methods in education and psychology: Integrating diversity with quantitative and qualitative approaches.* Thousand Oaks, CA: Sage.

Mertler, C.A., & Vannatta, R.A. (2005). *Advanced and multivariate statistical methods: Practical application and interpretation* (3rd ed.). Glendale, CA: Pyrczak.

Miles, M. B., & Huberman, M. A. (1994). *Qualitative data analysis: An expanded sourcebook.* (2nd ed.). Thousand Oaks, CA: Sage.

Miller, L.K., Fielding, L.W., Gupta, M., & Pitts, B.G. (1995). Case study: Hillerich and Bradsby Company, Inc. implementation of Just in Time Manufacturing. *Journal of Sport Management, 9*(3), 249–262.

Milne, G., & McDonald, M. (1999). *Sport marketing: Managing the exchange process.* Sudbury, MA: Jones and Bartlett.

Misener, K., & Doherty, A. (2009). A case study of organizational capacity in nonprofit community sport. *Journal of Sport Management, 23*(4), 457–482.

Misener, L., & Mason, D.S. (2009). Fostering community development through sporting events strategies: An examination of urban regime perceptions. *Journal of Sport Management, 23*(6), 770–794.

Mitchell, R.B., Crosset, T., & Barr, C.A. (1999). Encouraging compliance without real power: Sport associations regulating teams. *Journal of Sport Management, 13*(3), 216–236.

Mitrano, J.R. (1999). The "sudden death" of hockey in Hartford: Sports fans and franchise relocation. *Sociology of Sport Journal, 16,* 134–154.

Mondello, M., & Pedersen, P.M. (2003). Investigating the body of knowledge: A content analysis of the *Journal of Sports Economics. Journal of Sports Economics, 4*(1), 64–73.

Mondello, M.J., Schwester, R.W., & Humphreys, B.R. (2009). To build or not to build: Examining the public discourse regarding St. Petersburg's stadium plan. *International Journal of Sport Communication, 2,* 432–450.

Morgan, D. (2007). Paradigms lost and pragmatism regained: Methodological implications of combining qualitative and quantitative methods. *Journal of Mixed Methods Research, 1*(1), 48–76.

Morgan, D.L. (2002). Focus group interviewing. In J.F. Gubrium & J.A. Holstein (Eds.), *Handbook of interview research: Context & method* (pp. 141–159). Thousand Oaks, CA: Sage.

Moriarty, D., & Holman-Prpich, M. (1987). Canadian interuniversity athletics: A model and method for analyzing conflict and change. *Journal of Sport Management, 1*(1), 57–73.

Mullin, B.J., Hardy, S., & Sutton, W.A. (2007). *Sport marketing* (3rd ed.). Champaign, IL: Human Kinetics.

Newman, I., & Newman, C. (1994). *Conceptual statistics for beginners* (2nd ed.). Lanham, MD: University Press of America.

Newman, J.I. (2007). A detour through "NASCAR Nation": Ethnographic articulations of a neoliberal sporting spectacle. *International Review for the Sociology of Sport, 42*(3), 289–308.

Nunnally, J.C. (1978). *Psychometric theory* (2nd ed.). New York: McGraw Hill.

Nunnally, J.C., & Bernstein, I.H. (1994). Psychometric theory (3rd ed.). New York: McGraw-Hill.

O'Brien, D., & Slack, T. (2003). An analysis of change in an organizational field: The professionalization of English Rugby Union. *Journal of Sport Management*, *17*(4), 417–448.

O'Brien, D., & Slack, T. (2004). The emergence of a professional logic in English Rugby Union: The role of isomorphic and diffusion processes. *Journal of Sport Management*, *18*(1), 13– 39.

O'Reilly, K. (2005). *Ethnographic methods* (4th ed.). London: Routledge.

O'Reilly, N., & Seguin, B. (2009). *Sport marketing: A Canadian perspective*. Scarborough, ON: Nelson Education.

O'Reilly, N.J., Rahinel, R., Foster, M.K., & Patterson, M. (2007). Connecting in megaclasses: The netnographic advantage. *Journal of Marketing Education, 29*, 69–84.

Olafson, G.A. (1990). Research design in sport management: What's missing, what's needed? *Journal of Sport Management, 4*(2), 103–120.

Parent, M.M. (2008). Evolution and issue patterns for major-sport-event organizing committees and their stakeholders. *Journal of Sport Management, 22*(2), 135–164.

Parent, M.M. (2010). Decision making in major sport events over time: Parameters, drivers, and strategies. *Journal of Sport Management, 24*(3), 291-318.

Parent, M.M., & Foreman, P.O. (2007). Organizational image and identity management in large-scale sporting events. *Journal of Sport Management, 21*(1), 15–40.

Parent, M.M., & Seguin, B. (2008). Toward a model of brand creation for international large-scale sporting events: The impact of leadership, context, and nature of the event. *Journal of Sport Management, 22*(5), 526–549.

Park, S., Andrew, D.P.S., & Mahony, D.F. (2008). Exploring the relationship between trait curiosity and initial interest in sport spectatorship. *International Journal of Sport Management, 9*(3), 286–301

Parks, J.B., & Olafson, G.A. (1987). Sport management and a new journal. *Journal of Sport Management, 1*, 1–3.

Paton, G. (1987). Sport management research: What progress has been made? *Journal of Sport Management, 1*, 25–31.

Patton, M.Q. (1990). *Qualitative evaluation and research methods* (2nd ed.). Newbury Park, CA: Sage.

Pedersen, P.M. (1997). *Build it and they will come: The arrival of the Tampa Bay Devil Rays*. Stuart, FL: Florida Sports Press.

Pedersen, P.M. (2002). Investigating interscholastic equity on the sports page: A content analysis of high school athletics newspaper articles. *Sociology of Sport Journal, 19*(4), 419–432.

Pedersen, P.M., & Pitts, B.G. (2001). Investigating the body of knowledge in sport management: A content analysis of the *Sport Marketing Quarterly*. *Chronicle of Kinesiology and Physical Education in Higher Education, 12*(3), 8–9, 22–23.

Pedersen, P.M., & Schneider, R.G. (2003). Investigating the academic openings in sport management: An analysis of the field's professorial position announcements and hires. *International Sports Journal, 7*(1), 35–47.

Pedersen, P.M., Fielding, L.W., & Vincent, J. (2007). A five-year content analysis of academic positions in sport management: Professional announcements and advertisements from 2001–02 through 2005–06. *International Journal of Sport Management, 8*(4), 447–462.

Pedersen, P.M., Miloch, K.S., Fielding, L., & Clavio, C. (2007). Investigating the coverage provided to males and females in a comparable sport: A content analysis of the written and photographic attention given to interscholastic athletics by the print media. *Applied Research in Coaching and Athletics Annual, 22*, 97–125.

Pedersen, P.M., Parks, J.B., Quarterman, J., & Thibault, L. (2011). *Contemporary sport management* (4th ed.). Champaign, IL: Human Kinetics.

Pedersen, P.M., Whisenant, W.A., & Schneider, R.G. (2003). Using a content analysis to examine the gendering of sports newspaper personnel and their coverage. *Journal of Sport Management, 17*(4), 376–393.

Pedersen, P.M., Whisenant, W.A., & Schneider, R.G. (2005). Analyzing the 2001–02 sport management faculty openings. *International Journal of Sport Management, 6*(2), 154–164.

Pedhazur, E.J. (1997). *Multiple regression in behavioral research* (3rd ed.). Orlando: Harcourt Brace.

Pelletier, L.G., Fortier, M.S., Vallerand, R.J., Tuson, K.M., Briere, N.M., & Blais, M.R. (1995). Toward a new measure of intrinsic motivation, extrinsic motivation, and amotivation in sports: The Sport Motivation Scale (SMS). *Journal of Sport & Exercise Psychology, 17*, 35–53.

Petty, R.E., Cacioppo, J.T., & Schumann, D. (1983). Central and peripheral routes to advertising effectiveness: The moderating role of involvement. *Journal of Consumer Research, 10*, 135–146.

Phillips, D.C., & Burbules, N.C. (2000). Postpositivism and educational research. Lanham, MD: Rowman & Littlefield.

Pishna, K. (2007, September 11). UFC 75 on Spike TV sets records. http://mmaweekly.com/absolutenm/anmviewer.asp?a=4677.

Pittman, A.T., Spengler, J.O., & Young, S.J. (2008). *Case studies in sport law*. Champaign, IL: Human Kinetics.

Pitts, B.G. (1998). *Case studies in sport marketing*. Morgantown, WV: Fitness Information Technology.

Pitts, B.G., & Danylchuk, K.E. (2007). Examining the body of knowledge in sport management: A preliminary descriptive study of current sport management textbooks. *Sport Management Education Journal, 1*(1), 40–52.

Pitts, B.G., & Pedersen, P.M. (2005). Examining the body of scholarship in sport management: A content analysis of the *Journal of Sport Management. Sport Management and Related Topics Journal, 2*(1), 33–52.

Platt, J. (2002). The history of the interview. In J.F. Gubrium & J.A. Holstein (Eds.), *Handbook of interview research: Context & method* (pp.33–54). Thousand Oaks, CA: Sage.

Poindexter, P.M., & McCombs, M.E. (2000). *Research in mass communication: A practical guide.* Boston: Bedford/ St. Martin's.

Puri, A. (2007). The web of insights: The art and practice of webnography. *International Journal of Market Research, 49*(3), 387–408.

Putman, W.H. (2010). *Legal research, analysis, and writing.* Clifton Park, NY: Delmar Cengage Learning.

Pyrczak, F. (2008). Evaluating research in academic journals (4th ed.). Glendale, CA: Pyrczak Publishing.

Quarterman, J., Jackson, E.N., Kim, K., Yoo, E., Koo, G.Y., Pruegger, B., & Han, K. (2006). Statistical data analysis techniques employed in the *Journal of Sport Management*: January 1987 to October 2004. *International Journal of Sport Management, 7*(1), 13–30.

Quarterman, J., Pitts, B.G., Jackson, E.N., Kim, K., & Kim, J. (2005). Statistical data analysis techniques employed in *Sport Marketing Quarterly*: 1992 to 2004. *Sport Marketing Quarterly, 14*(4), 227–238.

Quelch, J., Nueno, J.L., & Knoop, C. (2005). Real Madrid Club de Futbol. Harvard Business School Coursework No. 9-504-063, 1–24.

Reed, T. (2005). *Indy: The race and ritual of the Indianapolis 500* (2nd ed.). Washington, DC: Potomac.

Rehman, L., & Frisby, W. (2000). Is self-employment liberating or marginalizing? The case of women consultants in the fitness and sport industry. *Journal of Sport Management, 14*(1), 41–62.

Reips, U.D. (2000). Web experiment method. In M.H. Birnbaum (Ed.), *Psychological experiments on the Internet* (pp. 89–117). San Diego: Academic Press.

Richelieu, A., & Pons, F. (2005). Reconciling managers' strategic vision with fans' expectations. *International Journal of Sports Marketing and Sponsorship, 6*(3), 150–163.

Riddick, C.C., & Russell, R.V. (2008). *Research in recreation, parks, sport, and tourism* (2nd ed.). Champaign, IL: Sagamore.

Riemer, H.A., & Chelladurai, P. (1998). Development of the Athlete Satisfaction Questionnaire. *Journal of Sport & Exercise Psychology, 20*(2), 127–156.

Riffe, D., Aust, C.F., & Lacy, S.R. (1993). The effectiveness of random, consecutive day and constructed week samples in newspaper content analysis. *Journalism Quarterly, 70,* 133–139.

Riffe, D., Lacy, S., & Fico, F.G. (2005). *Analyzing media messages: Using quantitative content analysis in research* (2nd ed.). Mahwah, NJ: Erlbaum.

Rinehart, R. (2005). "Experiencing" sport management: The use of personal narrative in sport management studies. *Journal of Sport Management, 19*(4), 497–522.

Roberto, M.A. (2005). Billy Beane: Changing the game. Harvard Business School Coursework No. 9305120, 1–14.

Roberts, J.M., Arth, M.J., & Bush, R.R. (1959). Games in culture. *American Anthropologist, 59*(4), 579–605.

Robinson, M., & Trail, G. (2005). Relationships among spectator gender, motives, points of attachment, and sport preference. *Journal of Sport Management, 19*(1), 58–80.

Rosen, M. (1991). Coming to terms with the field: Understanding and doing organizational ethnography. *Journal of Management Studies, 28*(1), 1–24.

Ross, S.D., James, J.D., & Vargas, P. (2006). Development of a scale to measure team brand associations in professional sport. *Journal of Sport Management, 20,* 260–279.

Rossman, G.B., & Rallis, S.F. (2003). *Learning in the field: An introduction to qualitative research.* Thousand Oaks, CA: Sage.

Rossman, G.B., & Wilson, B.L. (1985). Numbers and words: Combining quantitative and qualitative methods in a single large-scale evaluation study. *Evaluation Review, 9*(5), 627–643.

Rudd, A., & Johnson, B. (2010). A call for more mixed methods in sport management research. *Sport Management Review, 13,* 14-24.

Sack, A.L., & Johnson, A.T. (1996). Politics, economic development, and the Volvo International Tennis Tournament. *Journal of Sport Management, 10*(1), 1–14.

Sack, A.L., & Nadim, A. (2002). Strategic choices in a turbulent environment: A case study of Starter Corporation. *Journal of Sport Management, 16*(1), 36–53.

Sage, G. (1977). *Introduction to motor behavior: A neuropsychological approach* (2nd ed.). Reading, MA: Addison-Wesley.

Sam, M.P., & Jackson, S. (2006). Developing national sport policy through consultation: The rules of engagement. *Journal of Sport Management, 20*(3), 366–386.

Sanderson, J. (2008). "How do you prove a negative?": Roger Clemens's image repair strategies in response to the Mitchell Report. *International Journal of Sport Communication, 1*(2), 246-262.

Sanderson, J. (2009). Professional athletes' shrinking privacy boundaries: Fans, information and computer technologies, and athlete monitoring. *International Journal of Sport Communication, 2,* 240–256.

Sands, R. (2002). *Sport ethnography.* Champaign, IL: Human Kinetics.

Scanlan, T.K., Carpenter P.J., Schmidt, G.W., Simons, J.P., & Keeler, B. (1993). An introduction to the Sport

Commitment Model. *Journal of Sport and Exercise Psychology, 15,* 1–15.

Scanlan, T.K., Simons, J.P., Carpenter, P.J., Schmidt, G.W., & Keeler, B. (1993). The Sport Commitment Model: Measurement development for the youth-sport domain. *Journal of Sport and Exercise Psychology, 15,* 16–38.

Schaefer, D.R., & Dillman, D.A. (1998). Development of a standard e-mail methodology: Results of an experiment. *Public Opinion Quarterly, 62,* 378–397.

Schensul, S.L., Schensul, J.J., & LeCompte, M.D. (1999). *Essential ethnographic methods: Observations, interviews, and questionnaires* (Vol. 2). Walnut Creek, CA: AltaMira.

Schramm, W. (1971). *Notes on case studies of instructional media projects.* Washington, DC: Academy for Educational Development.

Schwandt, T.A. (2003). Three epistemological stances for qualitative inquiry: Interpretivism, hermeneutics, and social constructionism. In N.K. Denzin & Y.S. Lincoln (Eds.), *The landscape of qualitative research: Theories and issues* (2nd ed., pp. 292–331). Thousand Oaks, CA: Sage.

Schwandt, T.A. (2007). *The Sage dictionary of qualitative inquiry* (3rd ed.). Los Angeles: Sage.

Seaton, A.V. (2002). Observing conducted tours: The ethnographic context in tourist research. *Journal of Vacation Marketing, 8*(4), 309–319.

Seifried, C. (2007). Introducing and analyzing historical methodology for sport management studies. *Proceedings of the 22nd Annual Conference of the North American Society for Sport Management* [NASSM] (pp. 300–301).

Shaw, S. (2006). Scratching the back of "Mr. X": Analyzing gendered social processes in sport organizations. *Journal of Sport Management, 20*(4), 510–534.

Shaw, S., & Amis, J. (2001). Image and investment: Sponsorship and women's sport. *Journal of Sport Management, 15*(3), 219–246.

Shaw, S., & Hoeber, L. (2003). "A strong man is direct and a direct woman is a bitch": Gendered discourses and their influence on employment roles in sport organizations. *Journal of Sport Management, 17*(4), 347–375.

Shilbury, D. (1993). Determining the problem of order in the Australian Football League. *Journal of Sport Management, 7*(2), 122–131.

Shilbury, D., & Kellett, P. (2006). Reviewing organisational structure and governance: The Australian Touch Association. *Sport Management Review, 9*(3), 271–317.

Shilbury, D., & Rentschler, R. (2007). Assessing sport management journals: A multi-dimensional examination. *Sport Management Review, 10,* 31–44.

Shinew, K.J., & Arnold, M. (1998). Gender equity in the leisure services field. *Journal of Leisure Research, 30*(2), 177-194.

Shore, E.G. (1991, February). Analysis of a multi-institutional series of completed cases. Presented at the Scientific Integrity Symposium, Harvard Medical School, Boston.

Sibson, R. (2010). "I was banging my head against a brick wall": Exclusionary power and the gendering of sport organizations. *Journal of Sport Management, 24,* 379-399.

Silk, M.L. (2005). Sporting ethnography: Philosophy, methodology and reflection. In D.L. Andrews, D.S. Mason, & M.L. Silk (Eds.), *Qualitative methods in sports studies* (pp. 65–103). Oxford: Berg.

Silk, M.L., & Amis, J. (2000). Institutional pressures and the production of televised sport. *Journal of Sport Management, 14*(4), 267–292.

Silverman, D. (1997). *Qualitative research: Theory, method and practice.* Thousand Oaks, CA: Sage.

Simone, D.J. (2006). [Review of the book *Indy: The race and ritual of the Indianapolis 500*]. *Journal of Sport History, 33*(3), 381–382.

Skinner, J., & Edwards, A. (2005). Inventive pathways: Fresh visions of sport management research. *Journal of Sport Management, 19*(4), 404–421.

Skinner, J., Stewart, B., & Edwards, A. (1999). Amateurism to professionalism: Modelling organisational change in sporting organisations. *Sport Management Review, 2*(2), 173–192.

Slack, T. (1996). From the locker room to the board room: Changing the domain of sport management. *Journal of Sport Management, 10,* 97–105.

Slack, T. (1998). Is there anything unique about sport management? *European Journal of Sport Management, 5*(2), 21–29.

Slack, T., & Hinings, B. (1992). Understanding change in national sport organizations: An integration of theoretical perspectives. *Journal of Sport Management, 6*(2), 114–132.

Slack, T., & Parent, M. (2006). *Understanding sport organizations: The application of organization theory* (2nd ed.). Champaign, IL: Human Kinetics.

Sloan, L.R (1989). The motives of sports fans. In J.H Goldstein (Ed.), *Sports, games, and play: Social & psychological viewpoints* (2nd ed., pp. 175–240). Hillsdale, NJ: Erlbaum.

Smart, D.L., & Wolfe, R.A. (2000). Examining sustainable competitive advantage in intercollegiate athletics: A resource-based view. *Journal of Sport Management, 14*(2), 133–153.

Smith, A. (2007). "Satisfiers," smokes, and sports: The unholy marriage between Major League Baseball and Big Tobacco. *Sport History Review, 38*(2), 121–133.

Smith, A.M. (2005). *Fundamentals of marketing research.* Thousand Oaks, CA: Sage.

Smith, C.B. (1997). Casting the net: Surveying an Internet population. *Journal of Computer-Mediated*

Communication, 3(1). http://jcmc.indiana.edu/vol3/issue1/smith.html.

Smith, R.E. (1998). The logic and design of case study research. *The Sport Psychologist, 2,* 1–12.

Snook, S.A., Perlow, L.A., & Delacey, B.J. (2005). Coach Knight: The will to win. Harvard Business School Coursework No. 9-406-043, 1–14.

Snyder, E.E., & Kane, M.J. (1990). Photo elicitation: A methodological technique for studying sport. *Journal of Sport Management, 4*(1), 21–30.

Sokolove, M. (2008, May 11). The uneven playing field. *New York Times Magazine.* www.nytimes.com/2008/05/11/magazine/11Girls-t.html?pagewanted=1&_r=1.

Sommer, R., & Sommer, B. (2002). *A practical guide to behavioral research tools and techniques* (5th ed.). New York: Oxford University Press.

Sosa, J., & Sagas, M. (2006). Assessment of organizational culture and job satisfaction on NCAA academic administrators. *Applied Research in Coaching and Athletics, 21,* 130-154.

Stake, R.E. (1995). *The art of case study research.* Thousand Oaks, CA: Sage.

Steensma, H., Jansen, S., & Vonk, C. (2003). Organizational culture and the use of influence tactics by managers. *Journal of Collective Negotiations, 30*(1), 47–57.

Stevens, J. (1992). *Applied multivariate statistics for the social sciences* (2nd ed.). Hillsdale, NJ: Erlbaum.

Stevens, J. (2006). The Canadian Hockey Association merger and the emergence of the Amateur Sport Enterprise. *Journal of Sport Management, 20*(1), 74–100.

Stewart, B., Nicholson, M., & Dickson, G. (2005). The Australian Football League's recent progress: A study in cartel conduct and monopoly power. *Sport Management Review, 8*(2), 95–117.

Strathmann, C. (2001). Audience ethnography, sport in the mass media, and men's talk. In C. Hallinan & J. Hughson (Eds.), *Sporting tales: Ethnographic fieldwork experiences* (pp. 59–69). New South Wales: Australian Society for Sports History.

Sugden, J. (2007). Inside the grafters' game: An ethnographic examination of football's underground economy. *Journal of Sport & Social Issues, 31*(3), 242–258.

Sutton, R., & Staw, B. (1995). What theory is not. *Administrative Science Quarterly, 40,* 371–384.

Sweeney, P.D., & McFarlin, D.B. (1993). Workers' evaluations of the "ends" and the "means": An examination of four models of distributive and procedural justice. *Organizational Behavior and Human Decision Process, 55,* 23–40.

Switzer, K. (2009). *Marathon woman: Running the race to revolutionize women's sports.* Cambridge, MA: Da Capo.

Tabachnick, B.G., & Fidell, L.S. (1996). *Using multivariate statistics* (3rd ed.). New York: HarperCollins.

Taylor, S.J., & Bogdan, R. (1984). *Introduction to qualitative research: The search for meanings* (2nd ed.). New York: Wiley.

Thibault, L., & Harvey, J. (1997). Fostering interorganizational linkages in the Canadian sport delivery system. *Journal of Sport Management, 11*(1), 45–68.

Thomas, J.R., Nelson, J.K., & Silverman, S.J. (2005). *Research methods in physical activity* (5th ed.). Champaign, IL: Human Kinetics.

Thomsen, S.R., Bower, D.W., & Barnes, M.D. (2004). Photographic images in women's health, fitness, and sports magazines and the physical self-concept of a group of adolescent female volleyball players. *Journal of Sport and Social Issues, 28*(3), 266–283.

Thrasher, R.G., Andrew, D.P.S., & Mahony, D.F. (2007a). The efficacy of the Theory of Reasoned Action to explain gambling behavior in college students. *College Student Affairs Journal, 27*(1), 57–75.

Thrasher, R.G., Andrew, D.P.S., & Mahony, D.F. (2007b). The impact of gender and varsity athletic participation on gambling attitudes and subjective norms of college students. *Journal of Contemporary Athletics, 2*(3), 291–311.

Todd, S.Y., & Andrew, D.P.S. (2006). The role of satisfying tasks and organizational support in the job attitudes of sporting goods retail employees. *International Journal of Sport Management and Marketing, 1*(4), 378–389.

Tornblom, K.Y., & Jonsson, D.S. (1985). Subrules of the equality and contribution principles: Their perceived fairness in distribution and retribution. *Social Psychology Quarterly, 48,* 249–261.

Tornblom, K.Y., & Jonsson, D.S. (1987). Distribution vs. retribution: The perceived justice of the contribution and equality principles for cooperative and competitive relationships. *Acta Sociologica, 30,* 25–52.

Trail, G.T., & James, J. (2001). The Motivation Scale for Sport Consumption: Assessment of the scale's psychometric properties. *Journal of Sport Behavior, 24*(1), 108–128.

Trail, G.T., Robinson, M., Dick, R., & Gillentine, A. (2003). Motives and points of attachment: Fans versus spectators in intercollegiate athletics. *Sport Marketing Quarterly, 12,* 217–227.

Trail, G.T., Fink, J.S., & Anderson, D.F. (2003). Sport spectator consumption behavior. *Sport Marketing Quarterly, 12,* 8–17.

van Wyk, J.G., Burger, S., Kluka, D.A., & van Schalkwyk, J. (2007, June 2). Sport students' background knowledge of the Olympic Games: The development of a holistic sport event management frame of reference. *Proceedings of the 22nd Annual Conference of the North American Society for Sport Management* [NASSM] (pp. 292–293).

VanderZwaag, H.J. (1998). *Policy development in sport management* (2nd ed.). Westport, CT: Praeger.

Veal, A. (1997). *Research methods for leisure and tourism* (2nd ed.). London: Pitman.

Veeck, B., & Linn, E. (2001). *Veeck as in Wreck: The autobiography of Bill Veeck.* Chicago: University of Chicago Press.

Velde, M.V.D., Jansen, P., & Anderson, N. (2004). *Guide to management research methods.* Malden, MA: Blackwell.

Verner, M.E., Hecht, J.B., & Fansler, A.G. (1998). Validating an instrument to assess the motivation of athletics donors. *Journal of Sport Management, 12,* 123–137.

Vincent, J., Pedersen, P.M., Whisenant, W.A., & Massey, D. (2007). Analysing the print media coverage of professional tennis players: British newspaper narratives about female competitors in the Wimbledon Championships. *International Journal of Sport Management and Marketing, 2*(3), 281–300.

Wann, D.L. (1995). Preliminary validation of the Sport Fan Motivation Scale. *Journal of Sport and Social Issues, 19,* 377–396.

Wann, D.L. (2002). Preliminary validation of a measure for assessing identification as a sport fan: The sport fandom questionnaire. *International Journal of Sport Management, 3,* 103–115.

Warren, C.A.B., & Karner, T.X. (2005). *Discovering qualitative methods: Field research, interviews, and analysis.* Los Angeles: Roxbury.

Washington, M., & Ventresca, M.J. (2008). Institutional contradictions and struggles in the formation of U.S. collegiate basketball, 1880–1938. *Journal of Sport Management, 22*(1), 30–49.

Watterson, J.S. (2000). The gridiron crisis of 1905: Was it really a crisis? *Journal of Sport History, 27*(2), 291–298.

Weese, W.J. (1995). If we're not serving practitioners, then we're not serving sport management. *Journal of Sport Management, 9,* 237–243.

Weight, E.A. (2010). The role of the entrepreneurial coach: Non-revenue sport survival within big-time collegiate athletics. *International Journal of Sport Management, 11*(1), 16-30.

Wells, J.R. (2005). Bally Total Fitness. Harvard Business School Coursework No. 9-706-450, 1–20.

Wells, J.R., & Haglock, T. (2005). Bill Belichick and the Cleveland Browns. Harvard Business School Coursework No. 9-706-415, 1–11.

Wells, M.S., Arthur-Banning, S.G., Paisley, K.P., Ellis, G.D., Roark, M.F., & Fischer, K. (2008). Good (youth) sports: Using benefits-based programming to increase sportsmanship. *Journal of Park & Recreation Administration, 26*(1), 1–21.

Wenn, S.R., & Martyn, S.G. (2005). Storm watch: Richard Pound, TOP sponsors, and the Salt Lake City bid scandal. *Journal of Sport History, 32*(2), 167–197.

Wenner, L.A. (2004). Recovering (from) Janet Jackson's breast: Ethics and the nexus of media, sports, and management. *Journal of Sport Management, 18*(4), 315–334.

Whisenant, W., Pedersen, P., & Smucker, M. (2004). Referent selection: How the women in sport journalism shape their perceptions of job satisfaction. *Journal of Sport Management, 18*(4), 368–382.

White, P.H., & Harkins, S.G. (1994). Race of source effect in the elaboration likelihood model. *Journal of Personality and Social Psychology, 67,* 790–807.

Whittler, T.E. (1989). Viewers' processing of actor's race and message claims in advertising stimuli. *Psychology and Marketing, 6,* 287–309.

Whyte, W.F. (1997). *Creative problem solving in the field: Reflections on a career.* Walnut Creek, CA: AltaMira.

Wilkinson, D., & Birmingham, P. (2003). *Using research instruments: A guide for researchers.* London: Routledge Falmer.

Wolcott, H.F. (2001). *The art of fieldwork.* Walnut Creek, CA: AltaMira.

Xing, X., & Chalip, L. (2009). Marching in the glory: Experiences and meanings when working for a sport mega-event. *Journal of Sport Management, 23*(2), 210–237.

Yin, R.K. (2003). *Case study research: Design and methods* (3rd ed.). Thousand Oaks, CA: Sage.

Yokum, J.T., Gonzalez, J.J., & Badgett, T. (2006). Forecasting the long-term viability of an enterprise: The case of a minor league baseball franchise. *Journal of Sport Management, 20,* 248–259.

Youngs, L.R. (2003). Creating America's winter golfing mecca at Pinehurst, North Carolina: National marketing and local control. *Journal of Sport History, 30*(1), 25–46.

Zeigler, E.F. (1987). Sport management: Past, present, and future. *Journal of Sport Management, 1,* 4–24.

Zhang, J., Jensen, B.E., & Mann, B.L. (1997). Modification and revision of the Leadership Scale for Sport. *Journal of Sport Behavior, 20*(1), 105–122.

Zikmund, W.G. (1991). *Business research methods* (3rd ed.). Chicago: Dryden Press.

Zwick, W., & Velicer, W. (1982). Factors influencing four rules for determining the number of components to retain. *Multivariate Behavioral Research, 17,* 253–269.

Index

PLEASE NOTE: Page numbers followed by an italicized *f* or *t* indicate that a figure or table is on that page, respectively.

About the Authors

Damon Andrew, PhD, is a professor and dean at Troy University in the College of Health and Human Services, which includes the school of nursing; the department of human services, rehabilitation, and social work; the department of kinesiology and health promotion; and the department of athletic training education. His academic credentials include an associate's degree from Jefferson Davis Community College, a bachelor's degree in physical education and a master's degree in exercise physiology from the University of South Alabama, two additional master's degrees in biomechanics and sport management from the University of Florida, and a PhD in sport administration from Florida State University. Before assuming the decanal role at Troy University, Andrew directed University of Louisville's doctoral program in sport administration and founded and directed a doctoral program in sport management at the University of Tennessee. He also taught at Florida State University, the University of Florida, and the University of South Alabama, where he was selected as a Distinguished Alumnus in 2011.

Andrew's research has been supported by over $2 million in funding via 25 grants and contracts. His scholarship includes over 50 manuscripts accepted for publication in peer-reviewed journals/books and 70 presentations at national and international conferences. His peer-reviewed publications appear in more than 20 scholarly journals, including the *Journal of Sport Management, Sport Management Review, Sport Marketing Quarterly, International Journal of Sport Management,* and the *Sport Management Education Journal.* Andrew currently serves as the associate editor for the *International Journal of Sport Management and Marketing* and as an editorial board member of the *International Journal of Sport Management, Journal of Issues in Intercollegiate Athletics,* and the *Journal of Sport Administration & Supervision.* He serves as an ad hoc reviewer for more than 10

other scholarly outlets. He was elected by his peers to serve as member at large of the North American Society for Sport Management (NASSM) and as chief financial officer of the Sport and Recreation Law Association (SRLA).

Andrew resides in Troy, Alabama, with his wife, Tera, and their daughter, Clare. He enjoys spending time with his family, reading, playing tennis, and watching sporting events.

Paul M. Pedersen, PhD, is an associate professor of sport management and the director of the sport management doctoral program at Indiana University at Bloomington. Previously, Pedersen taught sport communication and management courses at several colleges and universities, including Bowling Green State University and Palm Beach Atlantic University. He received his PhD from Florida State University.

A former sportswriter and sport business columnist, Pedersen has researched, published, and presented on the activities and practices of many sport organization personnel, specifically those associated with the print media and affiliated with intercollegiate and interscholastic sports. He has lectured and presented worldwide on sport communication and management topics. His primary area of scholarly interest is the symbiotic relationship between sport and communication. Pedersen has published 60 peer-reviewed articles in journals such as the *Journal of Sport Management, Sociology of Sport Journal, International Journal of Sports Marketing and Sponsorship,* and *Journal of Sports Economics.* Pedersen has coauthored *Strategic Sport Communication* (2007) and *Contemporary Sport Management, Fourth Edition* (2010), and authored two sport history texts.

Founder and editor in chief of the *International Journal of Sport Communication,* Pedersen also serves as an editorial review board member of five national and international sport journals. He is a research fellow for the North American Society for Sport Management (NASSM), a member of the North American Society for Sport History (NASSH) and the European Association for Sport Management (EASM), and a charter member of the Sport Marketing Association (SMA). Pedersen lives in Bloomington, Indiana, with his wife, Jennifer, and their four children. He enjoys spending time with his family as well as traveling, photography, cycling, and watching sporting events.

Photo courtesy of Chad D. McEvoy.

Chad D. McEvoy, EdD, is an Associate Professor at Illinois State University, where he is the coordinator of the sport management graduate program. Prior to pursuing a career in academia, McEvoy worked in marketing and fund raising in intercollegiate athletics at Iowa State University and Western Michigan University. He has conducted research projects for clients at various level of sport, including professional sport, intercollegiate athlet-

ics, Olympic sport, and sports agency organizations.

McEvoy holds a doctoral degree from the University of Northern Colorado, a master's degree from the University of Massachusetts, and a bachelor's degree from Iowa State University, each in sport management/administration. His research interests focus on revenue generation in commercialized spectator sport settings. McEvoy has published articles in journals including the *Journal of Sport Management, Sport Management Review, Sport Marketing Quarterly*, and *International Journal of Sport Management and Marketing*. McEvoy's research has been featured in numerous media stories and interviews including *The Wall Street Journal, Sports Illustrated.com, ESPN.com, Chicago Tribune, Philadelphia Inquirer, Atlanta Journal-Constitution, Portland Oregonian*, and *Kansas City Star*. McEvoy appeared as a panelist before the prestigious *Knight Commission on Intercollegiate Athletics* in 2008, and he is currently the Co-Editor of the *Journal of Issues in Intercollegiate Athletics*. McEvoy co-authored *Financial Management in the Sport Industry*, a textbook published in 2010.

McEvoy and his wife Kerry live in Normal, IL with their sons Andy and Luke. In addition to spending time with his family, McEvoy enjoys playing sports and games, cooking, and watching sports.